REFORM!

The Fight for the 1832 Reform Act

REFORM!

The Fight for the 1832 Reform Act

Edward Pearce

JONATHAN CAPE
LONDON

Published by Jonathan Cape 2003

2 4 6 8 10 9 7 5 3 1

First published in Great Britain in 2003 by
Jonathan Cape
Random House, 20 Vauxhall Bridge Road,
London SW1V 2SA

Random House Australia (Pty) Limited
20 Alfred Street, Milsons Point, Sydney,
New South Wales 2061, Australia

Random House New Zealand Limited
18 Poland Road, Glenfield,
Auckland 10, New Zealand

Random House South Africa (Pty) Limited
Endulini, 5A Jubilee Road,
Parktown 2193, South Africa

The Random House Group Limited Reg. No. 954009
www.randomhouse.co.uk

A CIP catalogue record for this book
is available from the British Library

ISBN 0–224–06199–2

Papers used by The Random House Group Limited are natural,
recyclable products made from wood grown in sustainable forests;
the manufacturing processes conform to the environmental
regulations of the country of origin

Typeset by Palimpsest Book Production Ltd,
Polmont, Stirlingshire
Printed and bound in Great Britain by
Clays Ltd, St. Ives PLC

For all the helpful people
at the
London Library issue desk

CONTENTS

Introduction

The idea of writing a book about the Great Reform Act, which I think deserves its ardent Victorian adjective, had been with me for some time. The chance of writing it came when my agent, Bill Hamilton, trawling possibilities with publishers, was asked by Will Sulkin of Jonathan Cape, 'What about a history of Parliament?' I modestly suggested that I did not have quite such panoramic ambitions, but, in return, what about the Reform Act? This was kindly agreed to and we proceeded.

There are two well-known and established studies of the subject, respectively by James Butler of Corpus Christi, Cambridge (Rab's kindly Uncle Jim), in 1914, and Michael Brock (co-founder of Wolfson, Oxford), published in 1973. Both are quite admirable books. Butler disguised very full scholarship under the dramatic cape of a rattling good yarn, which this heroic tragical-historical knockabout surely is. Dr Brock wrote a wonderfully concise and reader-helpful piece of intense scholarship, making the narrative instantly coherent and clear.

The justification for a new book – apart from the fact of a new book persuading people to read any subject at all – is that there was room for a fuller account of the debate, for the parliamentary side of parliamentary Reform. It is entirely proper to recount what happened and what was at issue as reported narrative with parliamentary advocacy paraphrased. But I am an old gallery man, working for the *Daily Telegraph*, *Guardian* and *New Statesman* alike. I have a prejudice in favour of debate. Also, the words and arguments actually used then take us to the mindset of another age. Tories really did believe that the French Revolution, terror and all, would be replicated if we once weakened, however slightly, the fabric of 'the most perfect system of constitutional government in the world'. The Whigs were not democrats and they did believe that they were producing a final constitutional document to follow that other finality, the revolution settlement. We know what men did; it is quite useful to know what they thought they were doing.

There were, too, all sorts of nuances which are heard most clearly out of the mouths of speakers. And there were stars, great speakers, who, despite cavils, sound superb still: Grey and Brougham at their best, O'Connell, and, flickeringly in this contest, Robert Peel. But some speakers have to be heard to be believed; it is not hindsight alone which makes Sir

I

Charles Wetherell a fulminating boor and Bishop Van Mildert an unpleasing instance of timid, wittering uncharity. But when one encounters a historic person speaking *in extenso*, it may become necessary to revise received capsule judgements. Henry Hunt in his own words is not the barroom windbag of comfortable assumption, but a man of great truculent courage, warm heart and sympathies far beyond his own class. By contrast, the Duke of Wellington, squirming from absolutist pronouncement to a sidling manoeuvre in pursuit of government, sounds as furtive as he does brazen, and with his extra-parliamentary talk about using troops against people he emerges as a startlingly unpleasant man. Against this, John Wilson Croker, for all his Enoch Powell-like rush for apocalyptic conclusions, is a shining, wrong-headed talent, principled throughout. And there are voices of men long forgotten – the prophetic liberal voice of John Hawkins, the ironies of Daniel Harvey, the plain religious madness of the younger Spencer Perceval. Any weave gains from extra threads.

All pictures of the past are sketches. Parliament, then as at most times, was full of personalities and differences. Extensive use of what they actually said ought to refine those pictures. And where Parliament leaves off, I have used contemporary talkers and jotters-down, the shrilling Mrs Arbuthnot, the comfortable and good-humoured Lord Holland and the lordly and magnificent Charles Greville, fascination with whom has persuaded author and publisher to bring out a paperback abridgement next year. Again, I make no apology for drawing on the literature of the time – Hazlitt, Galt, Peacock, Lamb and Dickens (the latter as both Pickwickian and parliamentary reporter). The writers of the day, starting as this text does with Peacock's sardonic account of the cities of Novote and Onevote in *Melincourt*, written fifteen years before Reform, are part of the debate and a very sharp part. The belief of this writer is that history being, for all the exegesis, a story, ought to be a readable story. The attempt here, as Bishop Phillpotts swells in his lawn sleeves and intolerable young Macaulay shows off, has been to tell it in that way.

I have thanks for my agent and publisher, Bill Hamilton and Will Sulkin respectively, for their reliable kind sense and helpfulness and Richard Collins, a minutely dedicated and considerate copy-editor. Finally, as with every book I write, gratitude to my wife, Deanna, who has done a vast job of footnoting, been by far the most accurate partner in text correcting and who tells me that I talk only about my work, is unlimited.

If anything is wrong, I got it wrong, but I have written to be read, and read for enjoyment.

Edward Pearce
October 2002

The Cast

Lord Althorp

The reformers divided into contrasting categories, radical and tentative, good- and ill-humoured, but, most instructively, the modest and the flamboyant. John Charles Spencer (1782–1845), heir to Earl Spencer with 'Viscount Althorp' as his courtesy title, was the captain of the modest party. The Spencers descended from Sunderland, Minister to Queen Anne and George I and ultimate political schemer and opportunist. Althorp earned cross-party credit for selfless disinterest, but he was a clever politician for all that.

In the Commons until 1834, he saw through the business of Grey's Reform Ministry (1830–34). Althorp's appointment in November 1830 as both Chancellor of the Exchequer and Leader of the House was derided. He was no speaker and lacked training in finance. A sincere reforming Whig and in his Cambridge days an admirer of Whitbread and Romilly, Althorp was also devoted to his Northamptonshire estate.

The bungling of his first budget confirmed the patronising opinion of onlookers, and parts of it had to be redrafted. But, as Derby later told Disraeli, 'They give you the figures', so Althorp got by as Chancellor. He would, though, be one of the great Leaders of the House! In a period of savage, partisan feelings, he combined a sweet, jibe-turning temperament with great standing in his own party derived from opposition days. When Grey seemed to have withdrawn, and with the party split and squabbling, Althorp was there, a warm, attentive listener, leading by sympathy.

There had been a risk before 1830 of a drift to the Canningite Tories. Althorp always resisted such despair. He told Grey by letter in March 1830, when access to government was not expected, that a group had been formed favouring the cutting of sinecures and dedicated to avoiding alliance with Huskissonians, but not seeking immediately to bring down the government. During Grey's withdrawals, he acted as convenor of the Whigs. He was a good party politician, yet the Tories rightly trusted him, as did Grey, and in March the Whigs in the Commons elected Althorp their leader there. When the government was formed in November 1830, it was Althorp who handled the explosive Brougham who balked at the Lord Chancellorship and aspired to be Master of the Rolls, highly paid and independent in the Commons. Althorp told Brougham that a government

3

could not be formed if he persisted. It was Chief Whip's rhetoric and nonsense, but it worked. Brougham accepted the Great Seal.

Althorp's self-deprecation deflated the other side. The Tory, Croker, made a speech, long and heavy with numbers. Althorp replied that 'he had made some calculations which he considered as entirely conclusive in refutation of the right honourable gentleman's arguments which he had mislaid, but if the House would be guided by his advice, they would reject the amendment'. They did!

He was in fact very competent, but the good-tempered, fallible style, reminiscent of William Whitelaw, was unanswerable. Having supported the ballot in early discussions, he later used it as a swap card to reduce the franchise qualification from £20 to £10 a year. Durham and Russell had prepared the Bill, Russell introduced it, but Althorp piloted it through the Commons. He handled negotiations with 'the Waverers', Lords Harrowby and Wharncliffe, Tories offering a compromise to moderate (or weaken) the Bill. He was also a line of contact to Thomas Attwood, head of the Birmingham Political Union.

Though he had little wish for office, Althorp was a remarkably good politician. The threads were held together, the temperature kept down and, like Clement Attlee, he placed himself to the left of centre of his party. But having acted disinterestedly as locum to Grey, he ultimately deferred to him in a weak line. He was the second man in the government, but in disagreement with Grey, when the Prime Minister would not press the King to create peers to carry reform in the Lords. Althorp had threatened to resign if this were not done. But it provoked a corresponding threat of withdrawal from Grey which sufficed.

There was a price to pay. Althorp had been stretched emotionally beyond reasonable limits and in March 1832 told a new colleague, John Cam Hobhouse, that he had removed his pistols from the bedroom, kept there as a temptation to suicide. Hobhouse's reply sums up ministerial feeling: 'For God's sake,' he said, 'shoot anyone else you like.'

Thomas Attwood

Conventional English history has not made heroes of its radicals. Tom Paine was describe by T.E. Uttley of the *Daily Telegraph* as 'that *evil* man, Tom Paine'. The fact of Francis Place being 'a woman's tailor' has been remembered more devotedly than his running rings round the Duke of Wellington. Every effort has been made to ignore the deep generosity of spirit illuminating Henry Hunt and promote the image of a trouble-making windbag. English historical writing is a rope twisted at both ends. Official history still likes a high tone; left-wing history goes sniffing after unsoundness. The Tories see machinators and upstarts, Marxists dismiss petty bourgeois relevant only to their class and era. The task they undertook and the heroic presumption behind the undertaking never quite get proper credit.

The point so rarely grasped is just how difficult it was to be Paine, Place, Cobbett, Hunt, Carlile and Attwood. To read the speeches of Bishop Van Mildert of Durham and, in his different but equally blinkered, socially conceited way, Macaulay, dismisser of 'the rabble', is to encounter a society settled upon assumptions of social distinctions whether come from God or the natural order of things. Anyone questioning them was a threat, an impudent interloper or 'that evil man' and clearly a suitable case for suppression.

At best, Attwood was a noisy adjunct to a process of reform conducted by gentry for the wider benefit. Cobbett went to prison, Hunt in much worse conditions went to Ilminster jail, Paine fled to exile; it was merely a measure of their low cunning that Place and Attwood stayed at large, making trouble within a law they were careful to know and measure.

Thomas Attwood (1783–1856) came from a family typical of the entrepreneur and radical type common in this period. His father, George, bought a farm in hope of mineral resources, found them, went in for nailing, a local trade, built iron furnaces, made money and opened a bank. The views of the family were diverse; Matthias, Thomas's brother, always close, was a happy Tory. Thomas added an opinion beyond his political radicalism, putting him at odds with miners and squires alike, a loathing of blood sports and any other cruelty to animals. The family had a strong attachment to the England beyond London. Rooted generations back in Shropshire, the Attwoods had become Birmingham people, and the trouble which Thomas would make turned Birmingham into the focus of revolt against a London Parliament rich in noblemen's nephews representing semi-derelict Cornish villages.

Birmingham was a town of many trades and small masters. It made nails, ironmongery and – a cause of anxiety to authority – guns. The temperament of people working for themselves or in small workshops left Birmingham short of deference and any sense of the place it should keep. The writ of the gentry and the moral authority of the gentry's clergy probably went less far among its metal bashers than anywhere in England.

But Attwood did not begin as a constitutional reformer. Like so many midlanders, he had been badly bitten by financial crises. Broadly, the financial part of the economy, money at interest for industrial purposes, was not equal to the ambitions and activity of the industrial sector. In 1819 inflexible credit, an actual shortage of money, had nearly destroyed the family firm, Attwood and Spooner. Thomas accordingly became the advocate of currency reform, finding an ally in Peel's father, the first Sir Robert. That crusade lasted all Attwood's life, taking him into extensive lobbying and barrages of publicity. He wanted cheap and plentiful money, a sort of Keynesianism at odds with the Ricardian orthodoxy of 'sound', confined and punitive money.

Currency reform was Attwood's heroic failure. His triumph was the marshalling of Birmingham for parliamentary Reform through a political union everywhere imitated. While Reform never did bring the fiscal/financial changes he had sought, it did something else. His political union, swiftly followed in Manchester, Newcastle and in smaller towns like Walsall, was the precursor of the modern political party, a series of autonomous local parties nationally focused – and corresponding! When 'democracy' was feared, the political union was democratic. When public opinion was commonly expressed by mob actions, the union remained peaceful. Attwood, a formidable speaker and dominating personality, controlled his audience – by persuading them. He had to succeed in that other highly democratic thing, debate.

The political force which emerged convinced the Duke of Wellington that a revolutionary spirit was at large. Tories followed Sir Charles Wetherell, former Attorney-General, shocked and horrified that an unconstituted and illegal organisation not only operated but conversed with ministers. The idea of suppressing the unions licked across conservative minds like weak fire but never found the occasion. The not finding followed Attwood's insistence upon impeccably legal conduct. No handle was ever given to the senders of cavalry detachments. Indeed, the nearby garrison was regularly visited by families wearing the union's colours, fraternising with men who might be used against them. The Bristol riots, following close upon first Lords rejection, had excited Tories and shaken mainstream reformers. Attwood saw to it that nothing like those riots happened where he had influence.

Without legislative power, operating from platforms at meetings, he had to use straw-free bricks and ensure that nobody threw them. Attwood turned the monster meeting and the resolution/petition to Parliament into moral instruments. He had no power except support displayed to maximum effect.

He revitalised the parliamentary petition. The preambles to almost each day's Commons and Lords debate on Reform showed Tories railing for columns of *Hansard* at 'disgraceful intrusion', 'attempts at intimidation' and a general getting above itself of the public. Attwood, like Francis Place in London, bombarded his allies in government. A lobbyist before the letter, he cultivated all sympathetic politicians. But in crisis, the Days of May of 1832, fearful that a Wellington government would try to put down the unions with force, he prepared for a resistance, barricades, which demonstrated defiance, not insurrection. The soldiers would have to attack them.

No one can precisely weigh the causes of Wellington's failure to form a government, but Attwood's preparations and Place's bank run illustrated the public resolution contrasted with the King's reluctance even to threaten the stalling Upper House with peer creation. The message that rejection of Reform was not an option came from an unenfranchised public will led by Attwood.

The rest of his career was anticlimactic. In Parliament, he did not make a major impact. His currency schemes came to nothing, his business interests turned sour, leaving him a quiet retirement convinced of failure. But he had succeeded, his life a prophecy of political democracy: and, unlike the better remembered Joseph Chamberlain, a blazing credit to Birmingham.

Lord Brougham

Henry Peter Brougham (1778–1868) was the outsider whose presence in the Cabinet could be explained only by merit. He was not popular, but, unlike the equally provocative Durham, he lacked social standing. Despite ancient pretensions to being a Westmorland squire, he owed everything to his abilities. Like his Tory counterpart, Lyndhurst, he was a clever lawyer where one was needed. Unlike Lyndhurst, he did not know how to make himself agreeable and he had ungentlemanly ambition and pride of talent in full strength. And Brougham, through his Robertson mother, was Scottish (and thus better) educated – Edinburgh High School and University – called in 1800 to the Scottish bar, eight years ahead of the English one.

Already a legal silk and noted Whig, in 1820–21 he remade his name in blazing lights as counsel for Queen Caroline. Adulterous consort of the adulterous Prince of Wales, Caroline had on George III's death returned from Italian dalliance as 'Queen of England'. His Majesty, in a fit of rage and folly, set his Prime Minister, Liverpool, to prosecuting the lady, the laborious excavation of a deep hole in the ground apparent to everyone except George IV. Brougham was, of course, King's Counsel, but not literally so here. As the Queen's retained advocate, he would now give Caroline enjoyable revenge and at the same time shake the throne.

Brougham had been personal adviser to the Queen, and though on her return he was almost bought off, he reverted to his commitment to her. He took the royal case and doused it with George IV's own rather degrading infidelities, turning the prosecution into one of the great own goals of history. The King cowered at Windsor, distracted, as J.H. Plumb puts it, 'to the point of nervous prostration',¹ and the House of Hanover fell to the lowest of many low points in public respect.

Brougham was hard to define: talent and ambition boiling over, brilliance, unreliability, naked careerism and dedicated conviction lend outline to his character. One of those convictions concerned education for the neglected public. Brougham worked hard and effectively for SPUK, the Society for the Propagation of Useful Knowledge, a proto-Workers' Educational Association. Thomas Love Peacock, not an admirer, called it the Steam Intellect Society'; Brougham he called 'the learned friend'! But he was indirectly the creator of the mechanics institutes whose buildings still stand in northern towns and the 'Godless Institution in Gower Street', otherwise London University. Given his Scottish connections, Brougham was early involved with Francis Jeffrey and Sydney Smith in producing the liberal *Edinburgh Review*. He wrote eighty articles for the first twenty issues of this sniping partner of the Tory *Quarterly Review* and *Blackwood's*, both virulent Tory publications.

Entering Parliament in 1810, Brougham introduced in 1812 a bill to make participation in the slave trade a felony. But although a reformer, he was relaxed about the rotten boroughs, sitting successively for Winchelsea and then Knaresborough, both satisfactorily rotten. Such tolerance was on the record long before the Reform Bill, and in 1831–2 Tories enjoyed quoting him. He had always accepted the argument that such places gave a start to 'lads o' pairts' like Henry Brougham. Nevertheless, when Brougham put his mind to radicalism, he was formidable, offending Grey by his populism and winning a popular recognition the old Whigs scorned.

In 1830 he became a new sort of candidate, campaigning, travelling, speechmaking, a style slowly adapted across the century. His candidacy for Yorkshire was taken up because this vast county seat, when contested, became a democratic affair. Pleading daily at York Assizes, Brougham sallied out into every reachable town, making furious and amusing political speeches before being returned in triumph.

Dislike of Brougham had many grounds, among them his modernity and gift for publicity. Once elected, he would discard the Commons. Brougham wanted major office, but, as a parvenu, was badly positioned for a high political place. Outsiders could, however, rise in the law, as Jacky Scott, Newcastle coal man's son, had done in becoming that most learned, dilatory and reactionary of Lord Chancellors, Eldon. Grey had good reason to worry about the royal response even though William had succeeded George, proffered the Attorney-Generalship, but Brougham allegedly tore up the letter, threw it on the floor and jumped on it. This was generally believed because it sounded like Brougham. Grey, bullied all round and with some notion of Brougham's worth, swallowed affront and suggested the Great Seal. Brougham had wanted the Mastership of the Rolls (it offered political freedom and £7,000 a year). As radical scourge and faction leader, he was both feared and wanted by the noble leadership. Althorp charmed and shamed him into stooping to the Lord Chancellorship. And as Lord Brougham and Vaux, he became a major player in the struggle and one of the great Chancellors.

There would be many quarrels, but in the Lords second reading he would contribute one of the great parliamentary speeches, though malicious report reckoned that, firing on mulled port, he was drunk at the end. In court he would be a total contrast to Eldon whose anxious pedantry had put the Court of Chancery years behind schedule, providing Dickens with Jarndyce v Jarndyce in *Bleak Horse*. Brougham cut contemptuously through procedural refinements and caught up on that schedule quickly. He would be one of the great law reformers, changing the law of libel and proposing what would eventually become the Law Reform Commission.

He was a profoundly modern man, without his age's reverence for precedent and history, a non-doctrinaire utilitarian and representative of the meritocratic middle classes. But impetuous, variable in allegiance, tempestuous and, as was said of George Brown, ebullient, Brougham attracted the word 'impossible', and a final quarrel in 1834 tipped him out. No brilliant, difficult man was going to survive under Grey's successor, the bland, idle, mediocre Melbourne. Brougham lived a long retirement, wrote spectacularly unreliable memoirs, travelled, and on those travels, with typical unpredictability, discovered and inspired the modest development of a small coastal village in the South of France called Cannes. There is only one word for Henry Peter Brougham – 'fascinating'.

John Wilson Croker

A Galway-born Irishman, son of a senior customs official, Croker (1780–1857), though a Protestant, was hardly privileged. The History Society's gold medallist at Trinity, Dublin, enjoying friendships with members of the landed elite, he was drawn to Tory politics and valuable to them. A natural conviction Tory, he was called to the bar, entering Parliament for Downpatrick at twenty-seven, helped by the influence of one Sir Arthur Wellesley.

Croker suffered from the malice of Disraeli who in *Coningsby* sketched Rigby, a political creature, henchman to Lord Monmouth, contrasting him with the all-wise Sidonia, Disraeli's idea of Disraeli. The idea is a nonsense. Croker was both a first-rate man of business and a devoted believer in an old ordered tradition. He handled Lord Hertford's affairs at modest advantage to himself, showing that self-destructive aristocrat a disinterested devotion. Croker was a man of intense, gloomy earnest. An intelligent modern comparison would be with Enoch Powell, a near-contemporary one with Edmund Burke, of whom he is perhaps an intelligent parody.

Croker held the standard country gentleman view that the British constitution, as concluded in 1688, was at once perfect and pitifully fragile, but held it more savagely and despondently, dreaming of apocalypse. He hoped that an inevitable post-Reform revolutionary regime would let Princess Victoria live quietly as Miss Guelph.

Man of affairs and backstage intelligence to senior Tories, including Peel, his only intellectual equal there, Croker was also the party's most effective parliamentary speaker and journalist, expanding bright, bitter scorn for decades, notably in the *Quarterly Review*. He seems to have been content as an eternal wheel donkey, but his absence from the command group was absurd.

Interestingly, Croker supported Catholic emancipation, about which a West of Ireland man knew something. His Toryism was romantic, not to say dramatic, with a layering of intellectualisation, but not mean-minded. However, he walked out of politics at fifty-two, refusing in absolute terms to contest another parliamentary seat if Reform should pass. Peel urged him to remain, but without warmth or insistence, demonstrating his own machine quality and confirming Croker's hard-edged purpose. Yet he continued to advise the Tory leader until finally alienated in 1846 by repeal of the Corn Laws.

Quite separately, Croker had the educated nineteenth-century man's disinterested love of literature, and he wrote movingly about snuggling down in the library of his beloved house on the river at Moulsey. But this devotion led to a bitter humiliation. During the Reform debates, he had exploded Macaulay's grand tirade about the French aristocracy provoking revolution by dumb resistance to all reform. Croker coolly pointed out widespread aristocratic liberal intentions, citing the Montmorency and Noailles families supporting the grandest radical proposals.

Macaulay's self-congratulatory blacksmith-bowling-to-squire notions of English superiority were demolished, provoking a clever, conceited man to savage revenge. It came quickly when Croker's edition of an assemblage of Boswell and Johnson was shown to have its share of silly mistakes and received in the Whig *Edinburgh Review* such contempt fuelled by hatred that the work was withdrawn. Croker could hardly complain; he was a fierce, contemptuous reviewer himself. Dying in 1857, he faded into historical marginality in the way of losers. But he was an intelligent, brave, always interesting man, more interesting indeed than many winners.

John George Lambton, Lord Durham

Lambton (1792–1840) came from a family aristocratic before it was titled. Ancestors included a crusader, a Knight of Rhodes, kinship with Edward II and Henry VIII and a Royalist knighted at Marston Moor. The Lambtons steadily provided Members for Durham after 1675, rich, exalted squires. The Lambton coalfields, exploited in the eighteenth century, gave a proud family something to be proud of. In the England of 1820, the £80,000 a year on which Lambton 'could jog along' was a formidable argument. A castle in Strawberry Hill Gothic proclaimed it. Its inheritor added devastating latinate good looks and a blazing temper. When a peerage came, Lambton was furious at a mere barony.

Against such preoccupation with fiddling degrees of precedence stood a natural radicalism, much of it derived from a beloved tutor, Dr Beddoes, driven from an Oxford chair for his opinions, some from an appealing lack of prudential group identity, some from warmth of heart. Coal-owners were detested in County Durham, the brutal Londonderrys hated. John Lambton had set about being a decent employer and established a rough and ready pension scheme. When he died young in 1840, miners would follow the coffin.

But menace surrounded the growing boy. The family was as consumptive as it was rich. His father, William, died when John was four. His first wife, Henrietta Cholmondley, suffered the same early death. It would return to him and his own. By his second marriage, Lambton was linked, naturally enough, to another northern liberal aristocratic family, the Greys. Louisa Grey was the daughter of Charles, 2nd Earl Grey of Howick, in Northumberland. Lambton entered Parliament in 1813 and went on to the attack. He offered his own Reform Bill in 1821, stronger than the Act of 1832. Durham was remote from the lounging cynicism of the Regency political scene, in his lordly way a moralist, regularly moved to burning anger at the immoralism of others. He was self-righteous in ways usually creditable, but as commonly hard to live with. The aristocratic conscience could be a useful goad and as disagreeable as anything supplied by the Nonconformists.

He was naturally a radical as Croker was a Tory. They are the two men of undeviating principle in the whole Reform struggle. When the yeomanry charged at Peterloo in 1819, Lambton, hearing of a meeting called in Sunderland by a cathedral cleric, Henry Phillpotts, to congratulate the

Manchester magistrates, summoned friends and by a vote, dissolved the meeting.

Yet when, in 1828, the peerage came, Tories assumed that he was being brought with his father-in-law into the Canningite and Tory coalition. But he had told Canning that he would be as hard on the Tories in the Lords as he had been in the country.

In 1830 Grey would give Durham the Privy Seal, a middling, if serviceable, office, before casually expressing a wish 'that you would take our Reform Bill in hand'. As chairman of a committee of four, Durham supported the sweeping removal of nomination boroughs, but he failed to establish the ballot. Eventually made law by Gladstone in 1872, this was considered likely to wreck all chances of the bill passing, a prudential Fabianism which Durham despised.

In government he would be assailed by shattering, tubercular-related attacks and the slow death of his son, Charles, *The Boy in Red* of Sir Thomas Lawrence's painting, a beautiful, ethereal, intelligent child at the apex of an intense triangle of love with his mother and father. The grief at Charles's death, shared by his grandfather, Grey, and an enforced absence while the Bill was modestly amended, triggered Durham into a furious verbal assault on his father-in-law at a Cabinet dinner. But he remained, took his full part in Lords debates, contributing not least to the annihilation of the Bishop of Exeter, Henry Phillpotts!

In 1834 Durham was moved, after Melbourne's accession, to Canada (as an Earl). Sent out of the way, he would, in a five-month stay, parlay a frightening revolt into a blueprint for the cohesion of the British Empire. Reconciling Upper and Lower Canada, French and British, by exiling ringleaders to the US and amnestying everyone else, he proposed in a report that the Canadians should govern themselves in all internal matters, entrenching attachment to Britain in trade, war and general sympathies. His phrase 'Benign neglect' was a message of concentrated good sense contradicting the follies of George III. Returning to England to much criticism, Durham was unmoved in his (correct) view that he had been magnificently right. In all his impossibility, Durham was the bright, peculiar star of Reform; and that soiled word, vision, actually fits him.

Charles Grey, Earl Grey

Tynesiders know the statue which stands on a pillar in central Newcastle as 'Grey's Monument'. The raising of columns to the celebrated was a short-lived fashion. To one of Nelson in Trafalgar Square was added another of the same in Dublin, subsequently blown up in the 1960s by the old, left-wing, minimally violent IRA. The York Steps figure overlooking

The Mall in London celebrates a royal nonentity, Frederick, Field Marshal the Duke of York, whilst in North Shields, Admiral Collingwood, local man, Nelson's deputy and successor, also stands high. Grey is alone in Britain, I think, as a civilian memorialised on a column. A City Council was anxious to celebrate the Ministry headed by Lord Grey which reformed Parliament, and with it the constitution of the United Kingdom.

They were commemorating in this rather Italianate way the least vainglorious, most English of politicians. Charles Grey's father had risen from large squireship (17,000 acres) as one of very few generals making a decent fist of things during the American War of Independence (and in the West Indies). But the family had held land in Northumberland since the fourteenth century, with estates at Fallodon and Howick, for which the Prime Minister would frequently abandon Westminster.

Grey was a sincere reformer and a twenty-four-carat aristocrat, socially far above such Tories as Eldon, risen from the coal trade, the customs officer's son, Croker, or Robert Peel, whose doctrine that it needed three generations to make a gentleman narrowly admitted Robert Peel. Even Wellington, younger son of the merely Irish peerage, was an arriviste. But the radicalism developed at Cambridge, where Grey studied very seriously without troubling himself over a degree. The family were Whigs, and Grey, like Althorp, came under the influence of the advanced circle of Romilly and Whitbread, then was subsequently swept along by the rackety, irresistible charm of Fox and Sheridan.

But before Grey, the idealist, had matured, an encounter in the same circle triggered Grey, the lover. It was an episode out of a bad novel and has taken its natural place on television. The young Grey fell into devouring love for a Duchess, Georgiana, sensational young wife of the Duke of Devonshire. Devonshire was something out of Rossini, a crotchety older man, tyrannising a young wife, preferring his mistress and his dogs, intended for the suitably operatic comeuppance of a grand affair between that lady and a suitably handsome and idealistic young man. The flight with friends of Georgiana to France to bear Grey's child followed. 'Always a fool about women' snapped Charles Greville thirty-five years later, as part of a general grumble at the man then wickedly putting through constitutional reform.

But Grey was very much the lover, not the womaniser, and the role paralleled the early ardour of his politics. He entered Parliament in 1786 for one of the country seats in Northumberland before the French Revolution and its hopes and disillusionments, but also before the King's Minister, Pitt, had established an ice floe of preventative reaction. As an illustration of his sane and moderate good sense, Grey tried unsuccessfully to stop further prosecution of Warren Hastings for alleged peculation in India. The mania of Burke would prolong it another six years, but Fox would quickly be persuaded by young Grey that the distasteful business was going nowhere.

The 1790s would become for all liberals a period of 'Never bright, confident morning again'. The September Massacres and the Reign of Terror were horrible rebuffs for all who aspired to better things. The temptation to follow Pitt and Burke into systematic reaction was great, but the best of the Whigs, Grey among them, painfully resisted it.

Grey was an active founder of the Association of the Friends of the People, in the company of Tierney, later party leader, Whitbread, Erskine and Sheridan. He spoke for the Association, entirely opposing all violence and revolutionary activity while sustaining belief in constitutional reform amid the new witch-hunting mood. In 1793, Grey would argue as he would in 1831–2. The Crown and the Lords were too powerful – too powerful in the Commons! Pitt in reply rehearsed the anti-Reform rhetoric of 1831: present dangers, reform no better than revolution and a general indiscriminate hanging on to nurse, a world view which in that House would command a great majority for years to come.

Grey's conduct of another reform motion, rejected in 1797, won him great standing in the little room of principled Whig opposition. He became, in his early thirties, Fox's effective lieutenant. But his role was one of conservation, holding party and movement together against a better day. Most of Grey's battles in office between 1830 and 1834 would rerun races earlier lost when the Terror or Napoleon underwrote censorship, State spying and right-wing hysteria, English style. Winning the second time round would involve thirty years of patience, intermittency and low hopes, opposition at its most dispiriting.

The Whigs had had a shallow ally in the Prince of Wales, transiently a liberal. But George, a man on whom his own intelligence was wasted, reverted as Regent after 1810 to screaming type. Grey's first concern had not been for parliamentary Reform, but Catholic emancipation, something less remote and one, moreover, shared with Tory friends like George Canning. But the Regent, despite his morganatic marriage to the Catholic Maria Fitzherbert, was now shrilly against. A bill for relief passed the Commons, but was killed off in committee, with Grey scorning 'this anti-Catholic prince who is much more anti-Catholic than the king'.[2]

The Whigs, with no friends near the throne, saw a new and militant radicalism emerging in the middle and working classes, also excluded from things, only more so. Sir Francis Burdett, Major John Cartwright and the City merchant, Robert Waithman, never mind Cobden and Hunt, at once annoyed Grey and put pressure on him. There would be bad feeling between him and the radicals, and, given his views at this time, 'so delicate, so faint, so evanescent, so equivocal [that] a man must have good eyes and close attention to find them out',[3] he looked for some time like a leader dwindling into moderation. Meanwhile, Brougham was stealing both popular backing and the initiative.

Grey's role was to survive and adapt. But instinctively, like many leaders of reform parties since, he felt that his own left wing was making progress impossible. Parliamentary reform he had long left as an open question; full-blown opposition by the outs was not then the norm. But Grey's standing with Tories and Canningites as a safe man in a Tory-led coalition would strengthen his hand when the Tory party itself began to disintegrate. The Canningites, sick of Wellington, could join Grey without scrutiny of his intentions. Yet Grey was a far better party man than Brougham supposed or than Brougham himself actually was. There is a touch of Asquith and Lloyd George here – steady but casual leader and mercurial, endlessly intriguing high talent. And the steady man had kept the party fit to form a government and agree a programme.

The granting of Catholic emancipation by Wellington in a crisis was the shooting by accident of Grey's fox and might have accelerated membership of a Tory-plus ministry, especially as Grey had cut an impressive figure in the debate. But Wellington, desperately imperceptive, made no offer and Grey escaped temptation. An early inhibition had been his dislike of Canning, to whom he extended a fastidious scorn not shown to men of lower rank. Canning to Grey embodied such counter-jumping charlatanism as no genius could mend. But with his swift death, Tory support for the Turks in Greece repelled him. Ironically, Canning had sympathised with the Greeks.

And however much Grey grumbled about the radicals, he and Althorp could work with them. It thus became possible for the Canning faction of moderate Tories – Goderich, Melbourne and Palmerston – to join Durham, Russell and Brougham, with Thomas Attwood and Francis Place at the door. Grey was not a devious man, but somehow he acquired all the advantages at which conscious finessing might have aimed. In fact, on Reform he would be motivated less by past convictions than present social and political crisis. He would accept the judgement that a modest, limited bill would be as gravel hitting a wall, and that large reform was a political necessity. It was the conclusion to which, after Lords rejection, riots and what is euphemistically called 'unrest', most people would come.

As Prime Minister, Grey gave Durham's group their heads in outlining proposals, then assented to a bill unimaginably more radical than anything expected from him, especially by the Tories who were horribly wrong-footed, failing to strike early with a motion on the first night when still at full strength in a fluid Commons. If Grey had consciously been planning to set an aroused public opinion against the majority of members opposed to Russell's bill, he could hardly have done so more brilliantly. Equally, the King would take from the gentlemanly Lord Grey things which, from avowed radicals, would have appalled him.

Betwixt luck, quiet skill, adjustment to the times and his older instincts, Grey and the equally respectable though more naturally reformist Althorp became the right man for a long moment in history. Having kept his party together in opposition, he kept it together for nearly four years before passing it on to Melbourne in working shape and with great and irreversible things done.

Henry Hunt

New readers starting here need to learn one little related fact about Henry Hunt. He was a gentleman!* The family had Norman roots and had been noted Royalists during the Civil War. His great-great grandfather, Thomas Hunt, a voluntary exile with Prince Charles, had enjoyed no restitution of lands confiscated by, ironically, Parliament. The family, having been genteelly frugal for a couple of generations on a very modest estate in Wiltshire, worked and married its way back to substance, 3,000 acres in the upper Avon valley, property in Bath and a splendid house in Chisenbury Priory.

Henry specialised in the most up-to-date methods of sheep farming and gained an excellent name for his grains. Socially, he could look Sir Edward Knatchbull steadily in the eye, the absence of a title being almost a social advantage in a county family of serious antiquity. Henry had been intended for Oxford and the gift of a living from his father. He preferred to be a hard-working and splendid farmer of the family land. He progressed to the radical side by way of the local militia and, as with Cobbett, a loyalist anti-Napoleonic phase, though he had learned wider sympathies from a tutor. His perfectly honourable but convention-slighting unmarried alliance with Elizabeth Vince played its part. She steadied him, ended the high lifestyle of his respectable days while dividing him from local gentry society less tolerant than the circle of the regularly in-and-out-of-love Charles Grey.

Radical gentry are nothing unusual in England. Today, Hunt could have

---

* For most of what appears here I am indebted to John Belchem's excellent pioneering life, *Orator Hunt*. All quotations not otherwise acknowledged derive from it.[4]

linked arms with Tony Benn or Tam Dalyell. And such men commonly attract the livid animus of right-wing newspapers and historians. Hunt's private life would be trumpeted by the Tory press in the way of our own delicate tabloids. His private life paralleled that of Charles Parnell, both having a lifelong attachment to a devoted woman. A rash and early broken-down marriage prevented him from making Elizabeth Vince his wife. But Hunt, the political figure, was hated and any mud would do.

As for history, it has patronised him. The very name attached, 'Orator' Hunt, suggests a windbag, a man consumed with the sound of his own voice. But while Henry Hunt *was* vain and did engage in petty, bad-tempered feuds with allies like Cobbett and Francis Burdett, he was a generous spirit and vastly more than a demagogue. Even Socialist historians have got him wrong, Edward Thompson writing, 'Hunt voiced not principle nor even well-founded radical strategy, but the emotions of the movement . . . not the leader but the captive of the least stable portions of the crowd.'[5]

This is wildly wrong and it is sad that Thompson, who immortally chastised posterity for 'its monstrous condescension to the poor stockinger', should slight the spokesman of poor weavers for whom he systematically and consistently argued manhood suffrage and the secret ballot, two pretty strong principles to be going on with.

Hunt's first major speech in the Reform Bill debates reflects someone identified body and soul with the solid men of the new working classes. Hunt did not follow the crowd, but he identified with, loved even, the people and the social groups making it up. He spoke shortly after the famous, and in places insufferable, oration of the young, and generally insufferable, Macaulay who had exalted the new, aspiring middle classes and dismissed 'the rabble'. Hunt, who knew the industrial working class in Preston, 'did not wish the rabble as the hon. Member called them, to have votes, but he did wish that those who paid a rent of £3 a year up to £10, the men who were the sinews and nerves of the country, should not be excluded'. At this time even the £10 franchise was seen by the limper Whigs as chancily progressive and by the Ultra, Wetherell, as 'seeking votes among paupers or in a *lazaretto*.'*

Hunt's historical problem is that he irritates the left by his rejection of revolutionary measures (he once headed off the radical Dr John Watson from a trap of illegal action fitted by a government spy), and he annoys Whig/Liberal history almost as much. Hunt supported the Reform Bill

---

* Since a lazaretto means a leper house, the insult to payers of rates by small instalments was extreme.

for its acts of disfranchisement which struck at the old ordering. In this he inverted the frequent House of Lords view approving the new constituencies but horrified at terminating ancient boroughs. Hunt was scornful of the Reform Bill, which got his steady vote for what it destroyed. It advanced the well-placed by enlarging the national elite. It did nothing, politically or economically, for the poor stockinger!

The central event of Hunt's life was his presence on a platform in St Peter's Fields, Manchester, on 16 August 1819. A troop of yeomanry and another of Hussars made for the platform, sabreing and riding down the peaceful gathering come to hear him. Eleven people were killed and hundreds injured. Peterloo is history, a legend which happens to be true. It was to that 'doing of their duty' to which Croker and Wellington referred longingly when facing a Reform Bill sustained against the noble veto by barricades in Birmingham.

But Hunt, with numbers of local allies, was, if not their inventor, the effective contemporary summoner of crowds to oppose the authorities. Manchester was where authority's self-control snapped. But speaking in public, Hunt had kept resolutely and infuriatingly within the law. The Home Secretary, Sidmouth, complained in resentful capitals before Peterloo of 'the unprecedented Artifice with which the Demagogues of the present day contrive without transgressing the Law to produce on the Public mind the same effect which used only to be created by means unquestionably unlawful'.

Peterloo was what should not be done, would not deliberately be done, but was done, by oafish, part-time military. Hatred for Hunt stemmed from his ability to outwit authority by observing the law and preaching effective, non-violent opposition by the display of non-electing, non-belonging but horribly evident numbers. Thomas Attwood, organising his political union in Birmingham ten years on, followed in one key respect the model of Hunt's northern tours.

At a time when the word 'democrat' was a term generally uttered with a disclaimer or contempt, Hunt was a democrat. He was also a man with socially transferred loyalties, a Wiltshire gentleman farmer dedicated to the working men of the North. Many people would be disappointed by the Reform Act, but not Hunt. He had expected nothing from it.

Sir Edward Knatchbull

Light dismissal of Sir Edward Knatchbull (1781–1849) is as easy as wrong. He was the ninth Baronet, a creation of Charles I, from a family settled in Kent since the thirteenth century, a country gentleman's country gentleman. In *Persuasion* Sir Walter Elliot had looked with pity upon the creations of the eighteenth century, and, oddly, Knatchbull was related to Jane Austen by his marriage in 1820 to Fanny Knight, her favourite niece. Sir Edward (1781–1849) voted against Catholic emancipation in 1828 and the Reform Act in 1831 and was also a noted opponent of the South Eastern railway seeking extension through Kent. He was classified as one of the Ultras who turned against Wellington after emancipation then factitiously brought him down in December 1830. Authors of their own fate at the hands of the consequent Grey Ministry, whose Reform Bill they would die fighting, the Ultras were Neanderthals and stupid with it, in *1066* terms, 'a Bad Thing'.

Such glibness is unjust. The Ultras embraced complexities and variations. Sir Charles Wetherell, despite some legal distinction, was a boorish buffoon, and his insolence towards the people of Bristol certainly helped trigger the riots there. Wetherell was no gentleman. Knatchbull was never anything else. Deeply Conservative from an ingrained belief in the fragility of society, he also had a social conscience. He voted happily enough for the abolition of slavery, which Peel accepted only late and under local pressure.

As distress deepened in the North, Knatchbull could see beyond class and region. A natural supporter of the Corn Laws, he had still voted in 1826 for a limited importation of foreign grain. He told a local farmers' protest meeting, 'You have no conception of the distress which exists in the manufacturing districts; your own county does not afford a comparison. Here we are not met by hundreds of human beings barely eking out an existence, affording the appalling but desperate truths of the wretched state to which the operatives have arrived.'[6]

His opposition to ending Nonconformist disabilities and to 'Catholic Relief' was anxious rather than bigoted. 'He would give religious toleration to every class of people, but he would not give political power to those persons who would not tolerate the religions of others,'[7] not good thinking, but not truly sectarian and par for the country gentleman's narrow course.

His anger over Peel's and Wellington's legislation of Catholic Relief was chiefly anger at an abrupt, non-consulting change of course. Neither Wellington nor Peel, in responding to the threat of social breakdown after O'Connell's election in County Clare had challenged the prescriptive (and vituperative) oath no Catholic could take, ever explained themselves. Peel had refused office under the candid friend of emancipation, George Canning. His concession to *force majeure* made the earlier line look like a bid for the country gentlemen's support, discountable in office. It affronted Knatchbull's formidable sense of honour. The move was 'utterly inconsistent and at variance with his former political life . . . a general feeling of distrust pervaded the minds of all men on this subject.'[8] In all his limitations, he was, and would remain, straight. Shock and a sense of personal betrayal by Peel left Knatchbull unable to see the damage of a split or rebellion. He and a younger man, Sir Richard Vyvyan, a lighter, more cheerfully irresponsible figure, worked to remove the Wellington government, something accomplished on a civil list motion in November 1830.

Never as adventurous as Vyvyan, he felt very uneasy at dealings with the real super-high right wing, the Dukes of Cumberland and Newcastle. And on parliamentary Reform he accepted from the start the principle of a middling bill. If it were for 'disfranchising those boroughs where the corruption . . . has been carried on to so great an extent and conferring it on large towns – when facts are properly proved, I will support the measure'.[9]

It even seemed possible that Knatchbull might join a Reform government. Things were very fluid in 1830. Grey and Althorp were very keen to recruit reputable Tories. The Duke of Richmond came in, to his own surprise, and, with occasional kicks and screams, stayed the course. Knatchbull was offered a choice of two Cabinet posts, declining both, as Greville admiringly noted: 'The offer was "a reward for the service done in giving the mortal thrust to the Duke" [but] as he is an honest man and wanted at that time the Duke's life rather than his purse . . . he never would have done on any terms (what Richmond and others did) so inconsistent a thing as to join a Reform Ministry.'[10]

He would, of course, be an opponent of the large-scale Bill presented, though never among the shrillest voices, and this would for a time cost him his seat in Parliament. But Knatchbull is best seen as a thoroughly reputable man, muddled and buffeted by events and given to making his judgements more of men than measures. Not a fanatic at all, he was a decent Tory shocked by the speed of the political track. Such a man, right or wrong, is part of the fibre of good politics, the follower refusing, from his own convictions, to follow.

Sir Robert Peel Bt.

'It was Peel's merit as a statesman that he normally adapted his policies to the need for change. It was his defect as a politician that he did so in a manner which combining as it did, prickliness, egotism, self-exculpation and unctuousness, gave a formidable handle to his enemies.' This comment comes from Robert Blake of The Queen's College, Oxford, distinguished Conservative historian, historian indeed, of the Conservative Party. It is possibly a little harsh, but certainly Robert Peel never found the words or sympathy for talking to his supporters. There may begin with him a recurring tradition among Tory leaders of actively disliking the generality of the Tory Party.

Logically, Peel should have been a Canningite, an open accepter of the new and the practical. But Canning was thought an adventurer and outsider, and Peel was the sort of new man devoted to convention, a new man defending old things. And he wanted, or believed that he wanted, to do so; he could exalt the old order as readily as any squire reciting Church and State formulae. But he was a new man for all that, a grandson of cotton and Lancashire, grandson also of a smallholder turned small-scale millowner, known as 'Old Parsley' Peel. Yet he lacked any collective conceit in the middle class. He was a paradox; he had been to Eton and Christ Church, gaining first class honours; and from his father, the first Baronet, a very large-scale millowner, he would share in a splendid fortune. But, said Disraeli, he pronounced 'wonderful' as 'woonderful' and struggled to control his aspirates. Although Disraeli, describing Peel's pronunciation of 'put', uses a circumflex, this seems not to have been the social death in the 1820s which it would be among late Victorians and for most of the twentieth century. Ultra Tory squires were unlikely to make much effort to keep Norfolk or Yorkshire out of their speech.

Much more damaging was Peel's evidential pragmatism. He would move against party prejudice on Catholic emancipation and the Corn Laws according to, respectively, a major crisis of order in Ireland and belief in the obvious sense of importing cheap food for the producers of exportable goods. His politics echoed his speech, aspiring to one thing but coming back gravitationally to another. He was a brilliant member of the urban commercial class leading a party of hereditary rustic immobilists, a rational man charmed by an unreasonable heritage. Such an attitude betrayed him on occasion into statements fitting neither his intelligence nor his essentially humane nature. Support, until the very last minute, for slavery in a modified form is a painful instance.

He was also given, perhaps because of this split nature, to emphatic commitments to causes he was most tempted to doubt. In the case of parliamentary Reform, he would severely defend the status quo. But he was too intelligent not to know that a reformed Parliament meant the increased influence of people like his father and grandfather, creative, intelligent middle-class men. He shared up to a point in the not irrational but overdone Tory fears of an English Jacobinism. But his whole performance throughout the Reform struggle was constricted, almost artificial. Essentially, he was doing what was expected of the second man and prospective leader of his party.

Less high-mindedly, the second man in that party heartily disliked the first. Peel and Wellington had in common cold formality, deficiency in warm words and, in Lord Blake's term, 'egotism', Wellington, for all the bluff-soldier-on-duty pose, being the more egotistic of the two. The Duke was also the man most violently dedicated to absolute denial of any parliamentary Reform. He had lost office for saying so. Peel had followed his about turn on Catholic emancipation, sharing recognition of a necessity, sharing also in calamitous non-communication to the ranks. Wellington, having then lost the Ultras, wanted them back, followed them over Reform and lost altogether. Peel despised the Ultras and left them with few doubts as to how much or why. He had no motive for accompanying Wellington into the quasi veto of the second Reform Bill by blocking its central clause in committee.

He thus took no part in the consequent requirement to form a government liable both to put through the essentials of the Whig Bill *and* provoke civil breakdown. Flatly refusing to remove so much as a necktie, he watched from the bank while Wellington stripped to swim in a dangerous river, paddled at the margin and scrambled ignominiously back. He would not have acknowledged the pleasure, but pleasure it must have been.

But Peel had, anyway, little talent for opposition. His very great distinction is for things done, the creation of a police force shrewdly kept relatively unpolitical, and adapted to local notions rather than those of the continental autocracies, and a superb Bank Act, stabilising an unstable, diffuse system of undercapitalised and overextended country banks. Finally, in the teeth of the squires whom again he did not consult, Peel would abandon agricultural protection, that service of unenlightened self-interest to the landowners whom he had long led with so little mutual affection.

Abolition was, like Catholic emancipation, which he had adopted, and parliamentary Reform, which he had woodenly resisted, the right thing. Like so much in his career, it was first-rate government executed by way of appalling politics. Peel, too, would go into the river, one which had to be crossed. And on the opposite bank, he would die.

Arthur Wellesley, 1st Duke of Wellington

As every schoolboy knows even today, Arthur Wellesley, 1st Duke of Wellington, beat the French in the Peninsular War and at Waterloo, thus obtaining immortal fame. As a diplomat after the war (British delegate to the congress of Verona), Wellington showed a great deal of good sense, making, as the war ended, a famous proclamation (in French) pre-empting all revenge where France was concerned, saying that the allies had only one enemy, Bonaparte.

Wellington had a unique place in Britain after the war. He was the victor and the hero, someone very difficult to criticise. And holding office under Liverpool after 1818, he did not attract especial criticism, but he resigned office in 1827 when Canning pushed partisanship towards the Greek independence movement too far for his taste. Wellington was essentially a status quo man in foreign affairs. But with the incapacity of Liverpool and the death of Canning, and a Tory split which made a united government impossible for Goderich, Wellington was the hero, perfectly constitutionally called upon to govern during a vacuum of civilian authority. Nothing is more startling than the contrast between what followed: Wellington 1, the emancipator of Roman Catholics, and Wellington 2, the stubborn immobilist, setting his face against all parliamentary Reform and bringing down his own government in the process. All this, accomplished in a period of less than three years, succinctly illustrates the difference between military and political genius.

Wellington, himself a fairly godless Irish Protestant, happy enough with the statutory injustice excluding the Irish majority from the government of Ireland, knew trouble when he saw it. The act of Daniel O'Connell, having collected a massive following across the country, then standing for a seat in Parliament for which he was disqualified by religion, was explosive, perhaps more so than O'Connell himself quite realised. Catholics having had mere votes since the Union, he was certain of a majority. The idea of rejecting the duly elected Member for County Clare on the grounds of a Catholic not being able to take the anti-Catholic oath, and doing so in the teeth of a Catholic Ireland roused to the edge of the sort of revolt it had been through thirty years before, was not wise. And Wellington, like the flexible soldier of the Peninsula, recognised the need for coherent, well-managed retreat, and duly retreated. Catholic Relief/Emancipation was put through Parliament by Wellington's Tory administration with enthusiastic support from Whigs and to the manifest grief of a great body of Tory members.

Wellington, the soldier, had been adaptive and flexible in cooperation with Spanish rebels busy inventing guerrilla warfare. But because he was a soldier, Wellington, though not a despot was not a consulter either. He had dismayed not only bigots and constitutional standers-pat; he had upset all the people he didn't tell, those to whom he made no concessions of forewarning or prior discussion. He had conjured a situation in which high-flying Tories could argue (correctly) that, where Catholic Relief was granted, parliamentary Reform and abolition of the Corn Laws would follow. The Tory Ultras were created at that point, often country gentlemen, by no means stupid or ill-disposed, but wedded to what they knew, convinced that clever fellows meant to take it away and certain that the

Duke, of all men, had betrayed them. They felt a dreadful sense of loss and a corresponding anger, which they directed with sullen inveteracy at the Duke.

If Wellington had been a good, devious, civilian politician, he would have played for time over all future issues involving change, perhaps pulling in the more office-hungry Whigs, playing things down the middle and staying open to a minimalist reform bill, all that the Whigs at this point were contemplating. Or he could also have been inscrutable, saying that many things were possible but that his concern was the continuation of the King's government. A twenty-seat bill exchanging rotten boroughs for northern cities would have bought him years of office and relative public quiet. But facing the tide of demand for Reform which was starting to move, in November 1830 Wellington stood up in the Lords and proclaimed in flat and resonating emphasis one of those 'nevers' which good politicians know better than to utter. Again there was no warning. Close colleagues like Aberdeen, his Foreign Secretary, were not consulted. After speaking, Wellington said to Aberdeen 'I haven't said too much, have I?', receiving the acrid answer that he had said quite enough.

His position had been formidable. Greville had recently seen no reason why he should not continue in office indefinitely; Althorp was having to hold back Whigs willing to support or join this apparently liberalising (and very strong) government. After his declaration, power fell away from him in days, and he was recognised in all sophisticated circles as finished. Where he absolutely needed (and had enjoyed) limitless opportunity to manoeuvre, he had chosen to fight. He had lost Canningite and independent support, he had freed the Whigs at once from their duty to acquiesce and from their despair, and he had antagonised a public and press opinion led by the radical *Times*, which now mattered a great deal. Yet he had not regained the respect and votes of the Ultras, at whose convictions the grand denial had been directed.

His Ministry fell at once. At the beginning of December Grey was able to form another, and Wellington became the object of large-scale crowd hostility. Apsley House, Number One London, home of the national hero, had its windows broken. Wellington had taken brave but precipitate action without securing, or at any rate soothing, his core party. He had then, on another pressing issue, done the exact opposite in a way which made it news to his colleagues. The one thread of consistency running through a course of right-angled contradiction was, as ever, the solitary and perfect secrecy in which he made up his mind. Wellington's judgement did not improve in opposition. Having joined the Ultras, he at first stayed with them, refusing to acknowledge error and proclaiming resistance to the Bill *à outrance.* He also panicked at the influence of the political unions and took the highly off-colour step of approaching the King with a call for a ministry pledged to suppress them. Throughout the whole course of legislation he maintained his implacable position, but in the Lords debate where his speech was judged a major failure he would ask their Lordships 'not to pledge themselves either way about reform', and dropped hints about the possibility of a (Wellington) government introducing a moderate reform bill. This provoked the deadly private comment of the Whig minister, Hobhouse, 'In short, his grace made a shabby, shuffling speech very like a man wanting office again.'

If Wellington was ready to stoop, he was not going to conquer. The opportunity of that office came in May when, facing a prospective second Lords rejection, Grey sought, and failed to get, a peerage creation from the King. The Tories, invited to form a government, found themselves unable to do so, not least because Wellington's alienated deputy, Robert Peel, refused to touch one. They were made to look like wreckers of central policy unable to provide a constructive alternative, the ultimate humiliating failure of politics. And the Duke of Wellington, *preux chevalier* of public life, cool, sardonic, brave and above all petty controversy, had dragged them to it.

ONE

The Old System

*'How high a value I set upon your voice,
you may judge by the price I have paid for half of it'*

'"Make it six hundred guineas to end the matter."

'"No" said I; "no guineas above the five hundred; but I'll make it pounds, which you will agree is very extravagant."

'Thus from less to more, we came to an agreement, and signed mutual missives to that effect; and a pawkie laugh we had together, as well as a fresh bottle of Carbonnell's . . .'

Archibald Jobbry, retired nabob of the India trade, has concluded in claret his dealings with the solicitor, Mr Probe, in business as a broker for parliamentary constituencies. Mr Jobbry is buying one. The money expended is for only the latter end of a parliamentary term; a sitting MP is to retire and for the remainder Mr Jobbry is 'to succeed him as the honourable member for Frailtown, when he had taken the Chiltern Hundreds'.[1]

The chapter-opening exchange comes from *The Member*, a grimly elegant satire on the pre-Reform parliamentary system by John Galt, published in 1831. In real life, Lord Ellenborough, an assiduous Tory diarist of the period, looking around to find a seat for his brother, writes in April of the same year: 'Had 2 letters from Henry. The case at Wells seems desperate unless they can buy the seat of an attorney.'[2] Neither Lord Ellenborough nor Mr Probe mentions the Act of 1809 making the sale of seats illegal.

'Frailtown' is based upon Higham Ferrars in Northamptonshire ('Vamptonshire' to Galt), a well-known article of parliamentary trade. In the novel, 'Frailtown' has six voters. The artistic exaggeration is very mild. In contemporary political reality, Higham Ferrars 'was in the hands of the corporation – which consisted of the Mayor (who was also the returning officer), seven aldermen, thirteen capital burgesses, plus freemen, being householders not receiving alms, these latter in a permanent minority since the total electorate did not exceed 40'.[3] Higham Ferrars was one of only five constituencies with a single member. The others were Abingdon, Bewdley, Banbury and Monmouth; Weymouth enjoyed four. The norm was two, as it was in the county seats. The Northamptonshire town was one item for sale in a thriving market, but that market was an adjunct to a system of borough ownership and borough bestowal, much of it vested in the landed aristocracy. The polite term for such a possessor was a 'patron', the impolite one a 'boroughmonger'; and such a borough would be described respectively as being 'closed' (or 'nomination') or 'rotten'.

The system was ancient if not venerated. In the time of James II, the Duke of Newcastle was reckoned to control sixteen MPs, Lords Aylesbury and Teynham eight each; Lords Huntingdon and Preston and Sir Robert Holmes (colleague and adversary of Samuel Pepys at the Admiralty) six each.[4] Calls for change and reform were not new. They had been made in the reign of James I and, like subsequent proposals, had come to nothing. Seat- and member-ownership had grown and flourished.

The status and degree of freedom of a Lord's member varied with the Lord and the member. Examples of enlightened tolerance of opinion exist. So does the brutal example of Sir James Lowther, later Lord Lonsdale. In the late eighteenth century, Lowther outreached almost all the patrons of a hundred years earlier, sending to Parliament a minimum of nine members. His influence on occasion stretched to eleven, but his MPs were generally known, on account of their dependence and servility, as 'the ninepins'. An account of his court in Carlisle appears in Adam Sisman's excellent study of James Boswell. Seeking a route into politics, Boswell had been made recorder of Carlisle on a stipend of £20 per annum. 'His task would be to rule on the admissibility of so-called "mushroom voters": non-residents admitted as "honorary freemen" to boost the support for Lonsdale's chosen candidate.' It was the most blatant election-rigging, of course, but only a little above the eighteenth-century norm.*

Boswell's duty was to consider the evidence and then decide in Lonsdale's favour . . . Lonsdale received Boswell courteously and after admitting forty new voters, they dined with half a dozen others in a local public house. Lonsdale did all the talking. Three of his MPs were present, all of whom were utterly quiet . . . every day the pattern was the same. Lonsdale harangued, and when anyone ventured to speak, even to express agreement, Lonsdale silenced him, ordering 'You shall hear.' One of Lonsdale's cronies whistled like a bird when he treated him with contempt.[5]

* In the election of 1787 Lonsdale's nominee won by two votes with a total of 554 votes, of which 407 were cast by 'honorary freemen'. It was too extreme a piece of roguery even for the Pitt era and would be reversed by an election court the next year, 1788.

Such had already been the usefulness of the ninepins to the Ministry that in 1784, the first full year of the Pitt regime, Sir James had risen from Baronet to Earl of Lonsdale in a single bound, taking in the usually intermediary steps of baron and viscount as courtesy titles.

The art of boroughmongering had been well developed in the early eighteenth century by great Whig proprietors like the Dukes of Newcastle and Grafton. But the younger Pitt, using Treasury influence and a ring of landed allies, brought it to a finished and resplendent condition. And, quite as important, he would leave behind a posthumous obstacle to reform of Parliament or indeed anything else, a House of Lords permanently and reliably tilted to reaction.

The idea of creating peers in order to pass through the Upper House, the legislation of Whig or Liberal Ministries approved in the Commons which had then been returned in general elections, would give intolerable grief, as unconstitutional if not revolutionary, to William IV, Edward VII and George V. To meet the wishes of Pitt, King George III assented to the creation of 140 new lordships in seventeen years. Pitt, who died a commoner, packed the House of Lords. Yet it would be no part of parliamentary Reform to change it, merely, as we shall see, to get round the road block erected by accelerated ennoblement on behalf of a sacred constitution.

Lowther merely set a standard. The message sent by Lord Sandwich in the early days of the crisis in the American colonies to his prospective candidate, an Irish peer and naval captain, for the family seat of Huntingdon, was a requirement of 'thinking and acting as I do on all American points and supporting the present administration in their whole system'.[6] Another Sandwich member, Rawlinson at Queenborough, who was in effect one chosen in the royal interest, wrote in 1780 that as he thought the American war disastrous, he could no longer support it and would therefore either abstain or resign.[7] The Member for Linlithgow, John Hope, would lose the seat bestowed by a kinsman, for rejecting the Ministry's correct line on John Wilkes and voting against his expulsion from the Commons.

The ownership of parliamentary seats was seldom a simple promotion of the owner's convictions. The judicious marshalling of subordinated MPs made for advances in the peerage à la Lowther. Also at a time when a serious tranche of tax revenue went to the funding of sinecure offices to be equally judiciously distributed among a ministry's friends, a borough owner could command better things than right thinking. Edward Harbord, Member for Yarmouth, reminded his brother and patron, Lord Suffield, who had rebuked him for a missing vote on a motion of censure, of exertions which mattered more. 'As to my being justifiable in abandoning the interests of my family after all the money that has been spent to bring me into parliament, I have only to answer that the money spent has been well spent. Your lord lieutenancy and Peter's receiver generalship have been the consequence. In point of pecuniary advantage, the receivership pays more than the interest of the capital sunk.'[8] Harbord could not only stand up to his brother and threaten to find another seat, but he spelt out what nomination to Parliament was for.

Borough ownership would be furiously defended in the early stages of the Reform Bill as property indistinguishable from a tract of land for cultivation. And Sir Charles Wetherell, crudest and least apologetic defender of the system, would in all seriousness accuse reformers proposing abolition of rotten boroughs of advocating larceny. The truth, which by that later date hardly dared speak its name, was that reliable votes on the Commons were exchanged for preferments and places in Ireland, England and India. And a pattern of practice in their allocation had grown in the market. When in 1774 a member of the Irish Parliament sought a sinecure worth £3,500, the Prime Minister, Lord North, demurred, worrying that he would 'have no small difficulty in carrying the King's business if I consent to part with the disposal of those offices which have been so long and uniformly bestowed on the members of the British Parliament'.[9]

Parliament was managed by a ministry through what Edward Harbord had called 'pecuniary advantage'. The contempt with which writers of the period speak of 'preferment', 'place' and 'pensioners' reflected a general understanding that there was no representation without lubrication. And at a time when taxation was flat-rate and levied on goods of general consumption, citizens of no great wealth were made involuntary and resentful contributors to the salaries attending Receiverships sold for votes provided by borough owners. To take a single example, the literary dabbler, courtier and boulevardier, George Selwyn, in return for two seats at Ludgershall and one at Gloucester, had enjoyed together with their stipends, but with no duties, the Surveyorship-General of Crown lands, the Registrarship of Chancery in Barbados and the Surveyorship of the Meltings and Clerkship of the Irons at the Mint. The notion of intolerable privilege, against which a general, cross-class indignation grew, was in such a context more than radical rhetoric.[10] The rough numbers of this power and influence indicate the primacy of eight great Lords. The Dukes of Devonshire, Newcastle, Rutland and Norfolk, the Marquess of Hertford, Earl Fitzwilliam, and the Earls of Lonsdale and Darlington (later Duke of Cleveland) were reckoned to command fifty members between them.[11] It is suggested that 355 members were returned on the direction of 177 individuals.[12] These numbers break down into aristocratic and commoner patronage. In the last ten years of the unreformed Commons, 90 commoners could guarantee the return of 137 members while 87 peers sent to Parliament 213 MPs![13] The furious and outraged resistance of the House of Lords to both drafts of a Reform Bill in 1831–2, a resistance which came close to provoking civil breakdown, was based upon assets as tangible as specie or shareholdings. Borough ownership was simply the cream of landowning. Influence did not stop at outright ownership. It is also reckoned[14] that there were as many as 200 seats in which 259 peers and 150 commoners had some measure of weight at election time this side of specifically naming the next member.

Among fastidious men unable to take on one of the open constituencies like Westminster or Preston, the idea of buying a seat as Mr Jobbry did from an attorney, able through trading contacts with the small huddle of voters to deliver one, seemed relatively creditable compared to becoming an MP on a landowner's terms. Samuel Romilly, a high-conscienced Whig, wrote in 1805, 'I formed to myself the unalterable resolution never, unless I had a public office, to come to parliament but by a popular election or by paying the common price for my seat.'[15] The relationship which was *only* pecuniary was reckoned more honest than one even intermittently instructing the vote.

Such powers could be exerted because of the nature of so many constituencies, specifically those in the boroughs. In 1831 there were 489 representatives of English constituencies in Parliament; all except the four returned by Oxford and Cambridge Universities and 82 from the counties had been sent by boroughs. All save the six boroughs mentioned (Higham Ferrars, Abingdon, Bewdley, Banbury, Monmouth and Weymouth) sent two members, as did the counties. Nomination boroughs were those in which no popular electorate existed in such numbers as to make for uncertainty. There was no uniform franchise, but four main categories existed: potwalloper or scot and lot boroughs, burgage, freeman and corporation boroughs.

Potwalloper boroughs accounted for 59, those with the freeman franchise 62; the corporation sort took up 43; and in 39 constituencies only the burgage holders might vote.[16] Ostensibly the potwalloper seats were the most democratic, involving possession of a home (and hearth for the use of cooking utensils). Occasionally, as when the old dispensation coincided with recent industrial development, as at Preston, such constituencies actually were quasi-democratic. And on the strength of them, Henry Hunt, most dedicated of radicals, would be elected there on the eve of Reform by cotton weavers whom, ironically, the uniform and higher franchise of

Reform would largely disinherit. But given demography and population shift, a hearth-owning franchise occurred readily in places with negligible but exacting populations. If the numbers were very few, a proprietor would likely take over. Failing that, the happy electorate sold itself to the highest bidder and an election took on a festival quality. Both borough freedoms and burgage holdings could function autonomously. But depending on varying local residence qualifications or the option of 'honourary freemen', both could be subverted from honest sale by a large landowner. With burgage boroughs this was done by acquiring properties or deeds to parcels of land, known as snatch-deeds, for swift transfers then putting them temporarily into dependent paid hands. For freeman boroughs, lawyers as amenable as Boswell sufficed, and in both cases, the patron having made provision, could then literally import voters.

The most famous election in literature, the one at Eatanswill in *The Pickwick Papers*, is based on Sudbury, a freeman borough. Corruption here was cheerfully augmented by the prospect of Reform. And the reformers as cheerfully paid it when, in 1831, the holders of that honour, recognising a keen contest and a wasting asset, put their price up to £10 a head. A Cornish parson writing nearly seventy-five years before the Reform Act had denounced 'the low luxury and drunkenness' brought about by the 'corruption of our boroughs at the electing members of Parliament. This infamous traffic,' he added, 'begins with intemperance and riot . . . the basest prostitution of the highest privilege.'[17] Potwallopers, freemen and burgesses, with their votes and financial expectations from that infamous traffic, are perhaps best seen as a livelier equivalent of the lists of deceased serfs conferring enhanced status on the fraudulent hero of Gogol's *Dead Souls*.

But in English terms, the notion was pushed to the satirical limit by Peacock in his novel of 1817, *Melincourt*, where leading characters ambling around England (as tends to happen in Peacock when they are not seated at symposium and dinner) come to 'the City of Novote and the City of Onevote'. In Onevote the electorate is literally singular: 'The hustings were erected in proper form, and immediately opposite to them was an enormous marquee with a small opening in front of which was seated the important personage of Mr Christopher Corporate with a tankard of ale and a pipe.' The election address of one of the candidates, Mr Simon Sarcastic, begins, 'Free, fat and dependent burgess of the ancient and honourable borough'; he then argues that

The monied interest, Mr Corporate, for which you are as illustrious as the sun at noonday, is the great point of connexion and sympathy

31

between us . . . How high a value I set upon your voice, you may judge by the price I have paid for half of it: which indeed, deeply lodged as my feelings are in my pocket, I yet see no reason to regret, since you will thus confer on mine, a transmutable and marketable value which I trust with proper management will leave me no loser by the bargain.[18]

Few seats quite met Peacock's terms, though places like East Retford and Grampound, which were the subject of individualised attempts at disfranchisment before 1831, came close enough, and Old Sarum in 1831 had seven voters. Numbers had often been restricted by drawing the town boundaries well within the lines of population. This was done effectively at Taunton, Guildford, Southwark and Bridgwater.

But where the numbers were manageable, simple corruption worked very well. Mr Corporation's pipe and tankard were multiplied manifold. Indeed, in some seats, parliamentary elections, as frequent as possible, were acknowledged as a form of income, a poor man's pension, a modest plebeian sharing at the trough yielding the Receiverships and Clerkships of the Irons extracted by their betters, a form of 'trickle-down'! In contemporary cliché, the corruption was institutionalised. The burgage boroughs, resting upon house tenancy, implied citizenship, and should again have meant a semi-popular franchise, but burgage tenure could be bought, and great men in the borough trade did buy them. In Haslemere Lord Lonsdale settled Cumberland miners, his tenants, in burgage houses with the single task of voting for Lord Lonsdale's candidate.[19] Old and derelict properties, not normally occupied, would have their chimneys looked after by a landlord to establish their continued hearth status. He would then bring in voters for quick qualification.

Much was made by Whig speakers in the Reform campaigns and debates about towns decayed from former healthy numbers and with the decline of a trade turning into shells, filled by the Treasury or grandees, and this argument was much directed to Cornwall. It was perhaps the weakest point in their case and implying something the Whigs shared with the romantic Cobbett – that things had once been better, fairer, more Anglo-Saxon. They hadn't been. Elections were something to be fixed as much in the late Middle Ages as under Walpole or the younger Pitt. In corrupt Cornwall, something might be owing to former tin and lead wealth though much of that continued in the eighteenth century. But that county bulked as large as it did, grotesquely overrepresented and blissfully rotten, largely because medieval kings, owning tracts of Cornwall personally by way of the Duchy, took care to enfranchise pelting villages of few fish and fewer people because they would readily comply. In consequence, Cornwall acquired early most of its forty-eight seats in Parliament, eighteen of them within 'a stretch 28 miles long by twelve miles deep around Liskeard'.[20]

This state of affairs had continued over a long period. There seemed until very late in the day no great prospect that it would not continue indefinitely. It reflected a social order in which the primacy of the landowning class was a general premise to life and politics. The economic changes of the industrial revolution had brought about a demographic shift. Under the rules which made St Michael's or Lostwithiel two-member boroughs, the fact of Oldham's population having risen from 400 in 1760 to 12,000 in 1801[21], by reason of the demand for its coarse cotton yarn, was of no account.

But the shift, of which those little numbers are emblematic, changed the whole nature of society. And it did so through a period of French wars subsequent upon revolution. It also followed an intellectual shift among the middle class and the loosely liberal part of the gentry. The idea of adjusting, perhaps purifying, the electoral system had been about in the time of Charles James Fox and had been looked on sympathetically in his early days by Pitt. It was an Irish ally of Fox, Henry Flood, who in 1790 had proposed a bill for the enlargement of Parliament by creating a further one hundred seats based in the more open counties. Parallel with such thinking on the radical wing of the political class lay a movement among the people, not least the people of the new unrepresented industrial towns. In a society as formally structured and calibrated as the Great Britain of 1790, 'parallel' is the exact word and a gulf lay between the two lines. The word 'condescension' at that time meant not offensive, *haut-en-bas* patronage, but kindly fraternisation.

The London Corresponding Society (LCS) of the Scottish-born shoe-maker Thomas Hardy and, among many examples, that 'company of poor mechanics' two-hundred-strong in Leeds, which lamented 'Aristocratic Tiranny and Democratic Ignorance' overawing that town, were a world away from the company in Brooks's. But condescending or not, the Friends of the People was a group formed to make a bridge between an enlightened elite and what was uneasily called 'the people'. Its founders were George Tierney, Samuel Whitbread and a close follower and friend of Fox, Charles Grey. How much 'the people' would actually benefit from a reform programme best suited to an urban middle class which employed and feared them is a large and melancholy question. This book is a study of the Reform Act we actually got and of the struggle to get it.

The people who would finally enact Reform in 1832 under Grey's leadership were Foxite Whigs. And in the contest to do so, the people and their societies, the unenfranchised people of towns unknown to Parliament, would reassert themselves in groupings called political unions, decisively led from Birmingham, but a presence throughout the country. But between the two notions, aborted and triumphant, fell the Paris Terror, twenty years of war and what Edward Thompson very reasonably calls 'a counter-revolution'. Fighting a hot war abroad, Pitt and his successors would fight a cold (and dirty) one at home. The old order would be sustained by a spy system, by the effective suspension of constitutional rights, by the diversion of a great war and by a general mood of fear, fear sophisticated until it was felt by most people for the French revolutionary enemy, by the possessing classes for any kind of change and by the leaders of Reform for the consequences of doing anything. It was an institutional paralysis slowly tempered by the exasperation of business at its landholding economic bias.

The prospects enjoyed in 1790 would come again only when that coalition of fear, repression and executive will lost its first legitimacy at the end of the Napoleonic wars. With that began the gradual fissuring by which a grand reaction slowly broke up and its sustaining institutions could be challenged again, not truly radically but successfully.

TWO

Tory Disintegration, 1827–30

'The Duke was intelligent, he was a Conservative, but not necessarily an intelligent Conservative'

'It is quite true about Ld. Liverpool. He had a fit of apoplexy at ten this morning. He is a little better, but politically dead.'[1] The observer, Thomas Creevey, an active Whig politician, writing to his niece on 17 February 1827, would two days later contemplate the succession and tell her masterfully, 'I think somehow it must be Canning after all, and then he'll die of it . . .'[2] Creevey was right. By the time Liverpool actually succumbed, on 4 December 1828, not only would Canning have both succeeded and died, but his successor, Goderich, would have found the holding together of a Cabinet impossible and the mighty Tory government of forty years would have come to die in the arms of the Duke of Wellington.

Robert Banks Jenkinson, 2nd Earl of Liverpool, had been Prime Minister for nearly fifteen years, longer than anyone except Walpole. He was the heir-at-law of a Tory majority put together in 1784 by Pitt the Younger with considerable royal assistance. With modest blips, during one of which the slave trade was abolished, it had governed for most of that time under four Prime Ministers – Pitt himself, Addington, Perceval and, after Perceval's fortuitous and unpolitical assassination in 1812, Liverpool. Its largest single asset had been war, war garlanded with fear of the French Revolution and resistance to the universal monster, Napoleon Bonaparte – the complete patriotic card. Latterly, it had survived post-war distress, unemployment, radical agitation and the deaths under sabres and hoofs of eleven peaceful attenders at a Manchester rally, a victory known to history as Peterloo. But it had survived in a condition of unease and many-fissured division. This was not a ministry of a single conviction, nor was it, in any sense that we would understand, party government at all. Country gentlemen supported ministers who gave first priority to the landed interest, and there was more general support for an anti-revolutionary government.

But the large tent was sagging. Fear of revolutionary influence from across the Channel was a wasting asset when France was governed by that

35

most preposterously absolute of absolute monarchs, Charles X, whose notions of sacred kingship had put derisive resonance into the name Bourbon. As for the landed interest, comfortable under war conditions and war prices, it had exacted terms at the end of it, protection from foreign grain which should not be imported at less than eighty shillings per quarter measure. High bread prices, intensifying urban hardship under these Corn Laws, were matched by no serenity among rural labourers, brutally low waged and suffering from enclosure.

Meanwhile, among the political class, the idea of not only free markets, but free trade, was no longer an idea – it was the conviction of a major part of the Cabinet. Men from trade, able to compete with the gentry and nobility, if still deferential to them, had come into politics, including Tory politics, but Tory of a different and distinct sort. The long maturing into articulation of their natural interests until they achieved repeal of the Corn Laws is a subdued melodic line in history, rising in crescendo in 1846. But well before that development, what might be called the unlanded interest formed an identifiable element within the Cabinet, and they had allies among men who enjoyed that advantage. They also had a formidable spokesman in William Huskisson, Liverpool merchant, practical man, deviser of a sliding scale for mitigating the Corn Laws, and their ally in George Canning, wit, dramatic proto-romantic, son of an actress who had then married up, someone with the flair to be both an Etonian and a complete outsider.

Canning was the star, but Huskisson was the prophetic figure, one of those resented men who recur as glib, patronising parodies – Mr Bott, Mr Bonteen – in the novels of Anthony Trollope forty years later. But by the mid-1820s, the outsider was non-fictional and winning, and resentment was raw. A Whig observer watched appreciatively in the spring of 1826 and joined in: 'I was one of the majority last night in support of his Majesty's Ministers for cheaper corn than the landed grandees will now favor [sic] us with . . . If a good ultra-Tory government could be made, Canning and Huskisson must inevitably be ruined by this daring step. You never heard such language as the old sticklers apply to them.'[3] Sir Edward Knatchbull, Kentish squire and, if there could be such a thing, a moderate Ultra, certainly at forty-five, an old stickler, told Parliament with polite resentment that 'if he were to sacrifice the landed interest – the basis of our prosperity and the foundation of our greatness – he should be acting in a manner that was disgraceful to himself and injurious to those interests which it was his duty to protect . . .'. If returned again to Parliament, Sir Edward promised that 'his object would be to secure to the possessors of landed property what they now possessed and enable them to hold that station to which they were entitled (applause), for he was convinced that their interest contained the interest of every class'.[4]

The measure had been a coup brought in quickly during a period of distress, on Liverpool's nod. And Creevey, the Whig in question, savoured a fight serving his party's principles and hopes and is quite clear that the struggle is one of interests: 'On Monday we beat the *land* black and blue about letting in foreign corn; but the Lords it is said, are not to be so easy beat as the booby squires. There is to be a grand fight – the Ministers and Bishops against the Rutlands, Beauforts, Hertfords &c. Liverpool gives out that if he is beat, he will give up the government which may be safely said as there is no one else to take it.'[5]

But when the boast of 11 May was tested on 12 May, Rutland, Beaufort and Hertford (two Dukes, a Marquess and a great many acres) found themselves beaten three to one. Creevey could jeer that 'the landholders, high and low, are the same mean devils and alike incapable of fighting when once faced by a government without any land at all'.[6] The move, the admission of half a million hundredweight of foreign grain in circumstances of scarcity, had seismic qualities. Creevey was exultant: 'The charm and the power of the Landed Interest is gone.'[7]

Again, since history is not Marxist-mechanistic, personal enmities and jarring ambitions had been added to the turmoil, leaving the Ministry a coalition rich in ill feeling. Canning, for example, on decent terms with Peel despite disagreement over Catholic Relief, enjoyed (if that is the word) a hopeless relationship of mutual distrust with Wellington. The utility of Lord Liverpool was an ability, through good humour and a nicely managed unobtrusiveness, to have kept acres and looms, Sir Simon Steeltrap and Mr Gradgrind, as well as mutual enemies, together in the same Cabinet.

Foreign affairs divided ministers too. Belief in resisting Napoleon did not, after the first euphoria of victory, carry into a belief in instant suppression of all liberalism everywhere before it could erect its first guillotine. That roughly had been the position, once the mystical language is stripped away, of Tsar Alexander I and his Holy Alliance. Alexander, demanding a coalition of support for all anointed royal government everywhere, however incompetent and barbarous, recalls John Foster Dulles seeking 'bastions against Communism' in the 1950s. Castlereagh, Foreign Secretary until 1822, came closest to endorsing the Holy Alliance, though with growing reservations. And Wellington maintained close ties with a ring of ambassadors from highly Conservative regimes. But foreign affairs soon provided the occasion for a bold if florid gesture, British support, if in broad and gesturing terms, for rebels against somebody else's oppression.

Noisy and declaratory, though with large consequences, it had been the

...ar vehicle for George Canning, the Canning whom Mr Creevey felt it had, after all, to be. Canning, to the sound of stage thunder, had recognised the South American republics and, in a style oddly contemporary, claimed the credit: 'I called the New World into being to redress the balance of the old.' Wellington was outraged, Whigs delighted. Only the hardest radicals were unimpressed. For Hazlitt, not an admirer, the trick word in Canning's shows of liberalism was 'legitimacy'. 'It is the foundation of his magnanimity and the source of his pusillanimity.' Legitimacy, said Hazlitt, was 'shown to be a middle term between divine right of kings and the choice of the people, compatible with and convertible into either at the discretion of the Crown or the pleasure of the speaker'.[8]

But Canning was quite enough of a liberal for many Tories. For if they were split over protection and foreign affairs, they were split as bitterly, with some differences of personnel, on 'Catholic Relief', the ending of effective denial of public office and full professional careers to Roman Catholics, something rooted in the days of Pope Urban's invitation to assassinate Queen Elizabeth, the exertions of Captain Fawkes and the confessional/constitutional politics of the late seventeenth century. Canning, an Irishman of Protestant provenance, but fully awake to Irish Catholic feelings and warmly liberal on the subject since the 1790s, had made his views clear and himself anathema to the steady men of Church and State Toryism. This issue constituted an interesting division between the obvious contenders for the premiership. Creevey had noted that 'unhappily for Toryism, that prig, Peel seems as deeply bitten by "liberality", in every way but on the Catholic question, as any of his fellows'.[9]

But it was an exception which counted. Seven weeks before Liverpool's death, Sir Francis Burdett had introduced a bill into the Commons to end Catholic exclusion. It had failed by only four votes. Together with Plunkett, Attorney-General for Ireland, and in company with the Whigs, including the most vivid of them, Henry Brougham, Canning had supported it. Prominent among those resisting had been Henry Phillpotts, the Bishop of Exeter, an extremist on everything, the Master of the Rolls, Copley,* and Sir Robert Peel. Peel had attacked Plunkett; Canning, more bitterly, had turned his fire upon Copley. All were members of the same government. Greville had noted 'a great expectation that Canning would resign' and he attributed defeat on the issue to his having 'lashed the master so severely'.[10]

---

* Sir John Copley, later, as Lord Lyndhurst, Lord Chancellor in several Tory governments.

Canning, definitively unsound on the Catholic question, now stood sharply contrasted with Peel, an equal in talent but less senior and surprisingly dogmatic against relief. This settled the issue for many in the governing group. Sir Edward Knatchbull simply knew that those refusing to serve Canning spoke for England. And as one of the two Members for Kent and ninth Baronet, he did speak for a certain definition of England. Applauding Peel's 'manliness of character and distinction of expression', Sir Edward said that he personally 'would give religious toleration to every class of people, but he would not give political power to those people who would not tolerate the religions of others'. In practising which denial of tolerance, he was following 'the principles of loyalty to the King, a determination to support the aristocracy . . . and to defend the rights and privileges of the people'.

He had a good point; the Catholic issue showed up a recurring grief facing all Prime Ministers of the time – how to contain the ocean-going unreason of the Crown. George IV came and went in the degree of his opposition to Catholic Relief, depending upon who had spoken most assiduously and last to that flickering spirit. His companion, Lady Conyngham, and his doctor, Sir William Knighton, were temperate influences. His brother, Cumberland, a villain out of melodrama, accused on the street *and* in the best houses, of both incest and murder, would descend upon Windsor, settle in, calling for good fires, and remind the King of their father, manic on the subject, and of his own constitutional oath, turning him into a tearful and interminable obstacle to political advance.

Confronted by the prospect of Canning as Prime Minister, George played for time and held out hopes that Liverpool might recover, until Lady Liverpool sent notice of his positive wish to resign. Finally, he floated the possibility of a Wellington government with Canning and Peel as its pillars. But for the King the problem was Catholics, not Canning personally. There was affection between charmers. And with the opposition murmuring that, since the King was withholding a Prime Minister, the withholding of supply might follow, George finally invited the senior member of the late government to form a new one on 9 April, seven weeks after Liverpool's collapse. Greville, never one to pass up the chance to be scornful, spoke of Canning, inaccurately, as 'nominally Prime Minister', adding more reasonably that 'no man ever took office under more humiliating circumstances or was placed in a more difficult and uncertain situation'.[11]

Canning might be all the showy and amphibious things Hazlitt thought him, but he was too liberal for Eldon, the Lord Chancellor, Lord Westmorland and several others, all of whom declined to serve under him.

They were joined in this by Wellington, who had earlier fought and lost that bitter quarrel over South America. Ironically, the King, whose prejudices they reflected, was angry at the departures, subjecting Eldon, who returned the Great Seal in person, to an interminable scolding. Those declining to continue in office were seven in all, mocked by the radical *Morning Chronicle* as 'the Seven Sages'.* But Canning hung on, saw off the Duke's opposition, the King's anxieties and the rage of the old sticklers. He was now Prime Minister.

But when Liverpool had been found on the floor of his London home, he was clutching in his hand a letter conveying the latest discouraging intelligence about the Foreign Secretary's health. For Canning was already a victim of royal procedures and requirements. Attending the funeral of the Duke of York on 5 January, seven weeks before Liverpool's seizure, he had endured savage mid-winter cold which put other distinguished members of the congregation out of action and appears to have directly killed the Bishop of Lincoln (George Pelham). Canning had been badly affected, and would develop rheumatic fever, his secretary, Stapleton, reporting 'every variety of form of which cold and rheumatism are capable'.[12] So it was a seriously sick man, deserted by half the Cabinet and inhibited by royal prejudice from his central objective, who attempted to form a government.

In a time when, despite a long hegemony, party lines were wavy and accommodations with leading men on opposition benches thinkable, many Whigs had been smelling the air for some time. Henry Brougham in particular was excited. 'Brougham was here last night in a state of insanity after the negociation [sic] between Ld Lansdowne and Canning was broke off,' wrote Creevey cheerfully. The idea of Canning coming together with the Whigs was attractive – to the Whigs who lacked office and to Canning who was short of competent colleagues. Brougham saw his reasoning as very sane indeed. 'A greater or more ruinous error never yet was committed or one more fatal to the Catholic question than by holding out on subordinate points and punctilios of honour, to throw again the Cabinet to the Ultra-Tories.' His judgement, in a letter to Lord Althorp, was shared by men less avid than Brougham for seizing office and doing things.[13] Sir James Macdonald, a Whig member, wrote to Lansdowne saying that the Irish MPs 'would be in perfect despair if, when all that is Orange and illiberal is arrayed against Canning, a distrust of the man were to limit your powerful aid to a mere support . . .'[14] Macdonald also thought that nineteen in twenty

---

* According to Creevey (3 April 1827), the group was joined by Lord Bathurst only after he had noticed the missing places at a Cabinet dinner.

Whigs wanted Lansdowne to do more than give support 'to a Government which should be formed *without any restrictions* on the Catholic question'. The only exceptions he found were 'some crotchets of Lord Grey's which vary every hour . . .'.[15]

Grey's reservations were not crotchets. Brougham, a frantic careerist in the eyes of his enemies, was quite as much an issues man. His liking for Canning, despite a flare-up in 1823 on the Commons floor which might have triggered a duel, went back to agreement on the questions of Spain and South America. Again, both were exceptionally clever men, out of a remote, if not a lower drawer, each with an interesting touch of idealism flecked with caddishness. Anyway, a distinction between liberal and illiberal mattered more to both than tight partisan feeling. Grey, by contrast, held Canning in a disdain not less biting from Hazlitt's. Snobbery came into it – the son of an actress could not, surely, become Prime Minister – as did the antipathy natural between the staid and the dramatic. But so did Grey's sense of party, a healthy dislike of his own Whigs forming an annexe to what would still be a Tory government.

In a speech in the Lords 'full of eloquence, he attacked Canning's life and political character and announced his intention of remaining neuter'.[16] He wanted Catholic emancipation quite as much as Brougham (and Canning) but lacked both the lawyer's yearning for office and his belief that the Ultras could be beaten only by quick terms at this juncture. And he was right. When negotiations broke down, Brougham pressed his case by calling a short-notice meeting at Brooks's at which he set out, with his customary contempt for finesse, the need to deal on full terms with the natural ally, Canning. The meeting sent a delegation to Lansdowne calling for the negotiations to be opened again.

They resumed through the Duke of Devonshire, the Whig leadership offered support for the new Ministry, but took its time in assuming actual posts. Lansdowne wanted supporters of Catholic Relief to hold the Lord Lieutenancy and Chief Secretaryship for Ireland, something the King would not have. Eventually, in late May, begged by Canning to wait for royal retreat on the Catholic issue, Lansdowne, Lord Carlisle and George Tierney, Whig leader in the Commons, took office in a government strongest in liberal Tories, with Palmerston entering the Cabinet for the first time to join Huskisson and his group. But this was a half-cock involvement only, something demonstrated by those Whigs not actually in the government, at first remaining on the opposition benches while casting their votes in its support. And it was slightly absurd that a Cabinet dominated by supporters of Catholic Relief was compelled to leave any move on that issue on ice to assuage the King.

So, with Grey threatening unconvincingly never to set foot in Brooks's again, the political water was muddied further as the profound and fatal divisions among Tories were shallowly matched by tactical and temperamental differences between Whigs. But the immediate significance of all this was put in perspective in a curtly melancholy sentence of Greville. He had attended a royal house party at Windsor Lodge, including an entertainment by Tyrolese singers and dancers brought by the Austrian ambassador, one which had set a delighted King George talking to them in German. 'Canning came the day I went away, and was very well received by H.My.; he looked dreadfully ill.'[7]

The Whigs, with a foothold in government, waited for Canning to do something decisive, but he was busiest with foreign affairs, chiefly Greece, and in domestic matters played for the time he did not have. He also suffered a reversal reflecting the political configuration of the time when the Corn Bill was subjected to a Lords amendment with wrecking consequences, though not intentions, moved by his late colleague, Wellington. The amendment passed by four votes and the whole Bill had to be returned and safely passed a second time. But seriously ill anyway, overworked, roundly abused by the Tory press, conscious of a degree of hatred from the Ultras which shocked him, his job made heavier by the insecurity of his spatchcock ministry, Canning would tell an anxious George IV on 30 July that 'he felt ill in every part of his body'. Still struggling with foreign policy (the crisis in Portugal), he moved over days from intensifying agony to a condition in and out of consciousness to a quiet death. Creevey, chronicler of such things, observed next day 'so goes another man killed by publick life'.[18]

What followed was more of an interim than a government. Frederick Robinson, a successful if lucky Chancellor and broadly of the Canning/Huskisson outlook, was the King's choice, intended to keep Lansdowne and the other Whigs in a broad continuation of the Canning Ministry. He was no longer mere Robinson, having gone to the Lords as Goderich to lead Canning's government there, together with running the Colonial Office. Politics by now were less fluid than deliquescent. The immediate alternative was a High Tory throwback ministry, but the impetus for broad liberalism was intense and intensifying. The centre could not hold. Goderich, never a leader and with no illusions about the fact, was burdened with family griefs; the death of his only child, an eleven-year-old girl, had bitterly distressed him. He had gone to the Lords in order to have more time to console his wife. She, having become pregnant,* was now hysterically

---

* The child would grow up to be, as Lord Ripon, a popular member of late Victorian Liberal cabinets.

dependent and importunate. In a tough age, such sensibility in a father and husband earned general male contempt. We might be gentler now.

The quarrelling amongst ministers which had burdened Canning intensified notably with a bitter row over his choice of Chancellor, J.C. Herries. All of which, together with the King's eager meddling in patronage, exhausted him. Not that nothing happened at this time. During the Goderich Ministry the Turkish fleet was destroyed at Navarino by the literal interpretation of orders (returning massive fire for a chance shot) of a British admiral leading a European force, and Greece was consequently set to become an independent nation. This event, flowing fortuitously from earlier moves by Canning, changed European history and horrified both government and opposition.

Canning had died on 8 August 1827, leaving an everlasting question as to what he might have done, might have been. Goderich, finally wearied by a quarrel between Huskisson and Herries over a possible further opening to the Whigs, lasted until January 1828. He had in fact tried to make way in December but the intended successor, Harrowby, would not touch the post. Greville noted, 'They say that the King is quite mad upon the Catholick question and that his real desire is to get rid of the Whigs, take back the D of Wn and make an anti-Catholick Gov.'[19] If that was George's intention, it could hardly have misfired more completely. But obliged to give up his position as Commander in Chief, the Duke did become Prime Minister, showing a short way with Herries whose niggling had brought down the previous ministry, demoting him from Chancellor of the Exchequer to Master of the Mint, something which Herries meekly swallowed.

This was not quite the return of Cincinnatus. This very Roman Anglo-Irish soldier had been securely in and about politics for ten years, but it was a falling back on the prestige, personality and habit of command of a national hero. The idea, despite preliminary essays in that direction, that Wellington could command the moderate men of trade in coalition with the arable Tories, hardly got started as an illusion. Indeed, Robert Peel apart, about to form his New Police, this was one man's government, inherently weak in parliamentary numbers, expectations and support in the country, barricaded behind a ducal military front of splendid and graceful scorn.

The Whigs, though sensing that their time was coming, were not rid of their own differences, dividing into would-be coalitionists and what were called 'Malignants', a group looking to Grey to uphold the pure Whig condition, looking also for a fight, and waiting upon the day when, as an uncomplicated government of their own, they could straightforwardly promote Whig policies. Significantly, Creevey, not a neutral diarist, but a bundle of strenuous partisan opinions and Brougham's dedicated enemy, grew ever more admiring of Lord Grey. Grey had stood out against coalition, his scorn for Canning was compounded by determination on clear focus on the Catholic question and quite as much upon parliamentary Reform. The Whigs might now be denied power for another three years, but in opposition they were shaping into a group with sharp and heightened purposes.

The government which Wellington formed in January 1828 was a purely Tory affair which, in May, became purer still. Huskisson, determined to protect the ground he had won over corn duties, remained only until May when he voted against the government on, ironically, an issue of parliamentary Reform. A bill to disfranchise the corrupt boroughs of Penryn and East Retford and give their places in Parliament to Manchester and Birmingham was resisted by the government, but voted for by Huskisson. He wrote to the Duke explaining it as a matter of conscience and offered his resignation *pro forma*. Wellington responded in the briskest military manner by accepting it. Huskisson was promptly followed out of government by three other liberals, Lords Palmerston and Dudley and Charles Grant. As Greville recorded on 12 June, 'We have now got a Tory Govt., and all that remained of Canning's party are gone.'[20]

Like so many acts applauded for decisiveness, it was a calamitous mistake, leaving the Cabinet stripped of two first-rate talents and identified with a dogmatic pose without the means of keeping it up. For, ironically, this Tory government would deliver the prize most sought by the Whigs and do so in the clenched and snarling teeth of Tory opinion. Catholic emancipation might have waited a long time if it had been a matter of recusant squires or English Catholic working men in towns like Preston, or indeed of the Irish in mainland Britain. But Ireland herself was something else and Daniel O'Connell, leader of the unnerving Catholic Association, charming and bombastic by menacing turns in his erratic but surefooted way, was *somebody* else. 'O'Connell is far too dramatic for my taste,' wrote Thomas Creevey, 'and yet the nation is dramatic and likes it',[21] and he confessed that he liked O'Connell too. A County Kerry small squire turned outstandingly successful lawyer, the leader of the Irish bar, now turned rather grand squire (rents of £4,000 pa), he was disposed towards and equipped for a fight, a man who understood constitutional niceties well enough to know just how close to sedition he could get without quite touching.

The Catholics of Ireland had numbers and occupied a position of general inferiority. The Catholic aristocracy, aristocratic first, offered little leadership. The still-remembered attempt at violent revolution, the Year of Liberty, 1798, when the French were on the sea, had, after the French turned back, been narrowly defeated with superior force followed by never forgotten exactions. But three years later, Union with England had been hustled through the Irish Parliament, which was to dissolve itself in a welter of bribery and promises to the Catholics, not then kept by reason partly of the obdurate devotion of George III to his coronation oath.

O'Connell's genius was to show Irish Catholics their strength and, through the Catholic Association, to put it on unnerving display. The Association was a power for violent disturbance kept under calculated restraint. And since some of Pitt's promises had been kept, O'Connell had the support of a priesthood bred up unadorned in culture, untravelled, narrowly Irish and at a social level with the masses. The Maynooth Seminary had been created and funded in 1802 by the Westminster Parliament. Creevey, who travelled assiduously though Ireland in September and October of 1828, blamed these priests on the late Prime Minister: 'This was a piece of Pitt's handiwork to have these chaps educated in a Catholic college at home to escape foreign contagion; and they turn out the lowest and most perfidious villains going . . .'[22] The point has been much disputed since.

Lord Donoughmore, a landowner and fellow Whig, spelt things out to him succinctly: 'When Pitt established the college at Maynooth, he gave to Ireland a Republican priesthood. Formerly it required some money to educate candidates for orders in foreign parts, so they were necessarily Catholic gentlemen's sons; and they returned from France, Spain or Portugal with the manners of gentlemen and strict monarchical principles.'[23] As Creevey saw it, in Ireland Pitt was responsible for 'an ultra popular franchise and a republican priesthood, given to the most bigoted nation in Europe with a population of *six to one* against the Protestants'.[24]

By another irony, Catholics had the vote in Ireland, and, on more lavish terms, that 'ultra popular franchise', than would be achieved by Englishmen when the Reform Bill finally passed. Under the terms following Union, they voted as forty shilling freeholders, minimal, not to say negligible, landholders, but they could not elect a Catholic. The laws did not forbid a Catholic from sitting in Parliament and, as O'Connell was about to demonstrate, they certainly did not stop him from being elected. What prevented him serving in the ordinary way as an MP was another oath, 'that the sacrifice of the mass, and the invocation of the blessed Virgin Mary and other saints, as now practised by the Church of Rome are impious and idolatrous', a form of words to stick in the gagging throat of any Catholic of conscience, as was the intention.

The idea of simply standing for Parliament and leaving the government to enforce an outrageous bluff was a simple, inspirational act. A sitting member, Vesey Fitzgerald, had just been appointed to Wellington's Cabinet and in the precise way of the times* was obliged to seek re-election in his constituency of Clare. Fitzgerald was a pattern of Ascendancy virtues, model landlord, supporter of emancipation, genuinely liked by Catholics. This had been the liberal way. An election in Waterford in 1826 had seen a Protestant member of the Catholic Association defeat the candidate of the Beresfords, another formidable Ascendancy interest.

The notion of now making a set at Fitzgerald flowed from two of O'Connell's oddest lieutenants. Tom Steele, a Protestant, is described as 'a paladin of reckless language and wild excitability with a total lack of reasoning power and common prudence',[25] yet he was the only follower with whom O'Connell never quarrelled. The 'O'Gorman Mahon', another squire, also duellist, fighter in South American wars and, across sixty years, a highly intermittent MP, has been described by O'Connell's biographer as resembling 'more an Algerian Corsair than a graduate of Trinity College'.[26] However, Mahon and Steele, on reconnoitring that barren, thinly populated stretch of Irish-speaking Connaught, reported that, despite personal popularity, Fitzgerald might be defeated. But it was Sir David Roose, also Protestant, who drove to the central point. Fitzgerald ought to be opposed, not by another Protestant who supported the Association, but by a Catholic, in which case, why not by *the* Catholic, Daniel O'Connell?

The election itself was a rough affair, O'Connell himself abandoning his courtly style for the blackguarding vulgarity he did even better. Priests were in hectoring attendance: a Father Murphy served up the sacraments from a field altar, much as an English borough proprietor might distribute beef and beer, while a Father Maguire offered the pastoral message, 'Let every renegade to his God and his country follow Vesey Fitzgerald and let every true Catholic Irishman follow me.'[27] Catholic emancipation was a proper liberal principle, but under that Maynooth priesthood it would vest local power in hands not altogether liberal. However, the forty shilling free-holders of County Clare now stood empowered by orator, Church and mood to vote against all received practice for their free choice. And by 2,057 votes to 982 they presented Parliament with O'Connell MP and the Duke of Wellington with a vivid dilemma.

Wellington was no kind of bigot, remarking that the majority of the soldiers serving in his campaigns had probably been Catholics. A man of

---

* It lasted until the early twentieth century and cost Winston Churchill a rebuff as a member of Asquith's Cabinet.

the eighteenth century, he was without serious religious belief, seeing in divine worship very much what he saw in marriage – a lightly confining form of good manners. Wellington's thinking on the emancipation question related mainly to social order in Ireland. Over this he was also engaged in a parallel dispute with his Lord Lieutenant, Anglesey, the General Paget who had lost a leg beside him at Waterloo, a man too familiar, senior, warm hearted, tactless, popular and on the spot to worry much about due subordination. Anglesey was on the side of emancipation and kept saying so. He made, and chatted about, policy *in situ*. And in letters and memoranda he answered Wellington back. Wellington, with as much pleasure as relief, finally got rid of the Lord Lieutenant, only to find that events obliged him to adopt the Lord Lieutenant's policy.

Anglesey was remarkably sympathetic to the Irish and had mixed socially as much as possible, infuriating Wellington by dining at Catholic houses. He rapidly became convinced that a parliamentary role in Westminster for the leaders of the Catholic Association in return for closing the Association itself, together with disfranchising that noisy rabble, the forty shilling freeholders, was the way to win control by conciliation. Ministers should, he wrote, 'show partiality to neither party and two years will see Ireland a happy country'. It was absurdly simplistic but better than all the alternatives.

Wellington thought in terms of order menaced and looked on the Clare by-election as the precursor to violence in the countryside and on the streets. The Catholic Association had done much more than advance constitutional equity between the Christian confessions. In Marxist terms it had raised the political consciousness of Ireland. As the Duke saw things, it had stirred up trouble, trouble which could get only worse. His phrase for it all was succinct: 'This state of things cannot be allowed to continue.'[28]

The only deal was that if emancipation went through, the Association would be wound up and the forty shilling franchise repealed. Since they were the stick of a rocket irreversibly launched, O'Connell would be game. This was, of course, the precise strategy of Anglesey. And after the Clare by-election, it had, through clenched teeth, to become Wellington's highly improvised tactic. Like too few English statesmen, Wellington now found himself pitching at the essential conservatism of small farming Ireland, and, amazingly, he took Peel with him. Working across the winter of 1828–9 with a close hand of Lord Chancellor Lyndhurst and Peel, he put the case by memo to the King, and George IV was finally squared. Emancipation would carry into law unimpeded by the King.

Neither public opinion nor the Ultras had been prepared. Back in October 1828, Sir Edward Knatchbull had called an open air meeting at

Penenden Heath in Kent to support a petition demanding that 'the Protestant Constitution of the United Kingdom might be preserved inviolate'.[29] And when the Duke came coolly forward to amend that constitution, Sir Edward was appalled. Like many country gentlemen, he was chiefly shocked by the change of front, by Wellington's emergence as a *politique*, willing under sufficient pressure to tack and unsay things said. And he specifically attacked Peel, now art and part of the whole change of front, for 'allowing himself to be cheered throughout England as the champion of the Protestant cause, although at the very moment he knew that he had changed his mind upon the subject and was about to take his present course'.[30] The Ultras were not clever men, but they were honourable and they valued level and consistent dealing above all things. The distinction between simple twisting and enforced shifts of policy undertaken for fear of worse happening was lost on them. And neither Wellington nor Peel was of a temperament to talk through the *reasons* for such shifts. The Duke's resources of humour and quickness of mind were buried under the military manner and a style which had frozen on his face, his real charm a private and involuntary thing. Peel, a technocrat *avant la lettre*, was shy and cold in layers. Either could have been the model for Shelley's Ozymandias.

The response of Creevey, who had astutely expected just such a move from Wellington, was a mirror image of Knatchbull's. Wellington's action had done him 'infinite honour'. And he noted his colleagues' pique. 'Our Whigs who hate the Beau (Wellington) and Peel and Grey with all their hearts . . . are mad to the last degree that the two former have taken the Catholick cause out of their own feeble and perfidious hands . . .'[31] When Peel presented the bill on 5 March, Creevey, though regretting the raising of the franchise to £10, was generally delighted. 'The Beau is immortalised by his views and measures as detailed by Peel last night . . .', adding 'there is an increasing satisfaction in all the friends to the bill, and the ranks of the bigots are thinning.'[32] The Reverend Sydney Smith, dedicated emancipator and author of *The Plymley Letters*, which, long before, had mocked such bigots, was cheerful, even complacent. 'Men are tired to death with the Catholic question,' he told a friend. 'And are they not upon the eve of getting rid of it?'

Such enthusiasm from partisan opponents commonly indicates serious statesmanship and terrible politics. The severe fire damage done shortly afterwards to York Minster, then the actual burning down of Covent Garden Opera House, were acts only of lunacy or God. But they caught a Wagnerian moment in politics. Quite simply, Wellington had split the Tories. What we (not they) would call 'the right wing' began to take nebulous shape as the party of Ultras, the agricultural interest and deep-dyed Church and State men. They were currently out of all love and respect for Wellington, but their greatest rage was reserved for the unfortunate Peel, turning a coat he had worn with such ostentation. Knatchbull in his plain way put clearly his wish for change. If a Church and State government, what he would most prefer, could not be obtained, 'I would keep as much as I could of the present government, with as large an infusion of good principles as possible. Peel and all belonging to him I will never support. I am not so clear of the policy as I have before insisted, of separating from the Duke . . .'[33]

Peel had been an opponent of Catholic Relief and it was his style of politics to make all his oppositions implacable. His habit of locking and bolting side exits would, of course, end in his being devoured by the flames of Corn Law abolition when they consumed his own government seventeen years later. For the moment, however, it would cost him only a parliamentary seat, easily replaced. Peel was an Oxford man, double first, late of Christ Church. He was also, with some pride, one of the members for the University.

Oxford at that time was more seminary than broad academic institution. It was awash with parsons and men studying to become parsons. Politically, this was the most theocratic constituency west of Isfahan. Oxford was, moreover, enduring the early fits of Tractarianism, an attempt by earnest young men to discover a continuous Catholic state in a religion which its followers had for 270 years innocently thought entirely Protestant. The case, as one modern historian (David Starkey), puts it, rests on the frayed thread of Kitchen, Bishop of Llandaff, having hung on to his job through the Elizabethan settlement. This was not a good time for a rigid Oxonian supporter of the Protestant constitution to turn flexible. In the middle of actually legislating for emancipation, Peel offered a statement to the Vice-Chancellor, then chairing Convocation, which was in the middle of petitioning Parliament against the bill. In consequence, like Huskisson writing to Wellington, Peel found the tendered resignation accepted. He sought re-election, was opposed by an Ultra, Sir Robert Inglis, and defeated. He quickly returned to the Commons as Member for Westbury, a pocket borough, but the whole episode, the unhorsing of the second man in the Cabinet, had been a nasty jolt for the Wellington Ministry.

But beyond Oxford and its clerical self-absorption, the Ultras busied themselves. Their great names were Eldon, Lord Chancellor for a generation and creator, through pedantic delay, of the Chancery marsh commemorated in *Bleak House*, and the Duke of Newcastle, a systematic reactionary. But the running around and conspiring was left in the hands of Knatchbull and his friend, Sir Richard Vyvyan, both members of the Commons and neither of them, by their private lights, unattractive people. Their position was complicated and not one exclusively of reaction. Their constitutionalism was rooted and sincere, but they were dismally prone to muddle. Knatchbull yearned for an older English tradition. A letter to the Chief Whip, anxious about his activities, from a go-between, the MP Joseph Planta, reported him 'very melancholy' about agriculture and the currency, and saying such things as 'If old England should go on . . . If we shall last for five years', but speaking kindly of Wellington and showing 'a most established hatred for the Whigs'.

Vyvyan, a Cornish baronet of twenty-nine, an antiquarian romantic who might have wandered out of one of Peacock's novels, rushed into the reconstruction of the government. Since the fear of the Ultras was that Wellington and Peel would now move on from Catholic emancipation to parliamentary Reform and free trade, they wanted, above all things, a government which would do neither of these things. Claiming much later in his memoirs that he had encouragement from the King, Vyvyan had begun manoeuvres to bring about a government dominated by High Tories, but tempered with moderate men to please George IV.

Reasonably enough, he made approaches to Lord Palmerston, a moderate only in the poster-paint terms of 1820s Toryism, and, they reckoned, no great friend to free trade. Palmerston, consulted in early October at the Travellers' Club, heard him coolly, but without rebuff. 'Finding Vyvyan at dinner at the club, I sat down by him and fell to politics and cutlets and the dialogue ended in his proposing me to be the leader of the House of Commons to a Mansfield, Eldon, Newcastle and Knatchbull administration.'[34] For pure political cool, this did very well, but Vyvyan had an ardent young man's quality of disinterested effrontery.

He also insisted to Palmerston, correctly enough, that the Duke was very weak and, quite wrongly, that the King was looking for a chance to be rid of him (though that impression might easily have been given in a conversation between two such mercurial temperaments as George IV and Sir Richard Vyvyan, one ardent to please, the other as fervent to believe). Palmerston, like a good government man, said that he thought the Duke was recovering, and privately commented that the Ultras were trying 'to mix with a preponderance of old fellows saturated with the brine of Toryism a few young men of the Liberal parties who shall not be able to set up objection to any course proposed'.[35] The possibility that such a ministry which might, thought Vyvyan, include such unlikely figures as

Stanley and even Huskisson, would serve the Ultras' purposes or even come into existence, was never strong. But it was steady political thinking compared with Vyvyan's next move.

He sought to bring the royal family directly into government, and not just the royal family, but its single most discreditable member. Vyvyan wanted to put the Duke of Cumberland at the head of his following. This was both absurd practical politics and an embracing of the most unpopular man in Britain, one who would later become the despotic King of Hanover. The effect was to win his faction the derisive name 'the Brunswickers'. The calmer and older Knatchbull wrote asking his friend, 'does not the Character of the Person in question, or rather the estimation in which he is held in the country, disqualify him from being the head of a party?'.[36] Yet the measure of Vyvyan's naivety and his decency is that, at the same time, he was looking with horror across the Channel to Polignac, Charles X's authoritarian Minister, citing him for comparison with Wellington's ministers. He feared that an alliance with Polignac (and with Metternich in Vienna) might be formed by ministers 'for the purpose of crushing popular liberty'.[37]

And such was the paradox of the time that, along with fearing a free trading assault on the Corn Laws and reform of the electoral system, the better country members were alerted to distress and anxious to respond to it. Knatchbull, as noted, had been on the record as early as 1826, begging assembled Kentish landowners to look beyond their own countryside and face up to impoverishment in the industrial towns: 'You have no conception of the distress which exists in the manufacturing districts: your own county does not afford a comparison . . . Here we are not met by hundreds of human beings barely eking out an existence, affording the appalling but desperate truth of the wretched state to which the operatives have arrived. For this reason the importation of certain descriptions of grain have been allowed.' This is a country member acceding to a relaxation of the Corn Laws, not a small thing. It was of a piece, though Knatchbull was not the man to see it, with Wellington's own retreat on emancipation in the face of an Ireland bubbling with revolt.

And it was an even greater distress which Wellington himself witnessed on a journey north in 1829, one which was producing a political response. William Cobbett in print, Thomas Attwood organising Birmingham and Henry Hunt preaching radical reform constituted an English parallel to the Catholic Association. For this Tory government existed between three fires – Ireland, its own outraged supporters, and, to use a Tory term, 'Radical Agitation'. Cobbett and Hunt had been travelling the country, instructing it from platform and newspaper. The latent violence, of which neither of them approved, had subsided mid-decade with economic recovery, the interim condition from which 'Prosperity' Robinson as Chancellor had taken his nickname. Prosperity had disappeared at the end of the twenties and violence was back.

In the midst of such a conflict, the Ultras made a very shrewd thrust at the Ministry but one consistent with earlier anxieties. The Duke had spoken in the hopeful way of all governments about the distress being 'partial'. On 4 February, Knatchbull put down an amendment to the address on the King's Speech, lamenting 'the existence of that distress which His Majesty informs us, prevails in some places. We are however constrained to declare to His Majesty our opinion that the distress is not confined . . . to some particular places, but that it is general among all the productive interests of the country, which are severely suffering from its pressure.' It was a motion which Holmes, Tory Chief Whip, feared would carry and it was in fact defeated by only fifty-three, after Whigs, radicals and other non-Tories, O'Connell and Joseph Hume among them, came to the rescue. 'The result,' thought Greville, 'shows that the Government has not the slightest command over the House of Commons, and that they have nothing but casual support, and that of course will only be to be had "dum se bene gesserent"'*[38] The situation was relished by the Whigs. Henry Brougham, about to become a major player, put it sweetly: 'I am clear that the said Beau cannot go on as he is. They can't get people to vote and there is tendency for other people to join in voting against them . . .'[39]

Any government at the seething turn of the third decade of the nineteenth century would have had to live by shifts and reactions. But a Tory government refined very early to a sort of irreducibly true Toryism, purged of Canningites and of William Huskisson, a government headed by a field marshal, was horribly placed for such shifts and reactions. It had struck an attitude and drawn the stern, unbending men around in fealty. Any common-sense accommodation with what Hazlitt had called the Spirit of the Age was certain now to be seen as straightforward treason. At the same time, Wellington, though not yet sixty, was physically exhausted. Recourse to the waters of Cheltenham did something for him, as did a trip to Doncaster races. But the soldierly dismissiveness was in collision with intolerable pressure, so the temptation to order that pressure to back off by a statement of categorical defiance was horribly tempting.

* More commonly, as a legal term, *quamdiu se bene gesserent* – 'for as long as they behave themselves'.

The question of parliamentary Reform had been moving up the political escalator. Both the government's weaknesses – lack of a secure majority or young talent – and its great achievement – the daring pre-emption of Catholic emancipation – had pushed the Whigs towards commitment. They could see a political opportunity and, having had one fox shot, were keen to chase another. Sir Francis Burdett, sponsor of so many initiatives on reform over the years, who had more recently been holding back, now judged that the time was coming. He stated 'that the only struggle really worth making was reform of parliament. He believed that the people of England were at last beginning to bestir themselves.'[40]

Might Reform perhaps be another prize for an astute Tory realism briskly adjusting principles? The Marquess of Blandford, despite being generally seen as an Ultra, thought so, and less than two weeks after Knatchbull's amendment, on 18 February, he put down a motion redistributing seats to the industrial towns, a common scot and lot franchise, and, very much the practical thinking of early twentieth-century reforms, repeal of the Septennial Act and payment of members. The motion, though attracting Burdett's intervention, failed, as in such gaudy form it was bound to. So too, by forty-eight votes, did a bill of the Whig, Lord John Russell, tabled five days later. This was a gossamer wedge for painless insertion, £10 *or* £20 household suffrage and the enfranchisement of Manchester, Birmingham and Leeds.

The economy was low, the weather in the early months of the year ferocious. George IV survived the weather but not for long. On 26 June 1830, the First Gentleman of Europe, selfish, tender-hearted, hysterical, erratic, ludicrously extravagant, cultivated in the arts above any king since Charles I, finally died. Greville had written words eighteen months earlier which make a terrible obituary, that 'a more contemptible, cowardly, selfish unfeeling dog does not exist than this king upon whom such flattery is constantly lavished . . .', adding that 'with vices and weaknesses of the lowest and most contemptible order, it would be difficult to find a disposition more abundantly furnished . . .'.[41] The change of head under the crown would matter. George was followed by his brother William, lately Duke of Clarence, former naval person, hot tempered, warm hearted, slightly cracked, but in ways dangerous only to royal dignity, and given to a sort of lumpen bonhommie which pleased the public rather than otherwise, together with a slightly erratic enthusiasm for being helpful to his ministers.

Meanwhile, foreign events demonstrated that constitutions bound up in treaties could be amended more drastically than Lord John or even Blandford had proposed. Late in August, the union of the Netherlands with the Flemish- and French-speaking southern provinces, created at Vienna, would fall apart, with the southern Catholic element proclaiming the state of Belgium. But something more important had preceded it by a month, another royal succession, but one heavily induced.

'Yesterday morning I met Matuscewitz in St James's Street, who said "You have heard the news?"' The news which Charles Greville learnt on climbing into his friend's cabriolet that morning was genuinely sensational. At the end of July, the France of the restored Bourbons had provoked street demonstrations, faced on behalf of the mystically proud heir of St Louis by unwilling troops under the command of an unfazed Napoleonic marshal, Marmont. It all happened very flatteringly, according to the classic Whig pattern. Charles X, through his Minister, Polignac, had behaved with the same thick-headed imperiousness as James II, suspending freedom of the press, dissolving the Chamber and changing electoral laws to suit the royal interest. Cheating not being cheating if it were done in the name of sacred majesty, Charles and Polignac had tried to abolish the modest rules limiting their government. What happened next would not have surprised men of more sense.

After a life full of conspiracy, Charles 'had ended by conspiring against himself';[42] other people, notably the great Talleyrand, whose career of enlightened duplicity went back to pre-revolutionary France, and the rising Adolphe Thiers, had made arrangements of their own. On 29 July, Talleyrand looked up from his whist in the Rue St Florentin at the sound of cheering crowds and said 'Hark, we are winning', 'Who are we?' 'Hush, not a word. I will tell you tomorrow.'[43] On the same day, he told the Duke of Orleans to come to Paris. On 30 July, Charles X left for Rambouillet. The three Days of July, though distinctly bloody, ran very smoothly: one monarchy was ended and another took its place with the facility of a well-managed ballet; the fleur-de-lis on its white ground came down and the tricolour went up.

Under the superintendence of M. Thiers, new, but hard hand at this sort of game, Orleans, senior and most ambitious Royal Duke, lethargic but intelligent and exceedingly good at public relations before the term was thought of, succeeded, first as 'Lieutenant-General of the Realm', soon after as 'Louis-Philippe, King of the French'. No privilege or financial interest would suffer in a silken and well-conducted affair for which the word 'revolution' seems overdone. To a Whig raised on the glories of 1688–9, it looked like imitation of the most gratifying kind. Greville had no problems: 'the game is up with the Bourbons, they richly deserve their fate'.[44] Wellington himself briskly ruled out any thought of intervention. He expressed a poor opinion of the 'mean' Louis-Philippe, but thought his succession the best thing in the circumstances and moved insouciantly on to talk about a domestic court wrangle over etiquette, one concerning possession of the gold stick. As for the King of the French, Louis-Philippe made for the pavements, shook every hand within reach and smiled a lot, evidently another, if more calculated, William IV. A democratic *style* at any rate had come in, even with kings. In England little shudders at the presence of Jacobins come again on to the streets, mingled with acknowledgement that moderate men, constitutional men, men of the commercial middle class, now looked very big indeed.

The late summer of 1830 was a time of extraneous events: in June the death of King George, in July the removal of King Charles and, on 15 September at the opening of that embodiment of all bustling modernity, the Manchester to Liverpool railway, the death, hideously half under a train, of William Huskisson. To his official opponents Wellington had seemed for the best part of two years unassailable. At the end of 1829, Sydney Smith had thought tolerantly that he was 'getting stronger every day. He is an excellent Minister and bids fair to be as useful in peace as in war, and to show the utility of beating swords into pruning hooks.'[45] Catholic emancipation back in 1828 had both pleased and stunned the Whigs, an act of pre-emption which had revived serious thought about coalition. For the year following enactment, they were a temperate opposition, treading water and wondering what might turn up, something particularly true of Henry Brougham, at once the most brilliantly partisan of Whigs, the most avid for office and the most mercurial. But with George gone, the Whigs suddenly saw Wellington deprived of a prop and themselves of an obstacle.

Within four days of the King's death, Brougham's rick-burning instincts were released. In debate, he indicated the Treasury bench and described Wellington's battered team as 'his flatterers, those mean, fawning parasites'. As for Wellington, he was to be compared (in unconscious parallel to the words of Vyvyan) with the Prince de Polignac, suppressor general of French liberties. Wellington had preferred conciliating the Ultras, whose enmity he had created through emancipation, to embracing the opponents he had impressed. One window, opened in 1828, was closing. The terrible death of Huskisson, literally under the wheels of progress, made another less accessible.

To add to the bitterness of the occasion, Huskisson died as the direct result of his leaving his railway carriage during a temporary stop and attempting to give his hand to the Duke of Wellington. In some eyes, this might have led to reconciliation with the head of the government. A man who should not have been lost to it and who, returning to office, would have made thinkable a broad coalition with the political middle, was 'crushed to death in the sight of his wife and at the feet (as it were) of his great political rival'.[46] There was no question about Huskisson's calibre. It was, thought Greville, 'probably true that there is no man in Parliament, or perhaps out of it, so well versed in Finance, commerce, trade and Colonial matters, and that he is therefore a very great and irreparable loss'.[47]

But a loss to whom? The immediate rush to judgement insisted upon the cynical award of advantage. Grey, seeing only the downside, wrote that 'here again, fate is on the side of the Duke of Wellington'.[48] For Thomas Creevey, 'The Canning faction has lost its cornerstone, and the Duke's government one of its most formidable opponents. Huskisson too, once out of the way, Palmerston, Melbourne, the Grants &, may make it up with the Beau.' He was wrong this time, but all opinions were legitimate. The Canningites seem, with hindsight, as certain to join with Whigs as, decades later, Peelites were sure of becoming Liberals. On the other hand, Huskisson was a *trade* liberal and the most marginal and tepid of parliamentary reformers. Again, he was deeply loyal personally to the memory of Canning, with whom indeed the Duke had struggled furiously, but then Grey had covered Canning in public contempt. A coming together of Huskisson and Grey is difficult to imagine.

The Duke needed talent as well as breadth of support. Accordingly, before the fatal accident, it was entirely thinkable that Huskisson, Melbourne and Palmerston might have been brought into a government which would make just enough modest reform concessions for show, proposing, say, the enfranchisement of the Manchesters and Birminghams at the expense of six to a dozen boroughs incontrovertibly rotten. The Duke would have seized the centre ground, drunk confusion to the Whigs and argued from a stronger redoubt.

Another consequence of the death of George IV was that, under the rules of the day, it provoked a general election, the process beginning with prorogation of Parliament on 23 July, its six or so weeks falling in perfect sync for influencing the political mood across the Days of July in Paris. Massive swings did not generally take place under the system of county membership and closed boroughs, but drifts did occur. And in 1830 a distinct drift took place for the Whigs. The emblematic contest, one involving a decent sized electorate, was Yorkshire. Henry Brougham, advanced Whig, *Edinburgh Review*er, chief trumpeter of the Society for the Propagation of Useful Knowledge, clever beyond any identified competition and triumphally aware of the fact, gave up the closed borough of Knaresborough which, at the whim of the Earl of Darlington, had incongruously returned him, and threw himself into a decidedly popular county race for Yorkshire.

It was a race which old practice, abhorring the expense, had discouraged from happening often; this was only the fourth contest in a century and a half. Yorkshire was also an interesting confluence of opposing powers. The great landowners had once run things very satisfactorily in their own interests. But there had sprung up among them the cities and towns of the wool trade – Huddersfield, Halifax, Bradford, Leeds – and of steel and coal – Sheffield, Rotherham, Barnsley and Doncaster. And now this middle-class lawyer was running for knight of the shire! Based in York where he pleaded at the Assizes every day, Brougham, one of those frantically energetic men, flung himself round every town within a thirty mile radius of the Minster and, according to his legal colleague, Denman, was addressing 70,000 voters a day before getting back to York at midnight. It was the beginning of a new and furious style which would not die out till the 1960s.

The polls were declared on 6 August. There were two places and though the first went narrowly to Lord Morpeth, a more usual sort of Whiggish younger son, Brougham took the second, both having been ahead of all opposition throughout the running count. He put on a sword, placed a cocked hat on his head and, clinging on to the horse he had mounted, rode out of York Castle and through the streets. But as the Whig MP for Newcastle, William Ord, put it, he was now 'the member for Yorkshire or rather one should say, the member for Leeds, Huddersfield and Sheffield'. This was what reform was about, and Brougham had fought his election on such terms. Apart from an impassioned pledge to bring about the abolition of the slave trade, he made a personal pledge on triennial parliaments, the transfer of seats to great industrial towns and the widening of the franchise to town-dwelling householders.

In arithmetical terms, the election still amounted to drift, heavy drift – on Grey's calculation, fifty seats in Parliament. The Duke still had a majority, but he headed a seriously weakened ministry. With Huskisson's death in mid-September, any prospect of a minor coalition with the Canningites had receded. The choice would now be a grand coalition with the Whigs or the march under fire of a Tory government fifty supporters down.

But the election was not the only expression of public opinion. Distress and protest at distress had ceased to be a thing of the remote northern towns or the far countryside. Enfield, now a pleasant enough suburb of London, was then something between a village and a small market town and place of resort, but it stood in Middlesex, near enough. Charles

Lamb, on a good pension from his East India House employers, had with-drawn there. Only four months after the election, at the year's end, the apolitical essayist, lightest touch of anyone then writing, had unwelcome news for his friend, George Dyer:

> Poor Enfield that has been so peaceable hitherto, has caught the inflam-matory fever; the tokens are upon her; and a great fire was blazing last night in the barns and haystacks of a farmer, about half a mile from us . . . We are past the iron age and into a fiery age undreamed of by Ovid. You are lucky in Cliffords Inn where I think you have few ricks or stacks worth the burning. Pray keep as little corn by you as possible for fear of the worst. It was never good times in England since the poor began to speculate on their condition . . . he writes his distaste in flames. What a power to intoxicate his crude brains, just muddlingly awake to perceive that something is wrong in the social system – what a hellish facility above gunpowder! Now the rich and poor are fairly pitted. We shall see who can hang or burn fastest.[49]

With Parliament harder to handle, Huskisson gone and the fire and violence of the fields intensifying, the need to stiffen the Ministry was imperative. Wellington might not care for it, but people had to be courted. Peel was telling him so. There was a general agitation among his friends, not least his long-standing female friend and dearest companion, Harriet Arbuthnot, and her husband, Charles, usually called 'Gosh', whom Wellington cherished. They were being lobbied at the Duke of Rutland's country home by Charles Greville, anxious that the Foreign Secretary, Aberdeen, should be a loser in any reshuffle. Greville in turn learned from Arbuthnot of the *froideur* between the Duke and his lieutenant. Peel, he heard, was 'so jealous that he could not endure that anybody should do anything but himself'.[50]

Palmerston, the object of Sir Richard Vyvyan's attentions and approached tentatively for Wellington once already, was at Peel's insistence in early October made the prime target. He was addressed through Lord Clive, a friend of both men, then invited to Apsley House and offered a seat in the Cabinet. The idea was to follow Canning's successful approach to Lansdowne three years before and hold out three places for keepers of Huskisson's flame, and painful preparation was accordingly made for vacating the places which should be taken up. As well as Palmerston himself, there might be Melbourne, even, it was suggested, John Russell, author of that freelance, moderate Reform Bill. But Palmerston himself wanted not just the Canningites, but leading Whigs, specifically Grey and Lansdowne, to enter the Cabinet. This meant a coalition of equals and Wellington rejected it.

The person suggesting John Russell was Edward Littleton, kin to the Duke but politically a Canningite, who had devised a brilliant scenario. Russell, an acknowledged first-class talent, and as acknowledged a Whig, should come into the ministry and bring his bill with him. It was a modest, unrevolutionary affair, a Louis-Philippe among reform bills. This, said Littleton, would mean general Liberal support for the government. They would achieve an end, take a share of credit and enjoy a piece of the equity of office. From the point of view of moderate men across party, it was almost perfect. However, these men all occupied the Palace of Westminster. In the light of the street feeling and the numbers of respectable citizens rallying to Thomas Attwood and his political union in Birmingham and his imitators in other cities, it is doubtful whether a Wellington–Russell minimalist reform of Parliament would have stuck without provoking a cross-kingdom demand for much more. But it is at least arguable that even after subsequent concessions at committee or a following bill, the anti-reformers might have brought the system out of the conflict less reformed than when Russell legislated for a Whig Ministry in a Whig parliament.

From the point of view of an intelligent Conservative, such a deal was the thing to do. The Duke *was* intelligent, he was a Conservative, but he was not necessarily an intelligent Conservative. He was also not far from the end of his emotional tether and critically aware of the response to be expected from the friends of Vyvyan and Knatchbull. Reflecting about the option to Lady Salisbury years later, when all the Reform water was under the legislative bridge, Wellington said, 'I saw it was a question of noses, that as many as I gained on one side, I should lose on the other, the Ultra Tories were beginning to take great alarm at the idea of reform . . .' Meanwhile, in another conversation, 'Peel declared on the Saturday to Arb [Charles Arbuthnot] that he would resign before Xmas . . .'[51]

But that Ultra alarm and its deep roots would be expressed by a more refined spirit than Knatchbull's and a sharper mind than Vyvyan's – the Tory Party's uncomfortable intellectual, John Wilson Croker. Croker, eyes and ears of Robert Peel, undertook to talk to Palmerston on 6 November, conveying a last offer from the Prime Minister. He asked him, 'Well, I will bring the matter to a point. Are you resolved or are you not, to vote for Parliamentary Reform?'

'I am,' said Palmerston. 'Well then,' said Croker, 'there is no use in talking to you any more on this subject. You and I, I am grieved to see, shall never again sit on the same bench together.' Far and away the ablest of all the Ultras, Croker was also a doctrinaire. At another time, under less pressure, the Duke is unlikely to have spoken like this. But circumstances had made Croker a perfectly faithful voice for the mood at which he had arrived.

Wellington, having kept up so long the mask of cool indifference and made imperturbability his house style, *was* reached by events, *did* feel oppressed by them and was correspondingly ever less willing to make adjustments. Yet no one expected any kind of explosion or collapse.

The general assumption was that the government, being weak, would be strengthened, that being under pressure it would make practical accommodations. Intelligent onlookers, including opponents, expected an infusion of talent and reinforcing of the government enough to see it through immediate, post-election anxieties. Sydney Smith did not even think the Duke needed to hurry. Was he not very well placed?

> There will be no changes in the government before Christmas; and by that time, the Duke will probably have gained some recruits. He does not want numbers, but defenders. Whoever goes into his cabinet, goes there as an inferior, to register the Duke's resolutions – not as an equal, to assist in their formation; and this is a situation into which men of spirit and character do not choose to descend. The death of Huskisson has strengthened him very materially; his firmness, powers of labour, sagacity and good nature and his vast military reputation, will secure his power. Averse from liberal measures, he will be as liberal as the times require.[52]

This judgement might have been wrong as to the outcome, but it rests on a profound assessment of Wellington: splendid but alone, short not only of defenders but equals. As Smith says, he would be 'as liberal as the times require'. So he had been over Ireland, winning admiration and losing allies in the process. He would make his decision on Reform equally alone and apart from serious, non-subordinate advice. It was to reclaim the Ultras by taking a categorical, evasion-proof stand against all reform.

On 11 October, Thomas Attwood, addressing nearly 4,000 prosperous middle-class citizens at a dinner in Brodsworth's Repository in Birmingham, having praised the July Revolution in France, invoked the political union's motto, 'The constitution and nothing but the constitution', and was received with continuous cheering when he asked 'Where is the man among you who would not follow me to the death in a righteous cause?'[53] His audience had made their point by lustily joining in singing the 'Marseillaise'. On 2 November the royal address to the new parliament congratulated Britain upon 'social happiness' and 'commercial prosperity'. But the real catastrophe came from Wellington's own lips. Answering Grey, who had spoken impressively of moderate reform, the Prime Minister said, 'I am not only not prepared to bring in any measure of the description alluded to by the noble lord, but I will at once declare that as far as I am concerned, as long as I hold any station in the Government of the country, I shall always feel it my duty to resist such measures when proposed by others.'[54] Greville knew immediately what this 'violent and uncalled-for declaration against Reform' meant. It had 'without doubt, sealed his fate. Never was there an act of more egregious folly, or one so universally condemned by friends and foes . . . I came to town last night and found the town ringing with his imprudence, and everybody expecting that a few days would produce his resignation.'[55]

All this was happening not in a clinically isolated Westminster, but in a London where the Lord Mayor had persuaded the Prime Minister that he and the King should not attend a banquet for fear of assassination attempts against both. And in Birmingham, government agents informed Whitehall of societies formed for the 'express intention of intimidating the government' with the political union 'a most dangerous body'. It was a time when the market in state financial paper was registering falls and recoveries in the funds of up to 3 per cent. Greville saw and noted that 'troops were called up to London, and a large body of civil power put in motion. People had come in from the country in the morning and everything indicated a disturbance.' He went out on the evening of 10 November and found 'a little mob in the west end of the town, and in New Street Spring Gardens, was drawn up a large body of the New Police in three divisions waiting to be employed if wanted . . . The Duke of Wellington expected Apsley House to be attacked and made preparations accordingly.'

Nothing immediate materialised, and, in the febrile way of the City, the funds rose next day. But the mood was not conducive to cool reason. The Duke, for all Greville's instant obituarising, ought not to have been in immediate danger. But since the elections, Reform had become the single, all-excluding issue. Gathering every other discontent under its shade, it faced and menaced a government which was now assaulted on all sides by petitions for its enactment. A motion was due for debate, but the day before it was due, another piece of business, the civil list, on which a resolution had been tabled in the old parliament, came up and provided the pretext for all the mistrust and personality politics of the last two years to find expression. Wellington had forsworn an excellent interim option, the Russell Bill, with or without him personally, together with a deal with the Canningites. He had done so because of his fear of losing the Ultra Tories.

He had lost them anyway. An amendment by Sir Henry Parnell on the civil list motion was seconded by Sir Edward Knatchbull; it carried by 233 votes to 204. 'The Duke of Wellington's administration,' said Greville, 'is at an end.'[56]

THREE

The First Bill

'This Monstrous Act of Spoliation – This Civil Sacrilege'

'At length we have broke down!" The words are those of Harriet Arbuthnot, Wellington's uncritical admirer and a dedicated Tory, recording the adverse vote on the civil list. She had been dining at his house 'when the Duke got a note telling him what had happened & that Peel, Goulburn & Mr Arbuthnot had come up to talk to him. He whispered to me before he went down what had happened & went away, saying nothing to anyone else. I stayed till they were all gone & then went down stairs and heard *all about it*. I never saw a man so delighted as Peel.'² Mrs Arbuthnot would be left to her griefs, and Peel, as she resentfully but correctly noted, to his satisfactions. The Duke called on King William the next day, 17 November, assuring him that 'he had better try another arrangement'.³

There was only one arrangement to try and that was Lord Grey. The coolest member of his party when the option of coalition with Canning had arisen, leader by evolved consent of a party which had done very well in the recent elections, he was now perfectly placed for succession. The concept of an official opposition and an official leader of it waiting to enter the vacancies as they happened was a convention still developing. Grey's primacy contributed to its establishment. On 22 December, as Mrs Arbuthnot, 'vexed and mortified beyond expression'⁴ would record next day, his government was formed and received its seals.

Grey's immediate and biggest problem would come from his antithesis, Brougham, the man warmest in 1827 for trade with Canning. It was initially proposed that he should have the proper reward of a solid lawyer and steady party man – the Attorneyship. But Henry Brougham was not a solid lawyer and steady party man; he was an intolerable genius. He knew his worth and, when offered less, he behaved in what Lord Grey (and Mrs Arbuthnot) would have called 'a thoroughly ungentlemanlike way'. According to one account, he took the Prime Minister's letter making the offer, tore it up and stamped on the pieces. Rather more usefully, he reminded Grey and his circle that the Brougham motion on reform still stood awaiting debate and vote in the Commons.

This was the issue which quick-minded Tories like Peel had most hoped to avoid, preferring to go down on the technicality of the civil list. Brougham was willing to postpone the Reform motion, but not the issue of Reform. Thomas Campbell, a colleague and future Lord Chancellor, remembered twenty-five years later the quiet menace in his voice; 'As no change that may take place in the Administration can by any possibility affect me, I beg to be understood that in putting off the motion, I will put it off until the 25th of this month and no longer. I will then and at no more distant period, bring forward the question of parliamentary Reform, whatever may be the condition of circumstances and whosoever may be his Majesty's ministers.'[5]

With the non-voting public, that electorate in historic prospect, Brougham, the 70,000 audience-a-day stump speaker, and Brougham, the promoter of working-class education, had registered as a force, however imperfectly defined, for their interests. A group of workmen quarrying on the Lothian coast 'heard a small boy approach waving a newspaper and shouting "The Tories driven from power at last." Those of us who knew least of politics knew enough to understand the importance of this announcement. We took off our hats and caps, and loud above the north wind and the roaring sea, shouted "Henry Brougham for ever!" At that time we knew little of Earl Grey.'[6]

Grey had tried his hand at fobbing off and Brougham was too successful at democratic politics for fobbing. The best escape was to take him out of democratic politics. Grey would have preferred to offer the Woolsack to Lyndhurst, a genial, underfunded and adaptive lawyer who approached office in the spirit of an English mercenary commander in a small, non-violent medieval Italian war. But Brougham in a political department and the Commons, promoting Reform further and deeper than the Ministry wished, or Brougham on the back benches making brilliant radical assaults upon them were a couple of unpleasing options. Brougham, elevated out of mischief, though not, as they would find, out of vigorous usefulness or fights with colleagues, seemed to be the answer. The democratic victor of Yorkshire should preside in the House of Lords. Essentially Brougham wanted to stay in the Commons to promote Reform and a thousand other causes. He had hoped to be offered the Mastership of the Rolls, a legal appointment still reconcilable with Cabinet and Parliament. Grey went one better and offered him the Great Seal which he rejected. A succession of Whig eminences pleaded and cajoled, the blackmailing tone being caught by Althorp. If he persisted in refusal, there was 'an end of the matter; and you take upon yourself the responsibility of keeping our party for another twenty-five years out of power and the loss of all the great questions which will follow, instead of their being carried'.

When Brougham, after the ministrations of Lords Grey, Althorp, Sefton and Denman, finally reflected that a reforming Lord Chancellor could effect a great deal and submitted to the Great Seal, the guineas of racing men said that his mouth had been stuffed with office. King William thought that, by his own ready consent to the appointment, he had helped extinguish Brougham. Greville, so often sweeping, thought that 'the joy is great and universal, all men feel that he is emasculated and drops on the Woolsack as on his political deathbed; once in the H. of Lords, there is an end of him, and he may rant, storm and thunder without hurting anybody'. [7] It was to prove the most vigorous of deathbeds, one in which a great reforming Chancellor rarely slept and afforded his colleagues as little rest. But something had been diminished. The great *different* man, the force of nature, had been contained, if in the most spacious and interesting of cages.

The final Cabinet was one of core Whigs and slow-evolving Canningites, plus, in the Duke of Richmond, a pure Tory wandering in out of a spirit of good-humoured contrariness. It contained a former Prime Minister in Goderich at the Colonial Office, and four future premiers in Melbourne, Stanley, Russell and Palmerston. The key radical would be Lord Durham, Lord Privy Seal, one member of Grey's family, his son-in-law, able to claim place on merit and, Brougham not excepted, his most difficult colleague. Grant, Stanley and Graham at, respectively, the Board of Control, the Irish Secretaryship and the Admiralty, were more or less Canningites. Stanley would become a Conservative Prime Minister three times, if never for long or to much point. Graham would rejoin the Tories as Peel's Home Secretary and leave them again as a Peelite.

Grey's government was old fashioned in the degree to which pure family connection commanded places. Sons-in-law, brothers-in-law and nephews were all advanced in a spirit of old world tribalism. At the same time he shocked Mrs Arbuthnot by admitting trade to office. Grey she remarked, 'has made two merchants, one Secy of the Treasury & the other Vice-President of the Board of Trade, and the same Gazette, which announced their appointments, notified the dissolution of their partnerships with houses in the City'. She ended in italics, greeting the development with Edith Evans-like horror: 'This is all *quite new*.' Not new at all, but the young representative of the cream and essence of historic Whiggery, Lord John Russell, stood as Paymaster General, only at the Cabinet door, something displeasing to other, grander Russells. They need not have worried; the immediate making, or at any rate proclaiming, of history would be put into his hands.

Meanwhile, the cultivated world, what Sydney Smith had called 'the great parallelogram' levelled between Piccadilly and Oxford Street, shuddered at the evidence of violence. Anxiety among the better sort was not diminished by renewed disturbances in Paris over the failure of the courts to bring Polignac and his ultra royalist colleagues to any conclusion sharper than life imprisonment. The term 'Jacobin' would have currency in England for the rest of the century. Back in October 1829, Mrs Arbuthnot had been indignant at the general worthlessness of the lower classes. 'In the manufacturing districts they *strike work* as they call it, when they can earn 35 shillings a week; they won't work above three or four days in the week and then they say they are distressed! I think we want stronger laws to govern an unruly population for, when the idle and turbulent not only strike work themselves, but intimidate the industrious by threats and violence, they ought to be severely punished.'[8] And she had found the eleven shillings a week earned by 'boys of 12 & 14' to be 'quite as much as it is desirable they shd gain'.[9]

Profound economic changes had seen the growth of the industrial economy, producing for some of the time and some of the urban working class the sort of wages which had distressed Mrs Arbuthnot. It had also seen conditions of black misery, especially among farm labourers in the South and West. A population which, despite some shifts to the towns, was fully replaced, became in the eyes of Malthus and his disciples a 'surplus population'. 'Surplus to what?' is a question which might have been asked. Surplus they certainly were to the rural labour market, witness one report: 'man and wife, willing, if you could engage them together, say man at 8s, woman at 4s'.[10] The old poor law, using the so-called Speenhamland system, subsidised wages as the price of bread moved up, but misery among farm workers was endemic.

Edward Thompson, not a cool neutral, speaks of the relationship thus: 'On the side of the gentry and overseers, economies, settlement litigation, stone breaking and punitive tasks, cheap labour gangs, the humiliations of labour auctions, even of men harnessed in carts. On the side of the poor, threats to the overseers, sporadic sabotage, a "servile and cunning" or "sullen and discontented" spirit . . .' He also records a view of the poor rates system among southern labourers that 'the farmers keep us here like potatoes in a pit and only take us out for use when they can no longer do without us'.

One can add to his second list the destruction of threshing machines, which reduced the work for which men were desperate, and the rick-burning, which Charles Lamb had recorded in the first days of the new government's life. Thompson speaks sadly of 'the Last Labourers' Revolt'. That revolt had the capacity to scare the non-poor, moving them to brisk and satisfactory action. In practice, people like the Duke of Richmond could, with a show of force, quickly disperse labourers congregating for revolt. And the courts were resolute, taking up the labourers for trial in the company of a sprinkling of conventional criminality.

'Unrest', as it was called, had been an intermittent condition since the early days of the century and laws had been passed for its suppression. When, back in 1812, the death penalty had been introduced for the destruction of machinery, Lord Byron had spoken his mind forcefully: 'Setting aside the palpable injustice and certain inefficiency of the bill, are there not capital punishments sufficient in your statutes. Is there not blood enough upon your penal code that more must be poured forth to ascend to Heaven and testify against you? Will you erect a gibbet in every field and hang up men like scarecrows?'[11] The legislation was the work of the prim Christian reactionary, Perceval, soon afterwards, in unrelated circumstances, shot dead. It would operate vigorously under the reforming Lord Grey.

> On the 9th of January, judgement of death was recorded against twenty-three prisoners for the destruction of a paper mill at Buckingham; in Dorset, on the 11th against three for extorting money, and two for robbery; at Norwich fifty-five prisoners were convicted of machine breaking and rioting; at Ipswich three of extoring money; at Petworth twenty-six for machine breaking and rioting; at Gloucester upwards of thirty; at Oxford twenty-nine; and at Winchester out of upwards forty convicted six were left for execution . . .[12]

If this was the dreaded Captain Swing, he was dealt with easily enough. Sydney Smith, writing in November 1830, had said, 'I am frightened at the state of the world; I shall either be burnt, or lose my tithes, or be forced to fight, or some harm will happen to disturb the drowsy slumbers of my useless old age.'[13]

By December, however, he could write with a characteristic combination of wistfulness and ferocious flippancy. 'Swing is retiring. He is only formidable when he takes you unawares. He was stopped in Kent before he reached us [he was writing from Combe Florey in Somerset]. I can give you no plan for employing the poor. I took great pain about these matters when I was a magistrate, but have forgotten all my plans. There are too many human beings on the earth: every two men ought to kill a third.'[14]

What frightened Smith frightened many people in government too. And the griefs of that surplus population, the very poor, were divided by no very precise partition from the anger of crowds gathering in support of Reform. These crowds responded to the radical journalism of Cobbett and Richard Carlile, to the Wesley-like speaking tours of Henry Hunt and, as events unfolded, to the skilful organisation of Francis Place and his National Political Union in London and Thomas Attwood and his Birmingham Political Union. Ministers still behaved with the pleasurable detachment of ministers before them, taking their own places, appointing bishops and filling vacant sinecures with their kin. But the wish of some new politicians for a species of Reform was augmented by a public voice confused as to what Reform should be, but determined to have it.

Historically, that demand looks as if it enjoyed a swift response, details of a Reform Bill being presented to the Commons on 1 March. But, to adapt Harold Wilson, ten weeks, even including a Christmas, is an unconscionable time in politics. The Whigs had spent a long lifetime out of office. They had other things to do, like a budget which could not be avoided and which, in Lord Althorp's hands, was not very well done, involving as it did a tax on transfers which City pressure, largely Whig, caused to be withdrawn. There were also textile duty adjustments, said to have brought hundreds of Manchester cotton brokers to London in swift chaises. Althorp, who in those less detail-oppressed days, combined the Treasury with leadership of the government in the Lower House, had also announced commitment to a Reform Bill which, he said, would be managed by Russell.

Greville, who, like any low journalist, delighted in instant judgements, commented that the employment of someone outside the Cabinet was the consequence of it being otherwise Althorp's own business, 'and he is wholly unequal to it; he cannot speak at all'. It was simply, he thought, 'an expedient to take the burthen off the leader of the Government'. Althorp would turn out eventually to be a superb manager of government business in general and the Reform Bill in particular, and Greville, always open to the evidence, would later say so handsomely. But his first budget (11 February), on which early judgement of the government would focus, was a mess. That stock transfer and land tax created a great fuss among people placed to trade in land and investments, and was denounced with some force by Peel, who looked to see it withdrawn in favour of a property tax. Following an emergency meeting at Althorp's own house on a Sunday, the transfer tax was withdrawn, but not replaced by one on property. Greville expressed a wide, if outsiderish, view: Althorp was 'a respected country gentleman'. Such a man with 'all the integrity of £15,000 in possession and £50,000 in reversion, is all of a sudden made leader of the H. of commons without being able to speak, and Chancellor of the Exchequer without any knowledge, theoretical or practical, of finance'.[15]

Greville's scorn was nearly universal. Observing that 'the exultation of the Opposition is boundless', he remarked that 'neither the late nor any other government ever cut so poor a figure as this does. Palmerston does nothing, Grant does worse, Graham does no good, Althorp a great deal of harm.'[16] He might have added that Melbourne, a fundamentally unpleasant man with the charm of the type, was, as Home Secretary, putting down the desperate labourers who broke threshing machines, happy to confirm, with complacent brutality some four hundred sentences of transportation.

Fortunately there would be, in David Hume's phrase, 'a deal o' ruin' in a government. But it had got off on the wrong foot, and Peel, massively and openly relieved at the fall of a Tory government seriously at sea, was able to make derisive play with the first unsteady paddlings of the new voyagers. But this is often the way with new governments. The ease with which James Callaghan, so recently a Prime Minister out of his depth, put Mrs Thatcher in her place in 1979–80, is an illustration from posterity. Reform was to be the test, and the business of Reform had been quickly put into the concerting hands of Durham, Russell, Graham and Duncannon. Durham was the radical, Graham, at this stage, his ally, Duncannon the specialist on Ireland, which difficult country had to be handled with some finesse.

Reform had been a topic of speculation for fifty years and intermittently a serious political issue. The questions of rotten boroughs, of a restricted franchise, and of varying qualifications for that franchise were familiar. Some form of reform was now acceptable across a very wide spectrum. Curmudgeons like Eldon might rail. Clever, perverse, younger men like Croker might construct arguments which elevated the ramshackle set of electoral laws and practices into a sacrament, but sensible men, starting with Peel, would become reconciled to moderate reform. So, not altogether surprisingly, would Vyvyan and Knatchbull. Even King William, through whose coach window a stone had latterly been thrown as he returned from the theatre, was ready to accommodate his ministers. The question was for how much he would be asked.

The argument in Cabinet, though brisk by later, deliberative standards, was also haphazard. Ministers resolved soon enough, on a far larger scale than Tories realised, to abolish and demote delinquent boroughs. And the idea of two schedules, A and B, to account for the loss of both members or just one, appeared quite early in their thinking. The only research on current populations came from Durham, who had looked up the 1821 census. This suggested that towns with fewer than 2,000 people belonged in Schedule A, those below 4,000 in Schedule B. New boroughs would then be created by allocation of the seats withdrawn. To think in terms of population was new and heretical even to most Whigs. The rationale of the old constitution, something which would spill into the final new draft, was that it was the property (definable) and the intelligence (more problematic) of the nation which should be represented in the Commons. And all such thoughts had to be combined with a judgement on the franchise in respect of which all realistic thought, however reformist, was disposed in 1831 towards property as the measure, if not quite of all things, then certainly of fitness to vote.

There was some argument for varying the property qualification as between old surviving boroughs and new created ones. Established boroughs surviving, but not by much, would with a lower test bring in more respectable numbers of voters. In the new franchised towns, by contrast, the concern was for respectable voters! The Whigs, with their feeling for the solid middle classes whom they were proposing for the political club, favoured a higher hurdle in places like Leeds and Manchester. But other people had views and might make them felt – people in Leeds and Manchester, people like Attwood of the Birmingham Political Union, whose enormous meetings would take very poorly to their city being offered a stiffer franchise than Taunton.

But these calculations were complicated by the issue of the ballot. As Michael Brock observes, 'The radicals needed a way of showing that they were democratic. Advocating a wide diffusion of voting rights was not safe; advocating ballot was.'[17] But its supporters, led by Durham, found themselves up against a steady delusion of the age, that keeping your vote secret was a low, sneaking thing, the act of a cad. It was not, in a favourite word much brayed until World War rather dimmed it, 'manly.' The fact that tenant voters and, in the working boroughs, employee voters, might test their manliness against a lease or a job never seems to have registered. So, if the ballot were to come in, it must be balanced by a tougher franchise. Russell accordingly offered a uniform franchise of £20.

But the ballot was not coming in. Although recommended by the four-man committee, it would have to be sold to a hostile King William and to their Lordships who were going to make trouble enough anyway, so it was dropped. This left Grey and Althorp custodians of a public hustings and the highest qualifying point for the franchise at any time considered. As Reform this was a thin, unnourishing soup which would send public opinion away hungry and make nonsense of Russell's favourite proclamation of 'finality'. It was conservative to the point of imprudence. On top of which, the Whigs learned that their statistics were all wrong. An enquiry triggered by an MP's request from the Office of Taxes showed just how miserable was the number of £20 citizens in the prospective Schedule B boroughs. In more than half of them there were fewer than thirty houses paying such a rate and in eight there were fewer than ten. Schedule B boroughs, stripped of the fancy franchises and local variations by the uniformity of the new system, would emerge from Reform with fewer voters than before it. They would look uncomfortably like government pocket boroughs. The way to decent sized constituencies was a lower franchise, and, with the King squared at £10, one was agreed.

This was compromise, order, counter-order and very nearly disorder. The filling up of Schedules A and B was nothing of the sort. It was incisive if not surgical. Much of this boldness derived from Charles Grey himself, a man both aristocratic and intermittently radical, if soft spoken about it, and he had the full support of Althorp, who named one hundred seats as the fewest which could be shorn.[18] The thinking of such mainstream Whigs was that any reform which reflected pressing public demand should be seen as the sort of change to which fortunate and happily placed individuals should rationally respond. The Catholics of Ireland had represented that force as O'Connell toured and spoke to tens of thousands. Not to respond was to court violent upheaval in Ireland while No Popery meetings in England could be brushed off as atavistic and irrelevant. There was something, if only a little, of Marxist historicism about this acknowledgement of certain tides as irresistible.

Similarly with parliamentary Reform. Cobbett, Attwood and Henry Hunt (who was to defeat a minister, Graham, seeking re-election at Preston after joining the Cabinet) were people the government took irritable notice of as men speaking a public will. The Tories, as speech after speech would make clear, believed that authority was for asserting. They excoriated their own leaders for having resiled from such an assertion over the Catholic Irish. They would now be as scornful of Whigs bent on deferring to public discontent, to the voice of what several of them, recalling Burke's chiselled insult, would call 'the multitude'. He, in his fraught way, had called it 'swinish'; they would be content with 'clamorous'. And the likes of Attwood, a banker leading middle-class demand with wider support, ranked for Tories as an agitator to be regarded in the same way as the men of 1819.

Everything was now done at speed under the pressure of a promise early in February to begin legislation at the beginning of March. It was also done under the misapprehension that, once commenced, a bill would pass quickly into law. Grey was operating in secret both as to what government revealed and what ministers themselves learned about parliamentary feelings. As Michael Brock points out, the Prime Minister was not in heavy attendance at debates, neither was he a great frequenter of Brooks's, the gentleman's club in St James's Street which had flourished since the time of Charles James Fox and the citadel of all Whiggery including the most lukewarm and fearful kind. An operation of the type done in our times by an astute parliamentary private secretary going round asking the right questions would have told Grey that some of the avowed support for Reform was confined to the least offensive and most genteel kind.

Again, he had become Prime Minister in a parliament in which Wellington had been able to form a government, about whose exact strength estimates and counter-estimates had been generated at the time. Wellington had been defeated on a token issue after he had slammed and snecked the door on any measure of reform whatever. But he and Peel had first alienated the Ultras by way of Catholic emancipation for itself and as an abrupt change of front, perceived as duplicitous. Sir Edward Knatchbull might have voted for a twenty-five seat adjustment. That leading Ultra had, after all, been offered a Cabinet post in the Reform government, but neither he nor his friends, nor yet the tepid men of the middle, were prepared for the St Just-like schedules of boroughs pricked for death which had been kept such an exciting secret.

The waiting opposition learned the horrid details on 1 March from Lord John Russell who 'rose at six o'clock and spoke for two hours and a quarter – a sweeping measure indeed much more than anyone had imagined'.[19] Sweeping it might be, and faultable on many details, but the bill was not unconsidered; the Cabinet had made its mind up with much argument over ten weeks. The radicalism lay in the number of places enfranchised, disfranchised and – with the innovation of something quite new, single seat constituencies – half-enfranchised and half-disfranchised. This was no mere hitch of the constitutional jacket, gratifying Birmingham, Manchester and Leeds with the spoils of the prize delinquents among corrupt boroughs. Out of a House of 658 members, Lord John proposed the despatch of 168 seats. But when Russell came to what he might not have called the crunch, the news boiled over: 'seven towns which are to send two Members each: Manchester and Salford; Birmingham and Aston; Leeds; Greenwich, Deptford and Woolwich; Wolverhampton, Bilston and Sedgeley; Sheffield; Sunderland and the Wearmouths';[20] he was already menacing fourteen seats. Piling on excitement and grief, he listed twenty towns to have their first single member. These were mostly northern and industrial, like Huddersfield, Bolton and 'Blackburne', the exceptions being Brighton,

Cheltenham and Frome. Then, since, 'It is well known that a great proportion of the Metropolis and its neighbourhood, amounting in population to 800,000 or 900,000, is not represented', he announced eight new members to sit for the four new London double seats of Tower Hamlets, Holborn, Finsbury and Lambeth with populations ranging from 128,000 in Lambeth to 283,000 in Tower Hamlets.

Russell could not at this point resist a jibe at the most truculent of anti-reformers, Wellington's Attorney-General, Wetherell, who sat for Boroughbridge in the North Riding: 'The two large, populous parishes of Marylebone and St Pancras which, no doubt, are entitled to be represented at least as much as Boroughbridge, are included in one of the districts I have named.'[21] Next he announced the establishment of two extra members for twenty-seven of the larger counties plus a member for the Isle of Wight. Russell also announced electoral machinery, the listing and registering of voters by parish officers, and, with an interesting and prophetic twist in a time of running shows at the hustings, expressed the private hope that 'the time may come when the machinery will be found so simple that every vote may be given in a single day'.[22]

This was all very important and exciting enough, but the House knew by now that, with so many new enfranchisements recounted, it was about to see a far larger bill of mortality than anticipated. It was in at the kill. Calculations had been done, Russell explained, on a population basis of 2,000 inhabitants, and it was proposed to take away the representation in Parliament of towns which had fewer inhabitants than that. Ministers, he insisted, were being purely arithmetical; 'we were not influenced by partiality, prejudice, or a wish to favour some in preference to others.' With the drum roll of his next sentence, 'I will now read the list of the boroughs to be disfranchised on this principle',[23] the temperature rose and Russell was now speaking to a House no less attentive, but bitten personally and making its own fraught contribution.

As *Hansard* doucely puts it, 'The noble Lord accordingly read the following list, in the course of which he was frequently interrupted by shouts of laughter, cries of "Hear, Hear!" from Members for those boroughs and various interlocutions across the Table.'[24] It was very much Gilbert's *Mikado* before the letter. *This* little list was a recital of small, often beautiful places, charter boroughs, towns of note in the reign of Henry VI, places of assured nomination, with a high proportion of names on any good map of the Royal and accommodating Duchy of Cornwall, long impossibly overrepresented: Bossiney, Bedwin, Camelford, Fowey, East Looe and West Looe both, Lostwithiel, Newport (along with Newport Lancashire and Newport Isle of Wight), St Mawes, St Michael's and

Tregony. (Liskeard, which had sustained a silent Edward Gibbon with a colleague, would be docked one member.)

Among the fallen was Higham Ferrars in Northamptonshire. Another was Wendover, which, as well as being represented by Canning, had across ten years given Edmund Burke no cause to worry about an MP's role as delegate or representative of the seat to which he had been presented by the Duke of Grafton. Others were Callington, a Cornish borough for which Horace Walpole had peacefully sat, whilst Castle Rising had accommodated not only Horace, but his father, Sir Robert, the ur-manager of the old system. Appleby had returned the elder Pitt. The deletion of Aldborough in Suffolk (now called Aldeburgh) would unseat the most intelligent if fanatical opponent of reform, John Wilson Croker. And to be savoured was the haven of the bristling Sir Charles Wetherell. Russell had got Boroughbridge on his list. Wetherell's own response had been clear enough when 'as the plan was gradually developed, after sundry contortions and grimaces and flinging about his arms and legs, [he] threw down his notes with a mixture of despair and ridicule and horror'.[25]

One or two names among the depopulated have actually returned, either, like Buckingham, as centres for wide rural catchments or as latter-day suburban or dormitory eruptions like Reigate and Petersfield. But it was in general a slaughter of the elders, including blatantly disreputable elders like Gatton, Old Sarum and Ilchester, all of them clear targets for Lord John's utilitarian arithmetic. To the roll call were added another forty-seven boroughs which should lose one of their two members. Many of these still function, at any rate under the same approximate name, 170 years later: Amersham, Arundel, Chippenham, Grimsby, Guildford (here Guilford), Huntingdon, Leominster, Morpeth, Richmond, St Ives, Sudbury, Westbury and Wycombe.

Russell read out the balance sheet of ministerial actions. From 658 seats in the current House, 168 would go by disfranchisement. The large towns now enfranchised would send thirty-four new members, the expanded county representation would add fifty-five seats, London would have another eight; Scotland, Ireland and Wales would gain respectively five, three and one seat, a total of 106 new members making a grand total of 596. Behind the membership numbers lay an increase in the numbers voting, one which would 'add to the constituency of the Commons House of Parliament, about half a million of persons'. Since this was not, despite some hopes in the street and many fears across the floor, a Jacobin revolution or anything like it, Russell added at once that such additional persons were 'all connected with the prosperity of the country, having a valuable stake amongst us and deeply interested in our institutions'.[26]

At the same time he stated what changes would not take place. There had been calls for triennial parliaments in place of the septennial system. Surely in a system growing less corrupt, the charm of paying the steep price in beer and cash would be diminished and the sovereign people have correspondingly more frequent direct influence over MPs. Russell swelled into orotundity and capitals: 'Sir, I do not think it behoves the people of a great empire to place their Representatives in such dependence.'[27] For it was 'inexpedient to make the durations of parliament so short that the Members of this House are kept in a perpetual canvass and not be able deliberately to consider and to decide with freedom any great question'.[28]

Then there was that other radical proposition – the ballot. Lord John was respectful in precisely the way people are respectful about something they mean to stop. 'Men of rank and title may still desire to have power over the multitude.'[29] But would the ballot really protect them? And he launched, in the way of politicians, on to the responsibility of other people: 'I am bound to say moreover, that above all things, it appears very doubtful that it would be at all advisable to have any class of persons wholly irresponsible in the discharge of a great public duty.' And if the ballot did succeed 'in concealing the voter, he is and must be irresponsible in the discharge of a vast power'.[30]

Reflecting more anxieties than his own, Russell grew Burkean: 'Men who follow courts advise an arbitrary king; persons enamoured of the distinctions of rank are willing slaves to an arbitrary aristocracy; men of a more generous and enthusiastic nature exalt an arbitrary multitude.' It was a splendid trope and unfortunate not to have made its way into ready quotation. John Russell would not have been John Russell, intellectual and cerebrator of politics, without wrapping the main proposals in an elaborate historical/philosophical cloak. And he was no doubt happy to get away from the ponderous conservatism which justified keeping the ballot and shorter parliaments at comforting arm's length. (They would become electoral practice respectively with the Ballot Act of 1872, within Russell's long lifetime, and the quinquennial provisions of the 1910 Parliament Act, shortly after the right-wing press of the day had accused the then Liberal government of Asquith, also engaged on curbing a Lords' veto, of plotting to abolish elections altogether.)

He launched instead on the doctrines of the anti-reformers. Some of these were designer straw men, but they reflected the intense historical impulse of debate in those days. 'Our opponents say our ancestors gave Old Sarum Representatives, therefore we should give Old Sarum Representatives – We say our ancestors gave Old Sarum Representatives because it *was* a large town; therefore we give Representative to Manchester which *is* a large town.'[31] This was a dubiously historical assertion shortly to be challenged in debate.

Russell next busied himself with the charge that the Whigs were undermining the aristocracy and made his case on the principles of Jane Austen – Mr Darcy contrasted with Sir Walter Elliot.

> Where the aristocracy reside, receiving large incomes, performing important duties, relieving the poor by charity and evincing private worth and public virtue, it is not in human nature that they should not possess a great influence upon public opinion . . . But if by aristocracy, those persons are meant who do not live among the people, who know nothing of the people, who care nothing for them – who seek honours without merit, places without duty, and pensions without service – for such an aristocracy I have no sympathy and I think the sooner it is carried away with the corruption on which it has thriven, the better for the country in which it has repressed so long every wholesome and invigorating influence.[32]

John Russell was speaking in earnest here. He was an aristocrat from a family which had risen out of wine shipping in the fourteenth century, drained the Fens, been admirals and gone to the scaffold in opposition to Stuart absolutism. They, like Lord John, had been serious men, and puritanical contempt for the parasitical nobility of display came spitting from the heart.

No one represented opposition to the Reform Bill more faithfully than Sir Robert Inglis. Sir Robert, who had defeated Peel at an Oxford seeking revenge for Catholic emancipation, has not left the impact of Knatchbull or Vyvyan and was a lesser advocate than Croker. But he was an intelligent man versed in historical argument, and historical argument weighed with all sides in 1831. Russell had used it that day and Brougham had famously proclaimed that he sought not a revolution but a restoration. This was a Whig variant of the view held strenuously by William Cobbett whose radicalism was woven into a notion of a lost and better England which stockjobbers had corrupted. For the Whigs it was the encroaching Crown and neglect of economic and demographic change which had led away from the golden balance of interests. This was an argument which men like Inglis and Croker could demolish.

Russell's simple but central point that Old Sarum had been given representation when it was a large town – so we were not breaking precedent in giving such representation to Manchester, which was now a large town – was an open goal to Inglis. Old Sarum had *never* been a large town. Its first precept, he pointed out, came in the time of Edward I (1295) in company with New Sarum or Salisbury, already going up as Old Sarum came down. For 'whatever Old Sarum is now, there is great reason to think that such or nearly such was Old Sarum in the first day of its parliamentary privilege'.[33] As long ago as 1688 it had been up for purchase to Governor Pitt, the diamond-owning first of the tribe. He quoted a contemporary view of the transaction: 'His posterity now have an hereditary right to sit in the House of Commons as owners of it . . .'[34]

The arguments could be multiplied. What of the constituencies dismissed by Russell as former large towns now decayed? 'Heytesbury has no market; Haslemere, Newport (*Cornwall*), St Michael's, St Mawes, West Looe have never been parishes. At no time therefore could their importance have required Representation, if Representation were ever dependent upon population . . .'[35] As historians, the anti-reformers, reverencing history, were the better men, and the reformers had advanced on to ground which would not hold them. As Inglis added in the next clause of his sentence, 'and as their insignificance did not in the first instance exclude them from the rank of parliamentary boroughs, their insignificance *now* cannot – to those who profess not to be innovating, but to be restoring the constitution to its former state – be any argument for its destruction'.[36] The point could, of course, be made back to front. The supposed poor pelting hamlets, which, through wool and cotton, had become large towns now worthy of sending MPs to Parliament, had not been hamlets for a long time. Quoting Camden or Leland, Inglis could show Halifax housing 8,500 people in 1548, rising to 12,000 in Camden's time forty years later; whilst Manchester could be computed from its registry statistics as having upwards of 6,000 inhabitants in 1580 and 'Sheffield, Leeds and Bradford were considerable places'.

Of course, for Inglis and the other Ultras, for opponents of reform generally, representation had never been and was not now dependent upon population. *Their* medieval kings, unlike the pageant kings of Cobbett's historic projections, were practitioners of power who picked sites for the exercise of patronage at first or second hand, and they had taken care to have 'well affected' members reliably returned. For a romantic Tory, Sir Robert could talk perfect *realpolitik*. Take Cornwall: the Whigs would have it that 'The immense disproportion of Cornish members to those of the rest of England was owing to the tin trade of their county, its then great importance compared with the commerce of the rest of England, and the necessity of watching its interests.'[37] Not at all! A number of places remote from tin workings or commercial harbours, negligible fishing villages in fact, were given parliamentary representation precisely because they were negligible and would accommodate the King's creatures. 'The fact is,' said Inglis in best Machiavellian style, 'that as the House of Commons rose into importance, the Crown felt it necessary to have its own prerogative guarded here.'[38]

He would also make the strong point that talk of restoring the authority of parliaments was nonsense. When had they been stronger? Henry IV had directed his sheriffs that no lawyers should be returned to Parliament. Queen Elizabeth had instructed the Speaker that the Commons should be 'restrained from even treating on some points: "If any Bill relating to matters of state or reformation in causes ecclesiastical be exhibited."' The Commons, calling itself 'Your poor Commons', had spoken of approaching James I 'on the knees of their heart'. Did members really think the Crown now had more power of interference than when James II was packing parliaments?[39]

On the historical roots of Parliament, Inglis and his friends had an unanswerable case for as long as romantic historicism and a desire to sooth fears of revolution left the Reform Whigs talking unhistoric nonsense to fit their own concept of representative institutions as a lost inheritance. That argument had been reached by back-formation, an imposition upon the sixteenth century of the youthful semi-democratic feelings of the disciples of Fox and admirers of the Girondins in 1790.

But if that wouldn't wash, neither would the central conviction in the intellectual baggage of the Ultras. Inglis proclaimed the non-popular nature of representation. He had begun in the classic apocalyptic terms of Conservatives thinking dark thoughts about change: 'I approach the discussion of this question with a sensation of awe at the contemplation of the abyss, on the brink of which we stand, and into which the noble lord will, if successful, hurl us.'[40] And he feared, as Conservatives had since the French Revolution, sharing the shrill anxieties of Edmund Burke.

Russell had talked 'not only of the myriads of petitions, but of the millions of those who now come forward "to demand their rights" . . . .'. He recalled the words of Horne Tooke, a radical of the late eighteenth century, who had said 'the people have hands'.[41] Inglis thought that Russell's language, if it was not unparliamentary, 'approaches as nearly to a threat as the forms of the House can allow; and if suffered will entirely annihilate our deliberative character and will reduce us to the mere function of speaking the will of others from day to day'. And he firmly reasserted Burke's doctrines. Members were not present 'about Newton in Lancashire or Newton in Hampshire, Newport in Cornwall or Newport in the Isle of Wight', but were to deliberate about 'certain arduous and urgent affairs concerning us, the state and defence of our Kingdom and the Church'.[42]

78

Together with his sound history concerning the boroughs electing members in the past, Inglis was arguing the fundamental unimportance of populations and their 'demands', a word which had horrified him. It was enough that we had an unwritten constitution, not like those foreigners. 'We have no formal document to which we refer as embodying it, Montesquieu and Delolme are not our authorities; not even Blackstone. Our Constitution is not the work of a code maker; it is the growth of time and events beyond the design and calculation of man; it is not a building, but a tree.'[43] In a moment of exaltation, Inglis scorned the abstractions of meddling radicals: 'men create theories and adore them; they make beautiful statues and fall in love with them; they raise a golden image and call on us to worship it.'[44] But he had his own golden image, one of a Parliament which deliberated in hermetic seclusion from events and men, let alone the demands of men. The notion of changing the make-up of Parliament to take account of new needs, and of men who *did* make demands, was simple sacrilege.

Ministers had 'thought fit to pledge themselves and endeavour to pledge their sovereign before his people, to the doctrine "that the House of Commons is unworthy of the confidence of the people", were unworthy to stand between their fellow subjects and the throne'. There had been threats in the past, and he listed the crises of the previous century. But they had all been seen off with a firm hand. Inglis was shrewd about Elizabeth's parliaments, but presented with Peterloo, that peaceful meeting of unarmed citizens broken up with eleven fatalities by a cavalry charge of yeomanry, he saw only the state in danger wisely defended. 'Again in 1819 the Manchester meeting was preceded, attended, followed by almost insurrectionary movements throughout the manufacturing districts . . . Yet the danger was met, averted and beaten down.' Men had cried for Reform through all these disturbances, but firmness had sufficed. This was not 'the first time that when the people have been represented as clamorous for Reform; they also prove that these clamours have been silenced without concession: and I can see no reason why they might not now, whatever be their present violence, be silenced with equal success by equal spirit.'[45]

Resonant speaking and easily done if one believed that the trouble was all a matter of 'faction', on which he naturally quoted Burke and blamed the recent examples of Paris and Belgium. Sir Robert was nothing if not consistent. 'If I were to admit the fact that the great mass of the people were now eager for Reform, I should deny the conclusion. This House would not be bound by the cries of a majority of the people to decide in favour of any change.'[46] This echoed the dictum, thirty years earlier, of Samuel Horsley, Bishop of St Asaph: 'In this country my Lords, the individual subject . . . has nothing to do with the laws but to obey them.' It was the ultimate position, the stone wall of the Ultras, a willingness to see Parliament in entrenched opposition to the people, otherwise the multitude, and kept there if necessary by soldiers. It was very far from being the centre, but it could not hold.

Another Tory contribution came soon after from Horace Twiss, King's Counsel, Member for Newport, son-in-law and future biographer of the twenty-six-year-Lord Chancellor, Eldon. Twiss made the usual expressions of shock at the extent of Russell's list of deletions, a sincere enough sentiment among anti-reformers who had expected much less. They were witnessing 'Ministers of the Crown proposing to remove all the proportions of the legislature, all the landmarks of the Constitution – calling on the House to sweep away, he would not say the charters of Corporations, but all the charters of the realm itself.'[47] Twiss went on to invoke the over reachings of Charles II and James II, and to bring in Judge Jeffreys. He was an advocate of what he called a mixed constitution, in which 'regal and aristocratic' powers had their full due. They were needed as 'security against the blind passions of the people who might otherwise pull down the Constitution which was the ark of the general safety'.

The pocket borough system was to be defended not only on the customary grounds that the owners frequently put up men of talent and few means, but that if their influence was diminished by reform they would still have some power and would feel 'obliged to nominate someone of their family or someone residing in the neighbourhood and distinguished for his wealth',[48] a reason, one would think, for removing all possibility of nominating MPs. This intriguing concern that money and wealth might intensify its authority was offset by the ministerial proposal to determine the franchise by a £10 rating. It would lower the tone of Parliament dreadfully. They would be enfolding into the electorate men of

> limited information, of strong prejudices, of narrow and contracted views, such as shopkeepers and small attorneys. He begged not to be misunderstood, he was not disparaging this class, but he did conceive that retired tradesmen inhabiting houses rated at £10, members of small clubs, and persons of that description; persons he repeated, of narrow minds and bigoted views, who were now to be called in to counsel the nation, were not the best fitted to execute that important trust.[49]

When this provoked laughter on the government benches, Twiss quoted the Bible 'on potters and men practising various trades "who trust in their hands and every one is wise in his work", but "they shall not be sought for in the public counsel nor sit high in the congregation"'. This class, said Twiss, was 'shallow and dogmatical, the supporters of those political principles which made light of public faith and thought nothing of public credit, who regarded reduction of taxation as every thing and looked at rents and tithes and taxes as mischievous burdens laid on them'.[50]

Taxation at that time was not, of course, the welfare and public service-led taxation of the last seventy or so years, but the kind against which Cobbett had blazed and which Sydney Smith had derided. Much of it was purchase tax, of random, not to say whimsical, origin, falling at a flat and equity-defying rate upon household goods much as the Corn Laws made bread dearer, the whole effect being one of regression. Smith had famously given an account of 'the dying Englishman pouring his medicine which has paid seven per cent into a spoon that has paid fifteen per cent [then] flings himself back upon his chintz bed which has paid twenty-two per cent and expires in the arms of an apothecary who has paid a license of a hundred pound for the privilege of putting him to death' before expiring and seeking repose in that haven 'where he will be *taxed no more*'. Twiss was objecting to the shallow and dogmatical resentment of modest men at taxes whose benefits to themselves were obscure.

He was followed by Althorp, about whom Greville had been so cutting, especially as a speaker. He was Leader of the House and with Russell generally charged with the Bill's passage. He was something of a reluctant politician, a kind which did not disappear with Reform, but which has perceptibly dwindled in modern politics. There was about Althorp a bland and pallid quality in debate (accompanying a stubborn determination to win the contest). But diffidence did not bar him from the riposte succinct. Twiss had said that the demand for reform was temporary. Were there no grounds for the people's complaints then? And 'if there were a good ground, they could not be temporary, having a permanent cause'. And, straightforwardly, he proclaimed the Bill, in terms, to be 'the admission to the franchise of the middle classes. The people of England demanded a Government of Lords and Commons [*hear hear from the Opposition*].* Yes, but a Commons not coming into the House by purchase or nomination.'[51]

However, the Whig purple, like the cloven hoof, had a way of showing. The heir of the Spencers thought that Twiss, in ridiculing the middle classes, had lived a protected existence and accordingly 'did not know the amount of intelligence which was to be found in the middle classes when

---

* The expression 'hear hear', as recorded in *Hansard*, seems at this time often to have connoted an ironical counter-cheer.

he talked to them as he had done'.[52] In 1831 the word 'condescension' did not have its current implication of slumming. And Althorp, a great nobleman, soon to be Earl Spencer, was far better placed for such social adventures than Twiss, a connection by marriage with a first-creation former law officer. Althorp also represented a distinct strand among aristocratic Whigs when he came to the issue of finality. The question of yet further Reform Acts bobbed about along with arguments about Jacobinism and sinister threats to the Crown, Lords and Church.

John Russell's denials had won him the nickname 'Finality Jack', but Althorp was equally settled on the topic. 'He thought it would be a final settlement; and that as the plan was found a full and effectual reformation of abuses, those who differed on minor points would now sacrifice them for the sake of unanimity and for the advancement of the public good.'[53] But Althorp's jog-along complacency was allied with an attitude always popular in England, one of practicality and moderation. 'He was one of those who had never much looked to theories. He wished to see a practical Reform of the abuses of the system of Representation in Government.'

And though Althorp used a radical sounding form of words – 'until that House was placed under the power of the people, they never could hope to see an end of many practical evils' – he left nothing said undefined. Drawing Peel into the mocking applause of the rhetorical question – did this mean 'a promise to the people of England of overpowering influence in the choice of Representatives?' – he came up with his own sound answer. 'The right hon. baronet cheered that sentiment; but he would remind the right hon. Gentleman that by the people he meant the great majority of the respectable middle classes of this country.'[54] In a House where the Tories felt themselves still in a majority, Althorp, with however little dazzle, was following the course for winning the vote.

If the second day of debate, 2 March, contained some notable speeches, that of Lord Stormont was not among them. Stormont was a figure embodying every backbench politician who has ever grasped his lapels and said that the country was going to the dogs. He could, however – a virtue of the age – quote Shakespeare, in this case *Coriolanus*. He had been put in mind of a passage while listening to Russell's speech. Russell's reference to the people's demands, which had shocked Inglis, moved Stormont to think that 'the prescient mind of that bard had dived into the obscurity of future time and perceived that the time must come – alas! a most dreadful day for England, in which the ministers would propose that dreadful measure which had been brought forward last night:

. . . Let deeds express
What's like to be their words: 'We did request it,
We are the greater poll, and in true fear
They gave us our demands.' Thus we debase
The nature of our seats, and make the rabble
Call our cares fears, which will in time
Break ope the locks o'th' senate, and bring in
The crows to peck the eagles.[55]

Not many people thought of Lord Stormont as an eagle. He was, of course, an interested party. He sat for one of the two Aldboroughs,* the Yorkshire one, about, as they say, to be let go. And he not unreasonably demanded to know, 'What about Knaresborough? Or Calne?' Knaresborough had been Brougham's seat before the rapid succession of events electing him for the County of Yorkshire then translating him to the Woolsack. Calne was the seat of an opinionated, hyperliterate young man soon to speak, name of Thomas Babbington Macaulay.† Both seats had survived Russell's axe. Neither was a centre of heavy population.

But on the central object of Reform, Stormont had no problems. Population didn't come into it. Though he had interests in England, he had greater interests in Scotland and he knew that the people of Scotland preferred peace to revolution and, under Scottish institutions, Parliament 'had never been intended as a popular representation, but a Representation of the land and the owners of the land'.[56] Stormont's growling manner is almost audible on the printed page and rises to a bark as he concludes that 'if he understood [Russell's] plan rightly, Reform would be revolution, possession would be spoliation, and, sooner or later, religion would become atheism'.

It was against such inflated notions of democratic doom that the clever new member for the embarrassingly small borough of Calne spoke soon after. The speech is, or was, a much-quoted classic, long in triple stress rhetoric of the kind which Professor Higgins noted in Alfred Doolittle, and it rises to a finale in which rhetoric and serious conviction touch hands. But Macaulay began this maiden speech (at a time when the tedious ban on contention had not established itself) with a ponderous cliché – 'It is a circumstance Sir, of happy augury for the measure before the House'[57] – and he followed it with a defence of himself and ministers from any charge of dangerous radicalism. Coming suddenly and crisply to the point,

* The other, in Suffolk, returned Croker.
† Printed by *Hansard* as 'Macauley'.

he found ministers' principle 'plain, rational and consistent. It is this – to admit the middle classes to a large and direct share in the Representation without any violent shock to the institutions of our country [*hear!*].'[58]

As long as they stayed poor, there was to be no nonsense about letting in the working class, or, as Macaulay called them, 'the lower orders'. He would contemplate such a thing only if the 'labourers of England were in that state in which I, from my soul, wish to see them – if employment were always plentiful, wages always high, food always cheap . . . Universal suffrage exists in the United States without producing any very frightful consequences.'[59] But in a country like this, money had to decide things. Frequently the lower orders suffered distress:

> We know what effect distress produces even on people more intelligent than the great body of the labouring classes can possibly be . . . It is therefore no reflection on the lower orders of Englishmen who are not and cannot in the order of things, be highly educated, to say that distress produces on them its natural effects . . . it blunts their judgement, inflames their passions, that it makes them prone to believe those who flatter them and distrust those who would serve them.[60]

We have to remember that the author of *Jude the Obscure* would not be born for another nine years, universal education of a nourishing and grudging sort not introduced for another forty. But with all allowances made, something about the grand manner of Macaulay sticks in the throat.

However, having established his non-incendiary credentials, he would now turn on the Tories and the argument, upon which, since Inglis, they had been straphanging. What was all this about the wickedness of Russell speaking of demands made on Parliament by the people? It was supposed to constitute a threat? Well, now, in 1817 Castlereagh had come to the House (he had actually been speaking for the Home Secretary, Sidmouth, in the Lords) and had proposed suspending Habeas Corpus. Furthermore, 'he told the House that unless the measures which he recommended were adopted, peace could not be preserved. Was he accused of threatening the House? Will any gentleman say that it is parliamentary and decorous to urge the danger arising from popular discontent as an argument for severity, but that it is unparliamentary and undecorous to urge that same danger as an argument for conciliatory measures?'[61]

And with this Macaulay came to the core of the whole argument. It was agreed that the nation should be governed by property and intelligence. 'Yet saying this, we exclude from all say in the government vast masses of property and intelligence – vast numbers of those who are interested in preserving tranquility . . . We do more. We drive over to the side of revolution those whom we shut out from power.'[62]

Macaulay was a Victorian in waiting. And the self-confidence, the sense of being at once right and all right associated with the Queen Empress's time, found expression in an account of the resources of central London as shown to an enquiring foreigner.

> I would conduct him through that great city which lies to the north of Great Russell-street [sic] and Oxford-street – a city superior in size and in population to the capitals of many mighty kingdoms; and probably superior in opulence, intelligence and general respectability, to any city in the world. I would conduct him through that interminable succession of streets and squares, all consisting of well-built and well-furnished houses. I would make him observe the brilliancy of the shops and the crowd of well-appointed equipages. I would lead him round that magnificent circle of palaces which surrounds the Regent's-park [sic]. I would tell him that the rental of this district was far greater than that of the whole kingdom of Scotland at the time of the Union. And then I would tell him that this was an unrepresented district![63]

There is an American quality to Macaulay's collective conceit, but it was a sure footing for seeing off Tory squires and the priests guarding the English social pyramid. It was no good Stormont or Inglis praying the rights of property in aid. Macaulay and the commercial middle class could trump them with their denial of property. The system they wanted to keep was *not* government by property: 'It is government by certain detached portions and fragments of property, selected from the rest and preferred to the rest, on no rational principle whatever.'[64] Had Sir Robert Inglis asked when the constitution had ever been better than it now was? 'Sir we are legislators, not antiquaries.' Did Stormont invoke his pocket borough of Aldborough in Yorkshire as no smaller now than when it was enfranchised? Growth and enrichment had been going on all around it. Aldborough might have been a place of relative consequence when we had a population of two million. We now had fourteen million and Aldborough stood where it did after a period in which 'villages swelled into cities larger than the London of the Plantagents'.[65] (The parable of the talents hovered over this part of the argument.) The old forms remained 'and then came that pressure almost to bursting, new wine in old bottles – the new people under the old institutions'.[66] The revolt was a natural one, certain of success.

In some lights Macaulay looks historicist and determinist, asserting the assured victory of identified groups, not indeed becoming a proto-Marxist, but standing upon the step to which Marx would stride. There were struggles which must end in successful rebellion like the one 'which the Catholics maintained against the aristocracy of creed. Such is the struggle which the free people of colour in Jamaica are now maintaining against the aristocracy of skin.'[67] Nearest his own heart was the struggle to be fought by the English middle classes 'against an aristocracy of mere locality – against an aristocracy, the principle of which is to invest 100 drunken potwallopers in one place or the owner of a ruined hovel in another with powers which are withheld from cities renowned to the furthest ends of the earth for the marvels of their wealth and of their industry'.[68]

But having done his bit for the masterful and not-to-be denied middle classes, Macaulay reverted to the poor, the people in the streets and the fields, and with them to the institutions – to Parliament itself and the distrust in which the current parliamentary system was held by the people, that generality of outsiders. The hostility was a fact and one of growing and clamorous importance. He built up his argument with a series of questions on past attempts at repression (a repression in which his Honourable friend, the Home Secretary, was at that time comfortably engaged). Not letting this trouble him, Macaulay worked himself up to a final dramatic question which, eighty years later, would be used as the title of a very famous pamphlet: 'Does there remain any species of coercion which was not tried by Mr Pitt and Lord Londonderry?* We have had laws, we have had blood. New treasons have been created. The Press has been shackled. The Habeas Corpus Act has been suspended. Public meetings have been prohibited. The event has proved that these were mere palliatives. You are at the end of your palliatives. The evil remains. It is more formidable than ever. What is to be done?'[69]

The grand rhetorical question, later asked again by Lenin, had a plain and modest answer. What should be done was that they should pass 'the great measure of conciliation prepared by Ministers of the Crown'. It might not be perfect, 'but it is founded on great and sound principles. It takes away a great power from a few. It distributes that power through the great mass of the middle order. Every man therefore who thinks as I think is bound to stand firmly by Ministers who are resolved to stand or fall with this measure.'[70]

One quality present throughout almost all anti-Reform speeches had been hysteria, the tight little whisper that revolution was coming and that we should all be murdered in our beds, something inherited from the old-woman aspect of Burke which co-existed with his elegancies and distinction of mind.

---

* The title inherited for the last few months of his life by Lord Castlereagh, known to history by that honorific.

Macaulay, knowing his middle classes, looked forward with great perception to the new, and, for those in it, comfortable order of society, the adjusted pyramid in which monarchy and all its show would sit comfortably atop a structure whose dominant middle would run from shopkeeper to financier. Inglis had told them that if Reform passed '"England will soon be a republic". The reformed House of Commons will according to him, before it has sat ten years, depose the King, and expel the Lords from their House.'[71]

If that were true, said Macaulay, then the case for 'democracy' – by which he meant something rougher and more prickly than the soiled cliché of today – would be even stronger; for monarchy and aristocracy would have lost their appeal to the middle classes. In which case – and there is here a flash of bourgeois steel from the Member for Calne, he would regretfully have to conclude 'that monarchical and aristocratical institutions are unsuited to this country'.[72] But that wouldn't be necessary. Monarchy and aristocracy, he said patronisingly but with cool truth, were still useful – 'valuable and useful as means, not as ends'.[73] It had to be understood that there could not now be a form of government in which the middle classes had no confidence. But once concede, and court and nobility would find that 'the middle classes sincerely wish to uphold the Royal prerogatives and the constitutional rights of the Peers'.[74] It was almost a threat, as casual a statement of certain development as his insistence upon a class of destiny. But if the elect of the earth showed some sense, they need not fear French revolutionary conclusions.

Macaulay approached conclusion by combining his determinist case with a useful party political dig based on the conduct of Robert Peel. Peel had been roundly abused by Ultras unwilling quite to sink blades into the Duke of Wellington for his pragmatic and sensible conduct three years earlier over Catholic emancipation. The smarter Whigs knew this and were lavish with compliments not intended to help. For Peel, in his emphatic, unincremental way, before legislating for Catholic Relief had committed himself up to the collarbone in denial of ever conceding anything to Catholic Relief. Professing the 'high respect which I feel for his talent and character', Macaulay proceeded to a loving recital of the whole St Peter-like sequence of denials – and tied it in with Reform, also denied. Peel had resigned from the Cabinet on Canning's taking the premiership 'and he declared that if the Ministers should either attempt to repeal the Test and Corporation Acts* or bring forward a measure of Parliamentary Reform, he should think it his duty to oppose them to the utmost.'[75]

---

* Seventeenth-century legislation upon which the exclusion of Dissenters from all office rested.

Four years, three of them under government by Wellington and Peel, had passed since then and what had happened? 'What is become of the Test and Corporation Acts? They are repealed. By whom? By the late administration. What has become of the Catholic disabilities? They are removed. By whom? By the late administration. The question of parliamentary reform is still behind.'[76] Well now: were we to go again through the whole pantomime of pressure, defiance, new pressure and new assent? Would we have to wait till the Tories 'have been brought into office by a cry of "No Reform!" to be reformers, as they were once before brought into office by a cry of "No Popery!" to be emancipators?'.

They talked about the threat of revolution. Did they mean by stubborn denial to risk everything until, in a self-induced crisis, they humiliatingly gave in? 'Do they wait for that last, most violent paroxysm of popular rage – for that last and most cruel test of military fidelity?'[77] Reform was too big a thing and too nearly incapable of being stopped for such antics. They knew what had happened in France and to Charles X – 'the roof of a British palace affords an ignominious shelter to the heir of forty kings'.[78] The message, said Macaulay, is 'Reform that you may preserve!'[79] Sydney Smith was to make a similar appeal to the enlightened self-interest of the Tories and the great possessors: 'Do it,' said Sydney, 'for your ease, do it for your rent roll.'

But neither of the next two significant contributors to debate had much taste for ease. Henry Hunt had preached radical reform across England, had gone to prison for it and looked coolly upon the Whigs and their middle class. Sir Charles Wetherell had been called 'the Achilles of anti-Reform' and would speak like a man looking for a last ditch to die in. History has patronised Henry Hunt, hot tempered, impolitic, talking too much, a man of words and platforms, but he spoke up for people who were dismissed with fear or contempt and did so under the noses of those doing the dismissing. He had also made an attempt a month before to protect machine breakers from the severities of Lord Melbourne with a motion 'recommending them to the mercy of the Crown', which, he said, 'gave rise to some lengthened talk of no moment. On a division, Hunt had 2 tellers and 2 voters.'[80] History should have more discernment.*

Hunt was sorry to have heard Macaulay 'assert in his eloquent speech,

* He was an object of horror to the gently bred. Mrs Arbuthnot records that 'It is a great scandal, but Hunt and Cobbett have opened a meeting house they call the rotunda near Blackfriars Bridge and there they assemble and harangue crowds of the lower orders in the most seditious manner, and from that place they issue in large bodies & come & alarm the peaceable people in the West End of the town. I can't understand why it is allowed.'[81]

that we ought to give Representatives to the middle classes to prevent the lower classes from having Representatives'.[82] He had always argued for equality of political rights and had always 'contended that every man who paid taxes to the State was entitled to a vote in the choice of his representation and that taxation and Representation should go hand in hand'.[83] Macaulay talked about 'the rabble'. Did he then mean, in denying them the right to vote, to 'exempt them from the paying of taxes, from serving in the Militia or from being called upon to fight the battles of their country'?[84]

On the operation of the old electoral system, Hunt discussed the political economy of elections in the Cornish mock boroughs and in Ludgershall and Ilchester. There was what *Hansard* calls *great laughter* at this, but Hunt had a reason for exposing his own misfortunes in that place. He had for his pains served two and a half years in Ilchester jail after conviction for sedition. 'That laugh I understand again but I repeat, I know the voters of Ilchester and they frequently ran up a score from £30 to £35 between one election and another depending solely on the candidates to pay the bills. Many of them, indeed almost the whole of them could neither read nor write, and yet it was to them and not to those really possessed of property that the noble Lord continued the vote.'

He is talking about the potwallopers, the minimal householders in certain, usually corrupt small boroughs, whose vote rested upon ownership of a hearth to contain a cooking pot. The noble Lord here was Russell, whose plans did not at this stage involve their disfranchisement. And one of these boroughs where the creditworthy potwallopers could be relied on by the borough owner lay rather close to home. Hunt was, he avowed, the spokesmen for 'the rabble' and a regular speaker at meetings where they might be found – 'Aye, public meetings composed of men a great deal more intelligent and better educated than the inhabitants of that most degraded and rottenest of all rotten boroughs, the borough of Calne.' How Russell, in his list making, 'could have passed over that rottenest, stinkingest, skulkingest of boroughs' he could not understand.*[85]

The supporters of the Bill, Hunt remarked, had said 'that if the measure before them was not carried, its rejection would lead to revolution and massacre. What sort of massacre?'[86] Henry Hunt knew about massacres. The compelling moment in his life had come when he was to have spoken in St Peter's Fields, Manchester, in 1819. And when he recalled it on 3

---

* Calne did not meet the guidelines of a 5,000 population irrespective of qualified voters, set by the Cabinet committee. According to Morpeth, a government supporter, speaking later in its defence, Calne had 4,549 inhabitants.

March twelve years later, a furious attempt at shouting down surrounded him in the Commons, one which *Hansard*'s then practice of using reported speech and making a fuller marginal description brings to savage life. When he had attended that meeting in Manchester, one

> as peaceable and orderly as that now assembled in the House of Commons for as peaceable and constitutional an object – the attainment of constitutional reform; when that meeting took place, there was a real massacre. A drunken and infuriated yeomanry [*loud cries 'No,' 'No!' and 'Question!'*] a drunken and infuriated yeomanry with swords newly sharpened [*reiterated cries of 'No!' and 'Question!'*] – with swords newly sharpened, slaughtered fourteen and maimed and wounded 648 [*shouts of 'No' and 'Question'!*]. Where was the man who will step forward and say 'No'. I say again (said the hon. Member in a tone of voice louder and louder still which was almost drowned by still more violent cries of 'No' and 'Order') that on that day, a drunken and infuriated yeomanry murdered fourteen and cut and maimed 648 as peaceable and well-disposed persons as any he saw around him.[87]

Hunt expressed bitter surprise that Lord John should have argued that the House of Commons had not taken up Reform earlier because there had been no demand for it by the people. What had they been doing in 1816, 1817, 1818 and 1819, if not demanding reform 'with this difference, that then the petitions were of the people were much more respectfully worded than now'. Hunt supported the Bill as far as it went; he would have supported, he said, a bill to disfranchise a single one of the rotten boroughs. Nor did he want what Macaulay called 'the rabble' to have votes. What he wanted (though the words were not used) was the enfranchisement of the working class. Hunt, though a prosperous and efficient farmer with every claim to the password of the age, 'gentleman', had spent long enough among the workmen, the skilled craftsmen and steady men of country and town, to identify with them. Why shouldn't such people have the vote – and cast it by ballot?

The Cabinet committee had resolved upon a £10 rating as the qualification. For Hunt 'the best vote was that which came from the industrious artificer or manufacturer who earned from 30s to £3 a week'. How, anyway, did the government expect the mass of people to support a bill granting a right from which they should be excluded? As for the ballot, he spoke from experience. He was now MP for Preston, but when he had stood there unsuccessfully shortly after the Peterloo massacre, '400 families were afterwards in the year 1820 expelled from their homes in consequence of voting for him'.[88] One customary argument for the open declaration at the hustings was that it was the 'manly' thing to do. But manliness did not extend to tolerating such evidence. Hunt's account was greeted, says the record, by '*Loud cries of "Question"*'. But never much troubled at the giving of offence, Hunt went on to answer the alternative squirming claim, that the ballot would lead to hypocrisy, observing that 'at the Clubs of the highest classes in England, the Ballot was constantly resorted to as a means of avoiding the odium of a vote; but if any man was to say in these clubs that the Ballot made its members hypocrites, he would have his heart made a very cullender [sic] with bullets'. He concluded as abrasively as he had generally spoken, by expressing his desire to hear Wetherell and Peel. For 'he had not as yet heard a singular argument or observation on the subject of Reform with which he had not been familiar for the last twenty years'.[89] He did hope that those who were going to oppose it would at least come up with a reason for doing so.

The Achilles of anti-Reform, if not adducing new reasons, was at least different. Furious, noisy, lawyer-learned with a large splash of bully and buffoon, Wetherell was given to a laboriously jocose public style. The Speaker, Charles Manners-Sutton, had remarked of a wild speech on Catholic emancipation three years earlier that, 'The only lucid interval he had was the one between his waistcoat and his breeches.' Greville drily recorded his triumph then in the eyes of Tories and their press, who 'lavish the most extravagant encomiums . . . and call it "the finest oration delivered in the Commons", the best since the Second Philippic. He was drunk they say.'[90]

Having joined Hunt on the issue of Calne – why should it be spared among the carnage of so many other small boroughs? – Wetherell proceeded to quote not Burke but Locke, who 'had said that the best way of describing a thing was to call it by its proper name'. So 'the Bill by which the noble paymaster [Russell] proposed to cashier sixty boroughs thereby occasioning the loss of 120 Members and forty-seven boroughs as to half of their members' was 'Corporation robbery'.[91] It all went back to Cromwell. 'Althorp and Co' took their precedent from 'Cromwell, Fairfax, Fleetwood and Co'. He was alluding to Cromwell's successive sweatings of Parliament to the Rump, a core of his own supporters.

Wetherell took a view of corporation rights as a form of property in which, ironically, he joined Hunt, who had reckoned that a vote in Ilchester rated £30–35 per parliament, say £1,500 in present money values. The Bill was, for Wetherell, quite literally a robbery, 'an extinction of 168 Members whose constituents were to be for ever, as long as the world should last, robbed and deprived of the franchise and privilege of returning 168 Members of Parliament'.[92] He wondered at the atrocity of it, and, since there was in operation a Special Commission for frame breaking, 'he had been turning over in his mind whether there might not be a Special Commission to try the present Cabinet for corporation-breaking'.[93] As for historical authority, 'the journals of the House did not contain a single precedent for this monstrous act of spoliation – this civil sacrilege'.[94]

However in the dust-flecked way of nineteenth-century lawyers, Wetherell could cite the depriving of Cambridge's corporation status – in the time of Richard II for what sounds like football hooliganism! But that loss of status and income had been rescinded. Wetherell began slowly to inflate his rhetoric, blowing its cheeks and enlarging himself as he asked what precedent there was 'for so gross an act of injustice as, by one compendious and confiscating measure of the noble military Paymaster to deprive so many towns and individuals without a single crime being alleged against them – without warning, without any species of trial whatever – of their most sacred rights as English freemen'.[95]

The one precedent for such atrocity occurring to Wetherell was the treatment by Henry VIII of the monasteries. He compared abbots hanged under attainder by Henry with the demoted mayors and corporations, an odd observation for a man who had fought Catholic emancipation as a threat to the nation, as a supporter of the monarchy and the rights of the Church of England. For Wetherell was worried about the Church. Where would it all end? The Church of England was a chartered body; the Bank of England, the East India Company, all held their rights and property under a charter 'which like that of the about-to-be-confiscated boroughs might hereafter be violated if the dangerous precedent were once admitted. They all knew too well that the men who coolly set at naught or destroyed the archives of town halls would not much hesitate to cross the portals of a church door or break into the cathedral.'[96]

For behind Russell lay the radicals with their further demands which ministers rejected, refusing to 'satisfy the reforming public out of doors, for their cry was "Give us more Representatives, we have not enough"'.[97] It was suggested that if the Bill were not passed there would be another election.

He must say in response to this most unconstitutional and insolent menace, that the man who would be influenced by it in his vote on the present momentous occasion would be nothing less than a recreant to his country. The man whom such a threat – particularly by a government so vacillating and individually contending and only united in this one monstrous measure of spoliation – would influence, was a man unworthy of the name of British Senator – was a recreant in morals – and a man wholly deaf to the call of conscience and of English liberty.

In conclusion the Member for about-to-be-confiscated Boroughbridge returned to the Roundheads and Puritans of the mid-seventeenth century, alluding to the expulsion of Cromwell's opponents at the hands of a Colonel Thomas Pride. He

> would call this Bill, Russell's purge of Parliament . . . the principle of the Bill was republican in its basis . . . destructive of all property, of all right, of all privilege; and that the same arbitrary violence which expelled a majority of Members from the House in the time of the Commonwealth, was now, after the lapse of a century and a half from the Revolution, during which the population had enjoyed greater happiness than was ever enjoyed by any population under Heaven, proceeding to expose the House of Commons to the nauseous experiment of a repetition of Pride's Purge.[98]

Wetherell, with his spoliations, civil sacrileges, monstrous acts and, a little later, his 'stigma of the blackest dye', seems irrational and incomprehensible in ways which the quieter Inglis, quite as remote in his own thinking, does not, largely because he parodies the bubbling rage of every fright-invoking, outraged right-wing Conservative in history. He invokes precedent and rights of property. If the one is lacking and the other infringed, no other argument is recognised, the liberties of England are insolently threatened with monstrous spoliation and there is an end of it. But his own side, the Tory squires, liked this sort of thing enormously. Greville heard Macaulay and Wetherell,

> the former very brilliant, the latter long, rambling and amusing, and he sat down with such loud and long cheering as everybody agreed they had never before heard in the H. of Commons, and which was taken not so much as a test of the merits of the speech as of an indication of the disposition of the majority of the House . . . The general opinion is that it will be lost in the H. of C, and then that Parliament will be dissolved, unless the King should take fright and prefer to change his ministers.[99]

Votes in the Commons, even exciting ones with defections, are rarely unknowable. But the government which succeeded Wellington's in a parliament where Wellington had been able to form a Ministry was a raft floating on a sea of conjecture. A widely held view was that if Peel had risen and forced a division in the House there and then after an evening suffused with the horrors of 168 seats despatched, he could have stopped legislation in its tracks. Then, went Tory thinking, the public appeal of half a million votes offered to the multitude would not have impacted. The natural Tory-plus-moderate-middle dominance in this House would have asserted itself. A bill for moderate reform could have been quickly brought in (Knatchbull stood ready to do just that), burying the absolutism of Wellington's grand refusal.

Writing to his patron, Lord Hertford, after the event, Croker expressed the general Tory view that the Bill should have been defeated, and blamed squeamish moderation on his own side.

The first night the proposition was met with shouts of derision, and if we had shortened the preliminary debate and divided, as I thought we should have done against the introduction of the *principle*, we should, I am confident, have carried its rejection by a considerable majority; but the first symptom of that terror (of which you will, I fear, see but too many subsequent proofs) was that Lord GS [Granville Somerset] and men of that calibre over-persuaded our leaders that we ought not to venture to oppose so popular a measure *in limine*.[100]

That outré and ruthless view was shared, strategically, by his political antithesis and fellow buccaneer, Brougham. The Lord Chancellor was giving dinner at the House to members of the Cabinet not involved in the debate and he relied, in an unelectronic age, upon half-hourly bulletins saying who was speaking, how they were received and who would speak next, all sent by his secretary, Denis Le Marchant. When a message came saying that Russell was near conclusion and the next speaker would be identified in the next note, Brougham offered a judgement. He had always said that in Peel's place '[he] would not condescend to argue the point, but would as soon as John Russell sat down, get up, get up and say I would not debate so revolutionary and mad a proposal and would insist on dividing it at once. If he does that, I used to say, we are dead beat; but if he allows himself to be drawn into a discussion, we shall succeed.'[101]

When the message came, Brougham read it and, in his own words, 'I flourished the note around my head, and shouted "Hurrah! Hurrah! Victory! Victory! Peel has been speaking for twenty minutes."'[102] In fact, of course, he had been doing nothing of the sort. Inglis had followed Russell, but, as Le Marchant explained, he had sent exactly that message. Having been busy away from the gallery, he had relied on wrong second-hand

information.[103] But with a civil servant's historically adaptive view of things
– he later became Clerk of the House – Le Marchant thought that Peel
could neither have moved a division nor have wanted to: 'So daring and
insolent a disregard of public opinion would have risked everything which
Sir Robert Peel and every wise man holds dear.' Perhaps, but Victorian
piety comes into the remark, and retrospective piety at that. Peel had been
caught on the wrong foot. He was staggered by the audacity of Russell's
list.

His biographer, Norman Gash, contrasts the exultancy around Peel in
Tory ranks with his posture, hands put in front of his face, and comments
that 'with his quick political sagacity perhaps he already realised that there
was now no room for compromise or moderation'.[104] He would refuse
assent to Knatchbull's move. Any quick victory in the House, even if
tempered, would tie him in with the Ultras, the last thing Peel wanted.
Across the middle of the century and driven by other causes, the group
identified with his name, the Peelites, would metamorphose by degrees
into Liberals. In 1831, Peel, though a devoted Tory, had held his party
back in hope of compromise. The terms of the Bill had closed the door
on that compromise. He may have seen a quick victory in the chamber
and a modest bill once Russell's words were out and on the street, as a
blind and dangerous alley. Modest reform could work as a first and only
proposal. In this sense Le Marchant had a point. Public opinion of a
furious and disappointed kind would gather against the Tory Party for
denying what had been held out.

Meanwhile, the debate which the fighting men of both persuasions
would have ended continued on its way. Greville reported admiration on
its third day, 3 March, for the contributions of Hobhouse and Peel himself.
But before them came George Bankes, MP for Corfe Castle, another Ultra,
former Admiralty junior, friend of Mrs Arbuthnot and voter against
Catholic emancipation. Bankes concluded a high and dry excursion –
Cromwell and the Long Parliament, the wisdom of Mr Pitt – on a great
harrumph about the dangers of revolutionary ideas which had 'spread
their malignant influence in almost every quarter of the globe and shaken
the fabric of every government'.[105] Bankes had once, long before, toyed
with the notion of reform. But in a sentence of thirty-one lines, three sets
of full colons, one semicolon and the ejaculation '– I say Sir', he recanted.
When he saw that the British Parliament and constitution had 'alone
remained pure and untouched in its vital principles', had 'resisted all the
efforts of Jacobinism, sheltering itself under a pretence of a love of liberty';
when he saw that 'it had supported itself against the open attacks of its
enemies and against the more dangerous Reforms of its professed friends',

he would 'be ashamed if any former opinions of mine could now induce me to think that the form of Representation which, in such times as the present, has been found amply sufficient for the purpose of protecting the interests and securing the happiness of the people, should be disturbed from any love of experiment or any love of theory'. Declaring 'the innermost thoughts of my mind', Bankes announced that 'even if the times were proper for experiments, any change in such a Constitution must be considered as an evil'.[106]

Parliamentarians of 1831 (and long after) paid the doings of antiquity (Cromwell, Charles I and, from time to time, Edward I) a degree of earnest attention strange even to historically minded descendants. But when J.C. Hobhouse had done duty by the regicides of 1649, the Cortes of Spain removing Ferdinand VII and events in Sicily, he usefully reminded Wetherell and Inglis that it was their own William Pitt who, in his brief liberal incarnation had proposed 'to cut off 100 Members from the House', and to take away or disfranchise thirty-six boroughs, 'monstrous spoliation' in an earlier form. He also dropped a hint no more subtly than necessary that the Tories, who had been dwelling on the vulnerability of the monarch to either revolutionary overthrow or Jacobinical enterprises, were doing William IV and his brothers no favours.

Sir Robert Peel (he had succeeded to his cotton-master father's baronetcy in 1830) was in the not unique position in England where the heirs of sixteen quarterings and better (Grey, Althorp, Russell) talked and acted liberalism and reform, of leading the Conservative cause from its remote margins. (The very word 'Conservative' was about to be invented – possibly the creation of Croker or John Miller in an unsigned piece in the *Quarterly Review*.) A brilliant adjective not readily turned into an abstract noun, it described at this time the landed interest, everything which was traditional, rooted and disposed to an established hierarchy. But Peel himself came from clean outside. He might be an Etonian and a member of Christ Church, but he was the grandson of a Lancashire smallholder turned small merchant and the son of a man, the first Sir Robert, who had turned a tidy sum into a superb fortune. He spoke with a northern accent; he was a man of business who would be happiest doing rational, arithmetical things like the Bank Act of 1844 and his abolition of the Corn Laws, chief shibboleth of all Conservative, land-owning and traditional interests. Peel spoke the more passionately against change in 1831 because he was part of it. He was a patriot of Tory England with the passion of an immigrant.

And his speech, concluding the third day of debate, reflected the fact. It was applauded and admired – and these were times when speeches were followed like sport, had indeed their own Fancy. It was a very gifted man's speech remote from the bullying cajolery of Wetherell or the puffings of small beasts of affirmation like Bankes and Twiss. And, unlike them, he was without venom or snobbery. Indeed, Twiss was given the back of Sir Robert's glove for dismissing the small attorneys and shopkeepers of the middle class. As he said, he sprang from the middle class and was proud of the fact. But for all that, it was high-flying Toryism, what someone in another context once felicitously called 'High Castilian nonsense'.

But it was also in measure a defensive speech. Peel, the facilitator of Catholic Relief, had to do that. After spending a lot of time over what Canning might or might not have done – Peel was sure that he would have continued firm against Reform – he reproached the Whigs for dragging the good name of William IV into their own schemes as if the Tory position for most of the century had not involved a regular dealing of the court card.

His essential message was that ministers were stirring things up. Like all Tories who took the point, he was on the firmest ground arguing that there would be no finality to this business. Though it is important to remember that what was denied, warned against and feared was not the incremental procession of nineteenth and early twentieth centuries, 1867, 1884 and 1918, but a large democratic push in the next few years. Even so, Peel's resonances, touching, like so many on either side, upon the risk of bloody revolution, have a touch of East Lynne: 'Did I taunt the people with their indifference to Reform . . . with having lived in the lazy enjoyment of practical good and disregarded the promises of visionary improvement?'[107] And he grew hyperbolically upset about a crowd from which someone had allegedly waved the French tricolour. He had not expressed 'misplaced admiration of the conduct of a crowd of many thousands who were supposed to have flaunted in the face of their king the emblem of a foreign revolution'.[108]

But Peel is at his least convincing when he is at his most ardent. He spoke of the constitution in terms of attained perfection and quoted Cicero, Tacitus and, finally, Canning to that effect. These ancient writers 'discussing a priori, the various forms of government, either despaired altogether of the formulation of such a Constitution as ours or described it as the most perfect of all'.[109] It was florid, hortatory stuff, an upmarket version of an editorial in the *Eatanswill Gazette*: 'Old Sarum existed when Somers and the great men of the Revolution established our government. Rutland sent as many Members as Yorkshire when John Hampden lost his life in defence of the Constitution.'[110]

And to this swirling style he added his regrets at the demise of the small voters, the potwallopers of Preston and the weavers of Coventry, of whom he thought it 'an immense advantage' that they 'should have a share in the privileges of the present system'.[111] It was a speech directed at the following he and Wellington had lost, a plea to the immemorial nature of the best things and the awful folly of trying to change them.

Rather more pertinently, ranging back from 1782, 1790, 1820 and 1821, he charged the Whigs with bringing forward Reform at times of economic or political distress which indeed it would not directly affect. But this was to deplore politics for being political, and Peel's concluding contrast was between England and France: 'Let us never be tempted to resign the well-tempered freedom which we enjoy, in the ridiculous pursuit of the wild liberty which France has established.'[112]

But despite the overdone tropes, Peel always had something intelligent to say. The Whigs were making a pitch for popular support, and doing pretty well. But they had started an auction which would never be stopped. The Whigs were enfranchising half a million men. You couldn't do that without gaining popularity. 'But these are vulgar arts of government; others will outbid you, not now, but at no remote period – They will offer votes and power to a million of men, will quote your precedent for the concession, and will carry your principles to their legitimate and natural consequence.'[113] So they would, but Peel was not quite as prophetic as this suggests. The time scale in contemporary minds of most debates on finality versus further change was not manhood suffrage in three bites over fifty-three years with a ballot after forty-one. It was for a telescoping of reforms in a period nearer a decade, a Mao-like condition of permanent Reform. By luck or management, Russell's Bill was going to prove quite satisfactory to moderate Tories. One of them, Gladstone, would bring in the ballot from which Grey pulled back.

FOUR

On to the Vote

'That corrupt and profligate thing, the daily press –
the vile daily press of England'

'Nothing talked of, thought of, dreamt of, but Reform. Every creature that one meets asks, What is said now? How will it go? What is the last news? What do you think? And so it is from morning till night, in the streets, in the clubs, and in private houses.' Greville, writing with his usual immediacy, dated his comments 7 March, the Monday after the Thursday upon which Peel had spoken. By the next Thursday, 10 March, noting the last day of the reading, he would declare 'everybody heartily sick of it, but the excitement as great as ever'. Inevitably in debate, speaker duplicated speaker, the better points were widely remade, as were some of the worse, but that excitement remained.

The expectation at first was that the Bill could not pass. It was too extreme, alienated too many moderate men. The Tory whips, Holmes and Bonham, were found by Lord Ellenborough at the house of another Tory functionary, Joseph Planta, on 3 March, working on a projected list of voting intentions. At this early date they were blithely reckoning on 356 against the Bill, 243 for, with 53 doubtful. Ellenborough, a personal friend of Grey, though the most conservative sort of Canningite, thought that they were too optimistic: 'I think they have counted some as against who will vote for. Such as the Barings who being the shabbiest fellows in the world, will vote one way & talk another & be convinced another.'*[1]

Ellenborough's own view was that everything rested with Peel's speech. But, unlike Croker and Brougham, he did not see the urgency of a pre-emptive division. 'I look to Peel's speech. He feels very strongly against the measure. If he makes as he will, a very good speech, he will carry a great many votes *ultimately*, for upon this question there will be no division. If he makes a successful speech we shall throw out the bill, then I rather expect a Dissolution. It is a fearful crisis.'[2] Two days later, after Peel

---

* They voted against.

had spoken 'effectively', Croker 'heavily' and Stanley for the government 'very much like a gentleman', Ellenborough reported from 'a dull dinner' at Peel's London house, one involving two Dukes, the Archbishop of Canterbury, the Bishop of London and assorted personages; Ellenborough observed buoyancy. 'I think there was confidence as to the final fate of the Bill', also that 'the excitement in the H. of Commons has been beyond example'.[3]

But back in the Commons, the doctrinaire negation of Inglis and, still more, the learned loutishness of Wetherell may have reminded moderate men what immoderation was like. The intervention of John Calcraft, a member of Wellington's Cabinet, was a straw in the wind. After some introductory grumbling, Calcraft, patron of the seat, Wareham, for which he sat, said that 'he would unite with several hon. Gentlemen who were of the same way of thinking as himself in requesting the house to allow the Bill to be brought in without a division, in order that they might see what it really contained'.[4]

This was the kind of thing at which we have seen Croker raging, the hesitancy of 'men of that calibre' under whose influence he would write to Lord Hertford on 15 March, 'we persevered in the same timid policy when the scheme was opened upon us in all its violence; and would you believe it? the same class of men, *now* give the same kind of reasons why we should pass the second reading, and reserve our opposition for the Committee'.[5]

By the 3rd, Creevey, who had the instincts of a football supporter, was cock-a-hoop. He had been personally delighted that it had taken such a bold and drastic form, the sort of thing he would have done himself if in the Cabinet. On 3 March he had asked his niece, 'Well what think you of our Reform plan?' It was all very well for a historian like Thomas Creevey to lay down the law, as he did in his pamphlet, that all these rotten nomination boroughs were modern usurpations, and that the *communities* of all substantial boroughs were by law the real electors,

> but here was a little fellow not weighing above 8 stone – Lord John Russell by name – who without talking of law or anything else, creates in fact a perfectly new House of Commons . . . What a coup it is! It is his boldness that makes its success so certain . . . A week or ten days must elapse before the Bill is printed and ready for a 2nd reading; by that time the country will be in a flame from one end to the other in favour of the measure . . .[6]

Here was Russell legislating to a purpose. By the 5th Creevey was talking the language of certain success. He had looked in at Crockford's (the splendid new premises of that celebrated gambling hell had been opened in 1828) and mingled with great lords, catching their dismay. 'At Crocky's even the boroughmongers admitted that their representative, Croker had made a damn rum figure.' And he proceeded to prophecy (correctly as it turned out) the electoral defeat of the Tory Chief Whip: 'Poor Billy Holmes! Both he and Croker will have but a slender chance of being MPs again under our restored constitution.'[7]

Remote from such exaltation, Calcraft acknowledged that there were 'large blots on the institutions of the country which ought to be cured. There were large masses of the country which ought to be represented.' His concern was that mass opinion should not get out of hand, 'an over-flowing influence of one of the estates of the Constitution, to the destruction of the other two'.[8] It was all too much, 'the difference between him and the new reformers who had sprung up was that he was for reform, they, with the noble Lord at their head, were for revolution'.[9] Like moderate men before and since, Calcraft was dithering, but unlike most of them, he would dither into tragedy. He would finally support the Bill, be found a seat by the government whips, but, feeling despised on all sides as a floor-crossing survivor, would negate all survival in September 1831 by cutting his throat.

In a floating House, Calcraft's drift to acceptance would be balanced by Charles Wynn's move in the opposite direction. Having resigned from the government, Wynn spoke sensibly, dismissing Wetherell's talk of borough status as a freehold. And without bombast, he argued in favour of piecemeal reform, the cashiering of venal boroughs in twos and threes on a case-by-case basis. He wanted the manufacturing towns to be represented and did not object to small measures of disfranchisement to bring this about. However, the government were taking on too much not to scramble the whole business. The boroughs should be looked at carefully and individually, largely as to population size but also as to property and wealth. This was the position of the tepid Whigs, of whom Charles Greville, heckling into his diary, was highly representative. In a sense they dithered as much as Calcraft, and as they dithered, events went past.

The heaviness of Croker which had wearied Ellenborough on 4 March consisted of an unanswerable analysis of the internal contradictions of the new allocation of seats by population. The rough and ready, back-of-an-envelope methods by which Durham and Russell had defined qualifications for borough status had stuck the legislation full of anomalies which Croker, technician as well as romantic of Conservatism, delighted to expose. The three boroughs of the North Riding, Thirsk, Richmond and

Malton, had an aggregate population of 10,084. The three new boroughs created in the West Riding, Huddersfield, Halifax and Wakefield, had a combined population of 36,500. 'Will it be believed that, when the 10,000 inhabitants of Malton, Richmond and Thirsk, are to send four Members to parliament, the 36,000 inhabitants of these three towns are to send only three?'[10] Croker also set about provoking a lifetime's quarrel with Macaulay by scratching the glittering surface of the Member for Calne's brilliant speech, chiefly by dwelling on Calne itself: 'Now Sir, it appears that Calne with 4,612 inhabitants, is to nominate two members, Bolton with 22,000 inhabitants is to return but one.'[11] He had enormous fun with the equity which the Whigs thought they were pursuing. Such changes, they were told, 'are made in order to satisfy the people; but this proposition is not only not what the people ask, but it is not what the people will accept; nothing like it – "they ask for bread and you give them a stone". They do not ask that Bolton and Blackburn with four times the population should have only half the representation of Calne or Tavistock . . .'

Calne, together with three other two-borough seats surviving Lord John's Herodiad – Knaresborough, Bedford and Tavistock – was a living in the gift of a Whig grandee, in this case the Duke of Bedford, the Minister's father. For the House of Russell served as borough owner, patron of great talents and walking contradiction, not least of the principle underlying the present legislation. Croker wondered why Lord John on his way to Callington (suppressed), in Cornwall, had not stopped at Tavistock (sustained), in Devon. But, of course, he mocked on, if such inequities as the one contrasting Calne against Bolton occurred as the direct consequence of what was called Reform, what should be the consequences? Was this 'a plan to make the system of representation more full, more free and more equal? Is it not on the contrary certain to scatter the seeds of contention and discord throughout the country?'[12]

Croker had the advantage of the natural, untrammelled Tory. He believed ardently in the Duke of Bedford's rights as patron and political Maecenas. Such good fortune in the proper hands of a great nobleman had nothing to fear from John Wilson Croker, son of a County Galway exciseman, Protestant Irishman (supporting emancipation), risen by merit, recognised by just another such aristocratic patron, and a better supporter than His Grace of the ancient and customary ways of the glorious British constitution. Croker was beautifully placed for irony:

God forbid that we should ever see the time when the natural influence of a munificent and beneficent landlord like the Duke of Bedford is to be annihilated. And yet Sir, such is the apprehended operation of this fatal Bill – such is the odium of the comparisons which it creates between such places as Bolton and Tavistock – that the heir of that illustrious house repudiates for the future an influence which is so natural and so legitimate that I hope and believe it is also inevitable and imperishable.

Croker was high, dry and impossible. But he was coherent, and the Whigs, blueprinting with one hand, drawing the map of the future free hand with the other, aspiring in one act, hanging on to ancient fixes in the next, were not. Macaulay, the inspirational orator held up to exquisite derision (as he would be again), who would pursue Croker with lifetime vengefulness through long and grindingly malicious reviews of his other work as scholar of Johnson and Shakespeare, had understood. Ellenborough, self-preoccupied Tory who found the speech 'heavy', had not.

But Croker's concluding message was a denial that the waters were rising. Russell had told them

> that the stormy tides of popular commotion were rising around us . . . and that it was time for us – and barely time, to endeavour to save ourselves from being swallowed up by the devouring waves . . . he invited you to embark with him on this frail and crazy raft, constructed in the blundering haste of terror, as the only means of escaping from destruction. No, Sir, no; . . . stand firm where you are and wait until the threatening waters subside. What you hear is not only a fictitious, but a factitious clamour.

The constitution was a wonderful thing, it was a perfect form of government, not least because 'the nation is always attentive to the voice of the House of Commons; in the long run the people acquiesce in its decisions'. The people had been aroused by voices from the Commons, so it was 'the moral authority of this House which again must quiet them'.[13]

But Croker's cool courage was as untypical as his doctrinal certainty. Ellenborough listens to the Duke of Wellington, still talking of tactical retreat by the government – a different, lesser bill after an election – and disagrees with him. The Whigs 'imagine things have turned in their favour the last few days and are in great spirits'.[14] In the same mood, Greville at one moment is writing and printing (anonymously) a 'declaratory tirade against Reform',[15] but the very next day, he finds it 'curious to see the change of opinion as to the passing of this bill. The other day nobody would hear of the possibility of it, now everybody is beginning to think that it will.'[16] Tory hopes, such they were, rested upon the Ministry modifying their proposals after an election in which they had lost ground, but Ellenborough began to expect an election of the Whigs' choosing.

Meanwhile, the second week of debate ground its way along with an inevitable silting up of used arguments. Lord Dudley Stuart was typical of the late intervener's dilemma, caught between fear of repetition and determination to join in. He made a suitably apologetic opening: 'After all that has been urged by both sides on this great question, I can scarcely hope to adduce any new argument for the consideration of the House; and it would be still more presumptuous in me to expect, by any thing I can have to say to influence in any degree its decision.' Such humility did not, however, silence a man who 'considered it my duty to give this important, this awful, subject my best attention', from going on about the Bill for three and a half reluctant columns. He was for it: 'Ours is certainly a noble, a glorious Constitution; but there are in it defects and a symptom of decay which if not cured, will cause the ruin of the whole.'

Sir George Warrender, speaking for 'his constituents, the pot-wallopers of Honiton', deplored 'the proposed Reform Bill because it was not a measure conferring rights on the people, but withdrawing and confiscating those rights they already possessed . . . it was a gross act of injustice to deprive any body of people of the elective franchise without any act of delinquency being proved'.[17] Cobbett and Carlile received an aggrieved bob of respect from Sir George. As an anti-reformer, he had 'thereby brought down upon him the vengeance of that most powerful and most dangerous engine, the diurnal press; but not withstanding that, he would still persist in his opinion, because convinced he was bound to do so, both by his duty to his country and to his King'.[18]

William Peel, Sir Robert's brother, having 'protested against the abominable injustice of the measure', took up Croker's arguments on the unequal representation of different boroughs. Tamworth, which William, now Member for Cambridge University, had represented for twelve years, had more houses in it than either of those Whig-owned boroughs, Tavistock or Calne, yet Tamworth (a Peel borough, bought by the first Sir Robert twenty years before) had been docked of a member while the others still sent two each to Westminster. And he drew out a column's length of metaphor about purges, soon to follow: 'a bolus in the shape of the ballot' from one reforming enthusiast, Warburton of Bridport; while 'Dr Hume would give them another dose in the form of Universal Suffrage and Annual parliaments'.[19] As for Henry Hunt, the Member for Preston 'would not sit in the House for three months without saying that Reform was well enough as far as it went, but it did not go far enough . . . and he would advise them a dose of Hunt's matchless composition'.[20]

Ironically, of course, Preston was an anomaly, a borough with enough unpropertied occupants (potwallopers) – 6,000 of them – to effect instead of the usual process of cash/coercive manipulation something very like a democratic election. The streamlining, not to say modernising, of the Reform Bill would reduce this glorious anomaly to a borough of 1,000 owners of property rateable at £10. But John Wood, Hunt's yokefellow in the seat, announced he would tell his constituents that though 5,000 of them would be losers, 500,000 would be gainers elsewhere. And he made the claim that 'At present a majority of the House was returned by about 300 individuals'. And adapting a rhetoric which would be familiar on the far left for the next hundred years, he invoked a demon: 'The people had the monster of corruption at bay; it had received a mortal wound; its frightful yells were heard in the last agonies of expiring existence, and they would soon be drowned in the triumphant shouts of the people.'*[21]

In similar style to contrary purpose, John North, Member for Drogheda, felt 'that this was only the first of those steps which would lead us day after day in our progress away from our ancient institutions – that it was the first abyss in the revolutionary hell that was yawning for us'.[22] North, who had also quoted Milton – 'in the lowest deep a lower deep / still threatening to devour, opens wide' – would, during nine closely printed columns of the record, also pick up on Dr Johnson and demand of ministers: 'Had they contemplated our constitution in a large and extensive view – these arrogant and self-conceited men! – who had given a verdict against institutions which had called forth the admiration of a Somers or a Locke, and to which we were indebted for a century and a half of felicity.'[23]

On day six of the debate, while Brougham as Lord Chancellor accepted in the Lords a petition from the City of London which expressed the Lord Mayor and Citizens' 'strongest approbation of the measure of Reform brought before the other House by His Majesty's ministers',[24] the Commons heard a speech which did not tread beside the customary furrow. Daniel O'Connell was the Liberator, also the agitator and the demagogue, prosecuted on and off for sedition, 'doing all he can', according to Mrs Arbuthnot, 'to rip up old sores and put Ireland again in a flame'.[25] Now Member for Waterford, it was as candidate for Clare that he had precipitated the Catholic emancipation which had ruined the Tories.

O'Connell was not brief. At twenty-nine columns of allusion, whimsy, legal learning, knockabout and earnest, he out-Castro-ed Fidel. And he had a very good press. Greville, always fair through his prejudices, rated

---

* A touch here of the Communist pamphlet prose parodied by Orwell: 'The jackboot has been thrown into the melting pot, the fascist octopus has sung its swansong.'

him 'very good and vehemently cheered by the government'. They had been prosecuting him six weeks earlier, before, as Mrs Arbuthnot saw it, 'to gain him for the election' they 'truckled' to him. The Tory, Ellenborough, was even more admiring: 'O'Connell seems to have made last night the best speech that has been made for the Bill.'[26] He came very quickly to the point: 'He was upon conviction, a Radical Reformer; and this was not Radical Reform. He was of opinion, that in every practical mode, universal suffrage should be adopted as a matter of right: he was likewise of opinion that the duration of parliaments should be shortened to the length stipulated at the Glorious Revolution; and above all, he was of opinion that votes should be taken by Ballot.'[27]

Even read today, the formally phrased but gunfire-delivered opinions create a tingle. Along the way of a great flashing and dazzling ramble, he enjoyed himself at the expense of boroughs employed as valuable exchange, drawing on Irish experience where certain towns had been disfranchised at the time of the Union. 'The borough of Askeaton was one of the boroughs thus disfranchised and £13,000 was given by the parliament to Massey Dawson as compensation for the loss he had sustained by the disfranchisement of it. Shortly afterwards his brother who was the other Member for that borough, claimed half that compensation money . . . the learned Judge on the bench told him that he must be non-suited and further told his counsel "I must tell you that your client is a most auda-cious man . . ."' However, added O'Connell, 'this very Judge, together with the father of the hon. Member for Limerick, were trustees named in a marriage settlement, by which it was provided that the nomination to the borough of Tralee should be set aside as provision for the younger children of Sir E. Dennie. And yet this was called the old Constitution – [An hon. Member, "Oh but that was in Ireland."]'[28]

O'Connell had the great politician's gift for enjoying himself and making opponents share in the enjoyment: He explained 'the miracle of Armagh', a borough in the gift of the Archbishop who first nominated the Chancellor of the Exchequer and was then burned in effigy by Orangemen, before giving a crisp justification for the dubious survival of a place like Tavistock: 'The Bill did give something to Tavistock, it threw the borough open and created 1,000 electors where at present there were but twenty-four.' He set about the scarifying of Edinburgh: 'There were thirty-three constituents in that great city, and this measure would turn the thirty-three into 10,000. Was that no improvement? There never yet existed a Representative of 100,000 constituents who had received so much of the public money for doing nothing as the member for Edinburgh.'[29]

However, moving out of his beguiling good humour, O'Connell offered an instructive view, an Irish and blazingly bitter one, of Edmund Burke, held out by all anti-reformers as the chief glory of the nomination system.

> The name of Mr Burke was alluded to – a high Tory name – none higher, none dearer to that class of persons who are opposed to this measure. But what did Mr Burke do for the country? He did something for himself – he rendered himself rich and comfortable by the course he pursued and the country, be it recollected, has to pay the pensions granted to him to this hour . . . He might have been a great man; but Burke was brought into this house by the borough mongers, and his greatness and his value were lost to the country.[30]

Mixed with the fun and the stinging asides was shrewd lobbying for specific extension of Irish representation, handy comparison between certain Irish counties and those English counties due in the Bill for expansion by two additional members. 'Fifteen of them possessed a population less than that of the County of Antrim; nineteen of them less than Down, twenty-two of them less than that of Tipperary . . . He respectfully demanded then another member for Antrim, another for Down, another for Cork, another for Galway, another for Kerry, another for Mayo and another for Tyrone, for he could show that everyone of them was above the line of 200,000.'[31]

O'Connell was, of course, more than an orator. He was a leader of men with votes, one with a larger holding than the Duke of Bedford. In his cheerfully sweeping way, he included in his claims Protestant citizens in Antrim and Down unlikely ever to follow him. From time to time in his career, O'Connell would urge repeal of the Act of Union of 1801. Quite how much Tories were tempted by Irish parliamentary excursions to undo the work of Pitt, and quite how far O'Connell, enjoying his powers in a playable Commons, was in earnest, are nice points. So when he concluded by calling on members to support the Bill 'for the people of England, also to do it for the people of Ireland', adding that by doing so they would 'secure the tranquillity of that country, and find an ample return in the contentment and gratitude of its people',[32] he was talking hard lobby arithmetic to the Whig whips.

For the government Sir James Graham took issue with Croker and his assurance that the waters of discontent might rise but that, when they subsided, 'the public vessel would right herself'. During the war, he had watched a new naval frigate, away from a dry dock, heaved ineptly into the water and he described the helpful intervention of her commander: 'Desirous to bring her somewhat nearer the surface and thinking he might safely order another turn of the capstan, he gave the word; when the vessel heeled, filled, and for ever disappeared.'[33] In Graham's view, 'when the waters of bitterness and strife had risen to a certain height, when the tide of discontent was full, a slight wave raised by a passing gust might, at moments when it was least expected, overwhelm and swamp the vessel of State'.[34] It reads well enough to the landsman, but all contemporary opinion, encouraged by the comments of the Tory admiral, Sir Joseph Yorke, speaking next, agreed that Sir James had adorned an ineffective speech with a metaphor making no nautical sense and which nobody understood. Ellenborough, in reckoning O'Connell's to have been the best speech for the Bill, thought that Graham had made the worst.[35]

An oddity in the debate was the contribution of a Mr Praed, Member for the threatened Cornish borough of St Germans. Winthrop Mackworth Praed, who would die young before the decade was out, was a poet of a satirical bent and some talent. Something of a costume Tory, he conceded that, 'It was such a manifest absurdity that Leeds should have no member to watch over its manufacturing interests, and that Old Sarum . . . should have two Members to die in its last ditch that . . . any man of ordinary observation must have been at some period of his life to a certain extent a parliamentary Reformer.'[36] Yet this terrible system had produced such good results and thrown up so many clever men. (The Tories were devoted to this argument, particularly the clever ones.) And St Germans was a classic rotten borough. The whole concept smacked of a Platonic elitism, elder wisdom and thoughtful privilege outreaching the vulgar mob in their perception to advance men clad only in their shining talents. The fact that Maecenas more commonly gave the seat to Maecenas's dull nephew did not stop it being a useful quarter truth. Trade union Maecenases pushing the recommended bright economist as well as the tired district secretary might later have echoed it.

Praed's second point was rather more original. He noted the decline of the royal veto. King William's compliance was still going to count for a great deal during the creaking passage of this bill, but he could hardly have directly vetoed it. That being so, he 'looked with serious apprehension at this Bill, as tending to make the House of Peers obsolete'. Only the fact of Lords having influence in the Commons kept those Lords at 'their station in the country'. Praed feared that 'the House of Commons would become surreptitiously supreme in this country'.[37] Getting higher and dryer yet, he asked why they did not 'increase representation in the higher, more enlightened classes? Why did they not . . . allow double numbers in the two universities?' And glorying in the quotation of Burke, he cited him on Parliament's being slower to want changes than the public.

Otherwise 'they would have, with the forms of representative government, all the evils of democracy'.[38]

He then launched an attack on a great feature of the Reform movement, its use of petitions to Parliament. They were being presented in large relays. On the day before, 7 March, the House of Lords had received petitions against slavery, against tithes, 'for a repeal of the duty on sugar made by free labour, in complaint of distress from the shipowners of South Shields, for repeal of the Union and for Reform'. In the Commons, there had been six petitions for Reform on 7 March from the Political Union Society of Bristol, from Hampshire, from Moffat, Canterbury, Bridport and both West and Market Lavington. Praed didn't know where it was all going to end. If the Bill became law 'there would be as many petitions laid on the table of that House for further Reform as there were now in favour of the Bill'. Anyway, these petitions were not specifically supporting Russell's Bill, they were about everything else. 'Some were for Vote by Ballot and others were dealing with the property of the church.'[39]

Praed provoked Whig and radical MPs with the grand statement that he 'utterly denied that these petitions had come from men to whose opinions, as contra-distinguished from their wishes, the House ought to defer [The hon. Member was here frequently interrupted by calls of "Question"]'. Praed blinked rather at this and quickly added that 'he did not mean to deny that some of the petitioners who had approached the House on the subject of reform were respectable and intelligent individuals'. He just thought 'they were not those persons to whose opinions he would refer on a grand legislative measure. He should have preferred more of intelligence and wealth of the community as a guide of their decisions.'[40]

At which point of High Tory splendour, the sixth day's proceedings were adjourned ready for resumption on what would be its last. This began with another batch of petitions from unsuitable people, beginning with one 'from the Females of Ryde who while they themselves were in the enjoyment of freedom, deeply sympathised with females of the West Indies in their unhappy bondage'. There were also petitions in support of Reform, whether or not from people of intelligence and wealth, in Gloucester, Stockport, Salisbury, Chichester and, piquantly, from Calne.

Members spent four columns squabbling about these missives and about what might or might not have been the opinions of the late William Huskisson. But the final day's debate proper began with the ultra Conservative opposition of one of Spencer Perceval's sons. The elder Perceval had stood, in his godly, evangelical way, further to the illiberal side of politics than anyone in the entire line of Prime Ministers. Young

Perceval did not disappoint. He opposed the Bill because he was confident that, the moment it passed, a deathblow would be inflicted on the monarchy. He had not a wavering or a shadow of a doubt on the subject.[41] Perceval's thinking, like that of many Tories, derived from fear of the Commons being intimidated by outside pressure. This accounted for the common resentment against petitions, though the principal organisers of the new public opinion were shrewd constitutionalists like Attwood and Francis Place, doing everything ostentatiously by the book, as indeed, for all his heat and adjectives, did Henry Hunt. People like young Perceval or Croker became very emphatic on the inherent powers of the Commons to do anything, while expressing grave fear that what they would actually do would be to flatter the 'clamorous multitude'. This clamour, said Perceval, was experienced most immediately in the comment of the press, 'that corrupt and profligate thing, the daily press – the vile daily press of England'.[42] What grieved him was that so many MPs 'were the slaves of the press, and he knew men who agreed with him, who in their hearts hated the Bill who did not hesitate in private society to say so, but who being the slaves of the press, dared not utter any such opinion in public'.[43]

The press at this time contained many radical sheets, from those of Cobbett out through Richard Carlile's *Prompter* and the reformist, but more respectable *Morning Chronicle*. The paranoia of such men as Perceval was to see the whole order of society, King, Lords and Commons, trembling on a precipice because newspapers argued that in due course the powers of Kings and Lords should be diminished. The constitution 'was framed in wisdom . . . its roots were deep sunk in the hearts of the whole nation . . . And yet now, Parliament was to be called upon by the wretched insanity of His Majesty's Ministers to knock this admirable Constitution to pieces and cast it to the Winds of Heaven.'[44]

Perceval was not well placed to talk about the insanity of others. Like Calcraft, he would have a dark future. A few years later, Gladstone would record his visit with a companion to Peel's home at Drayton Manor as that of 'beings from another world'. Always, like his father, an evangelical Christian, Perceval had become an Irvingite, evangelism's craziest manifestation, and, progressing, had convinced himself that he was the personal instrument of God directed to act as his ambassador to the leaders of the nation. Peel, eminently sane and moderate on religion, would treat him then with great patience, for Perceval, far more than Calcraft, *was* mad. But in 1831, in the febrile state of so much Conservative thinking, his talk that 'There was a great conflict about to begin in Britain; there was in fact a conflict of principles going on similar to that which ushered forward the downfall of Roman liberty' alerted no one. The widespread apocalyptic hysteria on what had barely begun to be called 'the Right' resembled the clown's account of England in *Hamlet*: "Twill not be seen in him there; there the men are as mad as he.' And with Perceval it did not show.

A good cynical speech from Daniel Harvey, Member for Colchester, dwelt lovingly on the solid profits of the sacred constitution. The reason Lord Darlington, MP for Saltash, was opposing the Bill unlike his father, Cleveland, 'was confined to the refusal of compensation to the owners of borough property. He had heard the hon. Member for Corfe Castle press, in a low voice, that point on the attention of his noble friend when he was speaking.'[45] If the government had come up with ready money to buy out the borough owners, 'many of the keen calculations, much of the constitutional apprehension and balance-striking arguments of hon. gentlemen opposite would have been spared'. He was certain that 'fears for the fate of the aristocracy and the dread of the popular power, would have yielded at once in hon. Members' minds to the weighty arguments of some thousand pounds sterling as the price of their boroughs and their patriotism'. Indeed, such boroughs should not be sold short, they carried other financial resources. Suppose Corfe Castle (part represented by the fervent constitutionalist George Bankes) were to be compensated, he should like to know 'at what sum they would estimate the enjoyment of the office of Cursitor Baron preceded by a Commissionership of Bankrupts which the hon. Member's son or brother had obtained solely from the posses-sion of that borough? [*Cries of 'No, No!'*] . . . the public had seen the long list of pensions, and the kind of persons to whom they had been granted.'[46]

The debate was winding down, but there were odd interesting chords struck before it returned to the home key with a government summing-up by Russell. Henry Goulburn, a close confederate of Peel, invoked the absolutism of James I and tagged it to the government. John Abel Smith, Member for the scheduled borough of Midhurst, had stated that he would support the Bill. Goulburn quoted James's conversation with two Bishops, Neele and Andrewes, on 'whether he might not take his subjects' money when he needed it without the formality of parliament'. Neele, in high grovelling form, had told the King that of course he might since 'he was the breath of our nostrils'. Andrewes, deftly equivocating, told the King, 'I think your Majesty may take my brother Neele's money for he offers it.' So Goulburn would say to Parliament, 'You may take the borough of Midhurst for the hon. Member for the borough offers it.'[47] As much as Wetherell, the Ultra, Goulburn at the heart of opposition leadership still saw borough status as a right, and, by implication, borough owner-ship, with all the financial perquisites which Harvey had illustrated, as inalienable property.

Alderman Robert Waithman, Member for London and a City figure prominent in the Reform movement, put the whole Reform case into a few lines, contrasting thirty-four peers who 'returned sixty members of parliament, all of whom held places of profit or pension under the Crown'. They were not true representatives 'yet the power they possessed was considerable and the Constitution was such that the government could not go on without their aid while they remained in it'.[48] Lyon, the Member for another doomed Cornish borough, Beeralston, reflected the fact at the start and finish of a succinct speech: 'Sir, The Noble Lord who has brought forward this bill has sentenced my constituents to be one and all, for ever wiped out from the list of voters.'[49] He followed just over a column later with the plain conclusion, 'Sir, so much of this bill as goes to disfranchisement, I shall oppose.'[50] Edward Stanley, a close friend and supporter of the radical Lord Durham, later Lord Stanley of Alderley, made an odd little speech from the back benches. It was a languishing attempt at the perfunctory. He rejoiced that the House of Commons would henceforward consist of real Representatives of the People. This was a subject of great congratulation to the country. It would afford him pleasure and satisfaction if he could in any way contribute in rendering so important and valuable a service to the empire.[51] Stanley would die in 1869 paying a tribute to the Tory tradition of anxiety by asking of some minor commotion outside, 'Is it a revolution?'

Altogether less languishing was the speech of Thomas Duncombe, Yorkshire country gentleman and radical who sat for Hertford, using as it did language which could have come from Hunt. 'The country had seen Ministers destroy the outworks of corruption; they had witnessed the way the citadel had been summoned, and did the House believe that the people of England would stand idly by were an attempt made to abandon the siege?'[52] This was a playing of the menace card at which Tories raged and which Whigs generally denied, Waithman, for one, insisting on the quiet and moderation of the people. But the existence of the possibility was a reason why the mood was changing, a reason why the Bill would pass.

It was not so much intimidation through the mob as intimidation through the electoral process. Even under the old system there had been a marked shift to reform candidates. Brougham's populist methods were admired and would be copied. The 'vile daily press of England' at which Perceval had writhed, would renew its thunder. Attwood's Birmingham Political Union had found flattering imitation across the country, though Attwood himself had been startled by the radicalism of the Bill itself. Electoral politics at any contest called after a rejection of the Bill would also be populist, the hustings heavily and unnervingly attended. The thoughtful Tories, like the Hedgehog, knew one thing and it was a big thing – that they were in retreat. When Duncombe advised 'the borough proprietors to listen to serious advice and open their gates . . . unfasten their rusty bolts' and added that 'although they might postpone, they could not prevent, the hour of victory from arriving',[53] he was presenting a mirror image of all those anti-reformers who had talked about revolution and civil war. He was rolling the logs of morale, seeking to induce in the opposition a losing side psychology.

Any vote would have to take place on the second reading, Peel, with no opposition from immediate colleagues, having committed the party to not dividing at that stage. Yet Creevey would still report cases of Tory triumphalism: 'The enemy is in the most insolent, crowing state possible today, perfectly certain, as they say, to defeat our Bill. Wetherell told me last night he was sure of their victory as of his own existence.'[54] In fact it was now agreed that any victory in a second reading would be a very small one; Holmes's early numbers, never credible, had melted. Dissolution after rejection by a handful would mean an election to hit the Tories amidships. At the same time, whatever Wellington had said about rejecting all reform, we were all reformers now. Everyone, bar a rump of super Ultras around Wetherell, wanted 'moderate reform'. Praed's comment about the absurdity of an enfranchised Old Sarum and an unrepresented Leeds summed up the new Tory consensus.

At the same time – good hedgehog thinking – they wanted to do everything slowly. Lord Wharncliffe, who would show himself the most tactically shrewd of Tories in the coming months, would have liked to waive opposition to the Bill at the second reading also and then, at prolonged leisure, cut it down to tolerable size in committee. Letting the country get bored was his recipe for holding on to that citadel. Unfortunately for Peel, the Tory Party was not so much split as scattered in diaspora. Holding them together for Wharncliffe's sort of sophisticated purposes meant persuading to further restraint the large section of that party most naturally responsive to the command, 'Up Guards and at 'em.' And many of these, the word 'betrayal' forming on curled lips, were already seething with scorn for Peel's caution. Meanwhile, much more reasonably but confusingly, the friends of Knatchbull and Vyvyan were preoccupied with their alternative scheme of a positive motion in favour of a moderate reform motion.

The last word lay with Lord John, deploring 'personal gibes' and 'a line of argument mixed up with vituperation'[55] and elaborately defending ministers' actions in having drawn lines where they had been drawn, explaining that to have included Tavistock, butt of so much opposition huffing on the schedules, there would have been not 168 but 240 seats deleted. There was no arbitrary cut-off point at which some injustice, probably one favouring the Whigs, might not be proclaimed. And Russell, taking the word 'democrat' in its 1831 sense of 'dangerous Jacobin', told Wetherell not to be afraid of that 'democratic assembly, the Ministers were about to create which would at no distant day, destroy the King and the House of Lords'. For Russell 'there was a fallacy in the word democratic . . . He denied altogether that the measure would have the effect of rendering the House a democratic assemblage in that sense of the word.'[56] He could not see 'why Manchester or Birmingham, should send democrats any more than Bristol or Liverpool. He was rather inclined to look upon the supposition as one of the same class of chimeras as had agitated the minds of hon. Members when the Test and Corporation Acts had been repealed, and when the Catholics had been admitted into that House.'[57]

It was true, of course, as was Russell's remark that after Reform 'The Crown would be more secure, more firm by being placed upon the affections of the people.'[58] Generations of Conservatives using the word 'democratic' in the smooth, emulsified sense which would creep into use would deliver the same sermonette across the twentieth century and after. Arguably, democracy happened in order not to matter. But to Perceval and Wetherell, Russell's cool assurance, something very Whig in its disdainful reasonableness, must have been intolerable. As he said, the anti-reformers cried 'Wolf' at any change, even a simple modification of the game laws. Or, rather, they cried 'revolution'. They quoted Burke, looked back to the Paris Terror and saw the Whigs, not without satisfaction, as Girondins blowing on the flame which should devour them. But Burke, like scripture, could be quoted by both sides. 'The distinctions made to separate us from the people are mischievous. Let us identify and incorporate ourselves with them. Let us cut the chains and cables which hold us from them and float into that harbour, whose moles and jetties extend to receive us.'[59]

Russell rightly thought that he was speaking for *successful* Girondins, an enlightenment able to shift things by adjustment without bringing on the terror, apocalypse or even democracy as Hunt understood it. But for all the constitutionality with which the constitution should now be amended, Russell did use democratic arguments, and frightening ones. He noted 'a want of confidence in public men. The people had been for some years separating themselves into parties and sects and unions and classes without looking to anyone in that House with perfect confidence and reliance.' What he next feared was 'a total separation between what he might call the constituted authorities and the mass of the people'.[60] His argument was nicely judged, both philosophically addressed to long causes and developments, and politically, threatening unpleasant consequences. Beat off Reform he argued, govern 'without the confidence of the nation', and the people who did that 'would be said not only to have denied Reform, but to have betrayed the people'. Do that and 'the country would come to a species of Reform which might indeed be termed revolution'.[61] Addressing the moderate and unresolved men in a House balanced on a sharp blade, John Russell was, in the most dignified way imaginable, trying to make their flesh creep.

When he had finished at the end of the seventh day of the first reading, *Hansard* would record the mute discord and quiet desperation: 'The question that leave should be given to bring in a Bill to amend the Representation of England and Wales was then put from the Chair. The voices which shouted out "Aye" were loud and many, but, when the Speaker in the usual form, put the question in the negative, there were only two or three voices cried "No," one of which was remarkable for its loudness[62] and the others scarcely audible.'[63] The leadership were now resting from debate and engaged in politics. The Tories worried about government strength and talked about what they should do. General Hardinge, close to the Duke, told Ellenborough that 'he calculated a majority of 37 supposing all the doubtfuls vote for the 2nd Reading . . . He had told the Duke he thought it too late to resist Reform *altogether*.'[64] Wharncliffe told him the same day that 'he is for not dividing upon the 2nd Reading & shipwrecking the Bill in the Committee'.[65] But, three days later, the Marquess of Graham, future Duke of Montrose, now MP for Cambridge, gave Ellenborough 'a bad account of the spirit of the H of commons & feared the 2nd Reading would be carried'.[66]

Ellenborough was something of an old woman. Charles Greville was his customary, abrupt, dogmatic self. It was 'universally believed that this Bill will pass, except by some of the Ultras against it, or by the fools'.[67] Part of the equation was the King. Dissolution was a weapon for the government to use if defeated and, given both enthusiasms and fears among even the old electorate, one likely to work. But dissolution was William's prerogative and, although he was on good terms with his ministers and far from the selfishness of Edward VII or the uncomprehending resentment of George V during the crisis of 1910, his assent had to be worked at. Meanwhile, the Tories calculated their chances very much in terms of 'Would he? Wouldn't he?'. If it were thought that the King would grant dissolution should the Bill be defeated at second reading, the opposition would probably recoil from defeating it in the first place. *Per contra*, if they could bring everything off inside a single parliament, with the government either limping on humiliated or making way for Peel and with no prospect of the election which the Tories feared, a division on second reading would have enormous charm.

Meanwhile, there was something the opposition could do by way of a shadow battle for morale. The government stood in a considerable bind over the arid but dangerous question of timber duties. Althorp's budget had been such an undistinguished and untidy affair involving a major resiling and there were issues left unresolved. The tariff on Baltic timber had been left higher than that on Canadian woods. The interests, notably the shipping trade, wanted an answer and lobbied hard for it. Sensibly enough in a rational (and free-trading) world, Althorp proposed a cut in duties on the Baltic imports until they equalled those of Canadian timber. The move was sprung on a House supposedly convalescing from its constitutional exertions. But the government whips used a light rein, the strength of protectionist and imperial preference sentiment was underestimated, as was a specific West India trade interest and an evangelical concern for native colonial welfare, all of them on this one vote, assembled against the Chancellor.

As Greville noted, 'On Friday night after not a long but angry and noisy debate, there was a division on the timber duties, and Government was beat by forty-three, all the Saints, West Indians* and anti-Free traders voting with the great body of Opposition.' And, as he added at once, 'Their satisfaction was tumultuous . . . they wanted to let the world see the weakness of government, and besides on this occasion, they hoped that a defeat might be prejudicial to the Reform Bill . . .' The question was resolved, he said truly enough, not on its merits 'but is influenced by passion, violence, party tactics and its remote bearing upon another question with which it has no immediate relation'.[68] As for Peel, he 'was what is called very factious – that is in opposition – just what the others were, violent and unreasonable as far as the question is concerned, but acting upon a system having for its object to embarrass the Government'.[69]

John Cam Hobhouse, newly appointed to the government, sat next to Grey at dinner that night, finding him 'out of spirits with the vote of the night before and seemed to think it would affect Reform'.[70] But the Prime Minister had only praise for William IV. For 'nothing could exceed the excellent, open conduct of the King'; there had been a three-hour meeting between them, 'a conversation of question and answer, not of mere listening as it used to be in the Time of George IV'. The King was decidedly for Reform.[71]

---

* Meaning white planters and traders, as in the title of Richard Cumberland's successful stage play, *The West Indian*.

Unfortunately for Grey the firstlings of his thoughts on this occasion would be the firstlings of his deeds. Immediately after the timber duties defeat he wrote a letter to the King's secretary, Sir Herbert Taylor, and did so before he had talked to his Cabinet. Badly rattled by the reverse, he did not play a cool long game, but much more than hinted at the possibility of dissolution: 'One material point will be the propriety of advising His Majesty to dissolve Parliament.' And straight off he asked Taylor for an account of the King's 'feelings' on the subject. Even in the third person this was not the way to handle William. Fundamentally friendly, he had to be stroked and spoken to in person. On top of this, the civil list, money for princes, which had been Wellington's nemesis, was due to come up. The provisioning of the royal family was a near and tender point, and delaying it for an election a worrying prospect. Indeed, Grey had told Hobhouse that the only point of friction in that three-hour conversation had concerned royal household expenditure, a piece of that retrenchment which the Whigs were making their badge of policy. And over a particular saving of £12,000, he had thought it 'not worth while to quarrel with him for that sum'.[72] A civil list vote delayed by an election was a vastly larger alarm; accordingly, the abrupt enquiry provoked an abrupt reply. The King could not countenance a dissolution, particularly in the light of the public unrest in England and Ireland.

Ironically, the second letter sent by Grey was much better judged. It had to be; there had been a Cabinet meeting first, and collectively the government had not panicked. They took the common-sense view that defeat in an ambush on an issue bringing several interests together did not necessarily imply later defeat on Reform. It made best sense to go on to the second reading and face a division. Duncannon, who had helped draft the Bill, told Hobhouse in terms 'that the Cabinet was resolved, in case of necessity to dissolve Parliament'.[73] Grey wrote to Taylor telling him this and, to an accompaniment of stable doors flapping on their hinges, asking him 'not to say anything to the king on the subject of dissolution'.[74] He had, said the Prime Minister, simply been sounding out the secretary as to advisability of asking the King for a dissolution.

Early nineteenth-century politics operated in a village. Attempts to keep the royal views quiet were fruitless, especially with Queen Adelaide's court bristling with diehard anti-reformers. The story went round and, in the manner of the stock exchange, created a market of sentiment. The larger question – would the King dissolve if the substantial Bill were defeated – had been neither put nor answered, something which did not stop avid Tories from assuming and proclaiming a negative. This, in turn, was likely to affect sentiment among the waverers. Nowhere was this more pronounced than amongst the Knatchbull–Vyvyan group. In one of three Tory huddles on 21 March (the others involved Peel's mainstream and Wetherell's following), they decided to oppose on second reading. But specifically, Vyvyan would do what he and Knatchbull had been suggesting to Peel without effect for some time – make a specific Tory commitment to moderate reform.

Before the House got down to a second reading, it engaged in an extraordinary spat about the conduct of that dangerous and inflammatory publication, *The Times*. Sir Robert Inglis rose to complain, in his lugubrious way, of a breach of privilege and to demand prosecution for criminal libel. The paper 'had attacked the Members of the House, depreciating them in the opinions of the people, and holding up large bodies of them, for the part they had played in the deliberation upon Reform as totally unworthy of occupying the seats to which they had been elected'.[75] He compared such heckling in print to the experience of the French National Assembly intimidated by a menacing claque, 'the *poissardes* [fishwives] in the gallery'. Members would betray their duty to the people, 'if they would betray their duty to themselves and to the whole Constitution, if as Representatives of the people, they suffered any member to be outraged in such a way – if they suffered Members to be insulted in the way in which they had been insulted'.[76]

Beginning to read from the paper, Inglis, not a deft speaker, started at 'The unanimous enthusiasm of the people of England in defence of the national rights and liberties [cries of 'hear, hear, hear' and, at length, loud and reiterated cheers]' but after an interminable denial of his intention to suppress free speech, the Member for Oxford University got back to *The Times* text, which continued in the same high melodramatic vein, proclaiming

'war against some public enemy. That enemy is now the usurer of the Peoples' franchises – the cut-purse of the peoples' money – the robber of the public treasury under the forms of law – of law enacted by the plunderer himself to favour his own extortion – his own systematic conversion of the fruits of other men's industry to selfish or criminal uses.' [hear hear] Sir R. Inglis turning round to Mr O'Connell, said that there was one lawyer and but one lawyer in that House, who cheered and that lawyer was the hon. Member for Waterford.[77]

Inglis then moved on to read his favourite bit: 'night after night, borough nominees rise to infest the proceedings of the House of Commons with arguments to justify their own intrusions into it', before adding, 'It is beyond question a piece of the broadest and coolest effrontery in the world for these hired lacquies of public delinquents to stand up as advocates of the disgraceful service they have embarked in.' It was all, said Sir Robert, 'a false and scandalous libel on this House, tending to deter Members from the discharge of their duty and calculated to alienate them from the respect and confidence of their fellow-subjects'.[78]

The Pickwick Papers was only five years away and the argument between *The Times* and Sir Robert is terribly reminiscent of the response to an editorial in the *Eatanswill Independent* (Buff) from Mr Pott, editor of the *Eatanswill Gazette* (Blue): 'Our worthless contemporary, the Gazette' – 'that disgraceful and dastardly journal, the Independent' – 'That false and scurrilous print, the Independent' – 'That vile and slanderous calumniator, the Gazette'.[79] There would be more of this – much more – Hunt giving general offence by saying that it was all true anyway, and a shouting match starting up between Sir Francis Burdett, the old if variable liberal sitting for Westminster, 'a degree of hypocrisy which made him sick at discussing it . . . the baseness, illegality and wickedness of the traffic'[80] and the uninventable Sir Charles Wetherell. 'Yes, he asserted without fear of contradiction that the dictatorship of the hon. Baronet, the Member for Westminster and man of the people – the tyranny transferred from the hustings to the Floor of the House . . . he had never seen equalled.'[81]

Mr Pickwick's advice during a small riot at Eatanswill had been, 'Do what the mob do.' And to Mr Snodgrass's query, 'What if there are two mobs?' he had recommended, 'Shout with the largest.' In the House of Commons in March 1831, the largest mob was the government. Accordingly, after twenty-seven further columns of small print including counter-charges of deliberate delay, culminating in Peel dissociating himself from Inglis, the man who had roused the reverend voters of Oxford University to turn him out, and a short, sensible comment from the Attorney-General about the inconvenience of going into such things and the interminable time it would take, the matter was dropped and the second reading finally begun.

A measure of the exhaustion induced by three weeks of crisis and seven days of debate is that, though Inglis's press complaint takes up thirty columns of *Hansard*, the second reading of the Reform Bill itself occupies only 173. Sir Richard Vyvyan moved rejection, making clear his own intention to move 'a resolution which will give an assurance to the country that this House is determined to increase its Representation [sic]'. Like King Lear, he did not have the details, but he acknowledged 'the great interests which have sprung up in large towns, celebrated for their manufactures, celebrated for their population' and stressing that 'I was never of opinion that such large towns should be without Representatives'.[82] It was the thinking of 1830 when reform by modest readjustment had been much contemplated – disfranchisement of the scandalous boroughs and a proper welcoming for Leeds and Birmingham – the option which Wellington had peremptorily scotched. It was the day before yesterday's advanced thinking, yesterday's moderation, today's impossible nostalgia.

Richard Sheil, O'Connell's lieutenant, who, a Catholic Irishman, sat for an English rotten borough, Milborne Port, and would be an elder friend to young Disraeli, quoted Byron and Latin, but showed a touch of his own brilliance. Speaking of borough ownership, he invoked an old Turkish custom: 'A Sultana on her marriage usually had one province awarded to her for her necklace, another for her bracelets and a third for her girdle. Under the system of parliamentary proprietorship, it would be no matter of surprise to see a lady of fashion receiving Old Sarum for pin money and Gatton for her dower.'[83]

But Sheil had an English point to make in Irish terms. Ireland at this time threatened to overflow into general violence. What had been true about emancipation was true now about parliamentary Reform. 'If Ireland were now in a state of evil susceptibility, the House should recollect that it was their own doing. These were the results of years of agitation, produced by the madness of delay. Let them beware how they put Ireland through a similar process of excitement.' What Sheil asked of the anti-reformers he put in a single sentence: 'He said concede; and, that they might concede in safety, concede in time.'[84] The pressure for concession was, of course, being invoked on both sides of the debate as either threat to be resisted in the approved manly way or irresistible force not wisely to be denied. Charles Grant for the government gently chided the opposition for not being proper anti-reformers after all: 'The opposition to the principle of the measure has been pretty well abandoned. Scarcely one Gentleman who has spoken seems prepared to take his stand on the principle of Anti-Reform.'[85] And as he sweetly pointed out when Peel himself regretted that Russell had not brought in a measure he could support, he thereby 'admitted the necessity of Reform'. And Grant had fun with the gap between empurpled Tory rhetoric and their ladylike aversion to anything so definite as a division. Hadn't they talked about 'a new constitution' and a 'measure tending to overthrow the Monarch' – 'when I heard these expressions applied to the measure by hon. Gentlemen opposite I did expect they would have barred the door against the measure. – But no, they allowed it to enter.'[86]

Grant was doing two things. By teasing Peel for his circumspection he was provoking rage against the baronet from his own right wing and proclaiming the degree of public support for Reform so as to engender defeatism opposite. 'The measure has been received by one universal shout of acclamation through the whole country.' The country wanted the Bill, the Tories were scared of stopping it. A footballing version of Grant's speech might have been 'You're not singing any more.' He was far too graceful and well judged to offer triumphalism in any but a pastel shade. But he was standing on its head the recurring Tory theme, just voiced again by Inglis, of the menace to a sovereign parliament of an uppity multitude. The Tories really should not persist in Peel's mistake of talking about public excitement 'being of a transitory character'. And, deftly, he advanced 'Now Sir I think even a transient excitement ought not to be entirely disregarded; but I think the excitement on this subject is not transient nor local, but partakes more of the character of a general and settled sentiment.'[87]

Grant was making a thoroughly persuasive speech, in effect inviting the Tories to acknowledge not only that the game was up, but that retreat would be the safest, most sensible thing to do. Now was the time for concession and conciliation. Rejection would alienate the people still further from Parliament. They had the examples of Europe (events in France, Belgium and Portugal): 'Do they not call upon us to ask ourselves if this is the time when we should disregard the complaints of our own people and exasperate them by disappointment?'[88]

His soft-spoken balance of reasonableness and warning was probably increased in force when followed by a piece of bloodshot passion-tattering from William, the second of the two Bankeses and Member for Marlborough. There were the usual seventeenth-century comparisons, in this case with Charles I, not exactly Grey's role model. He confronted the eloquent Stanley with the Caroline nobility, also dangerous experimenters. Did Stanley believe 'that my Lord Essex and Lord Northumberland and Lord Warwick, he who stopped at last to carry the sword of state before an usurper, when they in their day talked of their reforms, ever dreamed that the blood of the head of the Church, the blood, the innocent and heroic blood of the rt. Hon. gentleman's ancestor, the Earl of Derby, would have reddened the scaffold and stained the annals of the country?'

This was the age of the bad historical novel, but Bankes pushed ambitiously back into time.

If indeed I were living three generations before the Flood, somewhere about the time of King Nimrod . . . I might then call about me a little knot of fellow workmen . . . and run up a snug little constitution for our compact society. But happily now we are not reduced to be theorists and inventors – we have before us the examples of ages to select from and to imitate. And shall we not select that which all times have conspired to praise, and all nations to copy? Shall not the British Constitution, this very parliament, which has been styled the noblest assembly of freemen in the world, be our model?[89]

Serious Conservatives like Peel, or indeed Vyvyan, were fettered by this sort of braying affirmation that the British constitution was best, so there! The contrast with an accredited extremist on the other side showed Henry Hunt hot tempered and provocative, but full of brutal evidence from street conflict, jail and the workplace. He might embarrass reformers, but by plainness not floridity.

Lawyers at this time supplied a good part of the most immobile and unreflective conservatism. Edward Sugden representing Weymouth, so long a four-seat borough, talked when speaking of the constitution of 'that perfection which existed now'. Sugden, who as Lord St Leonards, would become an undistinguished Lord Chancellor having already been an outstandingly poor law reporter, performed a small circle to reject Grant's view of public opinion: 'he would take it on himself to say that the people did not want the Reform which had been forced on the House. The Ministers were forcing this Reform on the Country and the people did not want it [*Cries of "oh, oh"*]'.[90] The former Solicitor-General invoked the example of France: 'and see what had been the termination of the popular struggle there? It had ended in the annihilation of royalty – it had over-turned some of the best institutions in the country.'[91] As for the middle and lower classes, Sugden 'would advocate their rights with as much zeal as any man. But he would not sacrifice the people of England to their own passions nor give up to their prejudices their own real interests.'[92] He concluded the first day in mild riot by accusing the government of doing a deal with O'Connell over additional seats for Ireland at the expense of England, something which Stanley rose to deny.

The last day of Commons debate on the original Bill came festooned with petitions – from Bognor, St Sepulchre's in the City and twenty-four other places as variable as Stockport, Glastonbury, South Shields, Dunfermline and Henley-on-Thames, and a handful, five in all, against. After some skirmishing on these, the House also learned that an Irish Reform Bill had been prepared and would shortly be presented, the occa-sion for O'Connell to make retaliatory swipes at Sugden and start an inter-esting fight with Wetherell, one which they had the good taste to keep wholly personal. O'Connell to Wetherell was 'a man who had dealt in spoliations and made them beneficial to himself by handing a begging box around among his friends . . . taking two pence from the poor man, a penny from the ragged man and a halfpenny from the starving man'. Meanwhile, in the view of O'Connell, Wetherell was a member 'remarkable for his extraordinary gesticulation – for a jumble of unmeaning words, enforced by violent thumps on the box on the table as if the rumbling noise from that empty box could supply the place of common sense'.[93] It was Peel who, with a nice dryness, got the reading resumed by suggesting that they 'proceed to the discussion of the important question fixed for that evening with as slight a degree of excitement as was consistent with the nature of the question'.[94]

Viscount Mahon of doomed Wootton Bassett, and a dedicated opponent, sounded a note of lamentation. It was all the fault of ministers: 'Who was it who had made the people clamorous for Reform? The King's Ministers. Who was it that by their agitation and complaints and their promises and their representations, had brought the House to that melancholy condition, that it could neither pause with safety nor proceed without ruin?'[95] Members, he added, were not sent there 'to gratify the populace at the expense of the people . . . If unhappily, they should act otherwise and the wishes of the government prevailed, then he would say he neither envied them their triumph nor the means by which that triumph was won.'[96] Sir John Shelley of Gatton, a heroically rotten borough, 'looked upon the bill as fallacious and revolutionary' and if it passed, 'the two other branches of the Legislature would lose their influence in the State; and the Members returned to this House would completely govern the country'.[97]

As rational argument, the debate was out on its feet; as excitement, it was doing pretty well. Greville, who had written that 'tirade against reform', now said urbanely, ahead of the second reading, that he expected the Bill to pass and that 'all things considered, it would be the best thing that could happen; it is better to capitulate than be taken by storm'. That was a wise view of the long term, a recognition that a tide was flowing best not resisted, a variant of what Grant had said. Greville put it with his special gift of concision: 'The people are unanimous, good humoured and determined; if the Bill is thrown out, their good humour will disappear, the country will be a scene of violence and uproar, and a most ferocious parliament will be returned, which will not only carry the question of Reform, but possibly do so in a very different form.' Greville's judgement had a conclusive ring: 'Reform the people will have, and no human power, moral or physical, can now arrest its career.'[98]

But William-Ormsby Gore (Carnarvon) had no time for urbanity. Invoking Bacon, Blackstone, a statute of Henry VI, Lord Burleigh and the eternal Edmund Burke, he spoke of 'the spirit of innovation stalking abroad through the whole of the continent of Europe'; and had not Burke warned that the government in evolutionary France 'had shown a greater disposition to attend to the suggestions of the people than at any former period of her history. It was the listening to projectors which had caused the ruin of that country. He would now conclude with a quotation from Lord Bacon . . .'[99] Speaking soon afterwards, Thomas Wyse of Tipperary anticipated the famous Shakespearean quip of Iain Macleod against Aneurin Bevan by 122 years. Ormsby Gore 'like his fellow countryman Glendower, had called up spirits from the vasty deep, but did they come when they were called?'[100] A whiff of radical brimstone expressed with blessed brevity came from Captain Frederick Polhill (Bedford), one of the left-wing military men about in politics at this time, who, in five lines, said that he would vote for the Bill, though it did not go far enough and he would have preferred a franchise of £5 to one of £10.

William Ward, a London member, confessed that a majority of his constituents disagreed with him – he had presented their petition for Reform – and argued in a style anticipating the New Labour government when charged with accepting donations for services. The present system was transparent. 'The accounts of the country were open to the people; in fact there was a balance sheet and every one could know how the last sum had been disposed of . . . what more a Reformed House would effect he did not know.'[101] Thomas Wyse, the Irish member who had ribbed William Ormsby Gore, made one of the interesting speeches of the debate, interesting in that, from a radical point of view, it used standard Tory technique, the appeal to history, before challenging them on the historical roots of revolution.

'Hon. Gentlemen seemed panic struck at the revolution or rather revolutions of France; but there was no analogy between that country and England. The elements of the French Revolution did not exist among us – our nobles lived with the people, half their year was spent in the country – they were the chiefs of the nation, not the servants of a court.' This is the cricketing squire metaphor, squire bowling to blacksmith, which would endear itself to Conservative social thinking for a century.

Wyse's dangerous Irish sense of humour would have less conventional appeal. 'William 3rd pursued another policy: he saw that men had changed – he changed the constitution imperceptibly with them. The reign of influence began, the Treasury was substituted for the Tower, men were not imprisoned but bribed. Under the first two Georges this revolution, soporific and stealing, but not less sure, reached its climax . . . This influence first in the hands of the Crown, soon fell into the hands of the oligarchy.'[102]

But Wyse's chief message to the anti-reformers was that they should learn from events in France instead of moaning about them. The terror in France in the 1790s was not brought about because the National Convention had been summoned, 'it was refusal, until refusal was no longer possible, vacillation in the king – treachery in the court, blindness in the clergy – and stupidity, arrogance and ignorance combined in the privileged orders'. Wyse invoked 'the fatal Congress of Vienna of 1815 [which] had bequeathed us the revolution of 1830. It tried to square mind and men like provinces and to set down the nineteenth century like the sixteenth.'[103] It was one more history lesson in a series but history as positivism and a relief from a great yardage celebrating accomplished perfection.

Lord Castlereagh, heir to the Marquess of Londonderry and representing what was then termed 'Londonderryshire', spoke the now standard Tory language. Some reform was necessary but not this reform bill. There was a touch of St Augustine about the argument. Castlereagh asked for 'a fair moderate reform – one adapted to the exigencies of the case, one restorative of the Constitution – but not, I repeat, such a sweeping, unconstitutional and destructive scheme as that proposed by His Majesty's Ministers'.[104] Frederick Shaw of Dublin, dripping cliché, 'was ready to vote for a moderate plan of Reform, but members should not therefore approve of a Bill which was neither more nor less than an axe laid at the root of the British constitution – a Bill which had been rightly described as 'a flagrant violation of the chartered liberties of British freemen'.[105]

Denman, the Attorney-General, and one of the most intelligent men in politics, sent all of this crisply up:

> It had been conceded on the other side last night, he believed for the first time, that some degree of Reform was necessary. No hint of the kind had been given during the former debate of seven nights duration; but now forsooth, the Bill before the House was to be brought into disrepute because hon. members had their measures of Reform, a secret to all but themselves, and even to themselves till within the last twenty four hours, Reform more moderate, more prudent and discreet, and by which the interests of all would be duly guarded.[106]

Sir James Scarlett, also an eminent lawyer, spoke for twenty close-set columns of ten-point print. He started by insisting 'I am most anxious that it should be fully understood that long before and ever since I have been a member of this House, I have been a friend to Reform',[107] getting to Edward I's acceptance of parliamentary consent to taxes on the fifth of them and to his chief horror, disfranchisement of boroughs in the present

Bill, in the eleventh. 'But what does this Bill do by way of disfranchise-ment? Why it disfranchises by one blow sixty boroughs entirely and muti-lates forty-seven others by taking one member from each. I own that the violence of the measure appals me.'[108] The practice of publishing debates 'which he was far from disapproving, nevertheless renders individual Members more sensitive to public opinion' and they should 'beware of adopting an important change in your constitution upon the mere ground of public opinion which upon a measure so recently propounded must be immature and undigested'. They should also beware of 'adopting upon the rashness of public opinion and untried theory in place of that insti-tution which, bottomed in long usage, and gradually improved to suit new exigencies, has produced in practice the most splendid and beneficial results'.[109] *Hansard* observed with a straight face that 'On the hon. and learned gentleman resuming his seat, the calls for "Question", "Divide" and "Adjourn" were loud and conflicting.' The next speaker, Sir Thomas Acland, a tentative government supporter, promised that he would not speak for more than five minutes and, at two columns, did his best. Sir James Scarlett may have spoken for all bores of all ages.

John Russell rose to end what he had begun, knowing that the vote would be settled either way in single figures. He kept to the core issue, seats bought and sold. And he 'put the same question to all who affecting to approve of reform, opposed the Bill, "Is it fit that the direct nomina-tion of Members by individuals and the sale of seats for money, should continue to be part of the constitution of the House?"'[110] This was the fighting ground of the campaign, the thing which no talk of anomaly, balancing Calne against Tamworth or vague generalities about modera-tion, could contest. The talk had been about a final account, but if moder-ation meant keeping, as Vyvyan had suggested, some nomination boroughs, there would be no finality. Russell applied himself to the theory and prac-tice of the great and perfect constitution. 'What did our ancestors do in 1688? First they declared that elections ought to be free and uninfluenced.' And, faced with an attempt by the Lord Warden of the Cinque Ports to nominate members, they brought in the Nomination Act, which said 'be it further enacted that all such nominations were contrary to the laws and constitution of this realm and are so to be construed and hereby declared null and void, any pretence to the contrary notwithstanding'.[111]

In Russell's view, very much a reform Whig view, the evil had set in after the accession of George II, the doing, though he did not spell this out, of those very different Whigs, Walpole, Pelham and the Duke of Newcastle. And he concluded on a note of healthy defiance. Beside all this talk of how they ought to have been moderate and have brought in a less offensive bill, there was a counter-option often charged against reformers 'of being too willing to act like their predecessors, of falling into their system as soon as they had got into place, and of forgetting all the pledges and promises they had given when they were out of office'.[112] Sounding a little exhilarated, the Paymaster acknowledged that he had been afraid that his beliefs out of office might come to seem unwise to him once he held responsibility. However, 'Now that he was in place, and called to take part in the Administration – when he and his friends were in power, and had responsibility, it gave him satisfaction to think that they had not hesitated to go the full extent of their opinions when out of power; that they had not hesitated to risk that power, to risk their fame . . . to improve largely, liberally, generously, and he hoped successfully, the Constitution of Great Britain.'[113]

It was a springtide speech made in a belief that his party's forty years of viewing all government painfully in the abstract was now being transformed into something substantial. Russell had been one of the voices for a bold measure. He had seen the anti-reformers go from expectation of anodyne tinkering to black, dismayed shock at the actual measure to cocksure certainty of successful rejection to final day-by-day recognition that reform was certain, combined with a moaning wish that strong had been weak. 'Exhilarating' was the word.

The irony was that such confidence did not turn upon assurance of actually winning the vote which would now take place, though the balance of the whips' thinking was for a single figure majority. If the Bill failed in the Commons, quite possibly King William might refuse a dissolution. But ministers, certainly not Russell, did not behave as if he would. The arguments increasingly weighing in the Commons, of Reform or worse, also weighed with the old electorate. If there were a dissolution they would win the election. If there were not, vast risks would be taken, risks which the sharper Tories as well as the King must see. Wellington would tell Greville the next day, 24 March, that 'a small majority for the Bill was on the whole the best thing that could have occurred, and that seems to be the opinion generally of its opponents'.[114] The under-truth of the last few days had been that the Tories knew that rejection would be explosive in the country. And ministers knew that they knew.

The vote was a dramatic occasion. Debate in a House where closure was unknown had run until 'exactly three minutes to three'[115] in Hobhouse's minute recollection. The vote would be on Vyvyan's amendment, 'That the Bill be read a second time this day six months.' Holmes, as Chief Whip for the Tories, and Joseph Hume, unofficial counter for the coalition of reformers, compared their arithemetic and 'brought them almost to an equality'.[116] It was also clear that participation in the vote would be massive, 'the fullest House that was ever known'.[117] Following an older practice, only the supporters of a motion, in this case the Tories, actually filed into a lobby, the opponents, here the reformers, remained seated to be counted.

Macaulay famously compared the event with Caesar's assassination or Cromwell sending away the bauble of a mace. It was 'a sight to be seen only once and never to be forgotten'. He also caught in that letter individual sketchings, J.C. Herries, one of the Ultras, 'looked like Judas taking off his necktie for the last operation'.

Uncertainty continued during a long vote. Greville quotes the government as thinking they had lost by ten and the opposition 'sure they were winning'. And in the way of the post-Regency the reform of Parliament was thought a suitable subject for a bet. On top of everything, the Ayes seem to have miscounted at one stage and given themselves 303 votes. In fact, they had 301 to the government's 302, an important difference. It was not without significance that, although the Bill carried among members for what was then very rarely called the United Kingdom, in England the vote went by 241 to 238 against Reform. Scottish members also rejected the Bill – by twenty-six to thirteen. But in Ireland the vote went much more decisively the other way, fifty-three for, thirty-six against. Tory opinion would be found fifty-five years later in the time of Gladstone's Home Rule legislation, at once resisting all notions of Irish autonomy and treating the Irish representatives in the Union Parliament as somehow not quite counting. But O'Connell's men were always going to vote for a change to the system which replaced nomination by election. They had, even without their old forty shilling franchise, more voters.

The absences were few, twenty-seven in all plus eight pairings, one of them Sir Edward Knatchbull, who was taken ill during the second reading. But the vote turned upon a very few late shifts. That of John Calcraft has been mentioned; owner of a Schedule A borough (Wareham) which must go, Whig turned Tory serving under Wellington, now very late turned Whig again in his vote. Calcraft had spoken against the Bill then voted for it. He would be elected before the Bill finally passed, for his local county of Dorset. Such mobility was less frowned upon when the notion of the independent member was prized, at least in theory, over the caucus. But as noted, it was mocked enough to turn Calcraft, clearly not in his perfect mind, to suicide in September of the same year.

Quite as eclectic, but much more robust, was Charles Wynn. He had resigned as Secretary at War early in the government's life and on 4 March spoken against the Bill. But now he voted for it. On the strength of his own claims, Wynn was thinking like a moderate Tory, roughly what he was when standing still. Moderate Tories wanted moderate reform. They also wanted not to have an election which they would lose, thus letting in immoderate reform. Wynn was a tactically minded version of Vyvyan.

Not that it mattered. His belief in 'a reaction against the bill setting in and thus wanting dissolution postponed for six weeks or two months'[118] was founded in fallacy. A reaction against the Bill was *not* setting in. Neither people nor populace, to follow Scarlett's interesting distinction, were going to change in wanting it very much and saying so. For the government any majority at all would mean that it talked to King William with quiet authority. It would mean that a subsidiary Commons reversal, equivalent to the one on timber duties, would be a mere hindrance to a government proceeding with major business, would mean something to entirely validate dissolution. The people had been sent a message. So had King William.

FIVE

Gascoyne's Motion, Dissolution and Election

'I am always at Single Anchor'

Charles Greville, like a sensible man, kicked his heels of 'the cursed bill' after second reading[1] and went off to Newmarket where, after a confusion among the judges, the horse he had backed and which came fourth was declared the winner, making him £900.*

But for those who insist upon being wholly serious, the politics of the interim turned a little upon retrospection and much upon the theory and practice of the committee stage shortly coming up. They were affected also by the general ill-speaking of Peel among Tories. Mrs Arbuthnot confided that 'Our difficulties in opposing reform are, however all aggravated by Peel's character. If the Conservative Party felt they could rely on him, they wd fight the battle; but they cannot. They all know he will yield some points on reform & the consequence is they all have their own crotchets, all want to gain popularity with their constituents by advocating at once that which from Peel's nature, they feel will be yielded sooner or later.'[2] Greville, who would on private acquaintance become an admirer of the man, confirmed her: 'I never heard anything like the complaints against Peel – of his coldness, incommunicativeness, and deficiency in all the qualities requisite for a leader . . . There is nobody else, or he would be deserted for any man who had talents enough to take a prominent part, so much does he disgust his adherents.'[3]

Peel, an intelligent, problem-solving man who responded to evidence, was leading a party, much of which shared the stubborn imperceptions of his old chief at the Home Office a decade earlier. Viscount Sidmouth had fallen into conversation with a Bond Street bookseller (also acquainted with Hobhouse, to whom he passed on the story). Sidmouth wanted to find out 'the feelings of those in his class of life, and his Lordship would not believe that the majority of them were not against the measure'.[4] The

---

* In contemporary sterling about £45,000.

bookseller, one Andrews, explained to Hobhouse that virtually everyone he knew in the trade supported Reform.

Mrs Arbuthnot talked of the opposition being 'at sixes and sevens'. For much of the time this had been true of the government, but at that moment they knew very well what they wanted. They should be ready for dissolution. They would very probably be defeated later in the Lords; before that they would likely suffer intolerable dilution in committee. So practical business, like the military estimates, was got quickly out of the way. At the same time, it made sense to wage psychological war over the King's intentions. Crassly, two royal household officials, also Members of Parliament, had voted against the Bill. Grey, not naturally a vindictive man, could see the point of tactical intolerance. At his request, the King dismissed both officials. The message was very clear: a King so responsive to his first minister would not break reform by refusing a dissolution. Thomas Creevey, ever the genial partisan Whig, was delighted: 'Horace Seymour and Captn. Meynell are dismissed from the King's household, their offence having been voting against the King's Reform Bill. They were both of them Lord Hertford's members. This is something like!'[5] Hertford, model for Thackeray's villainous Lord Steyn, was the patron of Croker at Aldborough in Suffolk, as of Seymour at Bodmin and Henry Meynell at Lisburne. The King's authority was now exercised against court officials beholden to a noble patron of boroughs. It was indeed something like.

The Tories were quarrelling amongst themselves, still very much divided into Peel's mainstream and the two variants of Ultra – soft (Vyvyan) and hard (Wetherell). And Peel was not the man to ask for graceful accommodation. The naively bouncing Vyvyan had made a clumsy attempt at reconciliation with Peel in a style suggesting too much a deal between equals, and withdrew frostbitten. But the Tories were not without resources. Of all the amendments which they set themselves to devising, one would have immediate impact. General Isaac Gascoyne, a Liverpool Member who had been paired on the vote, put down a motion for maintaining in any reformed Parliament the exact share of specifically English members as currently obtained. The House was set to fall from 658 members to 596, but the heaviest fall lay in England. Given the concentration of pocket boroughs in Cornwall and other parts of the West, this was inevitable, but complaining about it was excellent politics. The initiative changed the subject from defence of nomination boroughs and their patrons by means of roast beef and 1688 arguments now growing thin and risible, to 'the enemy at the gates'.

Not for the first or last time in Tory thinking, the enemy was Ireland. The discontent there was real. Even the generous Anglesey, back as Lord

Lieutenant, wanted coercive measures. The Ireland of between seven and eight million people which had gained emancipation and lost the forty shilling freehold, was swaying with violence, actual and prospective. The Tories from natural reflex blamed everything upon O'Connell. Since January, O'Connell had been facing charges brought against him by the Whig government. But all sophisticated opinion knew that O'Connell, precursor of generations of national revolt leaders, wanted the good things Ireland could get from Reform, something which made him the unacknowledged ally and prop in the lobbies of the Whigs who currently had him on charges. The agitator was extremely concerned to contain agitation. As for Reform itself, as Michael Brock writes, 'Despite his incessant complaints about the Irish Reform Bill, he wanted to see it on the statute book.'[6]

The government had to manoeuvre between a dissolution which they needed, an election which they could expect to win, Ireland so tricky and explosive that it might preclude an election and William IV, worried about Ireland, not happy about dissolution or anything else involving major risks, but readily drawn to his ministers when they were under fire. An opposition-wrecking motion which, after spirited resistance, then carried, might suit ministers rather well.

And the Tories were not the only ones amending. Ministers were sensible of the imperfections with which quick drafting and population arithmetic done on the back of an envelope had cluttered their legislation. Quite separately, there was a case for general retreat being made by weaker brethren. Palmerston, always the coolest of reformers, and one who also thought shrewdly – he had a seat to lose at Cambridge University – was for withdrawal on a broad front, reversing all or most of the curtailments in Schedule B. Neither that nor talk of a flexible franchise, a sort of variable geometry design for constituencies, got very far. In for a pound, the government saw no point in only staying there for what reformers and the public would see as small change. They settled instead for careful reconsideration of the less hopeless Schedule B seats, ones which might be expanded by taking in a larger parish. But they combined this with giving a welcome to a clutch of additional northern industrial towns. Ironically, the enfranchisement of individual towns and the general ground plan of Reform itself turned upon shifts and growth in population. And one of the late additions would be the capital of coarse cotton spinning, Oldham, which would soon be represented by the most eloquent radical of them all, William Cobbett. In 1833 Cobbett MP would speak with high plangency, during debate on Ashley's Factories Bill, of the labours of 'thirty thousand little girls in Lancashire'.

On 18 April Russell announced the amendments. Something of the sort would have happened anyway, but these had the effect of pre-empting Gascoyne's motion by increasing English representation. There would now be, he announced, thirty-one additional seats above those in the original bill and, of these, twenty-nine would be English. Certain boroughs in Schedule A would, with some boundary stretching, be removed to the haven of Schedule B. Buckingham, Malmesbury, Okehampton and, with some reluctance, Reigate, would receive this treatment. The two doomed Yorkshire boroughs of Aldborough (Yorkshire) and Boroughbridge would be brought together as one Schedule B, single-member constituency, promising news for the Vesuvian Charles Wetherell, currently one of two Members for Boroughbridge.

The anomaly of Calne, one of whose seats was held by the luminous Mr Macaulay, was recognised, not by treating it as roughly as similar boroughs falling on the other side of the line, but by rescuing *them* from Schedule B, from single to double membership. Rescue and promotion were to be the principle mechanisms of amendment. Leominster, Morpeth, Northallerton, Peel's own Tamworth, Truro, Westbury and Chipping Wycombe were to be taken out of Schedule B and restored to double representation. More satisfactory from a reforming point of view was that batch of new single member constituencies. As Russell put it, they 'proposed a counterbalance to the pure principle of population to give Representatives to large towns possessed of manufacturing capital and skill, such as Bury in Lancashire, Oldham and Rochdale'.[7] To the three great towns of the Spinning Crescent, he would add a member for 'that part of Staffordshire known by the name of the Potteries and situated at Stoke-upon-Trent'. Whitby would also achieve a seat, as would Halifax, Salford and Wakefield, the latter cheerfully acknowledged to have been left out by mistake! There would also be some upward adjustment in county membership. A new population norm was set here, one of 100,000. This would justify the addition of members, something now proposed for Berkshire, Buckinghamshire, Cambridgeshire, Dorset, Hertfordshire, Herefordshire, Oxfordshire and Glamorgan. With five additional members going to Scotland and Ireland both, Russell had improved Parliament to the tune of thirty-one members. There would now be 627 MPs, only thirty-one down on the present gathering.

If Russell had any hopes that sensible amendment would assuage the Tories, he was soon very much better informed. This was indeed a wrecking amendment. What Gascoyne wanted was postponement; and almost drowned out by heckling, 'he saw no reason why he should not at once submit his motion'. It did not take the snappish Gascoyne or the ranks

behind him much effort to find a patriotic tune to sing. For the propor-
tionate increase in Irish representation had been very sourly received by
the side which had lost the second reading by a single vote, when amongst
Irish the Bill had a majority of eighteen. Gascoyne was concerned with
'the spoliation of the English Representation'.[8] Like all men who dislike
other nations, he denied hostility to the Scots and Irish. But they didn't pay
enough tax to warrant their representation, and Irish representation was a
'dangerous influence'. Ministers, by 'conciliating it, might carry any measure
they pleased, no matter how it might affect the interests of the people of
England'.[9] To reverse Sir Thomas Beecham's dictum about the English
people and music, Tories at that time might think they liked the Union,
but they didn't like the noise it made.

It was, as Hobhouse noted, a 'violent and foolish' speech.[10] And the one
which followed from the Tory, Michael Sadler,* at thirty-seven columns
and nearly three hours, outran Scarlett and verged on the interminable as
he told the House that 'The people of England like not sweeping nor
dangerous experiments; their sober judgment is in favour of their ancient
and happy institutions . . .'[11] But the debate had its high points: 'A tall
ungainly young man with a strong squint in one eye, spoke with great
fluency and precision during nearly an hour, gaining much upon his audience, until the House became quite silent.'[12] This was John Hawkins,
member for St Michael's, itself a nomination borough, and Hawkins saluted
its inclusion in Schedule A. But he was about to deliver arguably the finest
speech – finer than Macaulay because free of his Ciceronian self-regard
– of all the Reform debates. Not to quote it at length is to miss not only
handsome cadences but, ahead of their time, essential arguments. Hawkins
held up to the light a particular rhetorical fork of anti-reform, identifying

> 'that class of antagonists . . . who always entertain a sincere conviction
> at any given moment that the present is not the right moment for the
> discussion of this question, and they arrive at such conviction by this
> ingenious dilemma. When the people are clamorous for Reform, they
> tell us that we ought not to concede such a measure to the demands of
> popular turbulence; and when the people are silent, that silence is proof
> of indifference and therefore the measure need not be passed.[13]

And Hawkins almost alone shook off the petticoats of historical prece-

---

* An Ultra, he certainly was, but Sadler combined constitutional immobilism with
passionate devotion to the child victims of industrialisation and was a heroic figure
with another Tory, the Dorset by-election winner, Ashley, in the movement for
factory acts.

dence, asking as he did so if the Revolution of 1688, 'the Sion of our political wandering',[14] was not a precedent against precedent, a changing of something because it had to be changed. 'We seek not this reform as a matter of abstract right, but of practical expediency.' It was 'not enough to tell us that our borough system is what it was 200 years ago. It is not enough to tell us that a system of tyrannical compulsion and corrupt influence which was in harmony with the violence and fraud of the political warfare of those days . . . suited alike to the selfishness of their political vices and the sternness of their political virtues . . . is not grown worse.'[15] Hawkins was that remarkable thing for his age, especially in England, a believer in a historical dynamic. We were better because more socially evolved than our ancestors. Now that 'the Sunday pamphlet has suspended the bludgeon of the mob, the newspaper taken over from the axe', it was 'too much to demand of us the continuance of those means of government whose worst corruption was unnoticed amidst the greater hideousness of the ends to which they were rendered subservient'.

Robert Southey, laureate, inferior poet and dedicated Tory publicist, had invoked on that side the spirit of St (then Sir) Thomas More. Young Mr Hawkins impudently wondered whether if More were 'to rise from his grave for the purpose of instructing a Poet Laureate in Political Economy, he might well ask us what do we gain by our superior knowledge and accumulated experience, when a few sounding phrases and a few hard names are sufficient to deter us from putting to practical use the results of that experience and the deductions of that knowledge.'[16] Faced with the short and repeated catalogue of great names which had been endlessly cited to show the beneficence of the nomination borough, Hawkins was unfazed. 'Hon. Members opposite string up their dozen or so of choice pippins in a golden row to win our admiration; but we have not been called upon to notice the bushel of crabs which have sprung from the same stock.'[17]

He objected to hereditary trespass in the Commons through peerage nominations and focused all attention on the word 'representation'. The best of the nominees might be splendid legislators, 'representative they were not'. So what was the point of being surprised if an underrepresented public periodically erupted? It was political immobilism which had levered up the public mood. This, he said, was why 'the press admonishes us by threats instead of advice; that the manufacturing artizan [sic] enrols his name in affiliated societies instead of subscribing it to petitions'.[18] However much the Tories 'might persist with a politic affectation of fear' it was due to their own long-dragging resistance 'that revolution had been called for when Reform was wanted'.[19]

It was a wonderfully eloquent speech, arguing that it was 'to the obstinate continuance of this antiquated corruption that we owe those periodical outbreaks of popular discontent which since the first French revolution' had kept people 'in a state of wonder at the continued existence of a Constitution which only throws off its peccant humours by this system of chronic convulsions'.[20] The Tories were really arguing, he said, from the point of catastrophe. Both sides to the debate agreed the old system was in tatters, 'but whenever we begin to thread the darning needle they say "Leave it alone in the name of prudence – in the name of Robespierre and Danton – it is so rotten that if you attempt to put a stitch in, the whole will fall to pieces"'.

Unlike many of the more tepid Whigs who still made much of the impregnable autonomy of the Commons, Hawkins crunched candidly on the phrase 'public opinion'. And whilst the word 'democrat' was handled by Russell and Grey, as much as Peel and Wetherell, with fire tongs – and denial – Hawkins was an avowed democrat. We came, he said, 'in the last resort to public opinion as the tortoise which is to carry the elephant . . . it is that popular opinion which is our best staff of support, though we will continue to insult it by clinging to a broken reed'.[21] Hawkins reminded the House of the instinct which at the Bourbon court had told the Estates General to wait at St Cloud, driving them to the tennis court and its oath and all that followed. The risk of going the Bourbon way was inherent in the rejection of reform. He identified a cast of mind which acknowledged 'the occasional personal, and constant moral corruption inflicted by our present nomination system' before arguing that 'it is the only way forsooth of keeping things quiet; the only way of saving the Monarchy, the Peerage and the Church'.[22] Hawkins in his own words then argued what first Gladstone then Churchill would express as 'Trust the people'. They were enjoying a summer interlude but were threatened with a harder season: 'I wish to exchange that suspicious safety for the holiday security of a people's love.'[23]

Argument did not continue at that level. Sir John Malcolm was terse in the way of an Englishman lately returned from India. He 'would not occupy the House by discussing the details of the Bill. He was opposed to the whole measure by which an example would be given for taking away the charters of Englishmen.' How otherwise than by the nomination of a friendly borough owner could someone like himself, long abroad, enter Parliament? He was, he knew, going against his constituents 'and he felt that in doing so, he was acting with the boldness and independence in which he had prided himself throughout his life'.[24]

Sir Robert Wilson of Southwark made a squirming speech. Not the first anti-reformist to insist on his devotion to Reform, he spoke chiefly of his own suffering: it was painful to him, he felt himself in a position of extreme difficulty. 'He had been sent into that House as a Reformer and he would not appear to his constituents as an enemy to Reform, by withholding his support from the Reform proposed by a government with which he was associated on the general principles of their administration, and on the general question of Reform.'[25] Nor was he 'the sort of Reformer who could change his opinions on Reform every week'.[26] Then again, 'he could not let mere personal considerations stand in the way of his zeal for the interests of his country in whose service he had spent the best years of his life, and in which he had shed his blood'.[27] 'He was not the one that could play the part of vacillation as it might meet the purpose of the passing moment; far less could he permit himself to be influenced by the most base and sordid motives.'[28] The admiration of Mrs Harris for Sarah Gamp as reported by Mrs Gamp could not have exceeded Sir Robert's discreet apologia for Sir Robert. John Hobhouse was there, noting 'the most disgraceful exposure that ever closed a life of pretended patriotism. It was a speech full of mischief and malice and at the end of all his vituperation he declared he should not vote at all.'[29] As Edward Stanley, coming next, laughingly put it, 'he had listened to the speech of the hon. and gallant member for Southwark with no ordinary amazement'.[30]

The debate returned to its natural territory, ill will over Ireland, with the intervention of John North (Drogheda), who said that not one voice was raised in Ireland for Reform, then corrected himself and indicated Daniel O'Connell: 'One voice, that of the hon. and learned member for Waterford, was raised in favour of Reform as a means of promoting the dissolution of the Union.' And with a reformed Parliament, 'a measure for the Repeal of the Union would not be impracticable'.[31] North raged against the level franchise throughout the kingdom; it reminded him of an ocean-going ship moving on a Dutch canal level and, more to the point, it enfranchised the £10 Irish renters, thus letting the Catholic Irish into far too much influence in preponderantly Catholic Ireland. 'This bill would throw all the inhabitants of the towns into the hands of the agitators of Ireland.' He, North, would support Gascoyne's motion because he was 'anxious to preserve unimpaired the English Representation as necessary to support and maintain the Protestant interest in Ireland for which he was anxious and which it was the duty of that House to support'.[32]

O'Connell, keeping up the pleasant mood, called North 'the Chief calumniator of Ireland at present', but otherwise stuck to the point that, on a town and population count, Ireland was getting less than its rights. There were fourteen towns in Ireland which, had they been in England, would have had representation. Both O'Connell and Hunt, who followed him, were in effect replying to the steady use by Tory members of their names as horrid warnings to the public. Hunt defended the government from charges of being, as it were, secret colluders with Henry Hunt. The government had declared the Bill to be final and if he or people outside petitioned for more 'the government would say "No, this is not fair, the bargain was that you should be satisfied with the measure we gave you and you shall have no more"'.

His speech highlighted a division among reformers and radicals. Hunt was one of those who regarded the Bill as a step before other steps and accordingly supported it as combined increment and stimulus. He was unhappy with the present Bill. 'In his opinion the only efficient Reform was Universal Suffrage and Vote by Ballot. That was the species of Reform which he looked upon as an unmixed good.' Much patronised by a consensus, amused and fearful at such excess, Hunt only finished with difficulty amid much shouting, but he managed cheerfully to snub the government. Gascoyne's amendment 'had appeared to him so preposterous that he did not intend to have voted at all upon it'. But he had heard that the government considered it a matter of great importance; 'and he resolved to give it his humble support, as he would, were it simply for the disfranchisement of one rotten borough'.[33]

By way of Peel and the Attorney-General, Denman, and their interrupters, the motion drew its slow length to an end, Peel saying wearily that he 'rose only for the purpose of bringing this discussion to a conclusion for it seemed to him that the attention of the House was exhausted'.[34] And mentioning O'Connell's speech, he spoke of 'the temporary excitement of the debate'.[35] The implication of what he said next was close to a rebuke to Gascoyne. Why was it necessary that 'Question of Reform should be mixed up with that of the relative proportions of the number of Members?'. However much he blamed the Whigs, that was exactly the purpose of Gascoyne and North. But a good deal of Peel's time passed in self-defence, and, wryly, he remarked that in speaking for the record, 'his mind vacillated between the vanity of having his words quoted and fear of being taunted with what he had spoken'.[36] He fretted about London with its enlarged and 'unfortunate' representation. The capital would now have 'no less than sixteen members'. They 'who would be always on the spot, who could always consult their constituents and support themselves by their opinions, would exercise in the House a power which no other Members in it could possess'.[37] It would be Tory tactics to enlarge on this in committee and attack the new metropolitan boroughs.

And joining a common Tory refrain, Peel disliked a uniform franchise. 'All aristocratic influence was to be destroyed while all democratic influence was to be carefully retained.'[38] He was troubled at the way things were developing in Manchester. The wrong sort of voter was getting on the register. 'The number of dwelling houses in Manchester rated between £10 and £20 was 1,770 while those rated above £20 amounted only to 851.' The property of the first group was assessed at £22,130, that of those in houses paying £20 and above was £29,300 . . . So 'the representation of Manchester would be placed entirely in the hands of the 1,770 £10 householders owning only three-eighths of the property of the 851 house-holders above £20. He did not say respectable voters would not be found, but he did say that superior intelligence and superior property would be overborne.'[39] Having been anxious about Manchester, Peel next grieved that London might suffer 'that species of influence which was so unjustly and perniciously exercised in Paris'.[40]

Peel, worrying that the assemblies of the Crown and Anchor and other dangerously democratic assemblies might turn into Hanriot's revolutionary guard in revolutionary Paris, was talking panic. When he fussed about the removal of the small boroughs, as something which would destroy the aris-tocratic influence, it is hard to warm to either speech or man, but we are in another age and have to remind ourselves of its assumptions and of the fears settled into conscious minds by Paris in the 1790s. Even so, this nagging little speech shows very little sign of Peel's undoubted grandeur. It was Conservative in all the wrong ways, timid, plaintive and facing foursquare in lament towards the comfortable past.

The amendment itself was anyway so drastic that the government could not have contemplated assimilating it, and Althorp, as Commons leader, said plainly that any decision would be final as it affected the Bill. The Ministry was on dissolution grounds and knew it. This debate, watched throughout by the Duke of Cumberland, Reform's most ferocious enemy, was less taut and exciting than the last day of second reading.

The House was by now irritable and possibly, at 3.30 a.m., the worse for drink. Denham for the government was nearly pre-emptively shouted down by late-night Tory noise. According to *Hansard*, 'The Attorney General rose amid cries of "Question" which, for a long time, rendered him totally inaudible.'[41] After inviting Gascoyne to show how he would make up the missing number of English seats – perhaps by dividing his own Liverpool into slices and declaring them constituencies – Denman's central point concerned the crisis which was being deliberately induced. 'It was doubtless the plain, but important statement of an undeniable truth, that if the Reform proposed by Ministers were rejected, the greatest difficulty in governing would result.' Very probably the division about to be called 'would be decisive for the fate of the Bill and of Reform'.

When Denman allowed himself a partisan query about actual Tory opinion of Reform itself rather than the narrow motion, the shouting, sober or otherwise, resumed and Russell had to intervene to demand a hearing. Denman mocked the opposition with the only clear Tory position made on the subject, that of the Duke of Wellington in November of the previous year. The Duke, like President Coolidge's preacher confronting sin, had been against it. In which case, if the opposition were about to bring down the government, what would they actually do about Reform?

What, for that matter, would they do about the Duke, now silent but a lowering presence in politics? And here Denman, speaking of a Tory administration without the Duke, used a figure of speech – 'It would be something like the play of Hamlet with the part of Hamlet left out' – which may have been the fresh minting of a brilliant simile or the old cliché already, in 1831, jumping through its hoop. As for the grief which Peel had evinced at the injury done to the moneyed interest – 'absurdly argued' thought Denman – he coolly reflected that 'money had both the means and the instinct of taking pretty good care of itself'.[42] Denman, far beyond the anaemic norm of law officers, was a good partisan, and he spoke up on behalf of the government: 'They executed boldly what they had conceived honestly.'[43]

But debate still dragged on into the morning following its second day and the result, announced in sudden calm and silence at 4.30 a.m., was a not unexpected defeat for the government of eight (299–291). The Tories, caught between not wanting an election and not wanting to let the Reform Bill pass, had finally chosen a way to jump. The government view came best from the phlegmatic Graham: 'Well never mind; then we must have it the other way; the process will be longer, that's all.'[44]

Only one thing stood in the way of a request to the King for dissolution – Ireland. For parallel with the progress of the Bill had run the matter of Daniel O'Connell, facing judgement for sedition in an Ireland ready to turn even more violent and create John Bull's other constitutional crisis. Back in January of 1831, O'Connell had written a letter calling for a run on the banks.* Anglesey, as Viceroy, felt his authority entirely undermined. A genial eccentric who thought he understood the Irish, he had taken the affront literally and personally. O'Connell had become for his adversary, 'the Arch-Fiend', the very same title which Creevey had jokingly settled upon Brougham!

---

* As the Reform struggle intensified, Francis Place, most law abiding of reformers, would do the same thing. (See Chapter 12.)

The authority of viceroys frequently survived tolerably without foundations, but Anglesey had persuaded himself that in the sophisticated Catholic Bishop of Kildare and Leighlin, James Warren Doyle, he had found an enemy of O'Connell whose authority would counterbalance the Liberator. 'This Prelate in his heart hates him.'[45] Thus deluded, Anglesey, the Irish Attorney-General and Stanley, Chief Secretary, had proceeded to 'firm measures'. At the end of January, under an Act fondly designated as serving 'for the Suppression of Dangerous Associations and Assemblies in Ireland', O'Connell had been arrested, charged and bailed. Anglesey congratulated himself that, with the middle classes and the Bishop all on the side of Dublin Castle, he could get O'Connell sent away for a year, while Stanley talked idiotically about the possibility of his being transported: 'and if he were, I really hope Ireland would be tranquil'.[46] It was not a clever way of handling the most popular man in Ireland who happened also to be its most astute trial lawyer and on excellent terms with the Chief Justice (Kendal Bushe) actually trying the case!

By deft delay, O'Connell put off proceedings until the government found itself anxious for the services of an arch-fiend. Conclusions were now due to be reached in horrid kilter with Gascoyne's motion. The notion of the January rhetoric of Viceregal Lodge becoming the sentence of a court in April was pure catastrophe theory. Like all sensible governments since, Grey's Ministry was concerned not to let the resolute approach actually get anywhere. They had arrested and charged him in January. They had needed his votes and voice in the Commons in March and April; they needed now not to be sending the leader of the Irish majority to prison, needed not to be firing on Irish crowds protesting at his sentence. They were on a hook and needed to get off it. Across the earlier part of April the talk had all been of delay; and, with desperate timing, on 20 April after Gascoyne's motion had passed at 4.30 that same morning, the Crown itself, the prosecution, went to court and had the business postponed until May.

That done, lawyers serving the Crown, otherwise the Grey government, would produce the blissful detail that prosecution of O'Connell could only be made under a statute which had just expired. O'Connell and ministers understood one another perfectly and, as we have seen, the votes of Irish members associated with him saw the Reform Bill through at second reading. Tory charges of ministerial collusion were entirely correct. The good sense of the colluders had narrowly rescued a government from the consequences of its right hand in Westminster not knowing what its left hand was doing in Dublin. Although Ireland would be some way short of peaceful, the greatest voice in the country was now raised for restraint and it would be possible to tell King William with a straight face that conditions were safe for holding a general election. Ironically, the upshot of all this would not be the domination of O'Connell and the advance of his professed cause, abolition of the Act of Union. Ireland would vote for Reform, for O'Connell's people and for the Whigs with whom they could at last do some business. And in the distracting process, the Union issue would also be postponed.

Back on the floor of the Commons, Hobhouse observed 'the greatest consternation in the enemy which by degrees was inflamed into rage'. A motion mischievously made by a government supporter, John Bennett, drawing attention to widespread corruption in Liverpool, Gascoyne's constituency, did its bit for parliamentary tempers and turned quickly into all-in irregular argument about the principle of Reform. In the middle of all this, Vyvyan tried to get the government to come clean about its intentions. On resumption he asked Althorp if he meant to abandon the Reform Bill and dissolve parliament. He answered 'Yes to the first question and as to the second, his duty commanded him to decline to give any answer.'[47] That made the prospect of dissolution clear and produced among the opposition a sort of dull fury. With no particular plausibility, a number of Tories, led by Vyvyan, protested that they had voted for Gascoyne's amendment not to kill the whole Bill, but to make the legislation fairer and more moderate. And Peel himself was drawn into the ring: 'He inferred from the silence of the noble Lord opposite (Althorp) that it was the intention of the government to risk that experiment which he thought at the present time was fraught with danger and might end in general tumult.' He ended a general complaint that dissolution wasn't necessary, and much harking back to reform resolutions of twenty and thirty years before, by saying that he 'admitted the necessity of Reform; but he again denied that it was an immediate necessity'.[48]

There was a desperation about his words. Having been the prisoner of Wellington's pronouncement against all reform, he now joined the rest of his party in bombarding government legislation with limiting adjectives or phrases, notably 'moderate' and 'not yet', and had added his own anxious talk about 'threats to public tranquillity', a charge almost that politics was becoming too exciting. A party leader who might have put up a set of reasoned amendments to embarrass the government with a credible alternative grew plaintive at the prospect of an election. Yet the same leader could have pulled his party back from precipitating it.

Comfortable with the way things were going, Stanley for the government observed that 'The dissolution had not yet taken place – it had not been announced – and the lips of the King's advisers were necessarily sealed.'[49] Dissolution was coming and there was nothing the Tories could do except complain, moralise and invoke history. As Greville put it, 'On Thursday Ministers were again beat in the H. of Commons on a question of adjournment, and on Friday morning they got the King to go down and prorogue Parliament in person the same day.'[50] 'This coup d'état was so sudden that nobody was aware of it until two or three hours of the time.'[51]

Defeat on the adjournment had the effect of denying supply and was bad tactics since a government without supply has a better case for dissolution even than one denied a major piece of legislation. But tactics was not a strength of Peel's opposition. Croker, who understood this, berated Gascoyne for having pushed on to his adjournment division, which, by denying the government the means of passing the vote on the ordnance, validated dissolution. However, Greville was wrong about foreknowledge. The Tories had known enough about dissolution to have spent most of the Wednesday saying that it wouldn't be fair; and the government moved quite as quickly as it did because it had been warned over 21/22 April that the opposition were looking for legal precedents to cite in stopping a prorogation. Any coup was directed towards frustrating a counter-coup. As it was, the Tories now retreated into the old Southern states tactic in defence of the indefensible – filibuster – attempting to make time through Commons speeches in which a motion might be carried in the Lords, praying the King not to dissolve. Meanwhile, the government took their chances on immediate business like the martial law, still reckoned necessary in Ireland despite O'Connell's helpfulness. It would have to be covered by indemnity in another parliament, one now almost certain, after such Tory blundering, to be more compliant.

William IV was generally regarded by his ministers as a great relief after the plaintive aesthete who had reigned as George IV. Nothing like as clever and, so far, nothing like as much trouble, the King could still dither and William was married, however incidentally, to the very fraught and authoritarian Adelaide. A memorandum justifying dissolution was next submitted to the King by Grey after Cabinet. After asking for a day's delay, William came back with a long-winded paper saying that he was not fully convinced, that there were weighty arguments against dissolving, not least the trouble in Ireland, but that in the absence of a credible alternative and in the interests of continuity, he would reluctantly comply. On top of which he would much prefer it if the new Bill were more moderate than the old one! As J.R.M. Butler puts it, 'The Bill's fate hung for twenty-four hours on the decision of a man whose natural common sense was warped by an ignorant and irrational fear of the working classes.'[52]

It might not be the warmest of approvals – William had lectured Grey with a passage from Bolingbroke's *Patriot King*, the text book supposed to have given George III ideas beyond his competence – but approval it was. The story quickly circulated and the Tories began to make all the trouble they reasonably could. Lord Wharncliffe, who would prove the most adroit of opposition figures, had a motion up in the Lords beseeching the King not to prorogue. The objective was to carry it before the King's commissioners could be admitted with the authority for dissolution. A split between Lords and Commons would have bitterly intensified the crisis and Brougham thought that, if such a motion carried, it might turn William back from his promise. Ministers flung an emergency meeting together on the morning of 22 April. Brougham asked the Duke of Richmond 'if he had ever seen a council of war held on the field just before going into action. He said "By God! Never."'[53] It was agreed that Prime Minister and Lord Chancellor should at once wait upon the King, asking him to forgo the delay of a commission and to come in person to prorogue Parliament.

The Tories had misunderstood William's nature. He disliked dissolution, but he disliked the hint of intimidation more. 'I took care,' said Brougham, 'to make him understand the threatened proceedings of the Lords, and the effect the proposed motion for an address was intended to have on his Majesty's proroguing Parliament. He fired up at this – hating dissolution perhaps as much as ever but hating far more the interference with or attempt to delay, the exercise of the prerogative; and so he at once agreed to go.'[54] The sluggard of the day before turned to breakneck alacrity. As Brougham tells it – and Brougham was never above giving verisimilitude to an otherwise bald and unconvincing narrative – the King required troops to accompany him to the Houses of Parliament. The Life Guards were an unhandy distance off. Brougham says that he had foreseen this and had taken it upon himself to order up the Horse Guards available at Knightsbridge barracks to accompany the King at one-thirty. He apologised profusely for this helpful presumption. William accepted the apology, observing that it was 'a strong measure' and later Brougham would more than once be ribbed for his 'treason'.

Another report has William shrugging off the need for the right kind of horses, cream-coloured ones, their manes to be painstakingly combed and plaited, and declared his readiness to go to Parliament in a hackney carriage. Allegedly, the Sailor King responded to Grey's apologies for his urgency in sailor's terms: 'Never mind that. I am always at single anchor.'[55] The Comptroller of the Household, Thomas Mash, was at once sent off in a carriage to the Tower to collect the crown and other regalia. Meanwhile, back at Parliament, the Tories, with fire in their nostrils, were trying to delay in one House and move frantically in the other. 'In the H. of Commons Sir R. Vyvyan made a furious speech, attacking the Government on every point, and excited (as he was), it was very well done.'[56] It was on every account a furious occasion, both Houses and their lobbies sparking with political animation, a mass tableau in need of its W.P. Frith. The Speaker, Manners-Sutton, had a furious set-to with Alfred Tennyson's uncle for challenging his judgement in declaring Vyvyan in order, then calling Peel next and getting into another dispute with the calm Althorp, who moved that Sir Francis Burdett, on his feet at the same time, should have been called.

As for Peel, in Greville's judgement, he 'made a very violent speech' treating ministers 'with the utmost asperity and contempt'.[57] Violent it was. He had been received, according to *Hansard* 'with loud shouts, groans, laughter and cries of "bar" from the ministerial benches'. If the Bill were carried 'they would introduce the very worst and vilest species of despotism – the despotism of demagogues. They would introduce the despotism of Journalism – that despotism which had brought neighbouring countries, once happy and flourishing to the very brink of ruin and despair.'[58] As for dissolution obtained from the King, 'If the Crown was to be so easily extinguished – it ceased to be an object of interest to enter into its service. He perceived indeed that the power of the Crown had already ceased.'[59] Hobhouse, not an unbiased witness, described 'a harangue of sound and fury, signifying nothing but his own despair and hatred of those who had overreached him . . . I who was opposite to him on the second bench behind ministers, was so much moved by his violence that I waved my hand and shook my head, as if to show him in no unfriendly manner that he was doing harm to himself . . .'[60]

One can see how soothing *that* experience would have been. But the speech reads dreadfully, an irrational rant seeming at that last point to become a tantrum directed at the King personally, not sensible in the leader of the Tory Party. And humiliatingly, Peel was still shouting when, in mid-sentence, Black Rod entered to summon the Commons to the Upper House: '[The right hon. baronet was here interrupted by loud and vehement cries of "bar!" He continued standing and speaking when The Usher of the Black Rod appeared at the bar of the house and said "I am commanded by His Majesty to command the immediate attendance of this Hon. House in the House of Lords . . ."]'[61]

The Lords had, if anything, been worse conducted, 'as much like the preparatory days of a revolution as can well be imagined'.[62] The Duke of Richmond was trying to slow down the drive to a vote on Wharncliffe's motion with a series of points of order of an excruciatingly heraldic/bureaucratic nature, about their Lordships arranging themselves according to rank, something made impossible by the removal for the occasion of the cross benches. Lord Londonderry jumped up, waving his whip (these were equestrian times), and 'four or five Lords held him down by the tail of his coat to prevent his flying on somebody'.[63] Even the urbane and cynical Lyndhurst shook his fist at Richmond, accusing him piquantly of 'disorderly conduct' and re-igniting Londonderry who 'screamed', as Brougham tells it, that, 'by a wretched shift', Richmond was obstructing Wharncliffe, as indeed he was.

Brougham had hurried over from his logistics meeting with the King and was briefed by Durham as to exactly what was going on and why. As presiding officer of the House of Lords he took over the Woolsack; as chief law officer he at once stood up to denounce the unconstitutional nature of Wharncliffe's address; and as party politician he started on his own bit of time wasting. As all this was happening, cannon could be heard at the Tower announcing the approach of the King. But the Tory peers were too keen to speak and not well enough organised to get through the disruptive vote they sought. Back in the Commons, Hardinge, Peel's friend and closest personal aide, normally a good-natured man, approached Hobhouse across the floor and said 'The next time you hear those guns they will be shotted, and will take off some of your heads.'[64]

When a message took Brougham out of the Lords' Chamber to receive the King, confusion took over. *Hansard*, less vivid than Henry Brougham, is lively enough: 'The Earl of Shaftesbury resumed the Woolsack amidst cries of "order, order!" "chair, chair!" "Order of the Day, Order of the Day!" "Shame, shame, shame!" "The King, the King!" It is impossible to describe the confusion, the noise, and impetuosity that prevailed from one end of the House to the other. The Peeresses present seemed alarmed. Some of the Peers were, as it appeared in the confusion, almost scuffling, and as if shaking their hands at each other in anger.'[65] A House not perhaps at its best, but certainly at its most interesting.

Wharncliffe, with good sense, had presented his motion in just over half a column before Brougham's arrival. But Mansfield, who had emerged from the cries of 'order, order' to declare that 'he never in the whole course of his life, had witnessed such a scene, and he trusted he never should see the like again',[66] was still denouncing government's conduct almost two columns later, in a speech which Greville thought 'prodigiously effective', as the King arrived, entered the Chamber and approached the throne. It was effective only in filling space for the government. Mansfield first proclaimed his certainty that an attack would immediately afterwards be made upon the credit of the country – upon the National Debt – upon the privileges and upon the existence of that House, 'adding that if in his warmth he had expressed anything that was personally offensive to any individual, he disclaimed . . . .'.[67]

Whatever it was he disclaimed was never identified: '[Here cries of "The King, – the King," were heard, and a loud voice sounding out – "God save the King." At that instant, the large doors were thrown open on the right hand side of the throne, and his Majesty, accompanied by his attendants, entered the House.]'[68]

William, having gone to robe in the Painted Chamber, with an unexpected touch of theatre went against practice and put the crown on to his head with his own hands, turning to his Prime Minister to say 'Now my Lord, the coronation is over.'[69] George Villiers, a friend of Greville, told him that 'as he looked at the King upon the throne with the crown loose upon his head, and the tall grim figure of Lord Grey close beside him with the sword of state in his hand, it was as if the King had got his Executioner by his side and the whole picture was strikingly typical of his and our future destinies'. The remark is worth quoting as one more instance of the enjoyable and hysterical self-pity into which Tories saner than young Perceval readily fell. When the Commons had been summoned and the Speaker had appeared 'accompanied by about 100 Members who rushed in very tumultuously', after Brougham had paid grateful and sardonic respects, and assent had been given to a clutch of bills (including one for the Civil List!), William began a speech, itself short and direct, by saying everything which needed to be said: 'My Lords and Gentlemen, I have come to meet you for the purpose of proroguing this parliament, with a view to its immediate dissolution.'[70] Parliament was dissolved to await the election which of all things the anti-reformers had not wanted.

The immediate public response out of doors to these events was, in a rough London tradition, geniality and menace in tandem. Illuminations were called for by way of celebration by the reforming Lord Mayor, Key. This, as Greville drily put it, 'produced an uproar and the breaking of obnoxious windows'.[71] Apsley House, home of Wellington, was approached and a gun with powder but no ball was fired from it at the crowd. Peel's house was also threatened, as were the St James's Street clubs. Later on, in May, Queen Adelaide returning from a concert, found her carriage surrounded by a crowd which her footmen beat back.

But such excursions did not alter the fact that the most important election of the century was still conducted under the rules which Wellington approved when he spoke of allowing no reform whatever. Patrons might still nominate candidates for what were still thought secure seats. Celebrating voters were still in the market for food, drink and hard cash though a sign of the democratic times may have shown at Sandwich, where the freemen voters insisted upon treating the candidates![72] What was different was the war of expectations.

Boroughmongers were still to be found trading avidly in nomination boroughs, but they were acting defensively, like men selling stock in a company likely to be investigated anyway. Lord Yarborough would sell his seats in the Isle of Wight to the government for a sum quoted between £4,000 and £20,000 for them to fill with men to vote for the disfranchisement of such seats. The notorious freemen of Sudbury, living up to its fictional future as Eatanswill, put up their prices.[73] The old order might be selling out to the new, but it was getting a good price. The new order might speak of purity but, with the old rules still standing, it gaily played by them.

Tories would also notice the grateful elevation of the King's eldest illegitimate son (by the actress Dora Jordan) to an earldom. But William, unlike his official consort Adelaide, was furiously popular, his name taken cheerfully in vain by the less buttoned-up Reform candidates, not least in a dreadful pun about a 'vote for the two Bills'.[74] He might not be a natural reformer, but the Reform side was happy to take the Court card from the Tory sleeve. And William had done not only himself but the monarchy (about which Croker wrote pieces suffused with its certain doom) no end of good. Steady decency and the fingertips of an honest, unsubtle man had brought an institution bruised by the insanity of George III and despised for the Queen Caroline affair into a phase of broad if temporary affection.

The rage of Peel had been directed at his precipitation into an election universally expected to strengthen the reformers. They were perceived as the winning side. Greville, back at Newmarket on 7 May, three weeks after prorogation, would report bad news: 'Nothing could go worse than the elections – Reformers returned everywhere, so much so that the contest is over, and we have only to wait to see what the H. of Lords will do. In the H. of C. the Bill is already carried.' Money was moving on both sides. The great landowners did their duty against Reform, notably the Duke of Northumberland, reckoned to have promised £100,000. Ellenborough, close in Tory business councils, quoted funds coming in – from the Duke of Buccleuch 'who has given £10,000 and promises if it should be necessary, £10,000 more. Ld Powis gives £2,000 and promises £4,000 should it be required.'[75]

Such funds were intended largely for doing business as usual, including remuneration and entertainment of freemen and potwallopers in constituencies on the schedules. Ellenborough also reported that 'The close boroughs rebel & Saltash, Hindon, Ilchster [Ilchester] &c require members who will not disfranchise.'[76] It was a straw at which to clutch. Such boroughs did exist but they were not a force sufficient to offset the popular current elsewhere. The response of some patrons was to bow to the spirit of the age by espousing Reform candidates. The spirit of fighting to the death, which Croker (intelligently) and Wetherell (buffoonishly) embodied, was rarely echoed by men with something to lose. Defiant and ideological patrons like the Dukes of Newcastle and Northumberland and Lord Lonsdale simply saw their candidates defeated where any sort of electorate existed, witness Newark, Carlisle, Stamford and the county of Northumberland.[77]

Another report tells Lord Ellenborough that Knatchbull, whose squire's authority in Kent had been oak-like, 'is not successful with his canvass'.[78] Even though Sir Edward was by this time talking Reform, two radicals, Hodges and Rider, would be elected for that county. There was bad news, subsequently confirmed, in Oxfordshire and Norwich, 'despite all our flattering expectations',[79] and hopes raised in Ipswich would be disappointed.

Success was forthcoming for the Tories only where they might expect it. Boroughbridge (two seats for the moment) returned Wetherell with Attwood's Tory brother, Matthias, Cambridge University ejected Palmerston, and Tiverton's voters rebelled against the patron whose own vote for Reform had threatened their expectations. But what was that to set against the early and highly symbolic rejection by the Liverpool which he had represented for thirty-five years and to whose anti-Catholic prejudices he had ardently deferred, of General Gascoyne himself? Ministers discreet beyond necessity had been keen that Gascoyne's seat should not be contested, but local reformers ignored the fearful discretion. Elections at that time took place over weeks and followed varying timetables. And in the absence of the ballot, results emerged in a species of slow motion as voters trooped up to make their declarations. It was often not necessary to poll for the full time allotted. Losing candidates, here often former sitting members, feeling the heat of their local kitchen, got out of it. After a mere ten hours at the hustings, Gascoyne withdrew.[80] Indeed, support for his amendment would lose members their seats as assuredly as a 'no' vote on second reading.

In the opinion of Reform's outstanding modern historian, Michael Brock, that first week in May told the extent of the Reform tide with London which quickly returned a ticket of reformers, giving the lead. By 11 May, Greville recorded bleakly, 'The elections are going on universally in favour of Reform; the great interests in the counties are everywhere broken, and old connexion dispersed.'[81] This was to be a central factor in the result. The English counties sent eighty-two men to Parliament, and county elections, whatever the sleepiness or deference of some of them, were not at a patron's clear disposal. In May 1831 they would be represented by seventy-six reformers. The reforming aristocrats, so far from following the Girondins to the scaffold (Croker's obsessive prophecy), rolled over the non-reforming aristocracy. In Worcestershire, a reforming Spencer had defeated a Tory Lygon, 'backed by all the wealth of his family'; while 'the Manners [the Ducal family of Rutland] have withdrawn from Leicestershire and Cambridgeshire and Lord E. Somerset from Gloucestershire . . . Everywhere the tide is irresistible.'[82] Hobhouse was understandably cheerful. After early monster meetings and celebratory dinners in Westminster, he would write, 'Everything going well. Indeed except Bucks and Shropshire, we have been defeated nowhere . . . Scotland and Ireland are doing well, but not so well as merry old England!'[83] A footnote to his observation of Peel in the Commons had been the attribution to him in a newspaper of two statements which brought Peel and the Whig diarist to the serious prospect of what the age called 'satisfaction', something messy and operatic, from which their prospective seconds extracted them.

What mattered was that even though the patron system and the complex of local practice and franchise variations which made up the American quilt of the old system still functioned, actual political opinion was coming through, and it was an opinion settled for the Bill. Frequently it carried against the resident patron. One source instances Reform victories in Dover, and 'that sink of corruption, Maidstone'; in Bury St Edmunds, unused to any contest; Cricklade, against strong Tory Church influence; Durham, where the whip-brandishing Lord Londonderry had a powerful interest; Huntingdonshire, where one of those 'supporters of Reform', sprouting on the Tory benches late in debate, was rejected after refusing commitment to the Bill; as well as in Westmorland, where Lord Lonsdale was denied in one of his seats. As for the newly enfranchised towns, in one of them, Oldham, on the list of late additions, there would be two radical MPs, the manufacturer, John Fielden, and the friend without whom he would not stand, a sixty-nine-year-old journalist soon to be prosecuted again for 'exciting the population to disturbance and discontent', William Cobbett.[84]

Scotland was significantly more corrupt than England and its working-class population correspondingly more angry. Sir Walter Scott recorded with approval the return of his kinsman at Jedburgh: 'Upwards of forty freeholders voted for Henry Scott and only fourteen [for] the puppy that opposed him.'[85] Sir Walter also took pleasure at the survival of the old ways in Selkirk whose voters 'had got a new light and saw in the proposed Reform Bill nothing but a mode of disenfranchising their ancient Burgh!'.[86] But he had passed a very rough day in Jedburgh. The populace gathered in formidable numbers, including a thousand from Hawick. 'They were most blackguard like and abusive; the day passed with much clamour and no mischief . . . I left the Burgh in the midst of Abuse and the gentle hint of "Burke Sir Walter". Much obliged to the bra lads of Jeddart.'[87]

Scotland, massively corrupt and near dictatorial in its concentrations of power, came close to explosion at several points. Glasgow staged a march 50,000 strong for Reform. Troops were begged for in Dumfries 'in consequence of the very great excitement among the middle and lower classes composing the boroughs of the county',[88] terminology which would have amused an earlier local notable, Robert Burns. Edinburgh's thirty-three co-opted town councillors did their duty against Reform. Francis Jeffrey, light with Sydney Smith of the reforming *Edinburgh Review* and now Lord Advocate, was run for the seat, but the councillors elected a member of the Dundas family, an event followed by a night-long riot. But Scotland still emerged with reformers and anti-reformers evenly balanced, a marked shift from the former House.

One entry by Greville is profoundly significant. Three days after he had spoken of the tide being everywhere irresistible, he reported that, with a prospective reform majority of 140, 'the Tories meditate resistance in the H. of L. which it is to be hoped will be fruitless', adding that it was 'probable that the Peers will trot round as they did about the great Cath[olic] qu[estion] when it comes to the point'.[89] The Lords didn't trot round, but Greville, who had written that 'tirade' against reform, was convinced of the destructive futility of further resistance and wanted to make the best of what could not be stopped. Greville's conservatism was of the pessimistic, not the fanatic sort, and he now saw more to worry about in the last ditch than in accommodation. He also speaks of the elections going 'languidly on' and remarked that 'contrary to the prognostications of the Tories, they have gone off very quietly even in Ireland, not many contests, the anti-Reformers being unable to make any fight at all; except in Shropshire they are dead-beat everywhere'.[90]

So they were. Figures are less precise than under a system of sharply defined parties, but a majority for Reform of 130–140 is not disputed. Croker, writing in the *Quarterly Review*, conceded that 'a House of Commons has been elected, in which of the 658 members, about 380 are said to be in favour of the Reform Bill, 250 against it and the rest have not declared themselves'.[91] A Reform Bill would now be presented to a parliament which had been elected to pass it. Schedules A and B would be imposed, the

£10 franchise would be set uniformly. The King, even though he still muttered soft-Tory things about moderation, was surely not going to be an obstacle. There must be new readings, first and second, of the new Bill, and a committee stage, none of which could remotely injure legislation which must then go to the House of Lords.

Croker had a view on what their Lordships should do then, and in the summer of 1831 he expressed it. '*Numerically* then the principle of the Bill may be considered as *carried* in the House of Commons; but it is in cases of this kind that it may truly be said that the race is not always to the swift nor the battle to the strong. The *numerical* force may be counter balanced by a *moral* force.'[92] Reaching his finale, Croker avowed that 'The Minority in the Commons will do its duty', but if it failed to stop 'the fatal bill, the Lords will not be wanting in theirs. They must know that this alarming crisis was produced by the *state of parties*, and not by the merits of the measure; and they will not allow temporary differences to subvert for ever the Constitution of England.'[93]

This recalled the Portuguese Communist leader Alvaro Cunhal, who, doing badly in an election, spoke dismissively of 'bourgeois arithmetic'! Croker came from the lower end of the middle classes, was an intellectual and an Irishman, as unlike the acred and unreflective norm of an English Lord as could be. But, like those other outsiders, Burke and Disraeli, he could think for them and was captivating in what he thought. His message, after so much airy talk of riot, disorder and general catastrophe, was that a narrow hereditary group should, by defiance of Commons and electorate, risk bringing about all those things. It was a Mephistophelean proposal to a Faust unlusting and incurious, but tempted none the less.

SIX

The Second Bill

*'You are asked only to give up that which is odious,
unjust and unconstitutional'*

The nature of Tory thinking in the large crisis of Reform might be measured by the language in which Robert Peel called on his party to respond to electoral reversal. They would be resisting, he thought, a majority 'unassailable by reason',[1] and he further declared that 'nineteen-twentieths of the country was against Reform'. The remarks spoke less about Peel's own altitudinous nature than the difference between periods of history. By our reasoning, an election held under the old system, the one which the anti-reformists cherished, had opted conclusively for reform. *A fortiori* the larger definition of 'the country' to be found in the Bill must register yet wider support.

Peel was looking at the country through the same lenses as Lord Sidmouth, certain in the teeth of his own bookseller's hard evidence that people 'of his sort', tradesmen, were against the Bill. Sidmouth was seventy-four, born in the reign of George II and accredited as an impenetrable pillar of frozen reaction. Yet Peel talked exactly the same language, either excluding the voting public from his definition of 'the country' or taking a grand paternalist view of the voters as misguided people whom their proper leaders should put to rights. For Tories, the House of Lords, and behind it, the King, remained after any election. The judgement, even of an electorate slewed towards 'property and intelligence', was no more than a kind of discountable opinion poll. The spirit, not just of Croker, but of Charles X of France, still flickered in the man who one day would abolish the Corn Laws.

But Peel also reflected the wider received view that, while an election influenced the choice of men to form a ministry, it did not create a mandate. This election had indeed been held about a single question, and a very great one at that. But elections generally were not so conducted. They concerned men not measures. These events would change all that, something which not even all the Whigs fully grasped. So, for the moment, politics went slack. The Whigs hesitated to take a triumphalist view and quickly ram the Bill through a second time to face conclusions. They also knew about the House of Lords and the King. Faced with such obstacles, there was an element within the Cabinet, best represented by Palmerston, which would still have favoured wholesale concession to the people who had lost the election.

With Durham away, attending upon the mortal sickness of his adored son, the risk of retreat was real. But Grey, despite his grandeur, and the quietly dedicated Althorp were perfectly solid about doing what they had set out to do. Modest accommodations there might be to keep William happy, but the new version of the Bill would keep the substance of the old.

The House of Lords stood at the end of a long, unshaded and sticky constitutional road along which the new Bill had to be carried: Cabinet and the major readings, then votes in the Lower House, lacking, it should be remembered, any closure procedure. As for the Lords, it had changed its own nature during twenty years of government by William Pitt who had steadily packed it. Lord Grey, consulting both a copy of the *Peerage* and Jane Austen's *Persuasion*, might echo that 'pity and contempt for the endless creations of the last century' felt by Sir Walter Elliot on reading the Baronetage. Pitt's House of Lords would stop a Reform Act; that was any reformer's starting assumption. What ought to follow next would be the creation of enough peers to enact legislation which people and Commons had approved. But the past is another country, and in the land of 1831 the old constitutional assumption rested upon a king whose prerogatives were leased to ministers only by a withholdable consent and a House of Lords which, if it rarely challenged the Commons, stood back for one very good reason.

Resistance to Reform had been as bitter as it had because the Lords' influence in the Commons through seats effectively owned by peers had given the landowning aristocracy two lines of power – vicarious and first hand. A nominee of the Duke of Newcastle, elected on his nod, was the tenant of a freeholder. Whatever liberties might be allowed him on other issues, he was expected to bark when the gates were threatened. And what the hard core of Tory peers did understand was the dynamic of power. To make the Commons the chamber exclusively of freely elected popular representatives was to take out the wicketkeeper and leave only the long stop. Any defeat the House of Lords suffered would be permanent. They had power, they were going to lose power. Their rhetoric about sweeping away tripartite- and aristocratic-dominated government for that abhorrent French thing, democracy, was directed towards fears, real and convenient, about it all happening in a very short time, like the Parisian 1790s, with or without the bloodshed. Their core prophecies would indeed come true, but so bloodlessly and at a pace so modest across a hundred years as to meet anyone's requirements of moderation.

The King, mindful of just such rhetoric, had in granting dissolution talked largely of moderation, of softening the Bill now. But after any Lords rejection, William would have to be asked for the stick of constitutional dynamite to break the log jam – creation of peers. When that happened, the Tories would cry 'Revolution' and William, a conservative figure who mixed lethargy with occasional helpful lunges, would have to be kept happy. The King had to be persuaded that his ministers had not been implacable and, specifically, that they had responded to his own generalised calls for moderation. And he had very little instinct for popular opinion, middle or working class, and an intense awareness of what his companions of Court and estate thought. That he might appease *them*, his ministers would have to make at least some show of appeasing him. But opposite the King and the aristocracy lay something neither assessed nor clearly defined – 'the people'. It was a term used variously of mobs breaking 'obnoxious windows' and burning down obnoxious houses, and of the new social forces, artic-ulate, organising and agitating: banker/trader/skilled man/radical jour-nalist: Thomas Attwood/Robert Waithman/Francis Place/William Cobbett. They might be disdained and, in Cobbett's case, put on trial, but they were that other fire, between which and their blazing Lordships, Lord Grey's government stood. The next few months would see the waging with increased intensity of a class conflict which risked becoming, literally, a class war.

The Tories for their part, though formally re-united, were still torn. Lords Harrowby and Wharncliffe, who would soon be known with their following, as The Waverers, favoured some form of accommodation. They set about putting flesh on the aspirational gestures of so many late contributors to the debate who had said that they approved of reform, but of more moderate reform. Against them stood, for the moment, the giant figure of Wellington, grand but sclerotic, content to see the Bill pass the Commons, as he had told Greville, but then apparently unwilling for the House of Lords to meet it with anything but rejection. Wellington's notion of the Upper House was of the British Army square which died hard and resisted everything. Wellington resembled the description which Hazlitt gave of the like-minded Walter Scott: 'His mind receives and treasures up every thing brought to it by tradition or custom . . . The land of pure reason is to his apprehension like *Van Diemen's Land*; barren, miserable, distant, a place of exile, the dreary abode of savages, convicts and adventurers.'[2]

For Wellington one might read the Court. Notoriously, Queen Adelaide detested Reform, and Lord Holland, now keeping a diary, was told by a lady-in-waiting of 'the aversion or rather terror which pervades the female Royalties of reform'.[3] It was a time when courts were taken very seriously by cabinets. The Bedchamber Crisis of 1839 would break the other way, to Peel's chagrin, and far more seriously, when the young Victoria declined the Tory ladies proposed to her by that Tory Prime Minister. Grey saw no reason why the Queen's Chamberlain, Earl Howe, should, by voting against the Bill, intimate Court hostility to government legislation, then boast of surviving Grey himself. The affair dragged on until October when Howe was finally dismissed, possibly a rebellion by William against Adelaide. 'I suspect,' wrote Holland (13 October), 'the act of vigour in turning out Lord Howe, although appalling beforehand, gratifies and exhilarates him, when executed.'

The episode, though a wearisome pettifog, is useful in defining the narrow, socially elevated focus of politics in 1831. Grey was facing a hostile House of Lords and, beyond that, the likely necessity of demanding creations to make it less hostile. Having court officials in either House working against him put an extra clog on to a long climb. But away from such noble preoccupations, other voices, plangent and tragic ones, were heard or perhaps not heard.

It had not been the intention to give representation to Merthyr Tydfil, though its steel works had made it a major centre of population. But when the owner of the Cyfarthfa works lowered wages he unsurprisingly started a riot, which penned magistrates in the Castle Hotel. The Argyll and Sutherland Highlanders shot dead twenty people, fighting continued for five days and after subsequent trials Richard Lewis, known to Welsh history as Dic Penderyn, almost certainly no more than one of the crowd, was hanged for wounding a soldier. An appeal to Lord Melbourne, even when made in person by an ironmaster, had naturally been turned down. Parliamentary representation was, however, created for Merthyr and promptly taken up by J.J. Guest, himself an ironmaster.[4]

Now the political unions, for which Attwood's in Birmingham had set the pattern, began to make themselves felt. Attwood, who had earlier coined the phrase 'the whole bill and nothing but the bill', had his own contacts with ministers. Desiring correct and peaceful practice in everything, he nevertheless understood the power of numbers.

He would apply that check to the limited weakening of the Bill which Grey and Althorp had agreed. The new draft would not divide counties and there would be at that stage no single-member constituencies. There was also an offer, later dropped, for University-style representation of the Inns of Court. But more importantly, the first draft contained an innocuous looking clause requiring the £10 freeholder, the new man of the Reform Bill, to pay those rates not more frequently than half-yearly. That raised the threshold of the vote very seriously. Attwood, with his banker's eye for small print, knew that most modest ratepayers in Birmingham could best afford small and friendly increments. He also knew that not more than ten per cent of them met the new clause's terms. He quickly made this point in a letter to Grey who undertook by return of post to delete the clause. Lord Ellenborough complained that Grey's response had been 'conceived in the basest spirit of concession to the Birmingham Union and the low press'.[5]

Weakening the £10 franchise was the sort of serious retreat attractive to Palmerston, whose membership of a Whiggish government was itself an accommodation. Palmerston, starting as a realistic Tory, flexible for real ends where someone like Croker was doctrinaire for the letter, readily urged dilution upon reforming colleagues still new to him. But Palmerston, though swiftly found a new constituency, was in the embarrassing position of suggesting from his personal ditch that there should be retreat down the main road. He had told Grey in a letter from Cambridge during the election that he had 'scarcely met six people who approve our Bill'.[6] In the University of Cambridge, hardly more in the popular swing than its sister at Oxford, that might well be so, and the University had duly rejected him. In London, Liverpool and the English counties, sentiment ran otherwise. Palmerston would have liked to see the franchise threshold raised. Whether the bi-annual payments were a nod in his direction or mere 'inadvertence', as Grey wrote to Attwood when accepting his complaint, they fuelled an encounter between Palmerston and Attwood, respectively temporising aristocracy and Midlands trade. Attwood won.

The divisions would show more sharply later in the year when the Lords had created the main crisis. Palmerston, together with Melbourne, would then want to deal with the option of compromise by way of serious negotiation. But the Bill which Russell (again) would present to the Commons in mid-June would leave the £10 franchise in an unamended, dangerously democratic state.

The last electoral return had been declared on 1 June. Three and a half weeks later, on 24 June, Russell returned to the Commons the second Reform Bill. Everything conspired towards tedium. Legislation certain of passing given the new majority, modified enough to dampen enthusiasm among supporters, but with its opponents as ever resentful and unappeased, the whole of it then traversing the open-ended longueurs of committee, did not make for excitement. And as argument refined itself, the argument would shift from end of the world talk to niggling practicalities. Time was going to pass during a long, dull summer, leaving in stale suspension the fervent engagement which Alexander Somerville (a private in the Scots Greys) in his barracks and Mr Greville journeying and conversing between St James's and the great Houses had both sensed. John Russell might make a fine opening speech and Croker in committee fling his febrile expertise at the small print, but the whole process of debate and legislation second time round is not one for exhaustive quotation.

First reading was almost perfunctory: a speech by Russell, the habitual historical/constitutional survey with which debaters would then wind themselves up, followed by some detail about calculation of population, on which the government in its haste had not distinguished itself during the first excursion. Peel responded by declaring himself happy to conduct debate at second reading. This stage is the occasion for at best broad principles, at worst knockabout. And, indeed, ennui was not universal. The Tory cause had not lost its disdain along with the election. Cumming-Bruce, a new member, spoke of 'His Majesty's Ministers, Whigs, Universal Suffragists, Ballotists, Revolutionists, Radicals, Infidels, Misbelievers' whose union reminded him of 'those vast and terrible pillars of sand which are sometimes seen galloping about the boundless horizon of the Arabian desert. It resembles them in the looseness and worthlessness and disconnection of the particles of which it is composed and in owing like them, the mystery of its temporary power to the state of the pestilent atmosphere and the force of the death-breathing wind.'[7] That was telling it to them.

And there would be flashes of the old animus. Sir Charles Wetherell existed for no other purpose, and he took up Attwood's discreet victory over frequency of rate payments with characteristic offensiveness: the 'class of men designated as £10 freeholders are in the habit of paying their rents weekly; not half-yearly – not quarterly, not monthly – but weekly. They are in fact for the most part, a class of men who will not be trusted by their landlords beyond a week.' Such a man was 'nothing more than a weekly tenant, solely dependent for his right of voting on the clemency of his landlord . . . Now will anyone attempt to say that it is desirable or proper to intrust [sic] this class with the elective franchise of England?'[8]

Wetherell, expressing detestation of 'any proposition founded on the sansculottizing principle of the French Revolution',[9] knew who was behind such flagrant democracy: 'I mean that body calling itself the Birmingham Political Union; – and Sir, having mentioned this body, allow me for a moment to digress while I express my sorrow and regret at seeing the Prime Minister of this country recognising that illegally constituted assembly.'[10] Having digressed, the former Attorney-General returned to his main trade of insulting people. He knew what was likely at Birmingham from his acquaintance with another city.

I know that in Bristol, of this class of the community there are many persons who are rated at the rent of £10, but who are in such a state of destitution and pauperism as to be unable to pay even the parish rates . . . I will tell the House that if this class be constituted by the Bill good voters, they will have to go back for their votes to the parish work-house; will it not be a degradation to have the would-be representative of the people obliged to canvass their constituents in a lazaretto or in Pauper establishments?'[11]

Later in the year Wetherell would go to Bristol pursuing his legal duties with consequences which would be noted.

On the other side, Macaulay had looked forward a hundred years. 'I have no doubt that those who may follow us in 1930 will be disposed to speak with as little contempt for this measure as we do now for that of the Great Charter.'[12] Macaulay made the routine point that Ultras and extreme radicals ('the friends of despotism and Jacobin agitators') needed each other for the purpose of mutual incitement and flesh-creeping. But his classic and rather comfortable Whig conclusion, that the sensible men of the middle had now taken care of all that, got him into a shouting match with the opposition back benches who took against his reasonable claim that the election demonstrated acceptance of Reform.

England has spoken, and spoken out, from every part of the kingdom where the voice of the people was allowed to be heard; it has been heard from our mightiest seaports – from our provincial capitals – from our populous counties AN HONOURABLE MEMBER. – 'No, no!'[13] MR MACAULAY. '. . . I speak from calculations made from the late returns, and I repeat that from all those places to which I have referred, a suitable answer has been given to the Royal appeal which sought the opinion of the people on this great question of reform. Sir, we are all now reformers – Several HONOURABLE MEMBERS 'No! No!'[14]

The shockingly democratic nature of the franchise, the votes falling to men who paid rent in a few weekly shillings, remained a preoccupation throughout second reading. Russell set himself to answer, reminding MPs of their previous readiness under the old system to 'go to a potwalloping borough where men of very low station in life are invested with the privilege of freemen and electors without entertaining the least apprehension'.[15] Yet faced with the new voters, they took them for a lot of Frenchmen: 'when Honourable Gentlemen talk of £10 householders, they think there is complete and total difference – they draw a comparison between them and the electors of France who in the year 1792 were invested with the elective franchise . . . And they immediately wander to the departments of the Seine and think that these £10 householders are nothing more than *sans culottes*, each with a bloody head upon his pike.'[16]

But despite such sparks and enlightenings, the second reading was not much more than an exercise in statutory grumbling, a limping jog round a required track with none of the racecourse buzz attending the contest of the first Bill. The outcome, a majority at 136, larger, said Greville, than the Tories had expected, showed 367 for the Ayes 231 for the Nays. As far as the Commons went, Macaulay had been right about the election having decided for Reform.

All this debate had been taking place in the middle of other preoccupations. In spite of having put the crown on his head while robing at the Lords, William IV was still required by convention to have a proper coronation with Handel and peers in costume. But the last coronation, that of the fussing aesthete, George IV, had taken a full day and cost £240,000. So in early July 'it was fixed for the 23rd and settled to be short and cheap'.[17] Rather more importantly, country and political class had been growing anxious about cholera, a disease about which doctors disagreed, dividing themselves into contagionists and non-contagionists. On the continent of Europe, numbers of people had ignored academic debate and died of it. Greville, who occasionally let sang-froid derange his judgement, observed that 'People are beginning to recover from their terror of the cholera, seeing that it does not come and we are now beset with alarms of a different kind, which are from Scotch merchants for their cargoes . . . The public requires that we should take care of their health, the mercantile world that we should not injure their trade.'[18] *Cholera morbus* and its attendant griefs would run its immediate course almost arm in arm with the later stages of the Reform struggle.

The date chosen to begin the sitting – 12 July – might have been a month before the glorious twelfth (of August), but it was still a hard time for an opposition of seigneurial figures and country gentlemen to endure the pains of a committee stage. The sporting country beckoned.*

No one seems to have been more vulnerable to the rural impulse than Peel. He would suffer the steady and much communicated animus of his rank and file. Not for the first time, he made off for his own country place, Drayton Manor, doing so on this occasion in mid-conflict, leaving the party he did not love to fight, fight and fight again to very little effect. During a debate on wine duties, he had left in the middle of the speech of an unvalued front bench colleague, J.C. Herries, and 'never voted, nor gave any notice of his intention not to vote'.[21] Leaderless, the opposition attendances both fell away and became dominated by the most eccentric and tiresome of the die-hards. Tory numbers on 17 July fell to 25 against the 180 maintained by government whips. Matters were left on this occasion in the hands of the extremists, Stormont, Tullamore and Brudenell (later the Lord Cardigan who charged the Russian batteries at Balaclava). Greville spoke of a 'rabble of opposition tossed about by every wind of folly and passion'.[22]

The Tories stuck to the rhetoric which had marked debates on the first Bill. In the face of so decisive an election, there was an irresistible impression of a sullen huddle prophesying doom by numbers. Meanwhile, the chief anxiety of ministers was the health of Earl Spencer. That aged peer, whose health, wrote Lord Holland, was 'very precarious indeed',[23] was to be cherished for keeping his son, Althorp, in the Commons. For it was now a general view that Althorp, despite being no virtuoso speaker, had quietly made himself a calm, competent, level-headed Leader of the House, the indispensable navigator of the Bill. Earl Spencer lived and Althorp was kept busy. Going into committee on 12 July, the House sat forty parliamentary days, concluding the stage on 7 September. It returned to the Commons and the final stage ended on 22 September, passing by a majority of 109.

The third reading was better timed for its opponents, coinciding with further and better riots in Paris which those susceptible to such things took for the start of another revolution. Very little had changed – in Paris or

---

* Later in the year, the Earl of Carnarvon would object to another piece of government legislation, The Spring-Guns Bill. A feeble enough piece of legislation in the hands of Melbourne, it forbad the setting of the spring guns which fired upon poachers in specified places without the licence of two magistrates. Carnarvon felt that 'such a regulation was likely to be productive of much inconvenience'.[19] Magistrates were concerned at Quarter Sessions with 'the claims of paupers, and he feared that the application of a farmer at such a moment, for liberty to set spring guns, might suggest to those paupers who might be in a state of excitement, the very crime which it was the object of the bill to prevent'.[20]

Westminster. There Sir James Scarlett made another interminable speech (fifteen columns) reaffirming that England, with a constitution in a state of advanced perfection, already 'enjoyed the greatest share of liberty and the largest proportion of prosperity that had ever fallen to the lot of any nation . . .' and saying of the Bill that 'instead of adding to our liberties and prosperity and glory, it would destroy all that which we already possessed'.[24]

One remark of Scarlett's was prophetic. He trusted the government to maintain the Corn Laws. These, maintaining the price of grain at a basic rate of seventy shillings per quarter measure (subject to a sliding scale introduced by Huskisson), were dearer to the country gentlemen who sat around Sir James than any constitution. And he asked, rightly, could a government continue to maintain them 'if the whole of the Members of that House were as much obliged to attend to the popular voice as the county Members? He apprehended not.' He also made the good ruralist point that a £10 qualification in a country town like Richmond in Yorkshire would indicate a much wealthier man than it would in an industrial town. When Sir James talked of the destruction of the constitution he meant the constitution which allowed producers to maintain protection. And he was right; in the hands of consumers it would in due course be destroyed.

John Hawkins was as luminous as in his first speech, but gave offence to a succession of Tories who would complain whinnyingly of his sarcasm. He raised the question which only Harrowby and Wharncliffe among Conservatives (with very little encouragement from Peel) were trying to answer. '"Some Reform" said the Member for Tamworth "must be". "Oh yes, we now see the necessity for some reform", echoed in ill-tuned chorus, his disorderly followers, "but this Reform is revolution." Well then if a Reform must be, and this Reform must not be, where was *their* Reform? . . . How could they reconcile this inaction to a sincere belief of the dangers which they foretold, he left to themselves to explain.' He concluded by raising the spectre of a Lords veto before strolling cheerfully through it. 'He was aware of no great measure of political improvement, in the acceptance of which the hereditary branch of our legislature has not shown that hesitation which in the theory of the Constitution was given out as their peculiar duty and virtue; but neither was he aware of any great measure of political improvement which they had not ultimately accepted.'[25]

Macaulay made a third contribution: 'a brilliant speech' said the committed Tory, Ellenborough; 'cut to ribands by Peel' wrote Greville, slowly becoming convinced of the need, if not to have Reform, then at least to pass it. The speech was like all Macaulay, written or proclaimed – brilliant indeed but also statuesque: 'Have they [the Peers] ever walked by those stately mansions now sinking into decay and portioned out into lodging-rooms which line the silent streets of the Faubourg St Germain? . . . Have they ever heard that from those magnificent hotels, from those ancient castles, an aristocracy as splendid as brave, as proud, as accomplished as ever Europe saw, was driven forth to exile and beggary . . .'[26] and so on. Macaulay, surely fluent in his sleep, was arguing through three lines of adjectives that the French aristocracy, unlike the British aristocracy who would know better, had 'refused all concession until the time had arrived when no concession would avail'.[27]

In saying that English Lords should make concession now and make it by accepting a good measure of parliamentary change as to a widened franchise, the ending of personal nomination to Parliament and a retail trade in constituencies, Macaulay was talking obvious sense. In claiming in a high style that the French nobility had not tried to accommodate times and people, he was getting his history wrong. And waiting to rise after him was the man who could prove it, John Wilson Croker. Croker could be obsessional, and warning of the death and destruction of civilisation was a sort of hobby with him. He denied the possibility that incremental reform might work in England as grand transformation had not in France. But he knew his history, and with deliberate politeness he instructed Macaulay. A large part of the French nobility had hurried to join the seceding *Tiers Etat* in what Croker dubiously called 'a Reform Bill calculated to increase the democratic and lower the aristocratical influence'.[28] Amid a number of other points, he ran through the *ci-devant* aristocratic enthusiasts for major constitutional change in the France of 1789. Who had offered 'the sacrifice of the privileges of the Nobility? A Montmorency! Who proposed the abolition of all feudal and seigneurial rights? A Noailles!' Both had, of course, gone to the guillotine.

The encounter would be famous as the foundation of one of the great literary academic hatreds, one traversing Croker's other and non-political work at the hands of Macaulay, the reviewer. Croker a ferocious controversialist himself, could not complain and much of the rest of the statistical elaborations in this speech showing the government's allocation of seats relative to population to be very inexact, were redundant, water perhaps cloudy, but long under the bridge. He also attempted to pray in aid the popular vote in the late election, much closer, he said, than that of the elected membership of the Commons. It was a premature call for proportional representation, not that Croker would have seen it that way. But in one shining moment, Macaulay the historian had been caught out, trapped in the toils of Macaulay, the parliamentary rhetorician.

Sir Robert Peel's early morning contribution to third reading came from the heart: 'Sir At this late hour, in this exhausted state of the House and exhausted state of the Debate . . .' He promised to dismiss the notice of every subordinate and extrinsic topic. '. . . I pass by the exciting topics of the French Revolution – I say not a word on the details of the Bill . . .'[29] This speech gives a far better sense of Peel's quality than his earlier interventions. He pointed out the contradiction between populist democracy and the classical liberal economics which by way of Huskisson, Canning and Robinson, had entered the political bloodstream.

He observed that a strong speech for Reform had been made by a member, John Williams, who had opposed Huskisson's liberalisation of the silk trade. 'Is the public outcry just at present for more free trade? Does the learned gentlemen really think that the new constituency of £10 householders is precisely the class which will insist on the free importation of foreign manufactures?'[30] And he invoked Coventry ribbon weavers and Worcester glove makers as the last people likely to welcome free trade. The irony of the landowners of all England proving, as Scarlett had prophesied in his long ramble, even more opposed than such craftsmen to Sir Robert's rational economics, remained coiled and waiting.

Peel's excellent reasoning led him into positions admirable in immediate debate, but flawed for the future. He gently chided the Whigs for stopping where they had. Denman had argued that every increase in voters increased security against corruption. That would inevitably be 'appealed to in favour of a more popular right of suffrage. What is the objection that you – the advocates of this bill – can make to the extension of it? Surely you will not say that resident householders who occupy houses below the value of £10 cannot be trusted with the elective franchise . . . your own arguments are conclusive against the stability and permanence of the arrangements you are about to make.'[31] So they were and ministers were general in their assertion that the Bill was to be not amendment, but a final act of a constitutional settlement. The idea of finality was a fallacy flowing from the precedent of 1688, itself held up as timeless. Another precedent, that of France after 1789, made reformers cling to the idea of a single decisive act concluding all things and pre-empting the social instability of a rolling and adjusting course.

Peel, though, was vulnerable to his own argument once he had declared for some reform but not this; he was vulnerable to every next step away from the castellation manned by Wellington and Wetherell. Peel was Janus-faced, looking forward and back, rightly picking out the utopian flaws in Reform, but obliged to fall back on the arguments of duller men to challenge the central principle. What was the necessity for Reform? he asked at one stage. To ask the question was to brush aside the constitutional crisis which had begun with Wellington's great denial of November 1830. 'If,' asked Russell summing up, 'there were no necessity for Reform, why did the Duke of Wellington and his colleagues resign?'[32]

The 'exhausted state of the House' and the 'exhausted state of debate' would soon be relieved. The crowds which had gathered in the Westminster streets in the early morning of 22 September broke into cheers as the message seeped through; by 346 votes to 237 the Bill had passed third reading in the Commons.*

There remained a single question: what would the Lords do? A letter to Wellington from an anonymous correspondent stated one doctrine, that 'when peers call to mind the circumstances under which the present House of Commons was elected, no decision of that House ought to have any weight with the Lords even if the Reform Bill passed by majority of 300'.[34]

In the country, those political unions whose recognition by Grey had so disgusted Wetherell would speak very clearly. Thomas Attwood had come to London to spend time in rooms near the old Houses of Parliament, unable to get into the overcrowded gallery, but joining in the happy mill outside. Though he did not expect acquiescence from the Lords, Attwood did not hurry back to Birmingham. Instead, he took a short celebratory holiday with his wife in Ramsgate.[35] But before that, with the debate concluded, he went with four of his radical London friends to a meeting with Grey. Attwood was chiefly concerned at the economy since, in the febrile mood of the day, bullion was being heavily sold. Grey, by contrast, wanted to know from the leader of Wetherell's 'illegally constituted body', what the reaction would be to a defeat in the Lords. And Wetherell would have been apoplectic to hear the Prime Minister hint demurely against too much quiet, suggesting that the union should now make itself publicly felt.

Attwood understood exactly what was required: a mass march, taking its time but entirely orderly, attended by as many people as possible, but with the union committee in iron-handed charge and all troublemaking elements excluded; supporters assembling in Birmingham to maximum publicity beyond that city; the approval of a petition couched in terms as civil as implacable, all this to be followed by quiet and peaceable dispersal. On 3 October, with a correspondent of the radical *Times* present, he got it. On the sounding of church bells at 10 a.m, perhaps 100,000 partici- pants, from leading merchants and bankers to a large body of Staffordshire

---

* Although Whig MPs also cheered, Hobhouse acknowledged that 'friends had been rather slack in their attendance. For example, Lord Uxbridge and Captain Byng preferred staying at the Doncaster races to their Parliamentary duties.'[33]

colliers, made their way, kept in good humour by street entertainers and led by the union's own band, to Newhall Hill where restrained but firm speeches were made and a petition for Parliament approved, after which the crowd went home without incident. Attwood had made himself the impresario of mass protest within the rules.

Next day he would present the Birmingham petition, along with seventy-nine others offered from around the country, and *The Times* reported the meeting and warned the aristocracy not to resist the people.[36] Birmingham was echoed, if not matched, by Manchester where Richard Potter, the local leader of the political union, had convened a meeting stressing the economic necessity for Reform as a step towards reduction in taxation. This, said Potter, with 'the immense debt by which it has been accumulated, is chiefly, if not entirely to be placed to the account of the aristocracy.'[37]

The Conservative leadership in the Lords, anticipating the passage of the Bill, had met on the evening of 21 September for dinner at Wellington's London home. It was to have been an affair eighteen strong, but two of the most gnarled and combustible anti-reformers, Kenyon and the former Chancellor, Eldon, shared a prior engagement (a measure of Tory solidarity and organisation), with the Duke of Cumberland, future King of Hanover. Chairs were left empty on either side of Wellington to accommodate their arrival later. Lord Dudley, who attended, informed Greville that 'Kenyon made a long speech on the first reading of the Bill, in which it was apparent that he was very drunk for he talked exceeding nonsense . . .' Lord Bathurst told him that Eldon followed 'and appeared to be equally drunk, only (Lord Bathurst told me) Kenyon in his drunkenness talked nonsense, but Eldon sense'. Lord Dudley summed up succinctly that 'it was not that they were drunk as Lords and Gentlemen sometimes are, but they were drunk like Porters'.[38] Meanwhile, on the same authority, Lord Lyndhurst, the Tories' best lawyer, was dining with neither Duke, preferring the house of the Whig Cabinet minister, Lord Holland, bidden there by his strong-minded wife, who was keen that he should support the Bill.

Ellenborough, earnest youngish Tory, *was* present and was appalled at the two peers 'who reeled into the room arm in arm'. He recorded something else – an attempt by Wellington, ten months late, to explain that pre-emptive veto of November 1830 on any kind of Reform which had reduced the Tories to misery. It was an attempt lightened by 'the recurring inebriety of the venerable old Chancellor!'. He reported Wellington saying 'that what had fallen from him in November had been misunderstood. He declared he had never yet heard of any plan of which he could approve – and he would never as Minister propose any – but he had never bound himself not to consider & not to approve of any plan which might be hereafter proposed.'[39]

With successful conclusion of the Commons third reading a certainty, all talk, however sober, was anticipatory. Lord Ebrington, an ardent Whig MP, convened a meeting one hundred strong at his house which resolved to push the government to strong measures after any defeat in the Lords, 'prorogation of parliament, creation of the Bill and suspension of Standing Orders',[40] something which Hobhouse, presumably intentionally, passed on to Sir Henry Hardinge, chief adjutant to the Tory leadership. On 24 September, a great dinner was given to ministers at Stationers Hall with 260 guests attending, 'as noisy and impatient', wrote Hobhouse, 'as our Westminster tradesmen at the Crown and Anchor, as though representing the greatest and proudest families in our Empire'.[41] On 26 September, Holmes, the slightly disreputable Tory Chief Whip, was dabbling in projected numbers in the Lords – 'He makes a majority of 45 against the Bill' – and the canvassing of the higher clergy continued, Ellenborough being told that 'The ArchB of Cy and the B. of London are now sure.'[42] Other matters intervened; on 24 September, Durham's beloved son, Charles, finally died, leaving his father and grandfather, Durham and Grey, distraught. Grey stayed away from the Lords in the middle of business for two days, causing a debate to be postponed.[43] During a Lords debate on foreign affairs, where the government were under fire for their easy toler-ance towards France, the two hottest tempers in the Upper House exploded when Londonderry called Brougham to order for chatting to the Colonial Secretary, Goderich, something which led to 'violent and vulgar language' from Brougham and an invitation from Londonderry to say that outside.[44]

And across this period a by-election was being fought and followed closely by Westminster. The suicide of Calcraft had left a vacancy in Dorset for which the Tory candidate was the young High Tory and evangelical Christian, Lord Ashley. Ashley (Shaftesbury as he became by inheritance) would die fifty years later, a hero to the left, and, as apostle of factory and labour reform, champion of the climbing boys and premature opponent, with his Ten Hours Bill, of 'flexible labour laws'. But his candidacy in September/October was the delighted preoccupation of every defender of immutable aristocratic privilege in politics. A victory would strike, they thought, a double blow against Grey's government. Ellenborough met Lord Aberdeen on his way to the headquarters which the Tories had established in Charles Street Mayfair. 'He told me that Ashley was 120 ahead of Ponsonby & that there was no doubt of success. We had some conversation about the consequences. I told him I thought Lord Grey would resign, with Althorp &c., and that Brougham would try to form a govt. offering anything to Peel . . . I told him I thought it not unlikely that Lord Grey would break down tomorrow . . .'[45]

Through all this, Lords Wharncliffe and Harrowby were trying to answer the taunt, 'Where is your Reform?' But the Tory party was still essentially taking its lead from a Duke of Wellington who, despite his rationalisations, remained as narrowly hostile and stuck in a hole as ever. The actual decision to use the noble veto and oppose the Bill in the House of Lords would be taken at Wellington's town house at the dinner distinguished by the conduct of Eldon and Kenyon. But Wellington himself was enraged on the subject and would write to Mr Arbuthnot, 'I recommend you to provide Means or Substance for yourself in another country.'[46] He had responded to the crowd violence earlier visited upon Apsley House with the observation, 'The people are rotten to the core,' and had said again to Harriet Arbuthnot that 'if we are in luck, we may have a civil war'.[47] He applied himself to the episcopal bench, trying to secure Church votes against Reform (talk of disestablishment of the Church as the next step after the £10 franchise was a steady theme in Tory speeches), and he told Ellenborough that 'he had reckoned on a majority of 90 at first, counting all the Bishops'. He later reduced this calculation to something nearer the final result.

The judgement of Greville on the Duke a few weeks later was sharp:

'He is a great man in little things but a little man in great matters . . . those mighty questions which embrace enormous and various interests and considerations, and to comprehend which, great knowledge of human nature, great sagacity, coolness and impartiality are required, he is not fit to govern and direct. His mind has not been sufficiently disciplined, nor saturated with knowledge and matured by reflection and communication with other minds to enable him to be a safe and efficient leader in such times as these.[48]

In simple terms, Wellington was used to giving orders. This worked in war because he was a first-class professional soldier, but did not work in government because he didn't know enough about politics and had no taste for either the asking or explaining so useful in that unmilitary activity.

Looking over these comments seven years later, Greville wrote a footnote asking if he had been unfair, something he often did, just as he often decided that he had been. But here his answer to himself was, 'On the whole I think not. He is not and never was a little man in anything, great or small; but I am satisfied that he has committed great political blunders, though with the best and most patriotic intentions, and that his conduct throughout the Reform contest was one of the greatest and most unfortunate of them.'[49] The conclusion was worse than sharper words would have been. On mature reflection it had gained a perfectly deadly moderation.

And when debate began in the Lords on 3 October it did so to national attention which it could meet only by the erection of additional temporary galleries. Ironically, the last time this had been done was at the state trial of Queen Caroline, the greatest mistake made by the British political establishment since the American War. The exertions of the political unions were felt before debate began in the Lords. While the Commons busied itself with the Bankruptcy Court Bill and the Select Vestries Bill, their Lordships, turning to the great matter, began with those petitions – in favour of the Bill from: Wellington in Shropshire, from Seaford; from 'places in Wilts, Kent, Renfrewshire, Cornwall, Somersetshire and Sussex; from Exeter and seven other places in Devonshire; from the Inhabitants of Carlisle, Castle Donnington, Maryport and Bedlington' and, borne by the Duke of Norfolk, from 'the Town and Parish of Sheffield (signed by 19,145 of the most respectable inhabitants there'). Petitions also came from Brighton, Dartford, 'the Town of Leicester', Kirkcudbright (2,000 signatures), Southwark (3,270), Denbigh, Penzance and Bury St Edmunds (1,844). Against Reform there were mustered petitions sponsored by a now steady Lord Eldon from Bridgwater and Weymouth. To the supporting documents were added batches of others, including eighty presented by Lord Chancellor Brougham himself.

The petition itself, an ancient form of parliamentary proceeding, had been taken up by the reformers of the industrial cities and had caught on in county districts and smaller towns. Operating from the earliest days of legislation, it was expanding and in the case of their Lordships' known proclivities, seemed the one effective method, along with the meetings launching such messages, of pre-emption. It was a form of substitute representation by which public could speak to Parliament. The passing of a resolution was also the one clear thing which a public meeting could do by way of both concluding and making a point. The procedure left anti-reformers reflecting sourly in the way of the Marquess of Londonderry who greeted the Durham petition by saying that 'he knew that a great portion of the people of property in the County were against the Bill'.[50]

Contemporary opinion lapped this Lords' debate in reverend admiration, Greville saying that 'by all accounts, there was a magnificent display, and incomparably superior to that in the H. of Commons, but the reports convey no idea of it'. Greville carried off this judgement with the heroic sang-froid necessary for a man who began that day's report 'At Newmarket all last week.' But at masterful second hand, he announced 'the great speakers on either side' – *for the Bill* Grey, Lansdowne, Goderich, Plunket, Brougham and Grey summing up. While *against Reform* he was recommended Wharncliffe and Harrowby, Carnarvon, Dudley, Wynford and Lyndhurst. The two first were, as noted, the core of the Waverers, Tories ready for a compromise, but having trouble designing it. Greville also felt competent to report Wellington's speech as 'exceedingly bad', that of Lord Harrowby 'amazingly fine' and Brougham, ambiguously, 'to have surpassed all his former exploits'.

What perhaps mattered about Grey's speech was its historical sweep. Forty years earlier, he had been a Foxite Whig. As Prime Minister at that moment, he was engaged in the high climax of Foxite Whiggism. He had, as he said, voted in 1786 for shortening the lives of parliaments and for Flood's Reform Bill, and he had introduced two himself. 'I stand therefore now before your Lordships, the advocate of principles from which I have never swerved.'[51] For Grey, the idea of Reform was one 'which had at times slumbered, but never been extinct during a period of more than eighty years'.[52] In an age which looked to its history first, even radical reform had its antique aspect and a genealogy to proclaim. And Grey, aristocrat and man of indisputable personal probity, was its guarantor.

But Grey was looking forward and could put a surprising edge on what he said. Men of learning had actually been found to argue 'that unless Members of the House of Commons are allowed to be, not the Representatives of the people, but the nominees of Peers, of loan contractors, and of speculating attorneys, all security for the happiness, the prosperity, and the liberty we enjoy will fall from under us'.[53] Then came a phrase which would take its place in history. Grey let himself suppose that 'at this hour – the nineteenth century – when the schoolmaster is abroad and when the growing intelligence of all classes of the community is daily and hourly receiving new lights', such things might have been 'met with universal derision and contempt'.[54] And he was very good at using the shibboleths of his opponents against them. Was it not the universal practice of the Commons at the start of every session to vote as one of their standing orders 'that it is unconstitutional and illegal and moreover a high breech of the privileges of the Commons House of Parliament for any peer to interfere in the election of Members to serve in that House?'.[55] The pure doctrine of the unalterable constitution was urged by the Crokers and Wetherells. But that constitution was clearly designed to separate powers and, while giving the aristocracy a great place, also to define it. One of those definings excluded the Upper House from playing any legislative part in respect of money bills, something acknowledged since Queen

Anne's time. 'Are your Lordships then prepared to say that this principle of the Constitution is not violated when peers are allowed to nominate and send into the House of Commons persons who being there, are competent to propose and to amend and alter their votes of supply . . . ?' It would have been a point too fine for the peerage of 1909 which, under the leadership of Eldon's heir, Lord Halsbury, would reject a money bill and injure the Upper House more grievously than any radical design of the intervening eighty years. And for a moderate Grey could be very emphatic. After running through the grotesqueries of Scottish representation and quoting the peer who had said 'that the Representative system in Scotland was too bad – that its doom was sealed – that it was too corrupt to last any longer', Grey contrasted England and found it insufficiently different.

And the record of Scottish atrocity was vivid: thirty-three voters in Edinburgh, thirty-three also in Glasgow; Invernesshire with 90 voters for its 95,000 inhabitants, and so many of these helpfully not the 'intelligent and propertied part of the nation' that Peel liked to talk of, but a biddable potwalloping ruck, a whisky electorate. In Bute, for example, there were twenty-one voters, of whom only one held any property. And topping the Dundas system of patriotic Tory nomination stood a single piece of damning evidence: 'The boroughs in Scotland are sixty-six in number, in which the electors consist of Magistrates who annually re-elect each other without any control by the people; and the whole number of electors in these boroughs is 1,440 or an average of about twenty in each borough.'[56] Allowing for plural voting, the number of electors sending forty-five MPs to Parliament was 1,250. The system generally had derived from the English one. And Scottish representation was 'strange, anomalous, monstrous and absurd'. How could one 'avoid the inference that the Representation of England in so far as it is composed of the members representing the decayed and corrupted bodies, is equally strange, anomalous, monstrous and absurd?'.[57]

However, Grey never forgot which House he was talking to. He had been twenty years in the Commons, but had sat in the Lords since 1807. Moreover, a man genuinely elevated and principled, he had a sense of the Lords' own position rank and duty. Sydney Smith might as noted tell the Lords from outside to pass Reform in terms of good-sense cynicism: 'Do it for your ease. Do it for your rent roll.' Grey, though he was very fond of Sydney, could not essay such levity and he had an idealised, but perfectly sincere notion of English aristocracy. Yet his argument was little different. Did he wish to reduce the legitimate influence of their Lordships? 'God forbid! The respect due to your rank and the influence which from property you necessarily possess will belong to you after the passing of the Bill as fully and in as great a degree as they do now.'[58] That, despite the graceful style, was the Sydney Smith approach, worldly and reassuring in practical terms.

But Grey tried also to communicate his high notions.

> The Peers of this country have not and I thank God they have not, any of those exclusive immunities or privileges which belonged to the old nobility of France. The nobility of this country are mixed and blended with the people. They share all their burthens . . . they are landed proprietors – they live on their estates – they perform their duties as Magistrates – they are known as neighbours . . . they acquire esteem and confidence which are given, not so much on account of their rank, as in consideration of their good conduct and the kind offices they bestow on those around them.[59]

It was high flown to the point of touching on the absurd, and the Hampshire poacher, Charles Smith, hanged in 1822 for winging the gamekeeper of Grey's colleague, Lord Palmerston, might have contributed a cool footnote. But it was not universal nonsense and it made a bridge to the audience which the Prime Minister had to persuade.

He was asking for a sacrifice and argued that it would be both creditable and uninjurious. They should give up what was neither. 'The odious power possessed by some of your Lordships does not help to increase the legitimate influence; and I verily believe that if you resolve to maintain the nomination boroughs, the whole Voice of the united Kingdom will be raised against you . . .' He then put his central proposition to this audience: 'You are asked only to give up that which is odious, unjust and unconstitutional, and by retaining which the security of this House may be shaken.' For if they clung to their old rights they would not long retain them. It was a state of affairs which 'in the present state of light and knowledge and when its effects are felt by the people, cannot I am satisfied, be maintained . . . for any considerable length of time'.[60] He then turned to the new Tory conceit of mitigated reform, the toned-down, moderate, not-frightening-the-horses option, upon which a relay of Peel's parliamentary echoes had fallen back. There had been an election had there not, making the point of a general desire for Reform? And he quoted *Hamlet*: '"Lay not that flattering unction to your souls". Do not believe that the desire for Reform will abate . . . the time is past when a smaller measure of Reform would satisfy the people. You must either take this bill, you must, I repeat, adopt this Bill or you will have instead of it, a call for something infinitely stronger and more extensive!' He invoked Wellington and Catholic emancipation: 'Following the Noble Duke, I would say "The time is come; things can no longer remain as they are; we must do something for the removal of a system which has long been odious in the eyes of the country.'[61]

It was a splendid speech, as everyone had told Greville, now back from Newmarket. Compounded of high tone and candid menace, the paying of tribute and the requirement of opponents to get out of the way, it also told a central truth which should not have been beyond the comprehension of the nobility of England. 'Disregard clamour then, I say again to your Lordships, but consider the importance of public opinion honestly expressed; and, if it be necessary, yield to it!'[62]

Had anyone ever talked to the House of Lords quite like that before? A great part of the traditionalist case had been the superlative autonomy of Parliament, its glacial impregnability in the face of street or counting house or tailor's shop opinion. It was not an attitude to die even after the Bill became law. Lord Salisbury's famous aside, that flicking of ash at the petty bourgeoisie, that he would no more be advised on policy by his valet than by Conservative Party conference, would, sixty years later, be its fleering echo. And having coupled the Duke of Wellington's practical submission to public pressure over Catholic emancipation (in which Grey had always believed), he drew connections. Catholic emancipation had been long resisted. 'You refused to concede however, and delayed until concession was extorted from you by necessity. You taught the people the consciousness of their power, and having attained that power, they were unwilling to lay it aside.'[63]

There was a lesion in Grey's argument here. Public opinion in England over Catholic emancipation was a very uncertain thing, not perhaps rabid 'No popery', but hardly fervent for relief. This cause was probably one of those entirely right things which only interfering doctrinaire liberals have the courage to care about. The public opinion here was Irish and straightforwardly violent. Fear of violence if O'Connell, victorious in the Clare by-election, had Westminster doors slammed in his face, had (very properly) influenced Wellington. The not quite stated, but earnestly contemplated element about public opinion over Reform was whether *it* too would become violent. Grey dropped hints by way of abhorrence. 'If the Bill is rejected by a narrow majority, I beg of you my Lords to consider the consequences. Do not flatter yourselves that it will be possible by a less effective measure than this to quiet the storm which will rage, and to govern the agitation which will thus have been produced.'[64] He, Grey, deprecated violence; freedom was vitally connected with order; as a minister it was his duty to maintain tranquillity 'but as a citizen, as a member of the Government and as a Statesman, I am bound to look at the consequences which may flow from rejecting this measure'.[65]

However sincere and in however great earnest, Grey was deliberately trying to make their flesh crawl. He also worked in a shrewd kick at the bishops then at a high point of prelatical distaste for democratic measures. The Church was *not* in danger from this legislation, but that Church, its privileges, revenues and other pleasant things, might not always be so sheltered after that other legislation which rejection might provoke at other hands.

But then Grey was serious. Quite happy to encourage Attwood to make all the constitutional noise he could through insistent petition and virtuous monster meetings, Grey feared real violence. He also wanted to disabuse the thicker-headed part of the Tory peerage from the dim notion, wearyingly repeated, that they could stop this bill, now in mighty national focus, replace it with a watered down ersatz and then govern quietly. 'May you therefore my Lords be wise in time – may your Lordships profit by the example set before you and avoid those dangers which inevitably arise from your rejection of this measure and secure by its adoption peace and conciliation in the country . . .'[66] More than any point about the franchise, the contents of the two famous schedules, even than the principle of Reform itself, this was now the question. What was the measure of the risk run by the Lords (and to be suffered by everyone else), if, using their certain powers in uncertain circumstances, they rejected the Bill?

SEVEN

The Lords: The Outcome

*'What must we expect when these lower classes
preponderate everywhere?'*

It was appropriate that Wharncliffe should speak next, after Grey, for he was, in a sense, Grey's first target. Wharncliffe was chief and earliest floater of the idea of alternative, painless, acceptable Reform, but not *this* Reform. And the central assumption of this debate was that some kind of Reform substitute rather than a Wellingtonian damning of eyes and furious defiance was now the objective.

Though as Mulgrave, a government supporter, speaking next, put it, 'the greater part of his speech belonged in Committee, was in fact, a major amendment, yet he had concluded with a motion which if carried, would preclude the possibility of the Bill reaching a committee'.[1] For Wharncliffe's amendment demanded that the phrase 'shall be rejected' rather than the usual 'be read this day six months hence' be inserted into the text, but whatever the tactics, his concerns were clear enough. There was too much popular, lower-class representation now in the offing for Wharncliffe, and the nomination boroughs helped to control it. For 'as the boroughs now stood, they were the only check on popular violence; and as they were going to send so large a proportion of that species of Representation – as this Bill constituted, so an additional number of popular members – he said that some check was the more necessary'.[2] Furthermore, the House of Lords was in danger: 'By the regulations of this Bill, the whole strength of the legislature would be in the Commons, the House of Lords would be nothing, and it would be well if the Crown itself could stand before it.'[3]

For a supposed moderate, Wharncliffe managed a remarkable echo of the ultimate Ultra, Lord Sidmouth. 'I ask the noble Earl [Grey] to walk down St James's Street or down Bond Street and then if he goes into the shops of those streets and asks the question, not of any person whom he may meet there, but of the shopkeepers themselves, I will undertake to say that he will find them ashamed of the measure; indeed so disgusted with it as to declare that they will have none of it.'[4] As for the petitions now stacking up, handy numbers of the not ashamed, they ought not 'to be taken as the signs of the sentiments of the people generally – they were rather the signs of the sentiments of the portion of the people which had long been accustomed to follow party views'.[5] In conclusion, Wharncliffe 'besought the Peers of England, as they valued their character – as they valued the station in which they held either by favour of their sovereign or by inheritance – to show that the Peers of England when called upon to do their duty, would not be intimidated by menaces or guided by interest'.[6]

The Ultra, Mansfield, produced a glittering doctrine of what might be called *noblesse n'oblige pas*: 'But the people will have Reform. Now my Lords, I do not mean to deny that a very great proportion of the people are for Reform.' But even if the people had been unanimous, 'I must answer that we are not here to answer the dictates of the people or to register the edicts of the House of Commons.' Rather it was their Lordships' business 'to examine with patience all that is suggested for the benefit of the people, and thus to impress upon their minds the truth which is not at once apparent to them, probably from the distance at which we are placed, that our interests are inseparable and that nothing whatever could be done without involving the peers'.[7]

Grey had asked peers to take the crisis seriously. The Tories varied between the fraught and the sublime, proclaiming, like Mansfield, either 'My lords the evil will not rest here; the wish for change extends to all your institutions – the abolition of a Church in union with the State, the division of property among all the children as in France . . . the fate of Europe is involved in your decision; if England should be convulsed, if she should suffer even bloodless revolution, the only barrier would be removed which opposes that spirit which attacks all ancient institutions'[8] or alternatively saying, with languid assurance, 'I must say, fain would I see this effervescence subside.'[9] Mansfield also prophesied the making of war upon Britain by her former allies, a threat which the next speaker the Whig, Lord King, characterised as indicating 'the rump of the Holy Alliance'.[10] Soon after this, the House was put into a mild and aristocratic tumult when Wharncliffe, for no clear reason, sought to withdraw his original form of words rejecting the Bill. He had been informed that 'as it stood, it might be interpreted in the light of an affront to the House of Commons. Now nothing could be further from his intentions . . .' And after the ball had passed back and forth between Wharncliffe, Holland, Mulgrave, Grey, Wellington, Richmond, Wellington and several others over six and a half columns of *Hansard*, he was finally given leave to withdraw it. As a name, Waverers seemed about right.

Again and again, the peers returned resentfully to the peers and the reduction in their own authority. The home key of self-interest was occasionally departed from for little rhapsodies about the public good, but their Lordships generally got back to it. Harrowby, the alternative Waverer, has had a brilliant press. Michael Brock considers him to 'have made the speech of his life'[11] and he quotes Martin Van Buren, later United States President, then ambassador to Britain, calling it the best anti-Reform speech he had heard in either House. One takes such views earnestly, but his contribution on 4 October was still rich in the irksome complacency and self-congratulation marking most anti-Reform offerings.

Nor was he immune to the Podsnappish theme of anti-Reform, the peculiar perfection of the British way, celestially perfect as he saw it: 'that happy form of government under which, through the favour of Divine Providence, this country had enjoyed for a long succession of years a greater share of internal peace, of commercial prosperity, of true liberty and of all that constituted social happiness, than had fallen to the lot of any other country in the world'.[12] And he was greatly concerned at the shop floor getting above itself. Power was going to be concentrated in the House of Commons,

> when that assembly which has already become the chief governing power of the state, attains to be not only the governing power, but the government itself, and suffers itself to be guided by other assemblies of another description such as have recently been formed in the north, and especially at Birmingham – when these come with their directions for our conduct thundering over our heads what, I ask, will be the kind of government then presiding over the interests of the country?[13] The principle and object of this bill are to make the constitution more democratic. Look to the consequences.'

That was the central sentence of the Tory case. Harrowby, long in cliché, invoked the 'the laws of the Medes and the Persians', speaking of the old system as something 'to which the people of England have been warmly attached'[14]; and when he attacked Grey, he did so naturally 'more in sorrow than in anger'. He had welcomed Grey's access to office in 1830 if the Wellington government could not be strengthened, but 'I trusted not in the Mr Grey of 1793, but in the Earl Grey of 1830'. It had been open to the Prime Minister to take a middle course. 'He was placed on a lofty eminence between two contending parties – those who wished to change everything and those who wished to change nothing.' Harrowby thought that Grey might have 'secured the valuable support of many of those who are called the conservative party'. 'He might have stood,' said Harrowby bathetically, 'as it were, between the living and the dead.' And 'in his conscience,' he added, 'I believe he might have stayed this plague'. Instead, the Prime Minister had followed the Roman tribune who 'periculum adduxit rempublicam'*[15]

The plague was a public agitation and Harrowby had seen it before when 'in 1780, 1793 and 1819 [it had] menaced the tranquillity of the country, but in time subsided; and prosperity, order and content succeeded to the violence of the storm'.[16] But the Bill had 'thrown the country into a state from which it will never entirely recover'. Aristocratic self-pity was part of the formula, so 'believing that a deadly blow has been inflicted on the vitals of the Constitution, I cannot consent to be an accomplice in the crime, though perforce I must be a sharer in the punishment'.[17] It is very difficult at this distance to read Harrowby's speech with much sympathy (Melbourne would call it 'eloquent but I must say, miscellaneous and sometimes contradictory'), but its undoubted success presumably derived from Harrowby's representation of his case in terms of a very British reasonableness, begging Grey to reconsider, in order to obtain 'a compromise between extreme opinions'.[18] It was fallacy, but fallacy couched in terms of sweet reason and full of Harrowby's personal pain at the divisions now existing. Certainly his anxious and grieving style showed to advantage in a context vividly lit by Mansfield and Wellington.

Melbourne, speaking next, had a good deal of form as an anti-reformer and he cheerfully marked it up. 'Wherever the flag of Parliamentary Reform was hoisted, I ranged myself under the opposite banner . . . I always opposed in the other House of Parliament the extension of the elective franchise to Manchester and Birmingham.'[19] Melbourne had taken that stand over Birmingham during the dispute which had led to the departure of Huskisson, something he very much regretted. But his new-found reformism was of the realistic sort. They should not now try to stop what they couldn't stop. And once you conceded anything at all, how and where could you stop? The Waverers, he said, would now go beyond the conservative Melbourne of the twenties. They would enfranchise Manchester and Birmingham. Why? Because those towns were rich and had large and growing populations. But so had many other towns.

Harrowby had pleaded for time so that people would quieten down as they had in the past, but if what the people wanted was reasonable and not against the principles of the constitution, then eventually 'the legislative and executive powers must yield to the popular voice or be annihilated'. He

* This translates as 'It brings danger to the state'.

made at this point an interesting comparison with the Catholic question. There were not so many Catholics, and their 'strength could always be seen and measured. But the spirit of Reform has been diffused through the whole population and the whole people may be said to be ready for commotion.'[20] And when Melbourne spoke of the Catholic question, however modest and measurable the number of *English* Catholics, he was alert to the alternative scenario in Ireland if Wellington had been as principled there as he now was about Parliament. 'I would beg leave to ask, what would now have been the state of Ireland had that measure not passed into a law?'

Significantly in a lukewarm reformer in a Cabinet which had contemplated concessions, Melbourne was anxious to have the Tories co-operate in a Lords committee stage, giving opportunities for amendment. They, being deep in a historic sulk, were never going to accept such an opportunity. At heart, Melbourne was a sensible Tory. He liked the old ways. He did not want Reform as such, and he utterly feared the street leadership. He saw resistance strengthening 'the party of agitation' and Reform taking the wind out of its sails. He too wanted Reform for his rent roll and his ease, and he spoke accordingly: 'Do not my Lords, arm a host of demagogues with the discontent of the people.' Then, rather anticipating the famous words of Franklin D. Roosevelt, he added, 'I implore you not to be guilty of the rashness of fear; I implore you not to be guilty of the greater rashness of delay.'[21]

Wellington, who concluded the second day's debate, was everything Greville reported. The splendid laconic style did not appear here. He began with a petulant defence of his own conduct in 1830 when rejecting all reform, and he dragged in as an objection to change, generalised words of Grey in praise of the Commons made in 1817. As for him, he had been the King's Minister and 'it is the duty of the King's Minister to support the institutions of the country'.[22] Graceful retreat seemed beyond him. His own statement – 'I spoke as a Minister of the Crown, and as a Minister of the Crown I meant to resist Reform'[23] – had not provoked the surge in opinion favouring Reform. For Wellington, 'the spirit of Reform in this country was the consequence of the French Revolution', and he complained that since the American War there had been a desire for Reform, one which was accentuated 'particularly when any disturbance or insurrection has occurred in any of the neighbouring foreign countries'.[24] He was convinced that things had been getting better until recent events in Paris. Self-exculpation and blaming foreigners are inevitable components of political speeches made when things go wrong, but in this instance they served Wellington poorly.

Getting round to the Bill itself, he observed that 'it altered everything – it changed or destroyed every interest in the country'. He made clear his bitter resentment of the King's acceptance that there should be a dissolution. There were precedents from the 1780s when minister and King had differed, ministers had retreated and been replaced by new ones so that the election was held on the basis of support for the King's act. This time round, the King had accepted the ministerial view and facilitated an election 'upon a particular plan of Reform which was accordingly discussed through the country'.[25]

Accordingly, Wellington, disregarding the commoner element in the Ministry, brought grave charges against 'the Noble Lords'. They had 'excited the spirit which existed in the country at the period of the last election'. Wellington also threw in the old Burkean maxim setting representation against delegation. His charge sheet against the government had brought about 'the unconstitutional practice, hitherto unknown, of elected delegates to parliament, delegates to obey the daily instructions of their constituents and to be cashiered if they disobey them . . .'[26] The reality behind the sonorous theory became clear when Wellington added his objections to the £10 freeholder. This, he thought, would mean most householders in the southern counties, shopkeepers, 'a class of persons of all others the most likely to combine in political views – and be acted upon by political clubs . . .'. All of which, the Duke observed, 'would be very injurious to the public interest'[27]; or, as he glossed it a little later in his speech, 'Throughout the Empire, persons in the lowest condition of life, liable to and even existing under the most pernicious influences, are liable to become voters or in other words, to exercise political power . . . What must we expect when these lower classes preponderate everywhere?'[28]

In fairness, what Wellington had in mind in this long grumble was the sort of noisy radicalism associated with the Rotunda and with the left of left groups connected with Richard Carlile. But to fear any such thing was imperceptive and somewhat windy in a man whose superb military career had rested upon implacable calm in far tighter spots than constitutional reform admitting a quota of lower workmen voters. Politically, the Duke was in something of a funk.

When he went on to say that they were establishing a democracy which had never been established 'without a war upon property and the public debt', and followed this by saying that they would now 'continue in the same course till you have passed through the miseries of a revolution and thence to a military despotism',[29] he was reciting the events of 1790–1815 in France, perhaps inevitable in a man of his generation, but the sort of catechism recital expected from a par-for-the-course country squire. Wellington had seen a wide world for twenty years of war and had functioned with brilliant calm as he demonstrated marked generosity towards France as a diplomat at the peace. Ironically for a conservative, he did not have either confidence in or knowledge of the rather more complex conservative nature of his own people. For a patriot, he had very little understanding of the English.

He gave a damning demonstration of his out-of-touch judgement by coming huffily to the defence of Wharncliffe, whose remark about the superior shopkeepers of Bond Street 'ashamed of the Reform Bill' had attracted some derision. Wellington could not understand this; they were '200 respectable persons, who are well able to form an opinion of the effect of the Bill upon resources of themselves, the middling classes and the poor as they supply the luxuries of persons in easier circumstances residing in that quarter of the town. Anything affecting property must affect them and they do feel that this Bill must affect property, private expenditure and the resources of themselves and of those whom they employ . . .' Were not such people 'interested in upholding the public faith and the system of property now established in England?'.[30] It sounded as if Lord Salisbury's valet was to have a say after all.

Yet for all his apocalyptic talk and rollings of French thunder, Wellington sounded at the end of his speech like a man looking to the possibility of resuming office. He wanted the House of Lords to make no pledges against any other measure which might be brought forward. From the man who had pledged himself against Reform in the smallest degree, this was rich. But the Duke wanted his supporters to keep themselves 'free to adopt any measure upon this subject which shall secure to this country the blessings of a government'.[31] Hobhouse knew what he thought of *that*: 'In short, His Grace made a shabby, shuffling speech like a man wanting office again.'[32] Hobhouse was a party activist on the other side, but the Duke's conclusion did sound like the prelude to some adaptation of a Waverers' moderate reform bill to be carried after the Lords had defeated the immoderate one proposed by the Commons. If Wellington thought that was possible, he did not understand the world he was living in, and he was amending sullen rejection with a gambler's terrible levity. Greville was right about him.

On the next day, Wednesday 5 October, *Hansard*, chattier than it would later become, drew readers' attention to the arrangements made for ladies. A few might in normal circumstances have attended below the bar, synagogue-wise, 'protected and screened by a curtain'. However, for this great contest,

> a considerable number of peeresses and their daughters and relations attended every evening, occupying a considerable portion of the space

below the bar where chairs were placed for their accommodation . . . they displayed all the ardour of their sex in their sympathy with the sentiments of the different speakers . . . Meanwhile the space near the throne was taken up by MPs and distinguished foreigners, among whom was present this day, the celebrated Hindoo, Rammohun Roy.[33]

Again there were petitions, overwhelmingly in support of Reform, brought in by sympathetic peers from places as disparate as Galway, West Ham, Perth, Cambridge, Flint, Bradford and the Parish of the Holy Trinity, Brompton. Also there was one against, from 'Bankers, Merchants and Traders of the City of London', not a group generally opposed to Reform. It was sponsored by Wharncliffe who, scorning the perfunctory, made another speech which included a long quotation from proceedings at the Birmingham Political Union's Newhall Hill meeting. Attwood, who had a line in biblical simile, had compared the old establishment with Leviathan and had said 'the Leviathan is hooked in the nose and with 150,000 men at the foot of Newhall Hill to hold the rope, Leviathan could not escape'.[34] Attwood had also asked his audience, 'Will the Lords Pass the Bill? I answer the question by asking another – Dare they refuse it?' At which piece of rhetoric, Wharncliffe went into an English nobleman's equivalent of orbit: 'Dare they refuse it?!! Such was the interrogatory which this individual put to an assemblage of 150,000 persons, and it was received by them with "Loud cheers".'

Wharncliffe relished the two phrases 'not dare' and 'loud cheers', and rolled them around much as Sergeant Buzfuz had contemplated the naked horror of 'Chops and tomato sauce'. If such a person talking to such a crowd could say things like that 'then he would say, and he thought he should be perfectly justified in making the assertion, that the revolution which they all dreaded was not only begun, but that it was in point of fact, actually accomplished'.[35] Wharncliffe might be an interminable old thing, but his pleasurable alarmism stood in the mainstream of the anti-reformist mood. There was no doubt about it: they would all be murdered in their beds. And it was quite enough to start a flurry of affront – at petitions, at public meetings, at persons making speeches on such occasions, the whole tone of which was caught by the aged and now sober Eldon who 'should be ashamed of himself if, after living so long in his profession he did not take that opportunity of saying a few words'.[36] The whole episode and all its sets of a few words each from a few noble Lords filled up twenty-four columns of the record.

History has given short and derisive shrift to Frederick Robinson, Viscount Goderich, largely on account of his yet shorter and more wretched

time, a few months of trying to hold together a Tory/Canningite government bent upon multiple fission. But his speech the next day, Thursday,
widely admired at the time, was a model of quiet sense. He tried to explain
to Harrowby, amid all his talk about 'a crime for which ministers would
pay the penalty',[37] that events had moved on. And anyway, the idea of
Reform was not new 'for it had attracted the attention of the country with
more or less intensity of power for a period of fifty or sixty years'.[38] In
those early days, 'it was a strange fact that when first it was introduced,
little comparative disfavour was entertained against it even in the House
of Commons'.

The French Revolution had created a general distaste for change: 'But
this was a question which from its nature might slumber, but could not
sleep; and if it were occasionally to sleep, there was something in the
constitution of the human heart that rendered it impossible it could be
extinguished.'[39] Goderich might almost have said that the times, they were
a-changin': taxation 'falling at this time more heavily on the less wealthy,
had increased, the war had concluded' and 'in the midst of all this glory
and prosperity, there were symptoms of the unstable nature of that very
prosperity', whilst the shift from war to peace had left 'scarcely an interest
in the country, mercantile or manufacturing, which did not suffer'.
Thousands 'were exposed to feel the effects of frequently recurring depressions'. People blamed everything on the existence of an unreformed House
of Commons. That might not be fair, but was it surprising? They had
hoped for better times from the peace but they had not followed. And
anyway, hadn't the old system grown scandalous, wasn't the sale and
purchase of seats disgraceful and, incidentally, illegal? As for moderate
reform, 'if they had refrained from legislating on this subject or had
produced a less extensive measure of Reform, so far from palliating the
discontent of the country, they would have prolonged it to all eternity'.[40]
Would the new county franchise diminish the influence of the aristocracy,
a throbbingly recurrent point? All too correctly, Goderich reckoned that
'the people of England would still be influenced by the aristocracy, among
whom they lived'.[41] He then went on to the offensive by giving a picture
of the real relationship between a candidate and the closed electorate of
a rotten borough, exactly what Galt had been describing in *The Member*.
It had been called 'a gross act of injustice to deprive corporations of their
right of sending members to Parliament'.[42]

Well now, he had wanted to advance an able and honourable friend, no
names, to a Commons seat. Understanding that money would return a
Member, he consulted a professional man who was acquainted with the

practice which there carried on. What was the exact amount of the douceur to be given? Having been told, he asked whether if he 'did not comply with giving the sum to out voters, they would give their votes to him?' The answer was 'not one'. And if the friend appeared 'at the hustings without complying with the terms whether he would have any chance?' The reply to that question was 'not the least'.[43]

And since patriotic triumphalism was a game which two could play, Goderich turned his attention to the France which Tories insisted upon as a model for all the massacre and revolution which must follow modest reform. 'What were the causes which led to those fearful events? They were to be traced to a corrupt court – a degraded nobility – a degraded nobility that insisted upon their exclusive privileges over, he might say, an enslaved people.'[44] The implied question to those assembled that night in the old pre-Fire House of Lords was clear if not explicit – *They* weren't like that, were they?

Falmouth, a Tory, would complain about the quality of the intake to the Commons at the last election. Wellington's 'What a lot of dreadful bad hats' is well known. Falmouth's threnody was for the recently fallen, for Knatchbull, Acland and Bankes, defeated Ultras, 'tried, experienced counsellors who had not only by property, the largest stake in the welfare of the State, but whose known integrity, talents and long services were unimpeachable . . . men whose characters could not be raised by any eulogy of his'. They had been rejected; 'and men more in the situation of pledged delegates than independent Members were sent up to support so violent a change'.[45] Falmouth also lamented that 'the vagaries of theorists and the wickedness of desperate men should be let loose upon them to work perpetual change and discontent'. Anyway, did Grey 'not know that the British system of government was the best that had existed in any age of country?'.[46] Falmouth also gave the bishops a little scare. He was sure that 'if any of that right reverend bench should be induced to vote for such a Bill . . . it could be from an error of judgement alone, but the right reverend prelates knew too well the essential connection between the Church Establishment and the balance of power in the State, to be drawn into so fatal a delusion . . . they would not, they could not, support that unprincipled Bill.'[47]

Part of the drama of the entire conflict lay in the determination of the Tory Lords to stress their qualities of manly immobility. John Waynes before their time, they knew what was right, and no threat or pressure, especially from the multitude, was going to shift them. The Earl of Carnarvon looked back to applaud similar firmness exercised by the

Younger Pitt when faced with 'the passing frenzy of the people'.[48] And he spoke with memorable scorn of the jiggery-pokery of Johnny Foreigner which had summoned up so many new models of government: 'They had had French republics by the score, they had Ligurian, Helvetian, Cisalpine, Transalpine and other republics of all sorts and denominations, the creation of the day's fancy and the victims of the morrow's spleen.'[49] All of these republics had been drafted with 'more care and philosophy . . . than had been devoted to the clumsy Bill he held in his hand; yet what had become of them? They had all passed away, leaving behind only the bitter recollection and great misery of the people.'[50]

Carnarvon's complacency kept talent and intelligence in their place. The Ministry contained 'men of the greatest talents – they had talents enough to overturn any country. Would to God they had one grain of common sense and common calmness . . . and they would have all that was necessary to save their country. The only hope of the country rested upon the firmness of their Lordships . . .'[51] He wanted them to make this stand in the way of the Waverers, not to stop all reform, but in the interest of what he called 'bit by bit reform'. He hoped that 'their Lordships would give it the breathing time which it required'. Then, if Ministers would work on 'a plan for reform less sweeping in its nature and more temperate, gradual and judicious, he would not be found in the ranks of their opponents'. A measure of his Lordship's earnest intentions was shown a little later when he acknowledged that 'with respect to giving the large manufacturing towns such as Leeds, Manchester, Glasgow, and Birmingham a share in the Representation, he was willing to take the point into serious consideration'.[52] Glasgow, if his Lordship had not noticed it, was already represented – by the votes of thirty-three mutually coopting councillors.

Much time had been spent by Tory peers denouncing the evils of 'abroad', with especial reference to France, but Carnarvon offered a novel argument drawn from French experience. One of Charles X's ministers, Martignac, 'before the late disasters in that country',[53] on being 'asked whether he thought the French charter* could be much longer maintained, had replied, "How can you ask that question; – how is it possible for us to contrive anything to stand in the place of your closed boroughs? and without that being done, it is not possible to carry on the government."' Having said which, and having concluded that 'never while he had a voice to raise in opposition, would he give his consent to a measure so pregnant with mischief', Carnarvon appears to have taken a mild turn. *Hansard* in

---

* The suspension of large functions of law, assembly and press by Charles and Polignac.

its confiding way says that, 'The noble Earl concluded abruptly saying though he intended to address some further observations to their Lordships, he found that his strength was exhausted and must therefore sit down.'

Plunkett, a reformer of whose speech Greville's informants spoke highly, argued that opponents of the Bill had made concessions. They too now thought 'with a single exception, that Reform, and in some considerable degree too, was necessary ['*no, no.*'] . . . the only person who had denied that Reform was necessary was a noble Lord opposite, the Earl of Mansfield ['*no, no.*']. The noble Earl was the only person of all that entertained such an opinion ['*no, no.*']. This rather unsatisfactory expression litters Plunkett's speech as he tries to give the Waverers credit for making not only Reform, but the Tories, more moderate. Accordingly, he moved on to contemplate the sanguine resolution of people like Carnarvon, happy to reject and damn the consequences. Would they think in the middle of the night that they were taking the safest course when they 'made violent appeals and called upon the Reverend Bench to attest their solemn appeal to Providence?' He reckoned that in the country at large there 'was a deep-seated sense of wrong ready to burst forth in the hour of danger which impressed minds of the utmost fortitude with a sense of terror'.[54]

Plunkett actually dared to speak for Burke's swinish multitude. 'He said there had been some smart sarcasms and polished epigrams thrown out against the people of England . . .' But the people who had sent in so many petitions to Parliament 'were no light, giddy and fantastic multitude – no rabble labouring under a temporary delusion, but a great nation, intelligent, moral, instructed'.[55] The Tories said that if the Bill carried, 'it would give the people of England the means of overthrowing the Throne and Church . . . what would happen if it were not carried?'[56]

A good part of the debate between the two sides had consisted of the Tories saying that the social fabric had been put in danger from that unreliable thing, the population, by the rash meddling of the reformers, and that it would be best protected by the wise refusal of the House of Lords to endorse Reform. To this Whigs had replied that the social fabric would be safe with the people, otherwise a reasonable bunch, providing the Lords did not enrage them by pushing their luck with a veto. For Plunkett 'the people of England were as much entitled by law to a full and fair representation in the House of Commons as their Lordships to their seats in that House'. The Lords' position was 'unintelligible . . . a claim by an oligarchy – to what? to a right to retain* a part of the democracy'.[57]

* The original text reads 'return', a near homophone which, in the context, makes no sense.

When it came to the regular sniping at the King for having granted Grey a dissolution, Plunkett abandoned the florid baroque of noble discourse and became refreshingly rude: 'He thought that what had been said on this subject was unconstitutional trash.'[58] He was no more polite about the Tories' attitude to the Church. When Falmouth had 'called on the Reverend Bench to defend the present system, he called upon Christian prelates to defend a system of hypocrisy'.[59] The anti-reformers and the borough owners wanted to uphold a system of constituency purchase 'for the exclusive benefit of themselves'.[60] And Plunkett, rather like Hawkins, had some historic feeling, a sense that things were perhaps getting better with the passage of time. 'What if our ancestors were as blind worshippers of their ancestors as noble Lords, wise in their generation, would fain just now persuade us to be of theirs, was no advantage to be taken of increased knowledge – of increased experience – of the relations of society being better understood because better contemplated . . . ?'[61]

Equally, would their Lordships please get into their heads the fact that the constitution, so far from being a great bundle of unalterable perfection, had spent its history changing. Where was the complex land tenure by which early Lords had been entitled to sit there? Where were the thirty mitred abbots present in the Lords until Henry VIII swept them out? As for the new gradualism, Plunkett refused to be impressed; such late-in-the-day moderation was now being shouted up from the hole out of which their Lordships had consented to move a very little. They had wanted to concede nothing, now they would condescend to yield something. What sort of statesmanship was that? 'Does it not teach the people that though nothing would be granted on the score of justice, much would be yielded to importunity?'[62]

That touched the centre of the Waverers' thesis, now by heavy hints adapted by Wellington, and, ironically, a masterpiece of bad strategy. Plunkett's idea of the statesman was someone who went aloft to get a better view of 'the people's rights and his own duties' and made his decisions on the principles of what he had learned. If he failed in that duty 'however he might win favour with noble Lords so – if we took their own word for it – infallible, disinterested in their judgment, he would be held in contempt by an enlightened posterity'.[63] His account was directed at the deathbed empiricism of men resentfully roused by the noise outside from inert conceit at their own virtue and devotion to things as they are.

Perhaps the best of all the anti-reformist arguments was that the election had been conducted with the public believing that every kind of change would come into their lives. Sydney Smith as a reformer said it better than any oppositionist: 'all young ladies will imagine (as soon as this bill is carried) that they will be instantly married. Schoolboys believe that gerunds and supines will be abolished and that currant tarts will ultimately come down in price; corporal and sergeant are sure of double pay; bad poets will expect a demand for their epics . . .'[64]

But for Lord Wynford, speaking on 7 October, such innocencies invalidated an election in which Lord Wynford's cause had done very badly. Parliament had been dissolved 'during the prevalence of a base cry'.[65] Given the limitations of the public, Wynford did not care to risk the vote on them. Plunkett had asked '"Are not the people of England to be trusted?" God forbid that he (Lord Wynford) should characterize them – taking them as a body – in any other way than describing that there was not a more respectable people on the face of the earth, but . . . they ought only to be invested with additional rights in proportion to their capacity for comprehending them.'

The trouble with people like Plunkett was that, if his argument for 'a massive confidence to be reposed in the great mass of the community meant anything, it was an argument for Universal Suffrage'.[66] And despite his denials of having said any such thing, Wynford was sure that it wouldn't stop there. 'He contended that if this Bill should pass, they would find it impossible long to resist Universal Suffrage and Vote by Ballott [sic] and Annual Parliaments[67] . . . Yes talent would find its way into parliament but it would be the talent of demagogues – talent which would not prevent the possessors of it from becoming the delegates of the wildest revolutionists.'[68]

His fears were echoed touchingly by the aged Eldon, self-made by enormous industry from coal merchant's son to Lord Chancellor yet wedded to the rightness of all things established, who cherished the closed boroughs on the grounds that judges of the past, Lord Holt and Lord Hales, had described them as 'both a franchise and a right'.[69] And Eldon was unhelpful to those keen to compromise and admit small, inoffensive elements of Reform. He was a believer in the calamitous powers of the little rift within the lute: 'My Lords sacrifice one atom of our glorious Constitution and all the rest is gone.' He concluded that 'this Bill will be found, I fear from my soul, to go the length of introducing in its train, if passed, Universal Suffrage, Annual Parliaments and Vote by Ballot'. Eldon was by now a very old man (born 1751), but he had anyway been all his life a believer in a sort of pedantic absolute. It had slowed his judgements in Chancery where he fussed them about in pursuit of perfection to a ruinous agony for the parties. The Reform Bill – rough, scrambled, failing to see ancient rights of property in a rotten borough, responsive to public movements and above all, thoroughly political – stood full in the face of all he had ever been. But it was the embodiment of Lord Chancellor Brougham. And Brougham spoke next.

His was a vast speech, three hours and fifty-four columns long. Grey would call it 'a miraculous speech'. Tories, then and subsequently, would allege that Brougham was drunk which, if true, would have made it an even more miraculous speech. It was the speech everyone talked about. Brougham, with his Scottish background, his vast energies and an interesting physical look – almost clean shaven with the thick grey hair cut short – was oddly modern, but there was a tremendous irony about this man's presence as chief advocate of radical reform. For the Lord Chancellor, despite his energetic small 'r' reforming in the Courts of Chancery, was eccentrically cool for a Whig on the sweeping away of rotten boroughs. As with the character in Disraeli's *Sybil* who said 'I rather like bad wine. One gets so bored with good wine', Brougham had a soft spot for them and had been firmly overruled by the Bill committee from which, perhaps for this reason, he had been excluded. The idea of clearing out the great body of patronage dummies by way of schedules A and B went against his own inclinations. He had sat without compunction for Winchelsea and Knaresborough and he would be embarrassed near the end of his performance to hear a letter sent to the Duke of Richmond quoted by the Tory, Winchilsea, in which Brougham had expressed his objections to parts of the Bill.

But not very embarrassed! Brougham was a great advocate as well as a fluid thinker on politics. If the circumstances demanded a high, scornful and devastating assault upon something about which he felt relaxed, Brougham was the man, and high, scornful devastation duly followed. Clever, explosive, devious, on the left of politics, yet suspected of being ready to cabal with the enemy, particularly disliked by Creevey, the uncomplicated good party man who called him 'Old Wickedshifts', Viscount Brougham and Vaux was, on his day, the most brilliant debater and orator in England. And this may have been his day.

It was a speech which ranged. Quite early, he contested the opposition's love of antiquity by himself going back 130 years to Jonathan Swift, not a radical, not a Jacobin 'but in the language of the times, a regular, staunch, thick-and-thin Tory'. It was Swift who had said 'It is absurd that the boroughs which are decayed and destitute both of trade and population are not extinguished' (or as we should say . . . put into Schedule A). Swift had also expressed a preference for short parliaments, what the furthest out radicals of the day, Colonel Jones rather than Attwood, were calling for. The ministers hadn't said anything on the subject, Brougham added,

'But if we had – what a cry we should have heard about the statesman of Queen Anne's day . . . how we should have been taunted with the Somerses and Godolphins and their contemporaries, the Swifts and the Addisons.'[70]

Brougham worked his way through a succession of Tory speakers in the manner of a summing-up, coming to Harrowby and his moderation. For the constant cry against this government was 'You are hasty, rash, intemperate men . . . See such a one – he is a man of prudence and a discreet . . .; he is not averse to all innovation, but dislikes precipitancy; he is calm and just to all sides alike, never gives a hasty opinion; a safe one to follow; look how he votes.' Lord Harrowby, said the Chancellor, 'is a Reformer and approves the principle, objecting to the details and, there-fore – he votes against it in the lump, details, principle and all'.[71] But having toured his opponents' speeches, Brougham turned to the closed boroughs. Anyone with means might

by vesting in his person the old walls of Sarum, a few pigsties at Bletchingly,* or a summer-house at Gatton, and making fictitious and collusive and momentary transfers of them to an agent or two for the purpose of enabling them to vote as if they had the property, of which they all the while know they have not the very shadow, is in itself a monstrous abuse . . . I will tell these peers, attorneys, jobbers, loan-contractors and the Nabobs' agents if such there be still among us, that the time is come when these things can no longer be borne . . .[72]

Drunk or sober, sincere or factitious, Brougham had hit a streak of furious, contemptuous passion. The anti-reformers looked upon boroughs as property, and withdrawal of that property as something between usurpa-tion and larceny. But this sacred title had had some interesting claimants. He instanced the former waiter at a gambling house who 'did sit for years in that House (the Commons) holding his borough property for aught that I can tell, in security of a gambling debt. By means of that property and right of voting, he advanced himself to a baronetcy.'[73] And he blazed at the charge of ministers having appointed like-minded peers, not some-thing the Tories had ever done.

His assault upon the creations of the previous half-century sets one back in the mood of all the Whigs who had endured the never-ending Pitt system. 'Service without a scar in the political campaign – constant presence in the

---

* It was a small irony, and surely intended, that Bletchingly was the temporary haven just found for Palmerston after his rejection at Cambridge University!

field of battle in St Stephen's chapel* – absence from all other fights, from 'Blenheim to Waterloo' – but above all, steady discipline – right votes in right places, these are the precious, but happily not rare, qualities which have raised men to the Peerage. For these qualities the gratitude of Mr Pitt showered down his baronies by the score . . .[74] The combination of such creations and the nominees of Lords in the Commons was what had held the system together for nearly fifty years.

Brougham, who could quote history with the best of the Tories, reminded them that the rotten boroughs were not the honourable dilapidations of antiquity, but had all too often been created rotten. (In his ingenious speech earlier in the Commons, Inglis had made the same point in their defence!) Brougham touched on the 120 creations of Queen Elizabeth's time and cited William Prynne, the Puritan pamphleteer whose ears had been cropped in the pillory for his writings, who had named 64 boroughs, 14 of them in Cornwall, 'as all new, and he adds, "for the most part, the universities excepted, very mean, poor, inconsiderable boroughs, set up by the late returns, practices of sheriffs or ambitious gentlemen desiring to serve them courting, bribing, feasting them for their voices not by prescription or charter . . . since the reign of Edward IV, before whose reign they never elected or returned Members to any English Parliament as now they do"'.[75]

Brougham finished his stroll in the mid-seventeenth century and observed, 'Such then is the old and venerable distribution of representation, time out of mind had and enjoyed in Cornwall and in England at large. Falmouth and Bosinney, Lostwithiel and Grampound may, it seems, be enfranchised by the crown. But let it be proposed to give Birmingham and Manchester, Leeds and Sheffield Members – and the air resounds with cries of revolution!'[76]

Antiquity did not hold the Chancellor long. He invoked new places and new classes. Lord Dudley, speaking earlier, had offered 'sneers at the statesmen of Birmingham and the philosophers of Manchester'. The actual speech was more inoffensive than Brougham implies, but it was too good a handle for a burst of concentrated class war. 'His noble friend was ill-advised when he thought of displaying his talent for sarcasm upon 120,000 people in one place and 180,000 in the other . . .' He did 'little towards conciliating for the aristocracy he adorns by pointing his little epigrams against such mighty masses of the people.'[77]

But Brougham, though a demagogue in the eyes of Tories, was not

---

* Site of the old Commons chamber, now of St Stephen's Hall, leading to the Central Lobby of the Commons.

talking about the great mass of people, what he, like most contemporary politicians, called 'the populace'. In order that Brougham and his colleagues should not be misunderstood as democrats in the sense which would grow respectable before it became first commonplace then cant, the Chancellor made his own demarcations. He was not talking about the Mob, though he had never abused them, and he had held out, always would, against their favourite remedy, 'the absurdity and delusion of the ballot'.[78] Rather, 'I speak now of the middle classes – of those hundreds of thousands of respectable persons – the most numerous and by far the most wealthy order in the community.'

At this point, Brougham launched into the passage which gets into the dictionaries of quotations, and, in its combination of resonant contempt and Gilbertian patter song, deserves to:

> For if all your lordships' castles, manors, rights of warren and rights of chase, with all your broad acres, were brought to the hammer and sold at fifty years' purchase, the price would fly up and kick the beam when counterpoised by the vast and solid riches of those middle classes who are also the genuine depositaries of sober, rational, intelligent and honest English feeling. Unable though they may be to round a period or point an epigram, they are solid, right-judging men and above all, not given to change.[79]

It goes brilliantly and perceptively on its way, rounding periods and pointing epigrams as it does, but also asserting truthfully the small 'c' conservatism of men in cotton, steel, wool and ceramics, in whose name the Manchester Exchange and Leeds Town Hall would be built. By contrast with this mass of virtue, Brougham was not solid, nor always right-judging, certainly not always sober. Steel and cotton had nothing to do with him. He was a lawyer and man of letters flecked with genius. He set himself to use the old aristocratic arts and eloquence to proclaim on behalf of the middle class a triumphalism they increasingly and reasonably felt, but lacked the flair and brazen nerve to assert. Brougham, confected of both, gave them words for the class equivalent of a national anthem. And, having said all this, he asked the huddled nobility of England if they understood what sort of opponent they had taken on.

Didn't they understand that these were people who, having made their minds up, could not be stopped?

> Grave – intelligent – rational – fond of thinking for themselves – they consider a subject long before they make up their minds on it . . . It is

an egregious folly to suppose that the popular clamour for Reform or whatever name you choose to give it could have been silenced by a mere change of Ministers . . . I do believe that no man out of the precincts of Bethlehem hospital, nay no thinking man, certainly not the noble Duke, a most sagacious and reflecting man – can dream of carrying on any government in despite of those middle orders of the State.[80]

That was the essence of it, the people not the populace, as he added (but with the populace not far behind), you could not govern against their concerted will. It was *realpolitik* with a touch of very necessary menace, and it stood upon the changed economic structure of the country.

Brougham then threw himself into the argument, common from the opposition since the whole process began, that whatever might be wrong with rotten boroughs, sale and purchase of representation and the rest of it, the system worked well. 'It works well does it?' enquired the Chancellor. 'For whom? For the Constitution? No such thing. For borough proprietors it works well, who can sell seats or traffic in influence and pocket the gains . . . It works well for the people of England? For the people of whom the many excluded electors are parcel, and for whom alone the few actual electors ought to exercise their franchise as a trust? No such thing.' The member sent to the Commons 'by a single man and not by a county or a town, he does not represent the people of England. He is a jobber sent to Parliament to do his own or his patron's work.' And Brougham next dealt with his own patron-launched career. 'My Lords, are we because the only road to a place is unclean, not to travel it?' Then they were regularly told how many great men had entered Parliament in this way. People using that argument 'do not, I remark, take any account of the far greater numbers of very little men who thus find their way into parliament . . . as docile and disciplined in the evolutions of debate as any troops the noble Duke had at Waterloo'.[81]

But the fulcrum of debate was not the long assailed and defended merit of a principle now twice (in two pieces of legislation) passed through the Commons. It was the question posed by the *Edinburgh Review*, 'What will the Lords do?' Brougham invoked their Lordships' own good sense in the recent matter of Ireland. The Duke of Wellington as Prime Minister 'had been told that the Irish demand would blow over and that yielding to it would be conceding to intimidation'. He had been told, 'It is no time for concession; the people are turbulent and the Associations dangerous.'[82] Spring had come and things got worse and what had the Lords done? 'Your duty – for you despised the cuckoo note of the season "not be intimidated". You granted all that the Irish demanded, and you saved your country.'[83] His demand of the Lords was now that they should concede early and gracefully in order not to find themselves conceding much more under the unquantifiable duress which would follow obduracy.

Then physically enacting his words, Brougham said, 'I solemnly adjure you – I warn you – I implore you – yea on my bended knees I supplicate you – Reject not this bill.'[84] Whether Brougham's subsequent difficulty in rising was gout, the ordinary aches of a man of fifty-three or the consequence of too much mulled port, the effect was not diminished. Even allowing for the swags and bows of the age's florid style, the speech exemplified the wit, erudition and force of personality which that age also thought the constituents of a great oration.

Lord Lyndhurst had a good deal in common with Brougham. A rascal quality made his fellow Tories as suspicious of him as were the Whigs of Brougham. Neither man was to be fully trusted; both were indispensable. Thus armed, they stood in the taxi queue of high-price silks, having preferences, but distinctly available. The son of the distinguished painter, John Singleton Copley, RA, Lyndhurst had cultivation and sensibility, but no family connection. He lived in an open marriage with a clever wife who inclined to Reform, and he is touted as the model from a backward glance for Gilbert's 'Highly susceptible Chancellor' in *Iolanthe*. Though no one would have thought so that evening, it would have been entirely thinkable for him and Brougham to have exchanged their historic places. But it fell to the cynical Lyndhurst to mock the equally cynical Brougham by quoting from a speech of 1819 in which the eradicator of rotten boroughs of 1831 had said

The borough of Old Sarum existed when Somers and the great men of the revolution established our government. Rutland sent as many members as Yorkshire when Hampden lost his life in defence of the Constitution . . . the principles of the construction of this House are pure and worthy. If we should endeavour to change them altogether we should commit the folly of the servant in the story of Aladdin who was deceived by the cry of 'New lamps for old'.[85]

Put in Lyndhurst's non-moralising, good-humoured way, this was formidable debating, a long way from the combination of bristling rage and self-pity favoured by so many Tory Lords. His larger case consisted of a cheerful acknowledgement that, according to the latest researches, the Commons had always been elected by a random mix of franchises and constituencies, but that the point of the 1688 revolution had been to get rid of the capricious powers of the King. That done, didn't the good old muddle work quite well? Then, picking on inconsistencies in the Bill: over-representation for Malton, underrepresentation for Huddersfield – what was so different about the new order that they should set themselves to so vast and disturbing a change. He, Lyndhurst, was not for rejecting all change or for a shift of government. He would be happy for Grey and his ministers to return with a milder measure.

Like Brougham, Lyndhurst was a gladiator, though one happy to fight with a buttoned blade. But he was enough of a Tory to play the Irish card. Of the one hundred members returned for Ireland, three-fourths were Catholics or supporters of Catholics: 'That number therefore are, or will be, agitators.'[86] He also looked forward with varying degrees of prescience to the things which a reformed Parliament, with its new, rougher element, English as well as Irish, might do. 'The Corn-Laws, our colonial possessions, all will be attacked in our reformed parliament.'[87] (Lyndhurst would live to serve as Peel's Lord Chancellor, helping fifteen years later to legislate for the repeal of the same Corn Laws and specifically informing protectionists in the Lords that none of their amendments could be accepted.[88])

He made an interesting historic parallel between the rebels of the seventeenth century and the radical and press opinion at that date: 'Out of doors we have been menaced in every variety of form . . . The cry of the seventeenth century, of malignant and rotten-headed Lords, has been revived and there have even been appeals to soldiers.'[89] He followed this with a quaintly passive and antiquarian notion of Parliament: 'We are placed here my Lords not to pass Vestry Acts or Road Bills, but for the purpose of guarding against any rash result from the acts of the advisers of the Crown, and against the wishes of the people when they might lead to destruction.'[90] Gracefully cynical, Lyndhurst invited his friends to reject the Bill because the people were 'noble and generous' and because, if the Lords did their duty and rejected the Bill, 'although that should be contrary to their inclination, they will abstain from all violence'.[91] Lyndhurst's cheerful complacency about the consequences of Lords' rejection would be more nearly right than the apocalyptic school, but he was whistling rather loudly.

One contribution not much cited was that of the Duke of Sussex. In the splendid words of J. H. Plumb, Augustus, second youngest son of George III, 'was given to ridiculous marriages, Whig principles and debt, but he was a warm-hearted man, foolish, extravagant, quaint, easy to caricature. There was no evil in him.'[92] Royalty had already intervened with some effect backstage in the general reactionary interest with the whisperings of Cumberland to George IV. Sussex contented himself with a short speech on the last day of the Lords debate. It did a warm heart great credit.

> In favour of that Bill numberless petitions have been presented; and I say therefore that the Bill is in conformity with the opinions of the people. It has been the fashion with some noble Lords to treat the people with disrespect. I can not agree with the noble lords in that sentiment. I know the people better than many of your Lordships do . . . I have gone to the mechanics' societies, I have visited their institutions and seen their libraries. At Nottingham they have a library that would do credit to the house of any nobleman . . . Now have not these men as good judgment as your Lordships? – And if they have, have they not a just right to use it?[93]

And on the French revolutionary influence, Augustus was surprisingly crisp: 'We have been told of the French Revolution, and of other foreign transactions as having created the present felling in the public mind. If I were to use an expression which is perhaps not very courteous in your House, but which nevertheless is strong and comprehensive, I should say this is a mere humbug.'[94] As for boroughs as immutable property rights, Sussex, sensibly disclaiming the antiquarian learning which had littered the speeches of Tory lawyers, observed, 'How particular boroughs got into the hands of particular noble Peers I do not pretend to say; but this I will say, that they have no right to them.' There is no need to patronise Sussex, a prince making a liberal speech. Unlike Dr Johnson's dog walking on his hind legs, it *was* well done, six columns, generous, sensible and to the point, if not a powerful precedent.

Debates at this time began late and went on to the delightful hours where late merges into early, and later speakers, by no means all of them tedious, have their *Hansard* text pocked with repetitions of 'Question'. Of poor Lord Barham, managing a mere third of a column, it is recorded that he 'supported the Bill and contended amid frequent cries of "Question", that their Lordships were called upon in duty to pass a measure which had come before them so sanctioned and supported'. Accordingly, when Grey rose to sum up, he spoke of 'the exhausted state in which I find myself at this advanced hour of the morning'.[95]

But Grey was in total earnest. He went back yet again to his Foxite, neo-Girondin past, to the letter severing his and his friends' connections with the more Jacobinical 'The Friends of the People'. But this had not been a lurch into reaction. The key sentence in that letter had been that great Whig mantra, 'We wish to reform the Constitution because we wish to preserve it.' That was what he wanted now, but the Tories had argued that the government, by seeking reform, had provoked public excitement. The excitement had been there before they came to office. It had relaxed with the prospect of reform, something brushed aside by the Tories as a factitious calm which the extreme radicals 'who look to certain results, have produced for the better attainment of their destructive purposes. But does any body believe that the feelings of a whole people can be so controlled, can be awakened, roused, excited, and then again be suddenly silenced by any individuals or any combination of individuals . . . ?'[96]

Grey was concerned to stress the affinities between a Tory government's response to that Catholic/Irish crisis of 1828, when outside pressure weighed so much, and the decision now waiting upon the House of Lords. 'Did the noble Duke then think he was bound as a Minister of the Crown, to resist a change from which destructive consequences were so confidently predicted? No my lords, his policy was more rational and withal, more safe . . . he came forward himself to propose that great measure of peace and conciliation, which he had until that time opposed.'[97] This was a charge which enraged Wellington, and the Whigs, holding an ace, saw no reason not to keep playing it.

Grey also invoked the King. He was 'bound to the king by obligations of gratitude greater perhaps than subject ever owed to a sovereign for the kind manner in which he has extended to me his confidence and support . . .'.[98] This was true, not least because all ministers with experience were grateful to William after the nightmare of Georges III and IV. (Mrs Arbuthnot put things another way: 'It is, one must acknowledge, true, the king had no alternative but to take Lord Grey. The fault he committed was in dissolving Parlt. For, at that time, he knew the Tory Party were reunited; but he was in the hands of his blackguard Ministers, who deceived him & he had not experience or character to resist them.'[99] But Grey was also telling the opposition that the Ministry was not looking for a way off the hook, and he made an assertion of his own dogged purpose. 'All that I can pretend to is an honest zeal – an anxious desire to do my duty in the best way that I can as long as he is content to accept my services on these terms, no personal sacrifices shall stand in the way of my performing the duty I owe to a sovereign . . . I had no desire for place, and it was not sought after by me; it was offered to me in such circumstances that nothing but a sense of duty could have induced me to accept it.'[100]

If that sounds a little prim, Grey was more entitled than most to speak in such terms. He had, as he also added, lived almost all his political life in exclusion from office and had formed no habits of office. He had the chance of doing something in which, whatever the flickering at midnight, he had always believed. The King's good sense was a bonus and much valued. But Grey was telling the Lords that he would not let the obduracy of their hereditary selves in the teeth of a public will create a vacuum in which that long purpose would slip away.

The vote was taken at six o'clock on the Saturday morning, not upon Wharncliffe's provocative total rejection, but upon the customary motion of a six month laying aside of the Bill. The result, at that early hour, including proxy votes, was rejection by 199 votes to 158, defeat by 41. The reaction of doomed, silly Mrs Arbuthnot was straightforward: 'we beat them by forty-one & in my opinion, the Lords never so faithfully served their country, not even when they obtained Magna Charta [sic] from King John'.[101] The wider response would be rather different.

EIGHT

Bristol, Birmingham and After

'Numbers were cut down and ridden over'

'The *Chronicle* is in mourning. The *Times, Herald* and other papers assuming an awful tone. The Common Council and Merchants are to meet immediately, and of course the Westminster Reformers.'[1] On the Monday (10 October) those Westminster reformers met at their habitual resort, the Crown and Anchor.* Hobhouse could not remember a larger meeting in its great room. As the local member he was carried shoulder high to the far end of the room, had his pocket picked in the process and observed 'the greatest spirit and propriety'.[3] But nothing that was said there is recorded. Not so the protest meeting at Taunton next day: Sydney Smith, co-founder of the *Edinburgh Review* and now Canon of St Paul's, most enjoyable and inventive of polemicists, sent from there his own message to the Lords. He invoked for comparison the eccentric lady, Mrs Partington, living near the beach at Sidmouth, who had responded to a flood in 1824 by trying to sweep it back with a broom. She

> had been seen at the door of her house with mop and pattens, trundling her mop, squeezing out the sea water and vigorously pushing away the Atlantic Ocean. The Atlantic was roused. Mrs Partington's spirit was up; I need not tell you that the contest was unequal. The Atlantic Ocean beat Mrs Partington. She was excellent with a slop or a puddle, but she should not have meddled with a tempest. Gentlemen, be at your ease – be quiet and steady. You will beat Mrs Partington.[4]

Unfortunately not everyone was quiet and steady. The Crown and Anchor meeting, with its spirit and propriety and pickpockets, was merely the respectable part of the response. Lord Ebrington had earlier told

---

* Oddly, the same hostelry had been, in the early 1790s, the regular venue of a Church and King, Death to the French assembly of High Tories, including James Boswell.[2]

Hobhouse that the bill was scheduled to end before the week was out although willing speakers could have filled out more time. They would do so, he said, because Saturday was pay day for workmen in the vicinity. Drink being the curse of the working classes, the feeling among people who had money at all times seems to have been that the 'populace' was more likely to riot when it could afford to. But the likelihood that somebody would riot was, in Whig and Tory minds, a fearful, fascinating part of the long gamble of Reform and resistance to it.

Wharncliffe's account of the shopkeepers of Bond Street who were ashamed of the Reform Bill now found a disputing echo on a placard outside a shoe shop in that select street which read '199 against 22,000,0000'. The shoemaker 'though very civil, was very firm and refused to remove the placard saying he had only done as others had done'.[5] And Hobhouse, on his way to court with constituents' addresses, keen reformer that he was, felt uneasy. 'I was surprised on going into the streets to find the shops shut and a great many ill-looking and ill-dressed people standing about. There was something in the look and manners of the crowds which I confess, I did not like.'[6]

Grey's instinct, like that of Asquith in two similar crises eighty years later, was to take his time. It was a dangerous approach. Peaceful protest with large numbers in choreographed attendance could be counted upon both as warning to the Tories and stiffening of the government. Attwood in Birmingham and Place in London would see to that, but the risk of gatherings neither orderly, nor peaceful, was serious. And on the London streets, as Lord Holland recorded 'the "populace" who on the whole conducted themselves peaceably, though they broke some anti-reform windows, shewed something like a savage thirst of revenge in pursuing Sir Robert Peel and the Duke of Cumberland, and struck Lord Londonderry on his arm with a stick and another on his head with a brick bat [sic] in consequence of his imprudent defiance and threat of carrying pistols about him'.[7]

But the immediate business of the organised radicals was skilfully managed and went well. The Lords' rejection of the Bill on the morning of Saturday 8 October* was followed on the Monday by a meeting, organised by the Marylebone Vestry, in Regent's Park, claiming 80,000 attendance. Francis Place, long an influence but now to emerge as a public player, remarked with convoluted menace that its resolutions were 'commendable as quietly letting down the exacerbation without impairing the disposition to use physical force, should it become necessary to employ it'.[8] On 12 October a march to the King's official levee was staged in

* Business of Friday 7 October.

support of the Bill. The numbers, though wildly disputed, were clearly very large and were a manifestation of working-class commitment to the Bill.

That same evening, Place was invited to meet at the Crown and Anchor a group of one hundred activists, delegates from London parishes supporting the Bill but at something of a loss about what to do beyond giving lame support to the government. He instructed them with quotations from ministerial speeches, with his own conviction that the prospect of a long-prorogued parliament signified retreat which in turn would spark popular action. The meeting took on a life of its own with a motion carrying there and then that a memorial should be put together and delivered directly to Lord Grey. Place swiftly set out the fears he had expressed, calling for the shortest possible prorogation and reintroduction of the Bill. He then, with seventeen of the delegates, descended on Downing Street at 10.45 p.m. and won admittance. Grey pleaded tiredness, the need for time and general difficulty. The quantifiable effect was slight, and Place uncharacteristically failed to get the episode the front-page-holding splash it deserved. But the 'midnight delegation', as it was called, came to be part of the mood-making legend of those weeks. To Tories it was an outrage as sinister as it was insolent in its design against order and all things decent. To others the excursion was proof that if the plain people of England had found a way of talking quietly to the Prime Minister, they would not now be stopped.

Meanwhile, the Birmingham political union had been monitoring events closely. Nobody feared violence more than Attwood. The psychology of reform, a thing sought from the possessing class by the not-possessing, involved an unquantifiable balance of sweet reason and scare. It was not enough to ask nicely. Minds like Mrs Arbuthnot's, for whom Lord Grey's government were 'blackguards', could never see Midlands shopkeepers as fellow citizens. It was necessary to drum very hard on the carapace of such contentment. But violence, however remote from the leaders of Reform, would provide a pretext for repression. Peterloo was only just over a decade past, and Tory MPs had reflected in the first Commons debate with satisfaction at how firm measures and a manly resolve had restored 'tranquillity'.

Men like Attwood and Place had in their minds' eyes a resort to soldiers, yeomanry and martial law, all the staples of firm measures, measures to be taken by a Wellington government, not against violence only, but against the whole intolerable movement in the country. Attwood dashed out an address which said what he wanted to say in its first fourteen words: 'The Bill of Reform is rejected by the House of Lords! Patience! Patience!

Patience!'[9] He went on to say that the people had nothing to fear 'unless their own violence should rashly lead to anarchy and place difficulties in the way of the King and Ministers. Therefore there must be no violence. The people are too strong to need violence.'[10] He had a terse, short-sentenced way which, in an age which liked stringing florid sub-clauses like beads, is as pleasing as it must have been effective when read round the city. And while riots would break out in Nottingham and Derby, and the castle/residence of the most gnarled of all Dukes, his Grace of Newcastle, was attacked and burnt, Birmingham got away with a scattering of broken glass and rough words to an uncompliant clergyman. But Birmingham also understood theatre. News of Lords' rejection came in at 5 p.m. on the Saturday. The response was Mediterranean: the tolling of the muffled bells of churches and chapels for the rest of the evening and night, what Attwood in a letter called 'a dirge for the oligarchs echoing in the heart of England'.[11]

But he was not organising restraint out of respect. Attwood feared back-sliding by moderate Whigs looking for a side exit, and so he coupled with this strict orderliness a second address directed beyond Birmingham, calling for the establishment of political unions throughout Britain to campaign for the Bill. And fifty requests for the union's rule book came in, something actively followed up in a number of towns. Birmingham was as smooth and unified an operation as it was, despite much bickering, because it was a city of many small workshops, many little masters and skilled men, with few great factories served by 'hands'. Birmingham had a natural democracy of its own and arguably fewer class antagonisms. Manchester and London both had political unions in opposition to one another and, as Edward Thompson points out, in Bolton, Lords' rejection led to a split in the union between incrementalists and advocates of manhood suffrage. The second group would stage a march 6,000 strong with banners proclaiming 'Down with the Bishops! No Peers!'[12]

The mood varied from place to place. Anger in Nottinghamshire owed a good deal to the character of the Duke of Newcastle. Henry Pelham Clinton was a character out of melodrama, ready probably to water the workers' beer and happy to meet Reform by evicting tenants known to support it with the words 'May I not do what I will with mine own?' After his castle and other property had been burned down in the riots, he demanded of Melbourne the chairmanship of the commission which should try his suspected enemies.* And the rougher end of the aristocracy

---

* Even without the Duke's assistance three men would subsequently be hanged for this outburst.

took to violent self-help, Newcastle himself emptying Clumber, another ducal seat, of all its encumbering finery and installing ten small cannon and a force of two hundred men. His brother of Rutland called up powder and shot from Woolwich and had his farm labourers and servants drilled and taught elementary gunnery.[13]

Under a different sort of fire at this time were the bishops. Wellington's canvass of his Grace of Canterbury had answered very well. Only one Bishop, Maltby of Chichester,* came out for Reform in the Lords' division, with another, the aged Bathurst of Norwich, registering support by proxy. Twelve princes of the Church had attended the Upper House to refuse Reform. Led by Howley of Canterbury, they were Bath & Wells, Bristol, Exeter, Gloucester, Llandaff, Lincoln, Lichfield, Oxford, Rochester, Salisbury and Winchester. Hostile proxies were recorded for the Archbishop of Tuam and the Bishops of Bangor, Carlisle, Cloyne, Cork, Durham, Leighlin & Fearns, Peterborough and St Asaph. On the reforming market, bishops became a distinct 'sell'. Richard Carlile, most extravagant (and theologically inclined) of reformers, wrote succinctly, 'The Bishops have done it, it is the work of the Holy Ghost.'[14] Van Mildert of Durham dared not appear in the county, full as it was of indignant colliers. When, in spite of the edginess on the streets, the House of Lords continued to function, its own burst of social unrest arose aptly over the conduct of a bishop.

Henry Phillpotts, Bishop of Exeter, was an exceptionally tiresome individual. An appointment of Wellington's, he had clung valiantly to a prebend of Durham worth £2,000 and had done nothing to his credit on the eve of a great wave of ecclesiastical reform. But there was nothing furtive about Exeter doing well for himself. He was a furious and outraged anti-reformer, the episcopal equivalent of Charles Wetherell and a defender à outrance of every last privilege attaching to the cloth of the Established Church. Sydney Smith would say, 'I must believe in the Apostolic Succession, there being no other way of accounting for the descent of the Bishop of Exeter from Judas Iscariot.'

Accordingly, a parliamentary wrangle about tithes on the Tuesday after Saturday's rejection, something which might at another time have passed with Regency good manners, caught ministers red-raw with anger at a Right Reverend bench contributing 18 votes to their defeat by 41. Lord King, who had brought in the tithes petition listing a number of abuses, said that the Dean and Chapter dealing with a Suffolk parish had appointed a vicar 'who was as might be expected, a non-resident' and added that

* 'That idiot Maltby' to his fellow reformer, Sydney Smith who had fancied the diocese.

203

the clergy 'professed to be against all changes and to be desirous that every-thing remained unchanged, but who when their own interest were concerned, became arch-disturbers of the peace'.[15] Argument rapidly shifted back to the debate concluded three days before.

Brougham blazed at them with his best Scotch dominie sarcasm: 'The Right Reverend prelates have acted with the greatest disinterestedness. Good God my lords, it is the last charge which I thought anyone would bring against them. They had a right to pursue the course they did. Who can deny it? They had a right to vote against the government; and if they thought that they had the opportunity of tripping up the government, my Lords, they had a right to do so.' Exeter promptly showed his head above the parapet, defying any one 'to state an instance when any Members of that House had been so vilified and insulted as the Bishops had been within the last week . . . notions were propagated everywhere against the Bench of Bishops and noble lords had moreover spoken against them in that House in a tone of sarcasm, if not of direct and positive censure, as a body actuated by self interest at variance with the public good'.[16]

Brougham did his heavy sarcasm, Grey his aristocratic disdain; 'a most tremendous dressing'[17] Greville called it. 'This,' said the Prime Minister was 'the most intemperate and the most unfounded insinuation that he had ever heard from any Member of the House. Was the charge made against him or the Lord Chancellor? How could he make an attack so intemperate and utterly without foundation . . . But the Right Reverend prelate was not content with this want of truth, but he had uttered it with all the appearance of a spirit that but little became the garment that he wore.' As to implications that the government were encouraging disorder by their legislation, 'The Right Reverend Prelate had uttered a foul and calumnious aspersion, totally unfounded in truth . . .'[18] As to Exeter's merely stupid words that day, the charge was unfair, but the rebuke amounted to a blast at all the peers, temporal or spiritual, who had made such charges of incitement steadily through the entire debate. And Grey, normally bound to elaborate civility by the graces of his order and personal reputation, must have felt much better for saying it.

But to contrast what passed in Parliament for fierce, bitter action with what happened outside is to touch on the strangeness of the times. Greville made an entry in his diary on 23 October and dated Newmarket: 'Nothing but racing all this week; Parliament has been prorogued and all is quiet. The world seems tired, and requires rest.' He added, fortunately for his sceptical reputation, 'How soon it will all begin again God knows, but it will not be suffered to sleep long.'[19] Sleep was permitted until 29 October. In the Lords, the Prime Minister had demolished a bishop. In Bristol a month later riots broke out which, running for three days, burnt down, amongst a great clutch of the city's central buildings, a bishop's palace, riots which saw the military first called up then lose their nerve, before reinforcements under new military men given *carte blanche* by Melbourne finally put down the mob in a distinctly Cossack way much applauded in the London clubs.

Bristol had got rid of its old Tory oligarchical corporation. It had sent two radical reformers to Westminster in 1831. It had its own, recently formed political union, though there was no hand like Attwood's to control it. It was ripe for provocation. And of all unsuitable persons to preside at its Assizes, Sir Charles Wetherell was the most unsuitable. It was not just that the Member for Boroughbridge was something of a buffoon, frequently the worse for drink and eye-catchingly vivid in all his political utterance, but that he had directly and specifically abused the prospective £10 suffrage holders of Bristol as pauper voters to be sought 'at a lazaretto'. But Sir Charles was Recorder of the degraded place. It was for him to attend and give judgement with all the processioning, public dining and show-making of the day in that city. In fact, intelligent voices from the city pleaded, sought, to avoid an obvious trigger. A deputation from the Bristol magistracy asked for the assize to be postponed; Wetherell, who had made himself even more obnoxious by his comments on the Derby and Nottingham riots, passed the issue to the Home Secretary. After two meetings, the second of which involved both of Bristol's two MPs and the Recorder, Melbourne ignored the warning.[20] Instead, he sent cavalry, not enough to contain riot, and more provocation than defence against violent protest. The local political union so resented the use of troops to protect the detested Wetherell that they denied co-operation to their commander, Colonel Brereton, a humane and nervous man. Withdrawal of the troops from the city centre added a vacuum to general public anger. Prolonged and destructive riots followed for which everyone except Melbourne was blamed.

The bishops were a point of departure in Bristol too. The public cry of one man, Charles Davies, was 'Down with churches and mend the roads with them.'[21] He would later be hanged for saying so. Books from the cathedral were burnt along with the palace. For the opponents of Reform, and perhaps not only for them, Bristol was the Marseilles of Britain, a maritime city standing in much the same relationship to London as the Mediterranean port did to Paris, with the advantage of being much nearer. A march on London was never contemplated and the mob spent a good deal of their time getting drunk, but, as a way of putting people into a funk, the Bristol riots did very well.

Greville corrected himself. 'The country was beginning to slumber after the fatigues of Reform, when it was rattled up by the business at Bristol which for brutal ferocity and wanton, unprovoked violence must vie with some of the worst scenes of the French Revolution . . .'[22] It certainly confirmed his own conservative instincts: 'The spirit which produced these atrocities was generated by Reform . . . it was a premature outbreaking of the thirst for plunder and longing after havoc and destruction, which is the essence of Reform in the minds of the Mob.'[23]

Though he was a man open to compassion, Greville's response to the counter-violence dealt out by the soldiery is instructive. He observed that 'More punishment has been dealt out than has been generally known, and some hundreds were killed or severely wounded by the sabre. One body of dragoons pursued a rabble of colliers into the country, and covered the fields with the bodies of wounded wretches, making a severe example of them.'[24] For a jittery and snapping Greville, at least at that moment, everything flowed from Reform and, moreover, from 'a mob-ridden Government and a foolish king, who renders himself subservient to the folly and wickedness of his Ministers . . .'.[25]

Colonel Brereton, faced with the fires and rioting, flinched from using full force to restore authority. His deputy, Major Mackworth, later reinforced by troops under Lord Hill, did not. 'Numbers were cut down and ridden over; some were driven into the burning houses, out of which they were never seen to return, and our dragoons after sabreing all that they could at the Square, collected and formed and then charged down Princes Street and again returned to the Square, riding at the miserable mob in all directions; about 120 of the incendiaries were killed and wounded here.'[26] Brock puts the total number of casualties over all at four hundred while reckoning that 'many more were wounded than killed in the cavalry charges. Though some rioters were driven back without hope of escape into burning buildings.'[27] All contemporary indignation was aimed at the rioters, but the impression remains of a degree of late-in-the-day ferocity worthy of General Lake in Ireland after the '98 or, indeed, of Haynau in Hungary in 1849.

Yet amidst such miseries, between Newmarket and a great house, on 11 November something else fell into Greville's consciousness. The cholera which had dallied so long in Poland and Germany as to be almost written off as a threat, and which had divided medical opinion about its contagious or non-contagious nature, proved contagious and cosmopolitan enough to land in England. The first cases were reported that day in Sunderland. The shipbuilding town on the River Wear had just been designated under the rejected Bill to obtain two seats in Parliament! The disease had been watched impotently for months. On 18 October Vyvyan announced the approach of 'Cholera Morbus'. And, since 'the fatal disorder had appeared at Hamburgh, within thirty-six hours "voyage by steam to this country" . . .' he asked 'whether, as the disease had now only to cross the German Ocean, any additional measures of quarantine had been taken against it?' Poulett Thompson for the Board of Trade announced 'orders enforcing a more strict quarantine with respect to all vessels coming from Hamburgh and . . . to vessels coming from any part of the coast lying between the North of Denmark and Rotterdam.'[28] After some to-ing and fro-ing, Henry Hunt intervened with the terse and sensible suggestion that the government should take the duty off soap. 'The poor classes would then be able to keep themselves clean; and cleanliness be found the best preventative of Cholera Morbus.'[29]

Ministerial replies had been careful not to promise that cholera would be kept in Hamburg. It was as well; on 11 November, Greville paused from his denunciations of weak kings and wicked ministers to record, with a note of self-pity, 'Nothing was wanting to complete our situation but the addition of physical evil to our moral plague, and that is come in the shape of the Cholera, which broke out in Sunderland a few days ago.'[30]

The same Greville who had talked with approval of the supererogatory brutality of Lord Hill's troops was stopped by reports out of Sunderland almost on mid-page. He recorded

a state of human misery, and necessarily of moral degradation, such as I hardly ever heard of and it is no wonder when a great part of the community is plunged into such a condition (and we may suppose that there is a gradually mounting scale, with every degree of wretchedness up to the wealth and splendour which glitter on the surface of society), that there should be so many who are ripe for any desperate scheme of revolution. At Sunderland they say there are houses with 150 inmates who are huddled five and six in a bed.[31]

A few days later he was sending £200 (£10,000 of our money) to the operation in Sunderland, remarking that 'we who float on the surface of society know but little of the privations and sufferings which pervade the mass; [and after all our boasting of our many national virtues, what does it all come to?]'[32]

The events at Bristol had their own impact on the debate of what should happen next. The Tories saw an advantage, calling them 'the Reform riots'.[33] Hobhouse, clear in his own mind that Lords rejection should be met by Lords creation, a wholesale elevation of enough new noblemen to vote down the old ones, was depressed by what he saw as Grey's drift and irresolution. Ashley had narrowly won that Dorset by-election, from which the Tories derived all sorts of hopes that a tide might be turning in their favour. Grey did not hurry to return to Parliament. Greville, placed to talk to both sides, heard from Richmond, anyway a fortuitous member of a reforming government, who agreed with his suggestion that 'nothing would do but a compromise between the parties'[34] and added that he would like to talk with Wharncliffe, the chief Waverer.

But Wharncliffe told Greville that matters were already much further advanced. Lines had been opened between Palmerston and himself, drawing in Harrowby and with Stanley from the Ministry meeting the Waverers with Grey's consent. This meeting led to a general statement of wavering principles on both sides, followed by a further encounter, this time between Wharncliffe and Grey at East Sheen on 16 November, the result of which was a minute presented to the Cabinet. This, as Wharncliffe told Greville, allowed for

> the concession of Schedule A, of representation for the great towns and a great extension of country representation on one side; the abandon-ment, or nearly so of Schedule B, such an arrangement with regard to the £10 qualification as shall have the practical effect of a higher rate and an understanding that the manufacturing interest is not to have a preponderating influence in the county representation, a great deal to be left open to discussion, especially on all the subordinate points.[35]

But in such scheming there was a bubble element. People who wanted as little reform as possible hoped from the Whig side to water the legisla-tion down. Wharncliffe and Harrowby, sensibly from their point of view, hoped for a smaller reform package. But beyond all such talk lay the country. And as Lord Durham told Sir James Graham, the King's support derived from mass public pressure. 'Do you think he keeps you in now because he likes you or on Whig principles? Far from it. He does so because the people would not sanction a Tory government for an hour.'[36] That was a remark in October prophetic of events the following May.

Parallel with such manoeuvring, the government's relationship with the political unions was coming under pressure. To the Tories, they were not worth distinguishing from the Parisian political clubs, the Vieux Cordeliers and Jacobins of the 1790s. Wellington was besotted with the subject and wrote to the King calling for the suppression of the Birmingham union which he accused of preparing to arm and form a guard. Fear that the unions might imitate the mobile troops which had underwritten the extremists in Paris during the Revolution was another preoccupation. Wellington's folly at this time reflected his extreme distance from any sort of popular feeling, however moderate. Like Wharncliffe and Sidmouth, he had his own definition of 'the country'. Writing to the Duke of Buckingham, he said, 'I was certain that nineteen-twentieths of the whole country would concur with me. I did it likewise at a period of the year at which I knew that if the king wished to get rid of the bonds in which he is held, I could assist him in doing so. There was time to call a new Parliament.'[37]

Wellington was wrong about the country, and wrong about the nature of the unions, but he was right, at least in theory, about military preparations. Birmingham, a city of metalworkers, included among them any number of gunsmiths. More easily than anywhere in Britain a Birmingham organisation with wide support could have armed itself. Thomas Attwood was the last man capable of doing anything which might be confused with French revolutionary activity. He was, though, balancing himself between the government whose nerve he did not wholly trust and which he wished to keep up to the mark, and his own rank and file, keen to see a show of metal.

In the opinion of his biographer, David Moss, Attwood was happy to talk openly about the option of a guard and did so deliberately. 'Proofs had been sent to public officials for approval and at the open council meetings, he had always taken care to emphasize his personal confidence in the king and the Whigs.'[38] It was all a long way from Wellington's excited communication to his circle that Attwood 'has given them, moreover, an organisation which is neither more nor less than that of the United Irishmen . . . if we do not put these unions down with a firm hand, they will destroy the country'.[39] But if Wellington feared Henry Joy McCracken and the '98 in Ireland, Attwood, as David Moss puts it, feared another French model: a Polignac declaring a present danger and suspending constitutional niceties to form a government of order as defined by himself. Messages were being sent, not saying that Birmingham was armed or wanted to arm but that it could if it wanted to, and that any attempt to suppress the unions would be resisted. To that end, everything was very public. The Duke did not have a scoop; he was reading what had been written out, not least for him to see. Not for nothing did Attwood hold almost daily and startlingly frank conversations with the Bank of England's Birmingham agent, George Nicholls, whose letters to the governor and excellent ministerial contacts were known to many more than Attwood.[40]

Attwood also had his brother, Matthias, Member of Parliament, devoted Tory and anti-reformer, from whom he must have had a shrewd knowledge of what the Duke might be up to. So when the time came to withdraw the military card, it was almost certainly a move which Attwood had prepared and was comfortable with. He allowed urgent requests from the trusted Althorp, passed through the sanctimonious and not at all trusted Joseph Parkes, to persuade him and what might be called his executive not to pursue the idea. Placed between the Duke and more militant activists in the country who disliked his long and careful game, he had fretted the one to gain credit with the other and was able to withdraw more or less gracefully. The Whigs, wiser and better informed than the Duke, did not discount French-style violence, but they knew well enough that the serious unions which Wellington wanted to suppress were a barrier against it. The whole episode was politics nicely executed.

Interestingly, King William had, at least initially, a better sense of the unions than the Duke who had excitedly communicated his fears in what Lord Holland called 'a paper, ill written and ill reasoned, containing some obvious legal and constitutional truths, loosely applied to unions and meetings, very vaguely described'. Holland, in the government as an advanced reformer, noted with approval William's observation that the unions 'had existed both for the purposes of raising wages and in some instances for political purposes too before the Duke of Wellington left office', and that their increasing political activity antedated the Grey Ministry or the Reform Bill being brought in 'and that it was idle to suppose that they had been created by the bill'.[41]

Grey took some credit for the retreat, however small his own part in events, and Althorp more. But the Prime Minister was going through his own crisis. The pressures of furious debate in which he had taken the central burden, the breakdown of ordinary law in two major cities, the hysteria for which Wellington spoke and the nagging, if reasonable anxiety of his more radical colleagues were bad enough. Then private grief over the death of little Charles Lambton produced a furious outburst from his son-in-law during a meeting at Althorp's house. Grey tried very hard to be a Roman in state matters and private, but the gifted and fraught Durham was altogether more extrovert both in grief and political responses. That open quarrel at Althorp's home involved savage recriminations from Durham and tears from Grey. None of this should surprise us. If the normally measured Greville, without private troubles and not an extremist, found himself talking of Grey, his colleagues and William as a 'mob-ridden government and a foolish king subservient to the wickedness and folly of his Ministers', panic was doing as well as cholera. But the dominant reforming part of the Cabinet was alert to the risk of resiling from its purpose, implicit in 'a less objectionable bill'.[42]

In conservative minds, optimism flared up. Grey had seen the error of his radical ways. The moderate members of the government would be split from 'the subversive party'.[43] The concessions to which they looked forward would mark Grey out as an enemy to the outsider radicals like 'Place and his rabble',[44] and ministers would suffer the humiliation of having to do a deal with Wharncliffe. Greville saw all this in prospect and took pleasure, though he asked 'By what process Althorp and John Russell were induced to concur, and how they are to set about swallowing their own words, I do not guess.'[45]

However briefly Grey may have been tempted in such a direction, it was all a splendid illusion. Althorp and John Russell were neither concurring, disposed to eat their words nor ready to suffer humiliation. The parallel account of the Whig minister, Holland, sees the same events in a very different light. A long Cabinet meeting lasting more than five hours had considered possible changes in the Bill, but waited upon missing ministers to make any decision. As for Wharncliffe, he had indeed 'had a long conversation with Grey in which he acknowledged his wish to agree with the government and the impossibility and even impropriety and danger of their yielding any material point much less any principle, to which they were pledged',[46] before listing what changes might be made. Wharncliffe made it clear that his authority to speak was very loose. The changes which would reconcile him might reconcile other peers, but he stressed that he spoke (Holland's italics) *without being authorized to say so*.[47] It was all a great deal softer-handed and more tentative than the grand accomplished retreat of Greville's wish-fulfilling imagination.

The pertinent division in the Cabinet lay on the question of recalling Parliament. Grey favoured delay and had created a widespread anxiety on the left by doing so. Holland, a witness, saw only 'personal inclination and the manifold inconvenience of a session before Xmas'.[48] He had the support of Palmerston 'faintly' and the Duke of Richmond 'earnestly', with the absent Lansdowne and Stanley said to agree. But delay was never going to be possible. Greville grumbled in his journal on the 23rd that a Tory informant, Bentinck, had 'confirmed my apprehension that Wharncliffe had been cajoled into a negotiation which the government intended should end by getting all they want'.[49] And he put Richmond, Palmerston and Grey into a minority of three over parliamentary resumption. It was a time for two-way suspicion between the main forces – suspicion of a feverish, gossipy, best-hoping and worst-fearing sort. By way of illustration, Greville blamed it all on Goderich! 'One of the most radical of the cabinet is Goderich. Such a thing it is to be of feeble intellect and character, and yet he is a smart speaker and an agreeable man.'[50] As Holland, who was there, tells it, on the occasion of that five-hour meeting, 'Goderich, who had been converted to the disagreeable necessity of calling Parliament immediately, gave that opinion, with his face covered with his hands . . .'[51] Either way, an early return had been voted through by eight to three. The thinking behind the decision was a combination of 'the representations of friends', anxiety about what the unions might do and a realisation that leaving a constitutional crisis bubbling without a Parliament troubling to assemble looked horribly careless.

In a way that underlined the key relationship of this government, Althorp told Holland later that, though he was certain they should go back, he had avoided arguing the point to avoid a conflict with Grey. The solicitous consideration and trust between these two men was a central truth of the Ministry. The government were not at this time fully in charge of events and they knew it. The House of Lords had put rioters on the streets. The political unions could choose to be cautious or revolutionary. The Cabinet supported a statement based on the law officers' judgement about the illegality of the unions, but, as Holland remarked behind his hand, nothing done by the courts against the unions amounted to more than 'scolding and railing – utterly unequal to prevent the formation of unions or to disperse them when formed, if there is determination in the people to persist'.[52] And when it came to the Speech from the throne, Grey headed off William's desire to say a few ill-chosen words of condemnation.

Perhaps in response to Wellington's memorandum writing, something dubiously proper in a former Prime Minister scrabbling at the edges of constitutional government and much resented by ministers, William was anxious to say a word on law and order and suppression of illegal combinations. He had wanted to identify the political unions (this was three years before the Tolpuddle case), but Ministers hauled him back and his speech as drafted would contain clear, unWellingtonian things about the people having 'a full right to discuss and represent their grievances'.

Having settled on a date for Parliament's recall in December, the Cabinet had made the big jump. Its own supporters would be relieved and their pressure would relax. It could now discuss its own modifications. The channel to Wharncliffe was kept open, but it was becoming clear to them that the authority he had assumed by an initiative was not underwritten by his party. Despite early friendliness, Wellington was obsessed with the political unions and in no mood for finesse. Wharncliffe, whom the affable Holland thought 'not exempt from some little vanity in acting as a self-constituted mediator without any positive authority and perhaps with very little concurrence of opinion with any body', had told Peel and Wellington the detail of his talks with Grey 'and the former returned a dry answer which he did not relish'.[53]

The Ministry had, since the Lords' rejection, been caught between fires. It was pressed by its social peers to temper the Bill more or less drastically so that their Lordships would let it through. Yet it was a government pledged to Reform and one sharply monitored by reformers, notably by the political unions. Dilution had been attractive to a minority of Cabinet ministers, particularly those whose conversion to Reform had been a pragmatic reaction to Wellington's immobilism of a year earlier. But it was no more than a minority. A steady plurality of the Cabinet wanted the substance of the Bill just sufficiently buttered to put the Tories in the wrong and to get compliance from the King when the alternative to dilution should be reached, as it surely must be, the creation of peers!

Wharncliffe and his enthusiastic admirer, Greville, thought in terms of a government seeking refuge in coalition with moderate anti-reformers. This was a turning back of the clock, a wish that what Wellington might have done in 1830 to save the Tory Party from split and defeat, should now be done by a Whig leader carried along by a popular tide for large and effective reform. Negotiation began and ended as a chimera. For a start, the riots in frightening middling people had not made them brave for a long drawn-out course of uncertainty, and such concern began to weigh with Tories. The Waverers' proposals, if accepted, guaranteed a split among reformers with an acquiescent Cabinet losing the core of its popular and parliamentary support. The alternative of long, wrangling negotiation to which Grey, by his preference for a January resumption had given colour, increased the prospect of crowds assembling, cavalry being made ready in barracks and of bloody conflict breaking out with no prediction as to its outcome. The charm of a swift conclusion grew by the day.

The Cabinet, looking at the odds, noted the remark of the Duchess of Gloucester 'to a female friend that as the bill must pass, it ought not to be delayed'.[54] They also savoured the regrets and retreat of one bishop (Blomfield of London, important), and contemplated the illness of another (Sumner of Winchester)* with un-Christian relish. Votes in the Lords were being counted.

Getting to a conclusion now had appeal even for Melbourne. Precisely because of his conservative instincts, he feared riot *and* the political unions in ways euphoric liberals did not. He had been most determined that the Birmingham Political Union should go back on its plans for drilled and

---

* He lived on, remaining Bishop until 1869 before dying in 1874 at the age of eighty-four.

possibly armed guards. He was troubled at the activity of the Rotunda group and he had read a spy's report that the National Union of the Working Class as this London group grandiosely called itself, had circulated to nearly six hundred supporters on 'the necessity of all the working classes to immediately arm themselves and form by their union a guard to themselves'.[55] Quite how seriously anyone needed to take the oratings of Richard Carlile and William Benbow, who had talked of teaching workers 'to march and the use of the firelock', is a moot point. But apprehension was real; Holland recorded 'Lord Melbourne's report on the state of the publick mind' and his somewhat reluctant but decided opinion that it would be aggravated very materially by a postponement of the meeting. Arguably, Sidmouth's old spy system now made its ironic contribution to the case for swift advance to full reform. By a vote of 8 to 3 it was agreed in Cabinet that the House was to be recalled early in December.

Grey himself, sensitive and tired, now had to be nursed through what was effectively a defeat in Cabinet: 'not perhaps so much hurt with us but low and oppressed at the prospect of business pressing upon him . . .'.[56] The sheer wear of bitter controversy and personality clashes, Grey's own sense of being bully-ragged over early return by Brougham (in which Holland thought him mistaken), must have weighed on a man of sixty-seven. He was to be battered further by that tirade and the loss of control exhibited at Althorp's Cabinet dinner by Durham, suspicious of scuttling during his absence and inclined to take everything out on the father-in-law who had shared the misery of Charles Lambton's death. Durham was a man of bright vision and good radical principles, but as a colleague periodically somewhere between impossible and intolerable. The quarrel was savage, and persuaded everyone but Durham that he intended resignation, something which seems not to have crossed his mind.

The changes agreed in the next few days did not represent a major concession to the Tories, and the Waverers' initiative has to be judged a failure. Like a good Tory, Richmond proposed votes for the colonies 'as a sure counteraction to the popular clamour',[57] something quickly knocked on the head. The £10 freeholder was now required to be a ratepayer, and the schedules were extensively withdrawn with new criteria for disfranchisement based on tax paid and the number of houses, with some boroughs enlarged in acreage to let them accommodate more voters. The number of that newfangled thing, the single member constituency, was reduced from 69 to 49. But the granting of new second seats largely benefited industrial towns north of Nottingham. Only Brighton and Stroud, the latter itself a busy textile centre, were outside the north in a list otherwise comprising Bolton, Bradford, Blackburn, Macclesfield,

Stockport, Stoke and Halifax. The number of seats to be disfranchised was settled at fifty-six, the number, as Russell would explain to the House, which earlier votes had determined to be 'of decayed and inconsiderable value'.[58] The counties became gainers, but once more the benefiting places tended to be counties which, like Yorkshire, were heavy with industrial development.

The debate when the new Reform Bill was introduced was blessedly short – two days – and surprisingly quiet. Indeed, Alexander Baring from the Tory benches observed, without contradiction, a general feeling that the matter should not be debated at that point. Russell, who introduced it, was almost entirely matter of fact though he said, with deliberate repetition, that 'the former system is now doomed to last no longer' and he ended on a note which would remain long after, begging 'to bring in a bill to amend the representation of the people of England'.[59]

The only important exception to the new mood of polite caution was Robert Peel, now, as earlier, showing no instinct for opposition. He had

> but one feeling, and that is a feeling of exultation at the escape we have had from the Bill of last Session . . . Numerous are the calumnies which have been put forth on this subject; but this Bill is an answer to them all. It is to the opponents of the late measure a most triumphant vindication – it is the noblest and most perfect tribute that could be offered in favour of the perseverance and ability with which time for further deliberation has been obtained for us.

He was not, said Peel, going to go into such details as why Schedule A was staying at the same level or why the number of single member boroughs was going down to forty-nine 'but, leaving all these matters for future discussion, I must congratulate myself and my Right Honourable Friends on the opposition we made to the last Bill, of the effects of which we now have such unquestionable proofs'.[60]

'I must congratulate myself!' It was pure Mr Toad and appropriate comment comes from Peel's sympathetic biographer, Norman Gash. 'It was true that various concessions had been made, including the maintenance of the existing numbers of the House for which the opposition had formerly fought in vain . . . But the essentials of the bill remained, and the knowledge that an increasing number of waverers on his own side were now prepared to support it probably infused a greater bitterness into Peel's speech at the opening of the debate than he realised.'[61] A number of Tories, Clive, Sandon and Warrender (who had been very hot before), made moderate speeches. Clive went out of his way to praise Althorp, a snub to Peel who had attacked him. The far right wing muttered a little, Sir Robert Inglis saying that he was 'no party to any arrangement, if arrangement there is, that the new bill shall meet with a more limited hostility than the old Bill encountered if on examination, the new bill should be found equally objectionable with the old one'.[62] And on the far left, Hunt, the one unreserved popular democrat in the House, remained his derisive, cynical self. He remarked that 'the bill (which is certainly improved) will exclude nine-tenths of the male adult population from any share in the representation whatever'.[63] And, significantly, he took scornful exception to Russell's change of terminology. 'On former occasions, all the talk was about the representation of the people of England; but now the Noble Lord only spoke of the representation of the intelligence and property of the country.'[64]

It is always good in the middle of Reform Bill debates to be reminded in Hunt's uncringing, plain and very intelligible way how very modestly the people of England would advance by any version of this legislation. But that had always been the case. Talk of 'the people of England' and Russell's own concluding phrase in this debate about 'the representation of the people' was radical rhetoric describing a class-limited bill. But Hunt, who actually did trust the people, has a near modern perspective. Yet by all the expectations of its day, this bill, like everything which had gone before, was drastic and sweeping, making Peel's triumphalism vapid.

The contemporary political world working in its own terms had a cool verdict. Denis Le Marchant, despite being Brougham's factotum and a friend of Reform, was not a furious partisan, but he dismissed Peel as 'very declamatory and very abusive – equally deficient in taste and tact – and ludicrously inconsistent, for after dwelling on the great improvements in the bill, and claiming all the merit of them, he declared his most determined opposition to it . . . The moderate country gentlemen were silent and, as I suspect, began making up their minds to act by themselves.'[65] And the attack made personally on the vastly popular Althorp did Peel no good. 'It was,' said Le Marchant, using an old Cromwellian term, 'cheered exclusively by the malignants.'[66] Quite apart from the Tory response, this reading was marked by the complaints of Irish members. Richard Sheil, O'Connell's deputy and Richard More O'Ferrell, whom Le Marchant called 'Mr Fowal', and highly complimented for speaking 'like a sensible and fluent English country gentleman',[67] objected that proposals for Ireland contradicted earlier promises for equal treatment with Scotland. Some backstage ministerial consciences were unhappy about this, but Grey, like many Prime Ministers after him, was exasperated by the Irish and categorically against granting the three seats demanded.

Despite all the devotion of the nineteenth-century Commons to measuring things by debate, the whole process was in the shadows this time round. The majority existed to pass any Reform Bill by large numbers. This was a version delicately adjusted to provide excuses for a Tory retreat, the signs of which had been made clear on the first day of the first reading. It was the Lords who had rejected the last Bill and the Lords which might reject it this time. Much of what was said in the Lower House was addressed obliquely to their Lordships, among whom replications of Tory retreat in the Commons were looked for; and by this time, an important part of the ministerial strategy there lay in the conversion of bishops. With the government muting its guns for a diplomatic victory and sensible Tories adjusting to retreat, the debate did not make for excitement. The economist T.R. Malthus, who had sat through the Saturday session, told a friend afterwards that 'he had never been so tired in his life'.[60]

The arena was thus open for the settling of private grudges, supremely that between Macaulay and Croker. The two most venomous men in public life had been for some months preoccupied with each other's throats. Both were historians and literary men, and educated hatred tends to grind heels in faces. The point-scoring and finding of slips between these two is irrelevant, but in a debate where the leading figures pulled punches and played tactically, there were flashes which spelt out the whole dilemma not just of reform but of social progress.

On the widening of the franchise, Macaulay contemplated a continuation of the status quo now that aspirations had risen. 'A narrow-minded pertinacious party above: an infuriated multitude below: on one side the possession of a certain degree of power is required by those who would obtain it – on the other it is denied by those who will retain power at all risks and all hazards . . .' These were sides 'both so totally ignorant of their own true interests that I say "God forbid that the state should ever be placed at the mercy of either"'.[69]

Croker, the most candid opponent of democracy, having denounced the 'death-like apathy' of ministers in responding to the riots,[70] set out his own dark vision of where it would lead. The Bill meant 'the placing of a large power in the hands of a mass of subjects whom if once excited, it is impossible to calm. It is one thing to excite the country and another to excite an assembly like this; but I have seen the consequences of the excitement of even so small a body: – and I say that the adoption of such a step as this would tend to the destruction not only of this House, but of civilised society.'[71]

Macaulay had spoken with glorious self-confidence of having 'no accusations to make against the working classes. I would refuse them nothing which I might consider would be for their own good; and I therefore, find with pleasure and satisfaction that the most industrious and intelligent portion of the community will, under this Bill be admitted to a share in the government.' Everything would come out well largely because of the wisdom of the Whig party 'composed of the vast and intelligent body of the middle classes. That party, with the flower of the aristocracy at its head and the flower of the working classes bringing up its rear, takes up its impregnable position between the main body of the aristocracy and the mob. It will have reform; it will not have revolution.'

For Croker dates mattered; the contest took place two years after the July revolution in Paris and shortly after outbreaks of more popular revolt in Lyons, something which had only been controlled 'by fifty thousand bayonets'. Couple this with Nottingham, Derby and Bristol, and in speaking so bleakly he had 'been urged by nothing but an imperious sense of the danger to the country, a danger which I know not how to remedy, but which I know will tremendously increase by the passing of the Reform Bill'.[72] It was a straight fight between euphoria and despair. Macaulay's grand complacency would be validated, but Croker spoke for the great part of opinion which saw the mob as heir-at-law to constitutional amendment. It was no accident that an article long attributed to him had appeared in the *Quarterly Review* identifying 'all that body of opinion which may be called Conservative'. He might lose the argument but was identified with a word bearing enormous weight for the future.

But that black view, the best summing up of hard Tory thinking, would receive a memorable reply at the hands of Stanley. He rose late after another vast perambulation by Sir Charles Wetherell, for whom it was 'the physical force which has driven us on. Thus a law is to be extorted by force and intimidation which cannot be justified by reason.'[73] For a man whose insults to the City, where he served as Recorder, had helped provoke a riot, this was brazen, but Wetherell was rarely anything else. Stanley had been in conference with Macaulay and devoted some space to scoring Macaulay's points off Croker for him, historical points about ship money and the abuse of prerogative by Charles I in which the early nineteenth century had a healthy interest.

But serious things underlay the history lesson. For Croker concession had destroyed royal government in King Charles's time. For Stanley, refusal of concession, the eleven years without a Parliament, between 1629 and 1640, had been the evil. The reader of the lessons of the past would recognise that 'Concessions from the crown in time – concessions to reason, to justice, to the advancing spirit of the age and the altered condition of society, are the firmest supports of the monarchy . . .'.[74] Stanley had not just talked with Macaulay, he had taken from him a notion of change being natural and of men in government – 'the Crown' was shorthand – adjusting to it. And he quoted Macaulay gratefully in asserting that 'forms of government must give place to forms of society; that governments were made for men, not men for governments'.[75] The notion was establishing itself among legislators that society and government were not a sterile fixed truth but had a dynamic.

But along with the philosophy of government, Stanley managed to get in some pleasant points of low politics, straws blowing to demoralise the other side. He gently mocked the resolute anti-reformer, Sir Robert Inglis: 'I really feel sir for my Honourable and consistent friend, the Member for the University of Oxford whose horror I well remember witnessing when he heard in another place the most Reverend Head of the Church of England admit that some reform might be necessary.' Did the Tories plan to fight in the last ditch, perhaps conceding the occasional Grampound or East Retford? Proceeding at that rate 'it would perhaps happen that about the year 1890, Leeds, Birmingham and Manchester would have representatives'.[76] With Robert Peel still touchily devoting much of his speech to a defence of his conduct on Catholic emancipation, the Tory (or Conservative) argument was on the back foot, worsted decisively on the large philosophical questions and slipping in the common politics of support.

And it was a sad thing for Peel, trying to demonstrate the impossibilism of the political unions, to quote the chairman of one (in Walsall) who had cheerfully looked forward to 'the instant and utter extinction of that abominable traffic in human flesh and blood, denominated Negro-slavery', and to comment as he then did. For Peel the prospect was that in a reform parliament, influenced by the political unions, there was little chance that 'negro slavery – *which perhaps ought to be carried on in a qualified and mitigated shape* [author's italics] will be dealt with with that care and caution and deliberation which this settlement so imperatively requires'.*[77] It was said about Peel by allies even more than by opponents that he was a man lacking sympathy or imagination. One had not thought he lacked them so much.

However, debate in the Commons had run its course and, after a brief intervention by Hunt, a division was called. As *The Mirror of Parliament* records it:

---

* Peel would finally pledge himself to support abolition of slavery at a constituency election dinner in 1832 when he also openly accepted what was by then the Reform Act.[78]

The House then divided, when there appeared for the Second Reading
  Ayes . . . 324
  Noes . . . 162[79]

The Bill was through direct debate and now faced the Committee stage. The liberal press came out of mourning. *The Times* proclaiming 'a great service rendered to the country – an inestimable source of encouragement, tranquillity and comfort'.[80]

However, at a moment of triumph it is worth registering one point which Hunt made in that late intervention: 'in one manufactury in the town of Leeds, in which 130 men are employed, at comparatively high wages – only three will be entitled to vote under this Bill'.[81]

With the Commons proceedings cleared, a course never doubted but something done handsomely at better than 2 to 1, the Ministry had to address itself to the Lords which given the lack of a majority there, also meant approaching the King.

NINE

The Second Bill and Hopes for Peer Creation

'Kings are kings, even the best of them'

The Ministry knew what had to be done, but were not agreed how, when or, in dark moments, if it should be done at all. Since the Lords as currently constituted would not pass the Bill, the Lords would surely have to be constituted differently. *The Times* was highly dramatic. There was 'but one course . . . a bold and powerful creation of liberal peers, or Great Britain, before the summer returns, will be one scene of blood and terror'.[1] Peers would indeed have to be made. It was the sort of drastic thing not readily associated with the Prime Minister, and even Brougham had been wobbling in the latter part of 1831. Le Marchant, his assistant, had remarked that 'the Chancellor begins to be alarmed. His opinions appear to have somewhat fluctuated as to the expediency of a large creation of peers. At first he said it would be absolutely necessary, but in the course of the debates he told me he had rather the Bill was thrown out than take such a step.'[2]

Durham did not wobble, and in his usual fierce way set out the strong line on creation in the first sentence of a letter sent on 29 December to his father-in-law. 'I feel it incumbent on me no longer to delay declaring to you my decided opinion that the Government ought to advise the King to create a sufficient number of peers to insure the passing of the Reform Bill.'[3] Durham followed a fierce political morality: 'To consent to or connive at any other course of proceeding, would not only be a breach of our pledges, but a gross act of duplicity.' Ministers already had 'the King's approbation, and a declared and overwhelming majority in the House of Commons. Our weakness lies in the other branch of the legislature . . . It is now, I believe, admitted that all hopes of conversions sufficient to enable us to carry even the second reading are abandoned . . . We may therefore fairly anticipate that we shall find a majority of twenty against the Bill on the second reading . . .'[4]

Perhaps the most compelling argument in a closely reasoned and lucid communication was Durham's appreciation that ministers had no excuse for a weak line. 'Are we then prepared to carry the Bill into the House of Lords in these circumstances knowing as we must do that its rejection or mutilation is thus inevitable? Ignorance of these facts and their consequences we cannot plead; and indeed they are not only notorious to ourselves, but the subject of general remark and discussion.'[5] He also met head-on all the arguments against creation, constitutional propriety, alienation of previous supporters in the Upper House and fear of undermining the institution itself, and flung them out with the usual cheerful Durham confidence.

But he was not alone in assailing Grey's ears. Brougham, characteristically, had changed his mind, back to his original uncompromising support for creation. While convalescing in Westmorland he set out the case. Two letters of 29 and 31 December show him thinking tactically. The best way of winning here was an opening salvo of creations, something to intimidate the Tory Lords, 'to begin with a partial creation, say of ten or twelve – some to be made, others, the greater part, called up – as for example say four creations and eight calls. But these are details, and whatever way you arrange them signifies little compared with the measure itself . . . I should not quarrel with fifteen in all.'[6] Brougham, advocating psychological warfare against the Tory Lords, expected 'a confident belief to get abroad first at Court then in the Lords that you can make as many as you please and this may prevent the making many, perhaps any more. But I think we must go further and contemplate the *possibility* of that necessity as not a very remote possibility, and we ought, I clearly think to be prepared for it.'

Equally, it was essential that the King should understand that the passing of the Bill was a single, absolute and unshirkable necessity. The instinct of constitutional monarchs in pursuit of their own comfort for splitting ineluctable issues down the middle, had, like the delay and confusion created by the buzzing intermediaries, to be closed off. Brougham had clearly had all he could take of Lords Wharncliffe and Harrowby, not to mention William's well-meaning talk of moderation. They had done moderation.

Brougham's second letter is a reflection of the anxiety of the times, and, even allowing for his own taste for the highly coloured, must have reflected a wider jitteriness. 'The state of trade and of the country is in my firm belief *very alarming*.' People were talking catastrophe, 'not whether the ministry shall be broken up or not . . . but whether the whole country shall not be undone . . .'. Anxiety was heightened by things already happening in Ireland. On 19 December *The Times* paused in its celebration of the Commons vote to quote 'events in Kilkenny where the captain of police and 14 of his men fell victim to the abhorrence of the peasantry towards the tithe system . . .'.[7] Avid with the prevailing mood, Brougham announced 'one very remarkable circumstance which I hear from all quarters: the Tories both in town and country (I mean not the highest of them as peers, but the middle and even upper classes of Tories), are desirous of the creation to secure the Bill'.[8]

But while Brougham and Durham, corresponding with Grey on the cusp of the year, 29–31 December/1 January, were seeing things clearly, they could not count on all the Cabinet. The Tories might be split between the last ditch of resistance and the double bed of acquiescence, but the flinching tendency flourished among the Whigs themselves. Grey had to tell his Lord Chancellor that the objections of Lansdowne 'are not at all diminished. He comes to the cabinet tomorrow. Palmerston and Melbourne are equally opposed to it.'[9] So, less pressingly, he added, was the Duke of Richmond.

But Grey's chief concern was the King. 'You know how strong his objections were.' Grey did not want William confirmed in his foot-dragging tendencies by knowledge of ministerial flinchers. He had conveyed to Grey his confidence that the Bill would carry both reading and committee, a comforting hope which provided an excuse for royal procrastination. And Grey knew what the Tories were saying. 'I hear their language founded on the assumption that the king will not make peers, is as violent and confident as ever; and Lyndhurst is becoming more and more an avowed and prominent supporter of their views.'[10]

Grey seemed to have few doubts as to what should be done. He had come, as he told Brougham on 1 January, 'nearer to your view of the matter of the peerage than I thought I ever could have done: and am much inclined to new creations at present or before the meeting of parliament, to the amount and in the manner you propose.'[11] The afternoon Cabinet meeting of 2 January traversed much of this ground, with Brougham's speeches read to the company, and it passed with civility and good humour.

But Richmond with real or affected optimism was sure the Bill would carry the Lords without creation. Palmerston 'still hankered after possible conversions [of opponents in the Lords] and manifestly would not personally grudge very great and even unjustifiable concessions to obtain them'.[12] Melbourne characteristically thought creation of peers 'a much more violent and permanent measure in its effects than a dissolution and exaggerated the magnitude, importance and danger of so extraordinary an expedient'.[13] The Cabinet settled down, as Lord Holland remarked, to the 'silly' question of how many peers should be proposed to the King – six or ten. Grey had opened with talk of 'ten to twelve or more', but would now close weakly on a maximum of ten. It might not be centrally important, but it showed Grey's style in Cabinet, clear on essentials but too aware of difficulties, too conscious of opposition.

And in this moderately firm spirit he went to see the King. With Brougham still unwell in Westmorland, the Prime Minister proceeded directly to Brighton where William continued use of his brother George's Pavilion. The meeting had been 'very satisfactory' wrote Grey, who had 'no doubt he will do what the cabinet may advise; but he desires to have it in writing. He is however, extremely anxious and even nervous as to this matter; but straightforward, confiding and cordial as usual.'[14] From the outer office Le Marchant saw everything in a young follower's radiant light: 'Lord Grey's visit settled everything. The king was very frank – gave him a long interview and at last yielded.'[15]

But keeping William on-side and coherent depended upon a united Cabinet telling him one undeviating thing and not telling its friends about their own divisions. Greville, an activist in the middle ground, had the evidence of ministerial tattle to state that 'the moderate party in the Cabinet consists of Lansdowne, Richmond, Palmerston, Melbourne, and Stanley', and to add as his own gloss that Palmerston and Melbourne, especially the latter, 'are now heartily ashamed of the part they have taken about Reform. They detest and abhor the whole thing, and they find themselves unable to cope with the violent party and are consequently implicated in a continued series of measures which they disapprove; and they do not know what to do, whether to stay and fight this unequal battle or resign.' The account given fitted with Greville's own prejudices, but his informant was Lady Cowper, a strong opponent of Reform and mistress, later wife, of Lord Lyndhurst, whose involvement with the last-ditch element had been noted by Grey. The climate in which such accounts flourished was viperous.

Palmerston and his group received few thanks from the *echt* Tories, but their accounts of the King matched Brougham's darkest apprehensions. Harriet Arbuthnot had snarled in mid-December, 'It seems that the King saw Ld Chandos several times at Brighton & pressed him to see Ld Palmerston (that faction true to their usual dirt, are now backing out and pretend to be afraid; they no doubt think the ship is sinking & like true rats are running away) & try whether something might not be arranged.' She then added with her customary dispassion, 'Ld Harrowby says the Ministers are the greatest rogues that ever lived . . .'[16]

Harriet Arbuthnot was a frantically silly woman and something of an upper-class fishwife, but if not wise she was well informed, at least about her own political sphere. She knew the Duke of Wellington for the closest confidences. When she says, on the evidence of Wellington, that in early December the King, as the Bill was coming up to Parliament, had 'clapped his hands to his forehead & exclaimed "God Almighty help me! What could I do? The Tories abandoned me"',[17] there is little reason to disbelieve her. Meanwhile ministers, 'the greatest rogues that ever lived', had to endure, and get an understanding of reality into, the man who had said it. But Mrs Arbuthnot would add very little more. In an entry of 6 December she would say in her best style, 'We have got the cholera at Sunderland. I think it a far inferior evil to the Reform Bill.' The diary ended almost immediately, but Mrs Arbuthnot lived on a little longer until, having survived the Reform Act, she died on 2 August 1834 – of cholera.

Wellington himself was fastidious about not directly intervening with the King, but friends had no such scruples. The Lord Chandos referred to by Mrs Arbuthnot was the eldest son of Buckingham, and a frantic anti-reformer. In fact, Chandos reached the King only by letter through the hands of Sir Herbert Taylor, secretary to the King, who passed it to Grey telling the hapless Chandos that he presumed that was what *he* intended.

The Tory buzz continued to contradict the cautious assumptions of Grey as much as the euphoria of Le Marchant. General Hardinge, Wellington's factotum, told Ellenborough (at a dance!) that the King was thought to have given assurances to Wharncliffe that he would not create peers. Hardinge had a theory of his own, that Grey was available for concessions 'but not to the Tories', hoping that supporters of the Bill would help him to graceful retreat by making 'motions of amendments to which he may accede'.[18] And Ellenborough, receiver of this dubious intelligence, fell to daydreaming about the make-up of a Harrowby/Wharncliffe government. In the name of moderation and some kind of little reform bill, it would have to do without Wellington and Peel who were giving little encouragement to the whole business. So the names of Carnarvon and Lyndhurst were mooted to support the chief Waverers in the Lords, while the Commons front bench might contain Chandos, Vyvyan, Leveson, Stuart-Wortley (Wharncliffe's son), Sugden and Lowther.

If the Prime Minister could talk to the King, so perhaps could Lord Wharncliffe, who made an approach through Sir Herbert Taylor. What the wavering case now amounted to was avoidance of the constitutional crisis, not to say public riot, likely to follow Lords rejection and to do so in return for ministers watering down the Reform Bill. To this end a weapon in the hands of Wharncliffe and his Cabinet allies was the threat of reversals of their past votes in favour by a number of peers. A list reached the right-wing press of twenty-four Lords headed by the Duke of Portland said to be contemplating that very course. It was a very brittle list and its assured purpose even more so, but in the racecourse mood of Court, Westminster and country house in 1832 it was very useful to Wharncliffe. He was able to contrast his own group, almost large enough already, he claimed, to help through an amended bill with the Portland list likely, he argued, to convert 'the support which they are now disposed to give to the second reading into the most uncompromising and bitter hostility to the government upon the whole measure and in every stage of it'.

From the ministerial point of view, Wharncliffe was far too close in his sentiments and intentions to everything that William wanted to hear. In practice, a game of bluff and threat was underfoot. How many peers might from outrage at the dilution of their purple withdraw support for the Bill? How frightened of that threat were the weaker ministers? How many of those disliking such a strong bill wanted to emasculate it anyway? Would the Lords, if stood up to, actually risk civil conflict? Would the public, if denied reform, go on to the streets? And lurking at the back of the bleaker minds, if they did come out would soldiers follow orders to shoot them? Language was fraught, imaginations were febrile.

The King's letter replying to the minute of their earlier discussion was reasonably satisfactory in that it set no limit on the ultimate number of peers who might have to be created. But in the way of royalty with its passion for blood and genealogy, William wanted to confine creations to eldest sons, collateral heirs and, slumming it, 'Scotch and Irish peers of large property'.[19] There was much keening about 'the value of the House of Lords' and nagging hopes that Whig ministers would not 'degrade' it. But Lord Holland, present at the Cabinet meeting where the letter was read out, thought 'the consent was explicit and handsome'.

However, the notion of ten immediate new peers was not pursued for the moment, a bad mistake. Greville would hear from Melbourne's brother, George Lamb, 'that they had resolved to make no Peers at present; that to make a few would be regarded as a menace, and be as bad as if they made a great many; but that as many as would be necessary for carrying the Bill would be made, if it was eventually found that it must be so'. Greville, who had been lobbying through his ministerial contacts and was in close touch with the Wharncliffe faction, regarded this as 'a great victory and I do believe mainly attributable to our exertions'.[20] Greville also took pride in 'the spirit we have infused into Melbourne himself'.

Holland, reporting the same decision at the same time, describes simply the postponement of a decision after a paper from Palmerston. This had argued 'the hopelessness of passing the bill without fresh creations'. Instead it offered postponement of creation plus all sorts of care and caution, but having at its core an insistence that if the Bill could only pass with the creation of peers, they must be created on a scale that would bring this about. The letter following this Cabinet meeting of 13 January tried to focus on the large numbers of peers which would have to be created in crisis and to avoid making William fret by a preliminary round of Lord-making. His reply assented to the prospective later, larger act – it was after all, comfortably in the future – but insisted that here and now there should be only three ennoblements, those already known about. But by the 15th, ministers had, for what it was worth, a royal promise to create enough peers to pass the Bill.

In the country, among people whom the Duke of Wellington did not recognise as the country, there was unease. Melbourne's special commissions, set up to try offences committed during the riots, had concluded their work and would be followed in the way of the times by public hangings. Melbourne would be untroubled. He had, after all, sought guidance from the most authoritarian European state outside Russia, asking Palmerston at the Foreign Office to enquire after 'the criminal code of the Austrian States, Hungary &c; what crimes are punished with death, and what punishments are fixed to crimes not capital; whether punishments are rigorously inflicted . . .' and 'whether there is any transportation or any equivalent to it . . . ?'.[21] John Hobhouse, who, newly made Secretary at War, had against his own conscience not fought the continuation of military flogging, was uneasy when approached by a petition for mercy finding that 'it was not very easy to refuse to sign and similar efforts were made to save the Bristol rioters; but if our criminal code awards death as a punishment for any crime, I could not see how these men could be saved'.[22]

On 19 January at St George's Square, Manchester, a meeting assembled to protest against the executions. It was a Sunday (not surprising given the six-day working week in the cotton mills) but, as one historian has remarked, 'respectable opinion was much shocked'.[23] When the meeting was adjourned for ten days on the direction of magistrates alarmed by allegations of the local union drilling men at night, the military intervened, broke up the meeting and made eight arrests, and four of the organisers were later imprisoned for a year. As James Butler further observed, 'Grey and Melbourne fully approved of the action of the Manchester magistrates.'[24]

But what concerned radicals in Manchester, like the carrying out of death sentences and transportations, were events going on in the wings.

On stage the Cabinet proceeded in hopes. Probably the Ministry lost a trick in the manoeuvres against the Tories by not following Brougham's end-of-year advice and making a demonstration shot, but as Palmerston's later conduct in crisis would demonstrate, such caution was not the triumph for Greville's friends that he thought it. Meanwhile, two sound Whigs, Osborne and Dundas, having been pre-approved for elevation, might go through. Business for the moment meant the committee stage in the Commons, set trudging on its way through. Nothing was under threat here though the committee stage provided an opportunity for seekers and prospective granters of concessions to try their hands.

There existed a deep division between different sorts of anti-reformists. William's letter committed him in certain circumstances to doing something he very much disliked. Given actual defeat for the Bill he would face wholesale creation, fifty or more, that thinning of blue blood which appalled right-thinking men decently endowed with it. For such temporising Tories, a softened bill pre-empting such horror was the obvious solution. But for the Duke of Wellington, the Lords' veto simply signalled a majority against the abomination and should be used. The forces of law and order stood ready, as they had at Peterloo, to deal with any consequences on the street. Wellington's fixation with the armed and military intentions of the political unions played a great part in this. The well-run unions like Birmingham had no such purpose and the ones which did have such yearnings were not organised in a way that would make the threat credible.

The Duke's Tories were looking for a fight, rejection and the defeat (or at any rate humiliation) of Reform. The friends of Wharncliffe and people near to the King wanted a bill sufficiently weakened to avoid Lords' rejection and creation, but not so slashed back that the next worse thing to creation would take place with dissolution and a further electoral appeal. The effect of this minuet of anxieties was to stretch out the crisis to the end of legislation.

It also put intolerable pressure upon ministers, especially Althorp and Grey. Ministers had amended their own bill to please the Lords and the Lords were not pleased. They had words from the King which they would pronounce satisfactory but they knew well enough that William wanted to do as little by way of creation as was humanly possible, preferably nothing at all. The step which should have put fright into Lords' resistance had not been taken. Ministerial allies and goads in the country like Attwood begged for creation as proof to their own extremists that something was moving. It *was* moving, but unbearably slowly. Yet Wharncliffe only had purchase and influence because so many Tories were very frightened indeed of the conflict which resistance to Reform had stirred up. Grey was trying to make progress on the strength of the King's pledge, but denial of any intention to create was a commonplace in the conversation of other Tories. Everyone was living on everyone else's nerves.

A sense of the hysteria which events could create in frail minds was highlighted by the strange episode of young Perceval. On 26 January, a quiet day, much of it spent discussing the Russian-Dutch loan, the son of a former Prime Minister spied strangers in Parliament. Spying strangers is an arcane power based on the high fallacy that the House sits, debates and legislates unobserved. It has been used in wartime to obtain hearings in camera, was used once (naughtily) to expel the future Edward VII, attending as Prince of Wales, but is generally the province of cranks being crankish. And the reporters remaining where they were, Perceval's motion was recorded. He rose 'to address the House in the name of our Lord and Saviour, Jesus Christ who is exalted King of kings, and in his name I implore the House to attend with reverence to one addressing you in his name.'[25]

Who, asked Perceval,

> looking at the state of the nation, society standing as it does on the brink of wild confusion – two great political parties in the State arrayed against one another – the two Houses of Parliament approaching an open conflict – Bristol burnt and in ruins, its property destroyed and trampled under foot – Ireland torn to pieces by intestine divisions, rendered still wider by religious divisions – who can see these things and refuse to recognise in them the judgments of Almighty God?[26]

He undertook to 'read from the Holy Book the promises and the denunciation of God's mercies and judgments . . . This country was formerly the seat of truth and of religion, but now may we apply to it the words of Our Saviour, "Woe unto thee Bethsaida, Woe unto thee Korazin; Woe unto thee, thou shalt be cast into Hell".'[27]

Perceval had other complaints against the ungodly. 'You sit here as a race of infidels. You do not consult your Maker. Where is the looking into God? . . . we hear of the march of intellect which claims such affinity to light; of the liberal mind that is marching through Europe and which arrogates to itself all the blessings that are enjoyed by man, but man owes to the giver of all good things. It is man-idolizing, God-denying idolatry.'[28] He was upset also about the Jews. An attempt had recently been made, an 'unchristian proposition', to admit Jews, like the lately indulged Dissenters and Roman Catholics, to Parliament. For Perceval the 'Lord and Saviour Jesus Christ is exalted King of kings, and Lord of lords; to call in the Jew to assist us in the holy work of government . . . is not admissible in a Christian country'.[29]

He was

> sensible that I have been speaking with noise and loudness though I am not conscious of anything approaching to violence But I am urging the truth on which I believe the safety of the nation to hang . . . Everyone of us is baptised unto Christ, in the name of the Father, the Son and the Holy Ghost. I plead on behalf of the country which took me up and nurtured me when left fatherless, that the House would lift up its cry to the foot of the Throne that from the Throne might go forth a proclamation for a day of fast and humiliation.[30]

The country was assailed with evils: 'The pestilence hath cleaved unto it and owing as I believe to our leaving undone this act of fasting, I will take care that the House of Commons shall speak out – I will now force them to do so careless of what ministers may do . . . It will not do to move the previous question. The act shall be done by the nation.'[31] And after another half column (there were three in all) of such stuff, Perceval moved 'that His Majesty will be graciously pleased to appoint a day for a general fast'.

The handling of the mentally disturbed is a delicate business but pre-emptive submission seems excessive. Althorp, present on Treasury business, and himself a sincerely religious man who did not make public show of the fact, murmured that 'discussion on such a matter is highly inexpedient' and did 'not tend to the honour of religion'. It was anyway unnecessary since it already was 'the intention of Government that a day of fasting shall be appointed'.

Hunt, whose sanity after a froth of rant was only matched by his scriptural fluency, remarked that they had all been called 'infidels, idolators and what not', and, turning to impious Jewish sources, quoted Isaiah: 'Wherefore have we fasted say they, and thou seest not! . . . Is not this the fast I have chosen? To loose the bands of wickedness, to undo the heavy burdens, and to let the oppressed go free? Is it not to deal thy bread to the hungry . . . ?'[32] But as Hobhouse observed, 'Mr Perceval made his foolish motion for a general Fast, and the government as foolishly gave way to the proposal.'[33] Perceval, catching a hysteria wider than his own madness, and armed with the government's response to the cholera which clean water supplies would eliminate sixty years later, withdrew his motion and strangers were readmitted. In due course 21 March was set aside for God's purposes.

The early months of 1832, despite promises and royal letters, were marked by jitteriness all round. Among the committed reformers there were fears about fixity of purpose in the leadership, fears of what might be negotiated away. John Cam Hobhouse is a voluble illustration of the uncertainties felt by Reform Whigs about their leaders. The anxiety started almost as soon as he took up his first job, itself a consequence of another small crisis. For while the Reform Bill might be a preoccupation and the only immediate thing to excite posterity, other political issues were swirling around and were more capable than Reform of undermining the Ministry. The motion of censure on the so-called Russian-Dutch loan for the government having paid the interest after Holland and Belgium had split back in 1830 is a piece of perfect arcania several planetary systems away. But the Tories dreamt of getting votes for that question nowhere available to them on Reform and perhaps fortuitously defeating the government. They had already carried an address in the Lords objecting to British acceptance of the treaty formally separating Holland and Belgium – standard scare stuff about the French menace – and had political hopes over the loan in a fluid Commons. Lyndhurst, a happy politician who enjoyed a fight, told Ellenborough that 'he thought these fellows might be turned out provided it were known that an Administration could & would be formed if they went out'.

It would come to nothing. Not for the first time in a difficult English moment, the Celtic vote would settle things. Like the Scottish Nationalists supporting the Callaghan government in the 1970s and the Ulster Unionists helping out the Major administration in the 1990s, Daniel O'Connell knew what was good for him. He spoke against the government and sent fifteen of his supporters away from the House to escape the temptation of helping the Tories. But the vote cast against the loan by another Irishman and a member of the government, Sir Henry Parnell (ancestor of the more famous Charles), lead to his dismissal and more insubstantial Tory talk of 'breaking-up'. Hobhouse had been the replacement, but, as a young politician, he was both worried and censorious. And in February, going unopposed through the re-election then required on assuming ministerial office, he told his Westminster electors gathered at Covent Garden that 'I should support the Ministers so long as they supported Reform . . . and that the Ministers looked to the public for support, and, if they withheld it, Reform might yet be lost.'[34]

He would go through a period of intense anxiety almost immediately after taking his Privy Council oath on 8 February. As a minister outside the Cabinet he was now placed to get himself briefed about what had been resolved on the Lords problem through a series of interviews with senior colleagues; and he would not be even half-assured until, having talked with half a dozen figures, he conferred at length over dinner with Althorp. He had heard talk of Brougham allegedly wavering and infecting Grey 'who I was assured, would be glad to be out of the concern. Lord Grey, he was told, had said "Damn Reform! I wish I had never touched it."' He was not made more comfortable by a conversation with Grey's loyal but strongly reforming heir, Lord Howick, who urged him to have a private meeting with his father rather than try to persuade him through a meeting of Whig MPs. As Hobhouse confided to his diary, a general disgust slashed with exclamation marks, 'This is the man to whom the destinies of this great nation are entrusted! . . . [a man] who looks upon it as a mere trick of state for the preservation of power and when he finds it disagreeable or not worth his while to retain that power, supposes he may abandon the cause with the same indifference as his house in Downing Street. This is incredible, but it is true!'

He shared his doubts serially with Sir Francis Burdett, Charles Grant and Lord Durham. He was told by Burdett that, if there was a risk of ministers pulling back from their commitments, he should resign at once. Grant urged him to go to Grey immediately, and pledged his own resignation from the Cabinet 'if I was not assured that the Bill was to be carried'.[35] Durham was more positive. He had himself threatened through his wife and mother-in-law to resign unless 'things were made quite safe in the House of Lords', but he reported that the Cabinet was settled and 'as many Peers as were thought requisite were to be made, either at once or by degrees; and on this the whole Cabinet seemed determined, though Brougham's illness made him flinch, and his flinching had raised doubts in Lord Grey; and both together revived the hesitation in that portion of the Cabinet that had originally objected to the creation of Peers'. All of which was very well, but Hobhouse's unease was not lightened when Durham observed that his father-in-law, the Prime Minister, was 'the most changeable man in the universe, and without a steady monitor at his elbow, would never persevere in anything'.

The obvious man from whom to seek a clear way ahead was Althorp. It may also have been very useful to the Leader of the House to hear the junior colleague who, representing the near democratic constituency of Westminster and attending Crown and Anchor meetings, was closer to the street than he was. Hobhouse was told that he and Brougham would 'certainly go out unless we have a moral certainty of carrying the measure'. But this was vitiated for the younger man by Althorp's relaxed view of departure: 'He seemed much pleased with this chance of quitting office.' This gentlemanly readiness to withdraw from the benches to the acres was exactly the kind of dilettante politics that Hobhouse had been rattling against; it was a readiness to lose with clean hands and dignity and hardly more reassuring than talk about accommodations with Wharncliffe. So instead of gratefully taking the word of his senior colleague as all the encouragement that a troubled junior need hear, he snapped back. Althorp would not be able to go out of office as easily as he had come in. And 'if it were generally suspected he might have carried the measure and would not do it, he would be stoned on the streets; and if the other party came in, I saw no small chance of his coming to the scaffold!'

One gets an idea of why Althorp was almost universally liked, often loved – even Greville would completely reverse his early strictures – from his reply to this absurd burst of excess: 'He smiled and said "I think so too. I have long thought so."' After all, forty years lay lightly between the men of '32 and the Paris Terror. However, before shooing Hobhouse away with 'an engagement [he] must have which could not be violated', Althorp undertook that Grey would indeed carry the Bill, 'but the mode of doing it must be left to him'. Perhaps Hobhouse was right and the Waverers were engaged in a trick. But in any case, unless ministers 'had a security amounting to a moral certainty the Peers would do as they promised, either new peers would be made or they went out'.[36]

From Althorp's point of view this junior interrogation was probably very welcome. He himself was a more dedicated reformer, or perhaps a steadier applier of himself to the task in hand than Grey. The young man's furious concern, obviously backed by allies as ready for resignation, was a counterbalance with the Prime Minister to the long, droning complaints of Palmerston, Richmond and Melbourne, and the King. He invited Hobhouse to dinner the same evening and was able to tell him that the Prime Minister had been given his views. Grey's message was 'Tell him he cannot be worse off than we are; if we cannot carry the bill we will go out.'

But Hobhouse was not to be smoothed over, partly because in the intervening hours he had heard from Charles Wood, secretary to the Prime Minister, that Grey had said to Howick that 'nothing should make him consent to a creation of Peers; and on Saturday morning he had desired Wood to make out as large a list of new peers as he could think of'.[37] Thus alerted, Hobhouse told Althorp that he did not agree with the Prime Minister. He had come in to fight for Reform and promised that it would be accomplished. Accordingly, if Grey 'went out now merely because he would not make an effort to do what he was promised he could do, he [Hobhouse] would be a dupe . . .'[38]

They would get no further despite talking until the then late hour of midnight, with Althorp again saying that they were sure of carrying the

Bill 'unless the King broke faith with them' and that 'Peers would be made if necessary; the King had solemnly promised it'. But it was during this late and intimate causerie that Althorp spoke of his fears of himself, the instinct for suicide which had made him put out of reach the pistols, kept for self-defence in his bedroom, 'for fear of shooting himself'.[39] It was not something to take lightly. Across the previous seventeen years Whitbread, Castlereagh and Calcraft had all killed themselves. Althorp was the admired model of English, liberal, aristocratic decency and good sense. *His* fears were a glimpse of something to worry about.

The confession came to Hobhouse man to man, and, though he was still worried about the ease with which high-minded nobles would forsake the vulgar stress of office when they should have been kicking the other side and winning, he was greatly drawn to the older man. When Althorp said that 'he was more attached to the Radicals than to any other party', he believed him. Hobhouse was, if by no means happy, then happier than he had been. And hearing from Durham next day that the King was enquiring whether even forty or fifty creations would suffice, he at least had evidence of a struggle taking place.

But the bombardment was not confined to Hobhouse. Althorp was also waylaid by Denis Le Marchant, determined to tell him 'what people say of the timidity of the Ministry on the peerage question and how the Tories said the king would not consent to a new batch'. Althorp replied that 'they would find themselves damnably mistaken'.[40] But he was getting the message.

Of course, anxiety was not confined to reformers. Three weeks before that earnest encounter, Ellenborough, dedicatedly on the other side, was noting that 'ministers think they are certain of being able to make peers as the Opposition think themselves of having the King's word that peers shall not be made . . .'.[41] For Grey had less to fear from the Tories than he seems to have thought. Underlying all the ardent campaigning of Harrowby and Wharncliffe was the fundamental scepticism of Sir Robert Peel. In the same month, February, in which Althorp was fending off Hobhouse, Peel was commenting with more ironic pessimism and insight than appeared in his speeches from the floor. 'Why have we been struggling against the Reform Bill in the House of Commons? Not in the hope of resisting its final success in that House, but because we look beyond the Bill, because we know the nature of popular concessions, their tendency to propagate the necessity for further and more extensive compliances.'[42]

It is a letter of serious Conservative wisdom, anxious to make reform difficult not because he confused it with revolution or thought of the ending of nomination boroughs as larceny, but in order 'to teach young inexperienced men charged with the trust of government that, though they may be backed by popular clamour, they shall not override on the first springtide of excitement, every barrier and breakwater raised against popular impulses; that the carrying of extensive changes in the Constitution without previous deliberation shall not be a holiday task'.[43]

It was excellent sense at a time when the word 'Conservative', having first made its appearance in that *Quarterly Review* piece,[44] was bedding down and aspired to further definition, but it was a flat acknowledgement that Reform would pass and would do so beyond Peel's specific words, fully into law. The practical implication of this was that if the government somewhere suffered a reverse, Peel was not available for office. He wanted, as his biographer succinctly says, 'to oppose reform in detail without opposing in principle' and in thus 'looking to the future, he forfeited much of the present'.[45] He held the Ultras in a contempt left unvoiced by the cold silences which were everywhere in Tory circles quoted as the arrogance of Sir Robert.

Perhaps Wharncliffe and Harrowby at their best had some sense of Peel's thinking, but Wharncliffe was a self-important little man given to writing round to his brother peers urging his own line of concession and abstention. It looked like an assumption of leadership on behalf of the new 'moderation',* something which in any official leader would cause affront; in the victor of the Peninsula and Waterloo it created contained fury. But there was, for that matter, little love lost between the Waverers and Peel. Greville who, for a chronicler, had become remarkably partisan on the wavering side, and would publish a pamphlet in their defence against an Ultra assault in the *Quarterly*, spoke bitterly of him as 'doing what he can to inflame and divide, and repress any spirit of conciliation'.[46] And Greville, missing the point of the noises which Peel had to make on committee, lumped him in with the High Tories: 'The obstinacy of the Duke, the selfishness of Peel, the pert vulgarity of Croker . . .'[47] Meanwhile, in Wellington's circle, caught between sullen resistance and the twitches of opportunism, Peel's grasp of the long term was altogether too deep, and bitterly resented. Ministers fretted and suspected, opposition leaders sulked.

And the implications for the Waverers' enterprise were serious. Were they trying to make Reform instructively difficult and perhaps mitigating its terms, or were they providing a territory, a new ground of debate, upon which through concession the government's split would lead to a break-up?

---

* A measure of Wharncliffe's moderation would be the furious lobbying which he would organise ten years later against the amendment tabled by Lord Ashley (Shaftesbury) against women in the mines working longer than ten hours a day.

Lyndhurst, not an Ultra but a partisan, for whom an opportunity to defeat the government meant office and a quick political coup, would settle for an attenuated reform bill without too much thinking about consequences on the streets. And what was 'moderate'? Wellington could have had a minimal bill and much credit back in 1830. He couldn't have it now. Arguably, any diminution at all might light a fuse, but Wellington wanted both to stop the Reform Act and perhaps re-run the minimalist script he had declined eighteen months before. He was, as it were, caught between getting it wrong on the last occasion and getting it wrong in a different way this time. And his associates still talked swagger, the renegade Whig Lord Rosslyn saying 'We shall beat the Ministry this time as we did the last.'[48]

But the idea was taking on that, because of the Waverers, perhaps the government would have a majority in the Upper House anyway.[49] To Le Marchant anything else was frightening: 'I confess I almost tremble at the thought of these promises not being fulfilled.'[50] Greville, for what it was worth, had been counting the numbers and reckoned on forty-seven Tories now ready to vote in favour at the Lords formal reading. Greville, not a man easily pleased, was also confiding to his diary a mirror image of Hobhouse's dismay at the Prime Minister. He was for the diarist far too attentive to his left wing. And 'such is his characteristic weakness and habitual subserviency to Durham (as it is to others who get hold of him, men or women) that he submits and does nothing.'[51]

Greville, giving passionate support to the two Lords lobbying furiously against a creation of peers, objected violently to Durham 'going about with a paper for Peers, being a requisition to Ld. Grey to make new Peers . . .'. As for Grey, he was 'a chief with an imposing exterior, a commanding eloquence, and a character below contempt, seduced and governed by anybody who will minister to his vanity and presume upon his facility'.[52] Grey, acquainted with the judgements from opposing premises of Hobhouse and Greville, might have concluded that he couldn't please (never mind fool) any of the people any of the time.

Ultimately he would trust to his own judgement. Grey was loyal to Reform though he would say old men's things against it long after. But he was also in an earnest, not a vainglorious, sense true to his status as a nobleman. Making fair-minded concessions to Attwood in a friendly letter or talking quietly with Place came easily, but he valued a serious aristocracy doing its duty and *deserving* its place above all things. Grey was as averse to creating peers as the King. The Tories talked promiscuously about disintegration of the order of society, whether from hysterical conviction or panic-starting motives. Grey regarded it as a real risk, to be set against the other risk of a different disintegration, revolt from below, street violence culminating in the crowd killing or being killed, one massacre or the other massacre. He believed that he could pilot the Bill, his government and himself between demotion of the peerage and the massive public provocation of throwing Reform out a second time. He believed that he would get the necessary votes, that it would be very tight, but was a chance worth taking. But given that dislike of creation he was ready to go further than any but the most conservative members of his Cabinet in making concessions.

Grey was not a broken reed but he did bend; wavering had a certain charm for him. He was personally ready to weaken on the metropolitan boroughs, the one issue the Waverers had been targeting with effect in Commons committee, to modify the £10 franchise and sacrifice Schedule B and its single seats. In a letter to Althorp of 11 March, Grey had said

> They are ready to acquiesce in Schedule A, in the enfranchisement of large towns and the £10 qualification only passing such regulations as might secure it against abuse and might be consistent with the intention of its proposers in making it a *bona fide* qualification. I am quite aware that under colour of such a regulation, the qualification itself might be injuriously affected. But surely this is a fair subject for consideration; and we should hardly be justified in proceeding to a measure of extreme force, merely from apprehensions that such an effect might be produced.[53]

The phrase is deadly and a perfect indication of Grey's narrow social vision; 'a measure of extreme force' is a strange and fearful way of describing the creation of sixty peers to pass the bill to which Lord Grey had set his name, and the Commons (twice) and the electorate had endorsed. But Grey feared a House of Lords in continuous revolt against such 'extreme force'. His letter to Althorp speaks of the Lords becoming unmanageable. It lead him to the conclusion, 'I really believe therefore that we should fail.'[54] And very typically of Grey with his sense of personal honour, he feared that ministers' characters would be damaged by events. He believed public anger would be redoubled after the failure he expected, worried about the French parallel and anticipated a House of Lords expanded by a successor Tory government; 'and then what would become of the constitutional character and efficiency of this branch of the legislature?'[55]

Grey was under pressure, of which Hobhouse's lobbying is a single example. Holland was for creation, along with Althorp, Brougham and Russell, a group Greville called 'the violent party in the cabinet'. So was his own son, Howick, as also, a little way off, was Sydney Smith who sent Lady Grey a preliminary list of suitable and talented men. Sydney's dozen included Francis Jeffrey, the poet Samuel Rogers and Viscount Ebrington, the motion-drafting Whig MP and heir to Lord Fortescue. Sydney Smith was hardly an extremist, but his advice was categoric. Grey should say 'I am sure this bill will not pass *without* creation, it may pass *with* creation, it is the only expedient for doing what from the bottom of my heart I believe the country requires. I will create and create immediately or resign.'[56] The bitterest opponent of Grey's course was Durham. He disbelieved in the list circulated of a likely Lords majority. He put no value in such a majority even if it did exist since it depended on 'the support of those who avow their determination to destroy the main provisions of the Bill in the Committee'.[57] He emphasised that a majority in committee for the key points was as important as one on second reading. Accordingly, to achieve such ends 'a sufficient creation at the present time is absolutely necessary'.[58] The first three points were not disputed but, on the conclusion drawn from them, the Cabinet voted 13 to 1 against.

Durham was right, of course, but he was right in his usual obnoxious, disdainful, puritan manner. Grey was leader and as leader had to be given backing. Also it was easier to deal with the prospect of Durham's resignation than Grey's. He threatened it, but Althorp telling him that the effect would be to bring the government itself quickly to an end and Russell offering to join him gave Durham a view of the chasm opening up. He may also have had actual impact since Goderich and Lansdowne were able to assure him that the metropolitan boroughs would not be given up and that the Cabinet was ready for wholesale creation of peers after second reading. And a couple of days later Grey himself was telling Creevey at a Downing Street party of his confidence of carrying the Bill. 'Oh certainly. We shall be able to carry Schedule A – to give members to the great towns and to carry the £10 qualification clause without any alteration',[59] a marked advance, despite any reference to Schedule B in his letter to Althorp of the 11th. The effect of the pressure was beneficent. The panic of the letter to Althorp did not determine policy. Grey was able to postpone creation of peers, but the concessions towards which his fearful spirit urged him could not be made against the obvious feeling of the Cabinet.

The conclusion of the Commons third reading was marked by Stuart-Wortley full of the horrors of property under threat: 'I therefore do not scruple to say that if in this country – which God in his mercy forbid! – it should ever come to a war of property, on the heads of His Majesty's present Ministers will rest the chief and original guilt.' He was having a last fling, on behalf, as he said, of the landed interest in opposing the Bill which his father stood ready in the next chamber to vote *for*. But the shared motivation was clear enough, and Stuart-Wortley spelt out what he meant by moderation. 'Sir I am convinced that a moderate Reform such as I have mentioned, giving Members to large towns and striking off an equal number of small boroughs would have fully and completely satisfied the people of England. I am not now speaking for the Radicals. I know they would not be satisfied. [Mr *Hunt* Hear hear!]'[60]

He also insisted upon the value of the Commons as a training ground for the House of Lords: 'I allude to the eldest sons or heirs-apparent of peers. I do think it of the highest importance if we are to have a House of Lords at all, that those who are to compose it should be trained in the habit of business – should be drawn from frivolous amusements; . . .' He could think of only one leading figure in the Lords, Holland, who had 'not received his political education here . . . I do think this system a great benefit, not to myself personally, not to us as a class, but to one of the three branches of the Constitution and thus to the whole Constitution and, therefore, to the whole country.'[61]

Sir John Malcolm called for colonial representation – 'The West-India interests required dispassionate and serious consideration.' (The chief West India interest was slavery.) As Wellington's man in the Commons, Malcolm hinted at a new flexibility in the Duke, speaking of 'a moderate and equitable and gradual reform' as a suitable objective. There was nothing flexible about Sir Robert Inglis. He quoted Grey's polite letter to Attwood, assuring him that the £10 franchise would not be confined to half-yearly payers. 'Would any man, knowing the character of the Prime Minister of England, have believed it possible to have seen his name signed to such a document and addressed to the chief of a Political Union at Birmingham?'[62] Violent demands had been resisted in 1819, 'but then we had not a government founded on the principle of *La Jacquerie*'.[63] Not just the Lords' veto but the peerage itself was under threat. And when that was gone 'the other House of Parliament would not save themselves though they threw up the National Debt, the Corn Laws, the Church and the Courts of Justice'.[64]

From the Reform side Macaulay asked the Tories to come out of the mists of undefined moderation and set out their own plan for Reform. Specifically, he challenged Peel to stop saying that he would 'assent' to a moderate Reform plan if the Ministry proposed one. Otherwise Peel, with all his virtues, risked going down in history as the man who 'hinted in general terms that something might be done, but never could be induced to explain what that something was'.[65] And did he think that he could ever again run a government on anti-Reform principles and maintain the current Parliament? The Tories coming to office at this point 'must dissolve the Parliament, and appeal to the people in a moment of fearful excitement; and they would then find that they had committed the same error which Charles committed when he dissolved the Short Parliament and exchanged it for the Long Parliament'.[66]

Macaulay was saying something with which Peel could never privately disagree. For he, unlike the earlier Tory speakers, had his eye on the immediate and viciously spinning ball, the Lords crisis. If their Lordships did reject the Reform Bill, who was going to govern? Not the Ministry; they had been defeated in Parliament. If it was to be Peel, he could hardly govern in this Commons and where was he going to get a more helpful one? And Macaulay threw back in Tory teeth their own nightmare patter of the mob and revolution. The public disturbances of 1817, 1819, the Queen Caroline affair and Wellington's latter and troubled time in office 'would be peace and tranquillity in comparison with the disorder and excitement which would immediately spread throughout the country. Tumults, seditions, agitators without end would arise.' And strong-arm repression 'from any government which attempted to smother the complaints of the people of England without redressing their grievances' wouldn't work either. 'There was only this simple alternative – Reform or anarchy.'[67]

For Macaulay the Reform Bill was 'the noblest measure that ever restored to health a corrupt Government, and bound together the hearts of a divided people'.[68] The Speaker, Manners-Sutton, possessed the sense of humour necessary in his position and impresario-like arranged for Macaulay to be followed by Croker, maintaining by popular request the long-running scholarly knockabout act, Pat and Mike with footnotes.

Once Croker had got over the hurdle of disingenuous civilities, no such simple alternative as 'Anarchy or reform' could be contemplated. As for the variant Reform scheme which Peel was begged to present, this was expecting him 'to take this most unfavourable and dangerous opportunity to cast new ingredients into the cauldron of dissatisfaction by proposing some idle and useless project of Reform, some scheme of our own, theoretic and gratuitous' which would only 'worse confound a confusion already, one should have thought, sufficiently confounded . . .'.[69] The vote in the Commons might be assured, debate at third reading a perfunctory ceremonial to be gone through before the real match a couple of days later, but Croker was an intellectual and a little thing like irrelevance was not going to stop him. Macaulay had taken fourteen columns. Croker went on for fifteen, including the observation that such were the beauties of Macaulay's oratory 'it would appear a sort of vanity in me to say how much I appreciated them',[70] before proceeding to compare Reform with cholera. Croker was comfortably and conclusively despondent: 'The appetite for change will go on increasing as long as there remains food on which it can be indulged; and will lie down at last like the wild beast, appeased and quiet only when it is satiate with having devoured all that is within its reach.' And 'indulged license [would] be followed by anarchy and anarchy by despotism'. There would he believed, ultimately be a new dawn, 'This great and glorious country, with all its recollections and all its hopes cannot long remain in oblivious anarchy . . . but before that dawn can come – O! would that I could disbelieve the prophetic warnings – we must have passed through a dreary, tempestuous and calamitous night.'[71]

Croker, that derivative Burke, was unlucky in his market. Let down by an abyss that failed to open, going bear for broke, preaching blood and anarchy in a pleasing style at the moment when the middle classes acquired deferential access to the legislative process, he would be hammered by history. It was suitable for his brilliance to be followed by that notoriously poor speaker, Althorp. Althorp, a professional anticlimax, got himself into a mild muddle over an article saying that supporters of the Bill were treated with ingratitude. 'It had appeared in some public paper, he did not know which [*a laugh*]. Gentlemen laughed but he assured them that not having much opportunity of looking at the papers, he really did not know which of them it was, nor even what were its politics.'[72] There may lie in Althorp's bomb-proof and bumbling oblivion to press comment a golden lesson for contemporary ministers. What mattered, he said conclusively, was that whoever else was ungrateful, supporters of Reform would get gratitude from their constituents.

Tom Duncombe, the radical Yorkshire squire, managed to be memorable by breaking through the stately quadrille of debate to be unironically rude about the Tories. They talked about the Bill bringing a revolution. But 'a revolution in the minds of men had taken place in this country. The people had awoke from their dream and were no longer to be imposed upon. Hon. Gentlemen opposite would have been glad if the people had still remained ignorant, but they could no longer impose upon the people. Hon. members might sneer and taunt [*Cries of 'No'*], he would repeat, the sneers and taunts offered by hon. Members opposite to the people [*Cries of 'No'*] [came from] those hon. Members who conceived that the middle and lower classes of society had no right to have a voice in political affairs.'[73] Duncombe concluded with a cheerful warning to the House of Lords: they should remember that 'a time was coming when they would no longer tolerate hoary-headed and inveterate abuses which could neither inspire reverence nor obtain respect'.[74]

It had been, almost by definition, a desultory debate. They had been here, most of them twice; even the new members, arrived at the late election, were horribly familiar with the arguments. It was rather like the ceremonies, general in the industrial North for more than a century, of the Whitsun Walks in which the children of the different Christian denominations processed to mark familiar places on a much-loved route. It was an occasion for small poseys rather than new plantings, though Wetherell, dragging into debate the foreign policy of France under Casimir Perrier (who had landed troops in Ancona), managed a rhododendron plot all his own. The French would never have dared do it if we had not been preoccupied with Reform. And like a number of other Tories, he wanted representation for the overseas territories. 'He might say the colonies were melting away . . . but then, those Gentlemen were not concerned in the colonies. They had no plantations to be burned down in Jamaica; no property in the East Indies . . . the Reform Bill would abstract England from herself, and all the world. Their foreign territories were in danger.'[75]

This sort of thing was different but not instructive. However, it was mild and constructive compared to the sad little storm about to break. Having meekly pre-empted Perceval by ordaining 21 March to be a fast day as protection against a water-borne virus, ministers would witness on the evening of the 20th the total emotional collapse of that apostle. Denman, the Attorney-General, was speaking late at night on the eve of the fast about the improved nature of the reformed constitution which 'would act on the only real conservative principle – the benefit of the people', when he was interrupted by Perceval 'looking as if he had just escaped from bedlam – his face pale as death – his eyes flaring'.[76] 'In whose name do you sit here? In whose name do ye sit here? In his name, at the mention of whom, with bitter taunts – [*cries of 'Question'*]; and think ye for one moment that sitting here in that forgetfulness of Him from whom all counsel, wisdom and might proceed – think ye – think ye – think ye . . . [*cries of 'Question', 'Go on', 'Divide'.*]

'We consulted,' wrote Edward Littleton, 'Whig and Tory together, and thought the only way of quieting him was for all parties to walk out of the House only leaving forty to adjourn it. We attempted this, at least two-thirds went away, but still he went on for at least half an hour.'[77] Indeed, as embarrassed MPs tried to leave, Perceval called, 'Ye depart do ye when the name of your God is mentioned? Ye would have sat till five o'clock and six o'clock in the morning had not his name been mentioned, listening to the tongues of men tinkling like idle cymbals.' Henry Hunt gently urged on him that, as the scheduled fast day was approaching, 'his object would be better obtained by the adjournment of the House'.[78] But Perceval ranted on for another two columns of the Record.

However intense the religious mania, there was a political context. Perceval had taken a fancy to the Reform Bill being an assault upon the King. But Ministers should beware! Easy, idle William with his ten children by Dora Jordan, was the special care of the All High. 'Therefore trouble yourselves not with this Bill; for this which I have told you is your doom . . . Ye have sworn to be faithful servants of your King. God looketh into your hearts and sees that ye care not for him . . . I tell ye that the rulers of the land think that their sovereign is in the net. But they deceive themselves for he is the Lord's anointed.'[79] It was all accompanied by what *Hansard* called 'Indescribable confusion' until, mercifully, Lord Sandon (Harrowby's son) spied strangers, the Speaker called for their withdrawal, 'and Mr Perceval instantly ceased and left the House'.[80]

The appointed act of humiliation kept the Commons away on the 20th when in Holland's dry words, 'Deference to publick hypocrisy prevented a Cabinet dinner on the fast day and compelled the Government to disperse with some broken heads the radical unions who had a plan for converting it to a feast and met in great numbers in Finsbury Square.' Holland thought that almost all reasonable men 'contemn in the hearts the observation of such superstitions and are equally conscious of their utter uselessness with the rabble; but each in looking grave, abstaining from his usual avocations and going to Church, tickles his own vanity by flattering himself that he is of the humbugging and not the humbugged portion of Mankind and so encourages the hypocrisy he despises'.[81] Actually the National Political Union, with a flash of humour rare on the far left, had decided to mark the fast day with a dinner. It was the National Union of the Working Classes which had called the meeting. This was reckoned at 100,000 strong and was followed by a march up West until stopped by Peel's New Policemen at Temple Bar and Holborn.[82]

The Commons reading continued on its way with speeches to be made. Some of them were striking, not least that of Hobhouse who, after accusing Croker of calling the people of England wild beasts, quoted Cicero and managed eighteen column lines of Latin. And some of them were significant. Peel was generally reckoned to have done well, admitting the Reform Bill to be 'the most important matter that ever agitated in parliament'[83] and acknowledging that 'there was desire, a permanent, a growing desire – for Reform among the sober and intelligent classes of the community'[84] also (a dig at Wellington), that 'it would have been difficult if not impossible for any administration to have been formed on the principle of resisting Parliamentary Reform'.[85]

This was obvious enough, but it was a long way from the raging Peel resisting dissolution a few months earlier. His whole style was one of wistful acquiescence. He could imagine a thoughtful nation in a few years' time 'scorched by the unmitigated blaze of a fierce democracy – panting for the shade and shelter of less popular institutions . . .'.[86] Reform, the speech said, was probably inevitable, but this was too much reform. It would not answer the expectations roused and the disappointment, combined with the new franchise, would create terrible troubles.

Peel spoke like a man not prepared to distress himself resisting something certain to pass. And in the Commons, certain it was. Accordingly, the minds of ministers were back with the problem afflicting them all year – precisely what to do when or if the House of Lords threw that Bill out.

At the Cabinet meeting of 21 March, the central issue was examined once again. If it were rejected by the Lords would they make new ones? There was a growing feeling that it would actually get through, but another consensus agreed 'that we ought to be prepared for the worst'. In such circumstances Grey, consistent with all his fears, 'evidently leant to immediate resignation'. But the group 'who contemplated prorogation and creation of peers as the course to be pursued' seems also to have amounted to a general consensus with even Richmond and Lansdowne joining in. Brougham favoured lucidity; 'the necessity of having our course clearly understood by ourselves and I think, explained to the king beforehand'.[87] Cabinet feeling was, however, against making this intention public, wanting instead to imply it, an odd and far from confident approach.

The Bill duly passed Commons third reading on 23 March and did so cold – 'in a very thin House, amidst no cheers, at about One o' clock in the morning'.[88] But before the Cabinet met again they had a warning of what they were up against from noble Lords. A bill to provide for the education of Catholic and Protestant children together attracted an effusion by a Lord Wicklow alleging that it meant 'the practical exclusion of the Bible from the education of the people', in Holland's view 'a notorious lie' which was sustained by 'the shabby and hostile conduct of the Bishops'. That full-time partisan Tory, Phillpotts of Exeter, was chief among them with what Greville called 'a furious speech'. The Duke of Wellington also flexed his muscles and 'studiously raised the standard of Protestantism, or rather Orangeism, in Ireland'.[89] The willingness of the cool Duke to blow hot and the scrupulous Duke to play dirty was noted. The government would have been defeated by a single vote, but was rescued by the proxies. Grey was counting on repentant bishops, but only three of them – Knox of Killaloe and the reliable liberal, Edward Maltby of

Chichester, with Bathurst of Norwich again sending his proxy – gave support here.

The Sunday Cabinet meeting of 25 March, the day before the Bill came to the Lords, was paradoxical. Resignation, Grey's preferred option as a response to defeat, was quietly dropped, but instead the King was to be told in advance that defeat would mean the inevitability of a major creation and prorogation of Parliament. Holland noted the enthusiasm of Richmond and other neo-Tories for this course and marvelled that they, who had cavilled at modest preliminary creations as a warning, were ready for a much bigger lightening of the purple if the fever reached crisis. *The Times* caught the mood. Following Lords' rejection 'a spirit more than insurrectionary will display itself in every part of England . . .'. It looked instead to creation, 'the Minister with the King's prerogative at his disposal . . . a natural and easy mode of averting so dreadful a calamity'.[90]

The procedure of the Bill in the Upper House involved its formal presentation to that House by John Russell on behalf of the Commons, to be followed by a second reading a fortnight later. It provided a happy interval for anxious speculation and head counting. Hobhouse resuming his conversations with Althorp, was told on the 28th that 'It is all right . . . the King will do it. If we are beaten, the Parliament will be prorogued, and we shall make eighty peers the next day. The Cabinet are unanimous on that point.' Althorp agreed with Hobhouse that 'they were on velvet',[91] adding that the King was grateful for not being asked to make peers any earlier than the Lords second reading.

Eight days later Althorp's optimism had evaporated. He still expected that second reading would be carried, if by a small majority, also that the first defeat would come on the first clause. This was the one disfranchising fifty-six boroughs. Ministers, he said, would ask William for sixty peers – and be refused! Ever eager to give up office, he envisaged without grief a sequence of resignation, a Peel Ministry and a Peel Reform Bill, a moderate one of course, which former ministers would support. It would do no harm to the party's character 'and something would be gained for the cause of Reform'.[92] He was speaking exactly the language of Grey. Althorp was a man of mood swings and fits of weary disengagement, but Russell, who joined them, confirmed the bad news. He shared the spirit of resignation, but not Althorp's readiness to throw in the towel, preferring concessions, arguing that 'as the Government had not carried their measure by force, they ought not to go out because they were beaten on the number of boroughs which Althorp thought ought to be the test'.[93]

The reasons for such diminished hopes were royal. The King had been sent the minute of the last Cabinet meeting and on 30 March Grey received his reply. As Holland coolly put it, 'If experience did not prove that on paper His Majesty is more difficult and controversial than he is in conversation or action, it would be the forerunner of a dissolution or dismissal of [the] Ministry.'[94] William was trying to shave his promises. Creation would take place if *necessary* but if second reading came through with only a very small majority, was it wise to make a major creation? William 'somewhat uncourteously hints at *some* of his confidential advisers being reluctant to recommend creating many . . . refers to former opinions that without modifications it could never pass to the Lords; and openly recommends in the case of rejection some understanding not only with the followers of Harrowby but with the moderate opponents of the measure, as the most eligible, not to say the only method of carrying it'.[95]

Ministerial reactions were illuminating. Brougham said flatly that the King was against them and ready to drop them once second reading was over. Palmerston wanted to accommodate the King's doubts and flinchings, and, if the Bill were rejected, they should follow him in 'accommodating matters with the more reasonable of our adversaries'.[96] Grey was clear and coherent. Even if a deal could be done, he and his colleagues were not the people who could do it. By trying they would be damaging their own repute and ability to govern. He would go to see the King, and Brougham was asked to draft a paper, but they would wait till he was back from the meeting to see if they needed it. The meeting, at Windsor, went according to Holland's appraisal of William's pattern of behaviour. He told Grey that his proposal for wholesale retreat and accommodation 'was only thrown out *as a suggestion* and did not imply a refusal to prorogue and create as he may be advised[sic]'.[97] He was friendly, spoke well of ministers and showed (his perfectly sincere) affection for Grey personally. But he worried very much about the number involved, seeming to shudder when Grey spoke of fifty to sixty. But the message reaching Holland from Grey's account was that 'should the case arise, he will handsomely and even readily acquiesce in the advice given to its full extent'.*[98]

Correspondence continued between the King and his ministers. Essentially, William continued to aver that he would make peers when the occasion arose but wrote in a tetchy, resentful way which as Holland noted, 'convinced us *all* that in that event we must instantly resign, unless He [sic] consents to prorogue Parliament and create Peers *instanter*'.[100] One long letter full of the details of what had passed between him and ministers

---

* As Holland would add in a wry afternote, it would not be so. A note written in the margin says, 'In this I was wrong, be it a proof of my simplicity or of the court's duplicity.'[99]

was later explained as the doing of Sir Herbert Taylor, and as the only way to have William remember just how firmly he had promised creation in the past. What happened, Taylor told Holland, was that the promises 'escaped the Royal Memory and was succeeded in his mind by an aversion to the measure stronger than ever and a *notion that he had been consistent in resisting it*'.[101]

Such elderly muddling explained much, but not quite all. The King was not a mischief maker, nor, unlike his brother George, a hysterical reactionary. But he lived in a court as fearful of the public as it was preoccupied with its own survival. His wife, originally Adelaide of Saxe-Coburg-Meiningen, was an absolutist for whom constitutional debate was the sort of thing soldiers were paid to shoot down. William was shrewd enough to beat off the worst excesses of court and spouse, but Holland was right – he was always more trouble on paper when surrounded by such people than in rational discussion with Grey. And by the time he descended on London for the Lords second reading on 9 April, he was once more full of warmth towards ministers.

But enfiladed as he was, William looked for compromise, in this case compromise between laws desired by the Commons, a large electoral majority with a clear public will, and the instincts of his own caste. The government had already been put off its stroke and badly shaken, then again given encouragement which would soon be withdrawn, behaviour by William well up to the historic standards of royal childishness. As Althorp wearily remarked to Hobhouse, 'Kings are Kings, even the best of them.'[102]

TEN

Back in the Lords

*'I ask is history ever to be a sealed book to
those noble Lords?'*

Debate on the second reading in the Lords would begin on 9 April. The King was in town, 'present to prorogue' said the Tories. Ministers had given up guessing what he might do and there was no more certainty of which way their Lordships would jump, though, as *The Times* put it, 'The Duke of Wellington and thoroughgoers of his kidney will of course resist.'[1]

The biggest problem was the first clause which read 'that fifty-six boroughs be disfranchised'. Such a plain statement of intent was generally resented and likely to be resisted. Wood, Grey's secretary, asked Greville to enquire of Harrowby about his response on this point. It was not something on which the government could give way, for any omission would look like retreat on Schedule A. When asked for consent, Harrowby threw a tantrum; 'he would not be dragged through the mire by these damned scoundrels. It was an insolence that was not to be borne; let them make their peers if they would, not Hell itself should make him vote for fifty-six; he would vote for sixty-six or any number like that, but he would not split from the Tories on the first vote'; and more in the same bristling vein.

Greville then spoke to Richmond, the most amendment-friendly Cabinet minister who wondered if the actual number could be left out in Grey's own opening speech to the Lords. At this point we get a sharp view of what is going on in ministerial minds and especially in Grey's. When Greville, who rather saw himself as the Messenger of Amendment, carried that suggestion to Wood, the Prime Minister's secretary was having none of it. Apart from the practical point of the Bill being already delivered to the Lords, he suggested that to be beaten on this clause would indeed be seen as defeat on Schedule A. In which case, the country 'would highly approve a creation of Peers and that, in fact, (if they wished), it would be the best opportunity they could have'.[2] This was *realpolitik* and related wholly to public opinion. Greville had grumbled that Wood 'harped about difficulty and his old strain of the country, etc'.[3] However, Wood, reflecting

Grey, was prepared to go along with not actually specifying the number in the text while making it clear that this must be the number, provided that Harrowby would say that the objection was only to the blatancy, 'the specification of the number in the clause'.[4] Such metaphysics belonged in palace politics. 'The country, etc' was going to be at the centre of the drama now stumbling legislatively towards an outcome.

Meanwhile, Grey took a Cabinet minute to William and, learning the gist of what transpired, Greville expressed it prophetically. 'It was probable (if he continues in the same mind and is not turned by some violence of the Opposition) that he will resist still more making peers when the Bill is in Committee to carry the details, some of which he wishes to see altered, but the difficulties are very great.'[5] This was exactly the direction in which William's faltering grasp of the plot and delusions of his own degree of choice were leading him. 'Difficulties' would indeed be what he got himself into. The debate mattered in every way. In an age which esteemed rhetoric and oratory, notably in a House which rated *its* rhetoric and oratory well above those found in the Commons, speeches might actually persuade. Charles Dickens, a reporter on *The Mirror of Parliament*, alternative to *Hansard*, then on the *Morning Chronicle*, might speak of the Prime Minister's 'fishy coldness, his uncongenial and unsympathetic politeness, his unsufferable, though most gentlemanly artificiality', but most insiders, as much Tories as Whigs, thought of Grey as the perfect man of honour, an undisputed gentleman in a society where the word was the highest form of approval. They also perceived high and gentlemanly qualities in his public speeches. Precisely how Grey impressed his brethren now would be supremely important. 'All depends upon the tone of Lord Grey,' said Lord Harewood, 'if he is moderate his majority will be considerable.'*[6]

Although the Prime Minister, when introducing the Bill, spent some time looking reverentially back to the seventeenth century – the right to representation of householders was something spoken for long before by a committee Report 'drawn up by Mr Serjeant Glanville' and 'it was well known that Selden, Finch, Noy (Afterwards Attorney General) . . . concurred'[7] – he tried hard to coax their Lordships into acknowledgement of the present and the menace surrounding it.

He had been accused of intimidating them but nothing could be further from his intention. But there were people out there. 'I never advised you to give way to the exorbitant and unruly demands of clamour, but what I did say then, and what I now repeat, is that the deliberate sentiment of a great and intelligent people, expressed after a long period allowed for

* Clearly, he was not moderate enough; Harewood voted against!

reflection, is entitled to your Lordships' attention – and the House will give me leave to say also – to your Lordships' respect.'[8] Effectively, Grey went to the window and pointed outside. 'My Lords, I admit that we have of late, heard none of that outcry on the part of the people which first marked the progress of this Bill. In its place a fearful silence at present prevails – a silence which may perhaps lead some persons foolishly to imagine that the people are no longer looking at this question with the same feelings of interest.'[9] They were looking as intently as they always had, and there were implications in that for their Lordships personally.

There was 'an opinion out of doors that the interests of the Aristocracy are separated from those of the people'. Grey denied that, arguing that the silence was 'the fruit of a latent hope in the bosom of the people that your Lordships will no longer oppose their often and loudly expressed wishes'.[10] To an astute anti-Reform peer, these remarks *were* intimidation. But so graceful and gentlemanlike was Grey in his expression of them, 'the perfect propriety and tone', applauded the next speaker, Ellenborough,* that his warning point was quietly taken.

Grey ended very solemnly, expressing quiet hopes that the Bill would both pass and prove a benefit, but if not, 'I pray that the consequences of my failure, may affect neither the security of my Sovereign, nor the prosperity of my country, and above all, I pray that the union between your Lordships and the people which is so necessary to the welfare of both and on which your Lordships' influence, authority and usefulness essentially depend, may not be weakened, but strengthened and confirmed.'[12] With which deft intimation of the suicidal potential of resistance, Grey moved that the Bill be read a second time. Le Marchant, in the government camp but with the qualities of a public servant always present, was impressed: 'clear, elegant, and dignified and singularly prudent and persuasive'.[13]

Opponents of the Bill who followed tended to address either detail, on which indeed they could find plenty of anomaly, and the vast and unspeakable future. The Bill, according to Ellenborough, 'must lead inevitably not only to universal suffrage, but to division of the country into particular parcels measured by extent and regulated upon theory.'[14] Both prophecies came true, but only after the lapse of comforting decades, in the case of universal suffrage, ninety-six years (following a Conservative Prime Minister's enfranchisement of women voters between twenty-one and thirty). But the general Tory case remained that Reform was simply revolution in

---

* Privately, Ellenborough told his diary that 'Ld Grey spoke feebly' before adding 'I followed' and concluding, 'I am glad I have made the speech, it places me where I ought to stand & certainly higher than I was in 1827.'[11]

immediate train. The lack, on both sides, of any sense of perspective allowing for increments and long-term change, is one of the oddities of the whole conflict.

Grey had put some hopes for apostasy among the bishops, but early interventions were not encouraging. Van Mildert of Durham saw a measure which 'provided only for further change and set a dangerous example of destruction and annihilation, without information and in spite of reason. It swept away privileges without necessity, without inquiry.'[15] As for 'the signs of the times', he had watched them and 'what was called the march of intellect, and he found abroad a restless disposition – a love of innovation – a wish to destroy institutions because they were ancient – a desire to set the subject above the ruler . . .'. The country was clearly going to what Mr Mantalini called 'the demnation bow-wows'. If the Bill passed, it would cause 'the deterioration of the House of Commons. Step by step, would that assembly decline till it came to the lowest point of descent . . . Atheism and infidelity, dissent and discord had already effected much mischief, and it would be worse than bad policy to make a palpably mischievous alteration in the Constitution merely because the destruction of that Constitution was clamoured for.' As for the advancement of knowledge, 'that species of knowledge when possessed by a person of inferior station, too often gave him an evil influence over his associates, one which under the Bill, would be dangerous to the State.'[16] Van Mildert, who lived in a castle next to the great Norman cathedral and was surrounded on all sides by disrespectful coal miners, would subsequently endure an unnecessary innovation all his own. Under subsequent legislation in the next parliament, he would be the last Prince Bishop of Durham.

Lord Wicklow, who had lately opposed the common education of Catholic and Protestant children in Ireland, thought that the Bill might do very well on the mainland, but 'If this measure should be passed, the separation of Ireland from the British connexions would be the consequence, and it required no prophetic spirit to foretell under such circumstances, the fall of this country.' He was against it.

The reaction of Viscount Gage was very different and spoke for the Conservative ability to survive. 'In October last, their Lordships had proved that they had the power to stop the progress further of the Reform Bill. He confessed he thought they possessed that power no longer and if they were to continue to oppose the Bill, their resistance would have the fatal effect of precipitating its adoption by the Legislature whilst they would lose the power they still, he thought, possessed of improving the provisions of the Bill in the Committee.'[17]

No such prudential reflection tainted Londonderry who rounded off the first day of debate in his best genial style. He denounced Harrowby and Wharncliffe for ratting and Grey for the ruin of the nation. 'They had a falling revenue – a discontented people – the inhabitants of Ireland were distracted – our West India colonies were in open insurrection – our foreign relations were distracted – and all these unhappy consequences had arisen since the period when the noble Earl had taken on himself the conduct of the government of this country; and he considered that the passing of this measure would prove the climax of all evils.'[18]

As for Harrowby, his triumphalist words last time round were flung back in his face. He had thought then that some improvements might be made in committee, 'But shall I, on that ground, consent to its going into committee? I think not, if I am satisfied that the principle of the measure is bad, I believe the principle on which the whole of this Bill is founded to be such, that no amendments made in the committee can so remove the objections to it as to make it our duty to pass it into a law.'[19] Against Wharncliffe he made a shrewd hit. That Earl had described his moving of the rejection of Reform as 'the proudest day of his life'. Now it was being said 'that the noble Earl had declared that he held in his hands a power which would enable him to carry the Bill through the House'.[20]

Both Waverers talked far too much early and late, but Wharncliffe's bragging of his influence with the King roused the simple landed proprietor's homely scorn: 'He could not conceive anything more unconstitutional than such a statement . . . He had heard it stated that the noble Earl had made use of the influence of the King's name to bias the opinions of noble Lords. If such were the case, he would say that the noble Earl's conduct was sufficient to induce an impeachment against him.'[21]

The second day, 10 April, began with a blasphemous little speech by the Whig and Roman Catholic Earl of Shrewsbury, blasphemous in that it denied the sanctity of the British constitution. 'It appears to me my Lords, that the Constitution of this country has never yet been anything but a beautiful theory, subject to perpetual contradiction in practice . . . We have been perpetually engaged in most wasteful and unjust wars . . . We have a poor and unemployed population – a population starving in the midst of plenty . . . we have always had a Government supporting itself by patronage and keeping up a large army of occupation and a numerous catalogue of useless and burthensome offices.'[22] Given the almost American conceit of Lords and Commons, Whigs and Tories, as to the superabundant all-rightness of that constitution, differing only over the presence or not of modest imperfections, this was desecration.

Lord Shrewsbury, Bertram Arthur Talbot, seventeenth Earl, was the premier Earl of England (created 1442), but that fact did not sweeten his view of the English aristocratic order to whom, following the procedures of the Upper House, he was free to speak direct in the offensive second person: 'Your extravagance, – your disregard of the interests of the country – your absolute tyranny over the people of Ireland – the bitter fruits of which you are now reaping – all these things are exposed in their true light until in my opinion, we now stand for judgment before the people.'[23] The remarks on Ireland were startling given the usual propensity of English Catholic noblemen to turn a light shade of orange in their concern not to be confused with the low, disloyal peasantry beyond St George's Channel.

For Shrewsbury, the Reform Bill was a lightening of the sky: it would be the start of what we optimistically call 'open government'. He looked forward very shrewdly to ideas of an incorruptible public service and an end to jobbery and the place system. He also took a passing swipe at the clergy. Having heard Van Mildert's lamentation the night before, he suggested wholesale reform on their part. 'They have been all too often the willing agents of every system of tyranny and persecution. They have been the promoters of that extravagance and spoliation with which this country has been afflicted at the hands of ambitious and self-interested men.' Were they now perhaps capable of 'appreciating the spirit of the times and of endeavouring as far as lies in their power, to remedy the evils which they have had too large a share in producing'.[24]

As for the Waverers 'who intend to vote for the second reading of the Bill with a view to bring it into a snare in which they will be able to defeat it', the Earl would respect them more if they would 'manfully stand forward in support of their own opinions, fight the battle boldly and desist from the desultory warfare which they are about to wage against the measure . . .'. Worst of all, Shrewsbury looked forward to later reform of the House of Lords itself. A government's majority in that House should not depend upon 'keeping up a disproportionate number of officers in the army and navy', nor should it rest upon 'translating a right reverend prelate from a poorer to a richer see or by advancing noble Lords from lower to a higher degree of the peerage – nor by reinforcing this House with every man who has voted for a certain number of years in support of the Minister'.[25] 'It appears to me,' concluded the Tony Benn of his times, 'that if the House of Commons be Reformed, this House must also be Reformed.'[26]

This was perfectly horrid, and Lord Limerick, who had voted, he said, for Catholic emancipation, reflecting on the ingratitude of both Shrewsbury and the currently tumultuous Irish, regretted that decision. But Limerick saw Reform and Catholic emancipation, events of the last four years, as a 'common catastrophe'. What had such liberation produced 'but insubordination, sedition and nearly rebellion? By agitation, a contemptible knot of low people had been enabled to convulse Ireland and dictate to England a measure which had shaken England to its centre and had mainly contributed to produce the melancholy crisis in which they were now involved.' As for the Reform Bill, its effect would be 'to return such Representatives to Parliament as would accomplish the two great objects the agitators had at heart which were the destruction of the Protestant Church in Ireland and the separation of Ireland from Great Britain'.[27]

As the debate progressed, partisans consulted, exchanged defections, made guesses at the outcome and awarded marks to speakers. Greville, the keen Waverer, was set worrying by his close friend De Ros:* 'He doubted how he should vote . . . his reason for seceding from the Opposition was the menaced creation of Peers.' Greville wrote to Harrowby 'and begged him to say something to satisfy tender consciences and moved heaven and earth to keep De Ros and Coventry (who was slippery) right, and I succeeded – at least I believe so for it is not yet over . . . Nothing can equal the anxiety out of doors and the intensity of interest in the town, but the debate is far less animated than last year.'[28] As to the outcome, Wood for the government camp projected a majority of sixteen, Holmes, Tory Chief Whip, interestingly was up on him, reckoning eighteen. As Le Marchant, to whom these numbers were confided, remarked, 'No pains are spared, no acts untried, to gain a convert. The Duke of Wellington is as busy as a recruiting officer.'[29]

After a very long speech by Mansfield rejecting all compromise, came Harrowby, admired by the scrupulous Le Marchant who was conscious of the difficulty of the position from which he spoke. Harrowby's speech had been awaited by Tories who believed he was jumping their ship and Whigs who reckoned he planned to demast theirs. As he remarked himself, he had been called both 'a deserter' and 'a treacherous friend'. Moderate men commonly look big in England, but Harrowby had a lot of presumptions to meet. His central point was plain: 'We cannot hope to again successfully resist a measure which the House of Commons has sanctioned for a second time by a large majority, and in favour of which the people of England had expressed a decided opinion.'[30] At the same time, he was solicitous towards Grey. He had seen in his speech a 'moderate and conciliatory tone, a disposition as he thought to adopt – at least not pertinaciously to resist such amendments as would not necessarily destroy its more important features'.[31]

If such bland words were calculated to irritate Durham and Brougham,

* Premier Baron of England and cardsharp.

Harrowby's next comments were a riposte to a central Tory nag and to the impregnable fortress theory of Parliament. They should not indeed yield to intimidation 'but he was also sure that they would not be induced by vapid declamation to confound a timely yielding to the forces of circumstances which was above their control with a cowardly shrinking to clamour'.[32] There had been an awful lot of vapid declamation in the previous thirteen months. Parliament's sense of itself as above opinion, especially the opinion it called 'popular' or 'low', had been present in extreme form as expressed by Wetherell, Londonderry, Croker, the Bankeses and a dozen more. Both Houses could be deathly proud. The call to retreat now came by diplomatic messenger speaking negative rhetoric, the kind employed to play something down. Harrowby was getting very close to Sydney Smith: 'Do it for your Ease. Do it for your rent roll.' And 'if they also saw that nothing less than an extensive measure of Reform would satisfy the public mind, were they not bound to forgo their own predilections and do their best to prevent the ill consequences of a too rapid and violent change?'. Government, he argued, using language he would not have employed the last time round, 'must ultimately rest upon the basis of public opinion'.

In sheer exasperation, he slapped down young Ellenborough whose diaries at this time bubble with the high opinions of his speech of various Tories, including Lord Ellenborough himself. He had argued, said Harrowby, 'that we ought, notwithstanding everything we saw, still to give a persevering resistance to Reform. He did not however know how this was to be done, and willing as he might be to do it, he still could not serve in any army, if one wing of it was commanded by the High Bailiff of Old Sarum, and the other was to be under the Command of the Mayor of Gatton.'[33] And Harrowby put himself at considerable risk with his own essentially Tory friends by giving credit to the threats of peer creation which Grey himself so abhorred thinking about: 'had they heard any thing from the noble Earl [Grey] which could induce them to believe that he would consent to a measure of less efficiency or extent?'

Here historic irony enters the discourse. The Harrowby who argued against taking government threats lightly went on in the same vein to ask what the consequences would be if noble Lords brought the government down.

Let them suppose the Bill rejected and that a new Government had succeeded to that of the noble Earl. Were the opponents of the present Bill foolish enough to believe they would gain anything by that change? Did they suppose that by a change of men they could get rid of the

Reform Question altogether? He would tell them not to deceive themselves for one moment by such a dangerous belief. Let His Majesty select
whom he might for his counsels. Reform must constitute a condition of
office, if those persons hoped to continue a single week in his service.[34]

That was a plain statement of realities. Yet less than a month later
among those voting against the first and central clause of the Bill – abolition of fifty-six boroughs, – was to be found the Earl of Harrowby. We
will come to that miscalculation, for miscalculation it must have been since
the whole burden of Harrowby's 10 April speech, widely praised by minis-
terialists, was not to give up frontal assault for discreet sabotage. Harrowby's
purpose in a lucid, percussive contribution was to avoid a crash and its
active public consequences.

That was not the view of the Duke of Wellington. Wellington was never
going to get over his obsession with the political unions. The distinction
between the militancy of some and the constitutionality of others was a
nuance too far. Instead, he pursued Harrowby, quoting what he had said
on the same topic during the previous second reading. The Waverers were
peculiarly vulnerable to this sort of point. They had started out as uncomplicated anti-reformers, had seen the extent of the crisis developing and
amended their view. It was most people's idea of empirical good sense.

But Wellington, who could be cunningly obtuse, simply quoted the text.
In 1831 Harrowby had complained of the assemblies of the political unions
and had asked, 'when these come with their directions for our conduct
thundering over our heads; what, I ask, will be the kind of government
then presiding over the interests of the country? What is it that we are to
expect from a Legislative Assembly so constituted and so directed?' So
how could Harrowby now 'say we must read this Bill a second time?' The
election, said Wellington sullenly, had proved Harrowby right, 'when he
said that it must cause the return to the House of Commons not of
Members but of delegates'.[35] Wellington was now the full-dress counter-
revolutionary fighting the revolution of his own projections. He sought the
destruction of the Ministry: 'their Lordships ought rather to address the
King to remove the Ministers from their places, and put things as they
were before, in order that the House might have a fair opportunity for
discussion, than proceed to read the bill a second time.' The Commons
might come back ten times with the same decision, 'but the country was
not to be abandoned on this account'.[36]

For Wellington everything was the fault of somebody else – generally
either Grey or the French. 'Now there could be no doubt whatsoever that
there was no opinion existing in the country, in the year 1829, and the

beginning of 1830 on the subject of Parliamentary Reform. [*Cheers*]' The cheers were ironic, but Wellington forged ahead none the less. 'Then came the French Revolution [of 1830] and the insurrection in Belgium . . . these events occasioned a very great excitement and alteration in the elections as well as greatly inflamed the people with respect to Parliamentary Reform.' The Whigs then came in. They could have had a bill for moderate reform, but instead they called a new election 'under a degree of public excitement that has never before been witnessed'.[37]

Behind Wellington's querulousness lay a perception of society which, like the unique and glorious constitution, should never alter.

> The opinion of the gentlemen of the landed property and of the learning of the country was against this Bill. The Bill was on the other hand, supported by the noble Lords opposite and their adherents, certainly not a numerous class; it was also supported by all the dissenters from the Church of England and by all who wished it would pass as a means of their attaining votes; but he would repeat that it was in fact, opposed by the sentiments of all the gentlemen, of the yeomanry and of the middle classes throughout the country. Yes, he would say, there was a change of opinion, and that the best part of the public were not desirous of the Bill, but were on the contrary, apprehensive of its effects. But they did not hear of this because no gentleman in the country could go to a public meeting and speak his sentiments secure from the attacks of the mobs.[38]

Wellington thought all amendment and thus all compromise impossible. The Bill was too full of 'gross anomalies' for that. But, essentially, his thinking did not differ from that of Wetherell. Reform threatened property and boroughs were property. 'The Bill went to destroy a number of boroughs – some holding by prescription, some by charter and for no reason whatsoever except that such was the will of the Minister of the day. There was no man who possessed property . . . but must run a great risk as to the security of that property under such a state of things as this measure, if it should be passed, was sure to introduce into this country.'[39]

As for another great fear, the prospect of a uniform right of voting, the Duke knew where that would lead. 'When they came to the larger towns, it would be found that the right of voting which this measure would establish there, would amount to neither more nor less than Universal Suffrage.' Some noblemen might linger on in their influence, 'but generally speaking, in those towns it would be the demagogue and not the gentleman of property who would possess the influence over the elections there'. Fearful, negative, intellectually frozen, lined with incurious prejudice and plain wrong, it was a dismal speech to anyone acquainted with Wellington the soldier, and at sixteen grumbling columns, with Wellington the one-line wit. Holland's diary, after praising the Tories, Ellenborough and Mansfield as speakers, observes that they and the Duke 'exhibited such practical ignorance of the nature and effect of popular elections as deprived their judgement of all authority in such matters with men of reflection'.[40]

Wellington was followed soon after by Wharncliffe 'greatly discomposed . . . and he came breathing fury to the Chancellor . . . begging that he might be allowed to answer his Grace'.[41] Brougham, though expecting to speak himself, cheerfully accommodated the request, allowing Wharncliffe to highlight the other side's squabble. As Le Marchant coolly remarked, 'He did it *con amore* heartily enough, and had he not spun out to almost three hours, he would have been very effective.' At just under fifteen columns, Wharncliffe was shorter than Wellington. The notion of six hours for two speeches, with a couple of columns of backwoods succinctness from Lord Grantham slipped between them, speaks of a stamina in orator and listener to which no successor can aspire.

But in important things Wharncliffe could be pithy. Wellington 'had said that before the revolution in France and Belgium in 1830, there was no such thing as a call for Reform. Good God! How could the noble Duke make such an assertion? . . . The fact unfortunately was that the noble Duke was entirely wrong on this subject.' The Duke had been a great and glorious hero abroad; he, a former MP, had merely been in Parliament representing people, 'and as long as he could recollect, this question of Parliamentary Reform had been proceeding'. As for refusing a second reading, 'if they did so, one day or other, this measure or perhaps a worse and more sweeping measure, must pass'.[42]

A casual listener would have supposed that this was a sustained wrangle with Wellington, which it was, but only as an unsuccessful attempt to make the field marshal think tactically. But Wharncliffe also said things in the Chamber which indicated the impossibility of compromise with any minister except perhaps Grey in one of his depressions. He insisted that 'because he or any other noble Lord might vote for the second reading, it could not be said they were bound to vote for the £10 clause or Schedule A in the Committee'.[43] There had at one time been members of the Cabinet who would have sacrificed the £10 franchise, but fewer who might have modified Schedule A. It was in the nature of long negotiations reaching no firm conclusion that such willingness had receded almost out of sight. Discussion had gone on too long – with Harrowby and Wharncliffe and within the Cabinet – for a defeat on such issues not to provoke either split or resignation. And the Cabinet, anticipating Melbourne's later remark about hanging together rather than apart, now saw every reason to make it the bold step of resignation. Over nearly fifteen columns and his share of sense, Wharncliffe was wasting his time.

The third day began with the Earl of Winchilsea, the same Earl whose abuse of Wellington at the time of Catholic emancipation had led to a mutual discharge of pistols respectively wide and high, but who, as a worrier about 'the democratic spirit which was wafted to our shores from infidel France and which if suffered to work its way would have involved the general civilization of the world in ruin',[44] seemed temperate by comparison with the next speaker.

The Duke of Buckingham who had, on the first day, made his own bizarre attempt to place a spoiling Bill before the Lords, followed next, making a comparison between Harrowby and Wharncliffe dealing with Ministers and Macbeth breaking in upon the witches:

> *How now, you secret, black, and midnight hags!*
> *What is't you do?*

To which the reply given to the noble lord was,

> *A deed without a name.*

Then, pausing only to applaud Charles I, 'a patriot king', he offered another simile: 'So will it be now if we break with the King, [government] will be in the hands of sullen Radicals, of Domestic tyrants, of canting Puritans or of some ascetic statesman who retires now because his plots are not ripe and spins his web until the country is fixed in his toils, that the destinies of England will be placed.'[45] The Duke concluded another two and a half hours/fourteen columns of historical pageant, the glories of England, with an assertion that under the £10 franchise 'All the beggars of London would vote', and by denouncing 'Republicanism'. That it was which 'had clothed itself in the garb and form of the British Constitution for the purpose of misleading the weak-sighted; and which in all the hideousness of Vampire deformity, had found its way to their Lordships . . . That House, he hoped, would be the Red Sea of this destructive enemy – drowned in which, it would no longer frighten from their propriety the constitutional feelings and good sense of the people of England.'*[46]

---

* Allegedly Buckingham, finding one of his spring-guns unloaded when he stepped on the trigger, berated his keeper for a negligence which would have spared a poacher.

Lord Radnor, something of a radical, had a nice phrase about government 'struggling for years against the growing intelligence of the people'. The Bishop of Lincoln in parodic Anglican style said that at the last presentation of the Bill he had been faced with 'a choice of evils'. That was still the case, but such was the state of general feeling 'that he believed now that the people would be satisfied with any modification which their Lordships, supposing they should concur in the principle of the Bill, should think proper to introduce into its details'.[47] Shopping around among evils, the Bishop announced that he would vote for second reading but could never support the £10 franchise. The Marquess of Bristol, speaking from a certain altitude, had 'hoped that deference for the opinion expressed by this House on the Reform Bill of last session would have produced such modifications in the bill before us as would have allowed of our considering in committee consistently with the important considerations on which our decision of last October was founded'.[48] Unfortunately, deference to such important considerations had been lacking and 'The Bill before us is quite as revolutionary in its principle as the former one and it contains the same sweeping and indiscriminate spoliation of charter rights which if sanctioned by this House, would shake to their foundations all the vested interest and ultimately all the rights of property in this great empire.'[49]

Very usefully for ministers, the Bishop of London after much havering – 'it was with inexpressible reluctance and concern he felt himself bound to express his dissent from many with whom he generally agreed'[50] – managed to reach a peroration in which 'he trusted they would be able, under the blessing of Him who had so long protected and favoured the country, to concur in a measure which would improve the representation, conciliate the affections of the people and adding strength and perpetuity to whatever was valuable in our constitution, cherish religion and consolidate the best interest of the country'.[51]

But the great event of the day, the prime explosion of the whole debate, now unwound in the person of Henry Phillpotts, Bishop of Exeter. That prelate, an extreme Tory, in effect Chaplain to the Ultras, is known to dictionaries of quotations from the observation of Sydney Smith that he 'must believe in the apostolic succession as the only explanation of the Descent of the Bishop of Exeter from Judas Iscariot'. Less famously but as devastatingly, Charles Greville wrote that 'It would be an injury to compare this man with Laud; he more resembles [Stephen] Gardiner; had he lived in those days, he would have been just such another, boiling with ambition, an ardent temperament and great talents. He has a desperate and a dreadful countenance and looks the man he is.'

Phillpotts was the ancient and cherished enemy of Lord Durham. They had violently clashed thirteen years before at Monk Wearmouth when Phillpotts, then a Prebend of Durham, joined to a delectable living, had sought to organise a public meeting in support of the Manchester yeomanry on the occasion of Peterloo. Loathing was not diminished and, as Exeter spoke, Durham listened. It was a mistake in 1832 to imply that a minister in the government had inspired partisan comment in a newspaper. *Nous avons changé tout ça*, but in the fourth decade of the nineteenth century saying so was a hanging offence. It was fine for the Bishop to quote *The Times*, in those days a startlingly radical sheet, on 'that horrid old mockery of a free government we have hitherto been enduring'; the trouble came from his description of the paper as one 'believed by many to breathe the inspirations, if not of the Treasury itself, at least of some high office or offices of the Government'.[52]

Phillpotts had a high notion of prelatical privilege, but failed to comprehend the height of either the parliamentary or the aristocratic sense of caste. Brougham, a mere talent at the social margins, could have (did have) a brother influential in Printing House Square and might have shrugged. Grey and Durham (though Durham probably shared the sentiments) could not. When outrage at the imputation was added, in Durham's case to decade-old contempt, the consequences had a headline quality enjoyable from here. The Bishop did not improve his chances by muffling his bomb in a flurry of appended ejaculations and weaselling a disclaimer: 'I do not say that this is belief well-founded – I do not say that I believe it – I only say that such a charge has been made, and that it is believed by many to be true. [*It is not true.*]'[53]

We are not told if those last four words came from Durham, but his full response, delayed until the following day, was worth waiting for. He began by briskly beating up the speaker preceding him, one Wynford, a lawyer, who inflicted twenty columns (about four hours) on the House. Durham had

> listened with the greatest interest to the long, and I may be permitted to add, desultory, speech of the noble and learned Lord who has just sat down . . . it embraced many topics and related to many subjects: but of these, some are entirely unconnected with the question itself and others with its present stage. In one portion he alluded to the household of their Majesties; in another to the inconsistency of the reverend Bench; in a third to the state of the Irish Church; and in a fourth to the state of the manufactures of India.[54]

The courtly elaborations and verbal bowings of English parliamentary discourse were not for John Lambton. He followed the principle that a gentleman never insults otherwise than intentionally. But for poor, interminable Wynford, he managed a residual compliment. The 'long and laborious attention' given to his speech had been 'in some degree at last repaid by the pleasure of finding that he at least has not adopted that tone of party rancour and personal animosity towards his Majesty's Ministers which has in so marked a manner distinguished the last two nights.' This had not been the case with the Bishop of Exeter. 'I shall only say that if coarse and virulent invective – malignant and false insinuations – the grossest perversions of historical facts – decked out in the choicest flowers of his well known pamphleteering slang – . . .'

According to the Record, 'The Earl of *Winchilsea* rose to order.' As well he might. His man was about to be knocked around the Chamber and a point of order was the best defence to hand. 'Did it,' he asked, 'become any such august assembly to deal in such violent personalities, to tolerate such personal invectives?' Lord Holland, who seems to have been occupying the Woolsack, later recorded having 'availed myself of my very undeserved, but high, character for knowledge of order to embarrass those who interrupted him as to his mode of proceedings'. Winchilsea came back and moved, by way of anachronistic fiction in the days of official and press shorthand takers, that 'a note be taken'. Buckingham, his own palate flowing with scarlet and purple, begged that the strong words should be softened.

Durham was delighted; they really must take a note and he would pause so that they could do so. Perhaps the words 'pamphleteering slang' were not 'the most elegant which I could have used. They do not perhaps suit the noble Earl's taste; but they are the only words which I consider can correctly describe the speech of the Reverend Bishop.' As for the term 'malignant and false insinuations' which Buckingham had asked should be retracted, he could only say that the Bishop, 'in the course of his harangue, insinuated that some of His Majesty's Ministers were intimately connected with the Press'. From the terms used and from parallel accusations 'in those weekly publications which are so notorious for their scurrility and obscenity', it was clear that the charge was made specifically against him. 'When therefore I found that charge repeated in this House, in terms which neither I nor any man living could misunderstand, I determined to take the earliest opportunity of stating to your Lordships that it was as false as scandalous. I now repeat that declaration and pause for the purpose of giving any noble Lord an opportunity of taking down my words.'[55] At which he briefly sat down, provoking a perhaps fearful silence.

Durham had other things to say before returning to the cutting and slicing of the Bishop. The gentry lived among themselves and simply did not know the country. Ellenborough, for example, had talked about 'the inferiority of intellect of the newly returned Members'. If he would go to middle-class meetings 'and enter into a discussion with them on political or scientific subjects, he would have no reason to plume himself on his fancied superiority'.[56] He recalled the panic measures of repression imposed a few years earlier, 'prevention of public meetings and petitioning – for fettering the press – for suspending the Habeas Corpus act, for granting indemnity bills'. They 'were proposed to the House of Commons and immediately adopted by that assembly'.[57] Tory Lords started to cheer as he listed the Gag Acts, all of them departures from the sacred constitution. Durham fixed them with his most scornful look and suggested that public anger with Parliament came from just such statutory acts of repression.

> The people, seeing their liberties attacked and their resources squandered through the instrumentality of a House of Commons theoretically the guardian of both, naturally directed their attention to the mode in which that House was chosen which neither represented their feelings nor protected their interests . . . They found one portion nominated by Peers – a second by Commoners – a Third by trafficking attorneys, selling seats to the highest bidder, a fourth to the most unblushing bribery and corruption . . .[58]

So what should be done about it? He contemplated the Tory Lords who had talked 'so loudly of the dangers of concession and the safety of resistance – and by the reverend Bishop who preaches to us the necessity of leaving the consequences to God. My Lords, I say nothing of the impropriety of these constant appeals to that sacred name in this place – especially from such a quarter – but I ask is history ever to be a sealed book to those noble Lords?'[59] Durham had surely read his Shelley, a highly sympathetic spirit. Although he was now talking about history, consciously or not, he was flinging in the face of Phillpotts, Van Mildert and the rest of the higher clergy the lines concluding a general denunciation of the established order: 'Religion, Christless, Godless, a book sealed.'

For the no-concession men he had not exactly Whig history, but a common-sense, rather moderate belief in making response to fair complaint. If Charles I, the Bourbons and the British in America had moved sooner and more intelligently, they would have saved themselves. But these sentiments were not summed up moderately. Whenever 'the consequences have been left to Providence, according to the suggestion of the reverend Bishop (Phillpotts), the course of events has always been uniform – in the first instance, bigoted resistance to the claims of the people – in the second, bloody and protracted struggles – and finally, but invariably, unlimited, disgraceful, but then useless concession'.[60] It was a different way of speaking from Grey's: combative, affronting but directed to the *res* and taking on the calcified part of the nobility with the necessary chisel. Yet it paid the House of Lords the great compliment of argument, and across the great distance in style and manner of 170 years it still has the tingling quality of a great speech.

Phillpotts now took centre stage again. The Bishop was in trouble for his remarks about press connections and, squirming in this hole, proceeded to dig a deeper one. It was a wretched performance. His voice dropped to a mutter, leading to calls for him to speak up. He excused Grey of having a connection with *The Times* which, as that newspaper had been roundly abusing the Prime Minister's caution and doubting his purpose, set people laughing. He then became specific, raising the subject of Buckingham's letter to William. Buckingham's stupid attempt at King management had been followed, it will be recalled, by William/Sir Herbert Taylor sensibly and properly passing the letter to the Prime Minister. It had then entered the public domain. This brought Exeter up against Grey, whose sense of honour and lack of partisanship could on occasion make him more dangerous than Durham. Buckingham had given assurance that he had not passed on a copy. Grey returned that 'on my honour as a Peer I can say I gave none'. He felt able to give assurances for his colleagues:

'But the right rev. Prelate said on a former night that he had heard these things and he believed them. I understood him to have say that he believed them . . . but if I am mistaken I beg his pardon.'
Exeter: 'I did not say that I had believed them, but that they had been believed.'
Grey: 'That they have been believed! . . . Now mark the charity of the rt. rev. Prelate – I say mark his charity – mark what he does not think improbable! That my noble friend near me . . . has been guilty not merely of fraud, but falsehood and has secretly and insidiously furnished newspapers with the means of attack upon the very government of which he is a Member. If this be charity – if this be the charity of a Christian Bishop, I am very much deceived in the true nature of that virtue.'[61]

It was 'an insinuation which I will not characterize further than by saying that I little expected it from any noble Lord, but least of all from one who sits on that bench'.

The Whigs had the high ground and Exeter was reduced to a further combination of apology and explanation of the kind Balliol College warns against. It was the kind of incident which, beyond the blue flash of the instant, relates to morale. The Bishop had bristled with audacity and assault now he had put the Tories generally into defensive mode. Goderich, a formidable debater, took him on gently but injuriously over other parts of his speech. Exeter had defiantly defended the nomination borough system.

> Why, he had asked, were those defects called the shameful part of the constitution? They were shameful because not agreeable to any intelligible idea of representation, because they placed in the hands of irresponsible individuals an influence which they ought not to possess . . . they were emphatically shameful because it was well known they were abused . . . Looking to human nature, they could only expect that individuals who gave money for boroughs would endeavour to make money out of them . . .

Against this it was argued that 'this power of nomination ought to be preserved as the best feature of the constitution without which their lordships and all their honours must tumble to the earth to be ground to powder . . .'[62]

Very long speeches mean very late hours, candlelight into dawnlight, and there were a few more hoops to be processed through. For the aged Eldon it was 'a bill so vicious in its principles that it is impossible to correct them in dealing with the clauses in committee'.[63] Tenterden, Lord Chief Justice, concluded by saying 'never shall I enter the doors of this House, after it has become the phantom of its departed greatness . . .'.[64] The Bishop of Rochester could never forget that his ancestors had sat 'as Members of their Lordships' House for 500 years . . . and would never disgrace their name or his own by voting for the overturning of a Constitution for which they were content to lay down their lives'.[65]

On the government side, Brougham, having made way earlier for the Wharncliffe fireworks, argued very credibly for the Bill's inherent caution. It did *not*, as Wellington and the Lord Chief Justice had claimed, 'subvert the whole parliamentary constitution of the country'. Indeed, as representation worked under the Bill, it 'served conservative principles'.[66] and he noted the extent of landlord influence which would survive. Following this line of argument he challenged Wellington's mutterings about the opposition of all the best and richest people to Reform. What about the City of London – 'the great body of merchants and traders and bankers of the city [sic] of London called together by public advertisement in the newspapers and openly congregated in the Egyptian Hall?' Brougham, speaking 'with less brilliancy than usual but great judgment',[67] was trying to soothe a parcel of diehards determined to hear in the broadening-down measures directed at the middle classes the rumble of drums under the social scaffold. It was a speech direct against the collective self-pity in which a large congregation of privileged but incurious men were indulging themselves.

Lyndhurst wound up on the Tory side, a gladiator politician, adaptive and self-made, though it was Grey who had made him Chief Justice of the Exchequer, something which might have (but did not) keep him silent in political debate. Lyndhurst, sexually fluent, never quite a believer in anything, was not for nothing an early friend of Disraeli. Like the bishops, he damned the Dissenters; they were for Reform. So were people without property; so were the popular press. Put them together and they could very soon mount an attack on the Church or anything else established. 'They could easily be brought to act in concert against the property of the Church – against the standing army – and against the legislative authority of this House.'[68] Lyndhurst knew what made prelatical and landowning flesh creep, and, very like Disraeli, he was an outsider with better talents who could speak for his huddled and fearful betters.

Another group keen on Reform were the Roman Catholics, a thought which led on to Ireland. Ireland, where there was real trouble, was a good card to play and Lyndhurst duly played it. The Catholics would return two-thirds of the Irish members. It was 'unnecessary to add that the conduct of those whom the Roman Catholics of Ireland have hitherto sent into parliament sufficiently shows that those Members will also be in the scale of extreme democracy'. With the effects of the wider franchise and deplorable prospects in Scotland, they would 'add at least 200 Members to the partizans [sic] of extreme democracy in that House. They might disband the Army, expel non-compliant Members in the fashion of Cromwell.' Accordingly, their Lordships should 'lay aside all temporising policy which must if you be weak enough to entertain it, prove your destruction. By voting against the second reading on the contrary, you will turn aside the dangers which menace the Constitution, and you will win the eternal gratitude of your fellow-countrymen and of all good men.'[69]

Grey now concluded, speaking into morning light for an hour and a half, from five till six-thirty. The scene was well described: 'The lights had grown yellower and dimmer in the fresh daylight, the faces of the wearied legislators had appeared more and more haggard and heated . . . The attendance of strangers was as full as it had been twelve hours before; for it was not a scene which men would miss for the sake of food and sleep.'[70]

By way of recapitulation, Grey returned to the events of October 1830 when the idea of Reform had first taken off. He had declared then 'that the conviction of the public was so strong that the present constitution of the House of Commons was so defective in practice and untenable in theory, that Reform must be granted to avert those evils which the further denial of it could not prevent from happening'.[71] And he turned to Lyndhurst resting from his appeal in the name of all good men. 'Did he not admit when he left office, that it was absolutely necessary to grant some Reform to carry on the government of the country? [Lord *Lyndhurst* made no reply].'[72] The silence echoed the 'Never' he had proclaimed last time round. A lie successful on one occasion should not be risked on a second. What Lyndhurst knew, Grey knew. And the political class was wise to Lyndhurst's quite recent belief in a Reform Bill and those earlier Girondin enthusiasms about which Denman had talked. Grey's words became, in this context, treble-barbed: 'Even the noble and learned Lord who now at last was a Reformer – who in the earlier times of his life had heard of or argued for or supported Reform – even the noble Lord who reluctantly consenting admits there is some necessity for Reform . . .'[73]

Close-mouthed and very much his own solicitor, Lyndhurst replied, 'I made no such admission; nothing I said could be construed into it.'[74] But Grey's conclusion was the most immediate part of his speech, a direction to the opposition of government readiness to create peers. It had been argued earlier in the debate 'that the exercise of this portion of the prerogative for the purpose of facilitating the passing of the bill would be an act worse than any committed by James II'. Yet 'a case might arise when it would be absolutely necessary to exercise it'. And he had learned authority for that view. 'All the best constitutional writers admitted that although the creation of a large number of Peers for a particular purpose was a measure which should rarely be resorted to, yet that cases might arise in which it might be absolutely necessary.'[75] Suppose there were 'a collision between the two Houses of Parliament and in which public opinion supported one branch of the legislature against the other . . . the power was vested in the Crown for the purpose of preventing the danger which might arise from a collision between the two branches of the legislature. More than this he did not think it necessary to say.'[76] Graceful men can do menace very well.

Debate in Chamber was now concluded and the division called at seven in the morning of 14 April 1832. What Lord Auckland, as government teller, returned was not much of a majority for the Bill, less than the Whips had contemplated. With Contents Present 128 and their proxies 56, there were 184 votes in favour; with Not Contents Present 126 and proxies 49, there stood against it 175, a majority of 9. For the record, counting proxies, the Opposition had won 2 to 1 on Royal Dukes, 10 to 9 on ordinary Dukes and 15 to 12 on Bishops.

One or two reactions might be noted. Charles Greville wrote on the same day, 'The tone however of the violent supporters of Reform is totally changed; at Lord Holland's last night they were in a very different note, and now, if the counsels of the Lords are guided by moderation and firmness, they may deal with the Bill *almost* as they please; but they must swallow Schedule A.'[77] Three weeks later Thomas Attwood told a crowd, reckoned by some in excess of 200,000, at Birmingham: 'I would rather die than see the great Bill of Reform rejected or mutilated in any of its great parts or provisions.'[78] From these irreconcilable premises the great question of Reform would proceed to conclusion.

ELEVEN

The Bill in the Lords

'I have the pleasure to tell you that we are no longer His Majesty's Ministers'

Greville had thought the violent reformists of the government chastened. It was a reasonable reaction. The slogan of the ardent reformers had been 'The Bill, the Whole Bill and nothing but the Bill.' After Lords second reading, they had the Bill, but with intelligent sniping in committee they would not have the whole Bill. Tory hearsay was upbeat, not least about the King's attitude. It was, though, third relay hearsay. Even before the reading was completed, Ellenborough had been told by Henry Hardinge, who had been told by William Ward* that he 'had had some conversation with the king. The king said that he was pledged as far as the 2nd Reading, but no further.' Ward also told Hardinge, who told Ellenborough, that the King wanted to get rid of the new 'three member counties, of Schedule B., of the Metropolitan members & to change partially the franchise'.[1]

That was as it might be. What ministers certainly knew was that, though they had obliged William by getting second reading without putting him to the pains of creation, his affection for them was cooling, largely over the conduct of foreign affairs. The Whigs, never a war party or given to bristling at old national enemies, had avoided making a crisis out of the new state of Belgium, which, dominated by French-speaking Walloons, was on easy terms with 'our enemies, the French'. The Whigs themselves saw the beneficiary of the 1830 Days of May, Louis-Philippe, not by any means fancifully, as a sort of French Whig, if a tricky one. Accordingly, they had tolerated French intervention against Dutch attempts to retain an unwilling province and had declined a shouting match over the demolition of frontier fortresses erected to keep back the next Napoleonic invasion. It was a sensible avoidance of patriotic neurosis which disturbed an old sailor (William) of ancient preoccupations and limited perspective.

* Financier and MP for the City of London.

Yet Holland found him 'in good humour with his Ministers personally,* but still harps on the necessity of distrusting France and preserving a cordial understanding with the other powers with a view to repressing her ambitious designs and counteracting her revolutionary principles.'² The 'other powers' essentially meant Austria and Russia, the former Holy Allies, police and spy regimes under absolute monarchs, bitterly detested by British public opinion.

But the immediate concern was the first clause of the Reform Bill and the number '56'. Rather like the Ultimate Answer to Life, the Universe and Everything, defined in *The Hitch-Hiker's Guide to the Galaxy* as '42', the actual number of two-member constituencies to be abolished under Schedule A of the Bill and spelt out specifically in Clause One, had taken on mystic significance. No Tory, no Waverer even, could bring himself to vote for the number fifty-six. It was disfranchisement; they knew there had to be disfranchisement, but they hated to admit it. Harrowby had gone into a passion on the subject when it was broached by Charles Wood, and Harrowby was the leading moderate. The probability that they could actually reduce Schedule A was negligible. It was core Whig business, unamendable to the parliamentary party, to political unions or government supporters in the country. But the number had shibboleth quality. The sort of things on which William Ward had quoted the King, some reduction in the number of metropolitan boroughs (at which the Tories had worked hard without reward in Commons committee), in the additional county members for industrial counties and a juggling with the £10 franchise, were the very best that might be possible. Ellenborough, bustling around among his Tory colleagues, gathered in a whole series of possible amendments. Only householders resident for a year should qualify at £10, suggested Lyndhurst. Alternatively, Aberdeen favoured a franchise for scot and lot payers resident for three years and able to prove payment. Ellenborough himself had notions for conflating metropolitan boroughs to reduce their number, while Croker, more ardent, would reduce the new members for towns to twenty-four.

But all this was contingent upon getting round that fifty-six. The only government response had been a readiness to remove the printed number if the whole of Schedule A were included in the clause, which was no concession at all. What about postponement until later in the debate? That option was favoured by a number of peers and endorsed by Peel (who had

---

* He soon afterwards rather embarrassingly gave the vacant see of Hereford to Grey's clerical brother.

deliberately kept out of Lords business), when he was asked. This was a time of consultations – consultations within parties, within factions, between factions and from time to time across party. Palmerston, able, and in some eyes too willing, to talk to the Tories, went as Grey's emissary to Wharncliffe to organise a meeting. According to Greville, Palmerston said 'that Lord Grey had now become convinced that he might make much more extensive concessions than had ever been contemplated'.[3] This does not sound like even the depressive Grey, and it fits oddly with the rest of Greville's story. Grey didn't want Harrowby present, finding him 'snappish and unpleasant'.

Wharncliffe regarded postponement as impractical and, when he finally talked to the Prime Minister on 28 April, he said so, and was promptly told that it was a non-starter. The Prime Minister said that 'the postponement of the disfranchisement at this stage and in the present circumstances would, in his mind, be *fatal to* the satisfactory termination of business and he could never consent to it'.[4] Holland could not see how anyone could take this plain statement as anything less than an undertaking to resign or demand creation of peers if postponement were carried in committee. Yet 'Lord Wharncliffe as well as Lord Harrowby had subsequently the face to impute trick, manoeuvre and management to Lord Grey!!!'[5]

But the one constant of a seemingly fluid situation was the rift running through the Tory Party. It was related to the split which had opened in the lifetime of Liverpool's government, was close to the one excluding Ultras over Catholic emancipation, was kissing cousin to the division which would come in Peel's time over the Corn Laws, and it would show again eighty years later when Hedgers and Ditchers fought one another over resistance to the Parliament Act. Parts of the Tory Party did not know how to retreat in their own interest. Periodically, there were flashes of coherence, but only after agonies of incomprehension. Wellington had difficulty getting a clear line from the Ultra peers. On 4 May he was certain that Eldon, Falmouth and the Dukes of Northumberland and Gloucester were unwilling ever to vote for disfranchisement, that central principle which practical Tories hoped to mitigate by a series of votes on specific constituencies. On 6 May, the penny seemed to have dropped when Eldon told the Chief Whip and the Duke of Cumberland that 'the ultras had placed themselves in his hands & he intended to vote as the Duke thought best, believing that he alone could save the country . . .'. But even such intimations of sense were mitigated by an insistence that 'they desired not to be hurried – wished that disfranchisement should not be promised on the first day'.[6]

Meanwhile, the working Tories were, quite properly, at work on the specific disfranchisements they would barter for. Peel was keen on giving more seats, six in all, to the County of Lancashire at the expense of Ashton, Rochdale, Bury and Oldham, and on drafting Tower Hamlets into the City of London and Marylebone into Westminster. On 6 May, just before the committee stage was to open, the Duke was entertaining Lords Rosslyn, Bathurst and Carnarvon to talk fine points about retaining three-member constituencies. Since they were rural, argued Carnarvon, they were a good thing and counties generally should have Tory support. Unfortunately, they also wanted to cut back the number of towns – nasty radical things – and in terms of negotiation could not expect to keep the first and not see the second returned. It took an evening meeting with Wharncliffe, to whose difficulties it impossibly added, to see off this proposal.

It was the concern of Wharncliffe to talk the diehards into a course which would soften Reform rather than stand to attention and be broken by it. But as they twisted and turned between their party's own factions, the credit of the Waverers declined sharply with those ministers to whom they had been speaking, not least with Grey. This had been apparent even before second reading. Wharncliffe and Harrowby had spent some time at an evening party forming, as Le Marchant put it, 'a quartetto' with Ellenborough and Lyndhurst, both identified with a hard line. Wharncliffe had pronounced himself 'quite easy' with the talk. Grey's reaction when told of this, as he was bound to be, was succinct: 'He said coolly "I am quite the reverse."'[7] In Le Marchant's view, the Prime Minister was thoroughly weary of the Waverers. They were a clog upon action and he actively disliked Harrowby; his natural friends and Cabinet colleagues were stretching points to accommodate negotiations with people who, being subject to the dull dragging of the diehards, could deliver nothing. It was a waste of time and bringing Grey no credit.

In a mirror image of this, by 3 May, as committee approached, Wellington had told Ellenborough that Wharncliffe's communication with Grey was upsetting the Ultras; 'there was such jealousy on the part of our people that it was impossible to communicate with him'.[8] Ministers like Palmerston talking about 'a good time to make concessions' were on marshy, potentially fatal ground. It was an impossible time for concessions. Upon nobody did Wharncliffe create a worse impression than Greville, at any rate as far as competence was concerned. He had 'contrived to play his cards in such a way from first to last, as to forfeit the good opinion of all parties, and to quarrel with Whigs and Tories in succession. With very good intentions and very honest, he has exposed himself to every reproach of insincerity, intrigue and double-dealing.'[9]

Originally the government, giving negotiation a little hope, but fore-seeing a hard time and wanting space to work out its strategy, had put off committee for Easter, a handy piety which allowed time for a swirl of consultations and contacts. But on 6 May, the eve of the first committee sitting, the Cabinet dined at Holland House and agreed to drop the actual words 'fifty-six' and instead to spell out the names of the doomed boroughs in Clause One, leaving each borough to be discussed individually. They settled at the same time against a deal of any sort over postponement of the clause.

As the crisis neared in the Palace of Westminster, so the acts of people outside began to run their rather different course. Birmingham had not rung its bells for the passage of second reading, but the council of its union had sat throughout the Lords debate. It waited for the worst that might happen. Cobbett, never on secure terms with Attwood, sent a paper warning Birmingham people against trusting their leaders. The distrust of Grey among reformers in the country was now being paral-leled. Attwood had one weapon against this and against all the enemies of full Reform – another grand meeting. It was called for the great day itself, 7 May. It was at this meeting that he would speak of preferring to die rather 'than see the Great Bill of Reform rejected or mutilated'. But it was the numbers which compelled. Organisation had always been good in Birmingham; it was now flung very wide, delegations marching from Wolverhampton, Bilston, Sedgeley, Willenhall, Wednesbury, Walsall, Darlaston and West Bromwich. This contingent from places north of the city alone was reckoned at 100,000 with the marchers stretching out for four miles. As before, it was fully covered by a sympa-thetic *Times* reporter, and other friendly papers like the *Morning Chronicle* were kept fully briefed.

In London, Francis Place and the National Political Union were concerned that further assault against the metropolitan boroughs, beaten off in Commons committee, and much fancied for Lords committee, should be resisted. And Place had been supplying Durham with statistical evidence to this end.[10] But there was to be no grand public meeting in London at this stage. There were reasons for this. London, still absurdly underrepre-sented in the Bill, never mind the deletions planned by the Tories, was a huge place. It was big enough to hold two major political unions, both fundamentally more radical than the one in Birmingham, and the NUWC more radical than the NPU.

Violence was a serious prospect in the city which had seen the Gordon Riots (1780) and a string of lesser unpleasantnesses during the eighteenth century. Place did not and could not have Attwood's strong-wristed grip on his people. When the NPU and NUWC consulted, the idea of demonstration on Hampstead Heath was approved. Place went to some trouble to put it off and keep it indefinitely that way from a genuine fear that it would bring out half a million, with sections of the crowd falling under the persuasion of violent factions, thus doing the cause any amount of harm, Bristol fashion. Attwood could parade numbers to scare the other side and be reasonably sure they would not confound his own. Place could not.

But as the committee proceeded, with the opposition still lethally incoherent, London crowds there could very easily be. The test for the Tories actually lay in Attwood's words. Were they going to reject the Bill or mutilate it? And to postpone the principle of disfranchisement after everything that Wharncliffe had been told by Grey was to proclaim an open-ended form of mutilation not worth distinguishing from rejection. When, on Monday 7 May, committee sat for the first time the answer came from Lyndhurst. The Duke of Sussex, the only Member of the House of Hanover to fully support parliamentary Reform, presented a Reform petition from the Lord Mayor and Common Council of the City of London.* Grey, as agreed the day before, announced deletion of the title and preamble and gave notice that the clause would stand thus: 'That each of the boroughs enumerated in the schedule A should cease to return any Member or Members to serve in Parliament.'[11] Lyndhurst then 'rose for the purpose of proposing the postponement of consideration of the Clause altogether'.[12]

Many Lords have risen to propose amendments in the Upper House, perhaps none with quite such thundering consequences. Lord Holland saw a straightforward conspiracy. 'That plot was obviously to get the Management of the Bill entirely into their own hands, to shake the confidence of the people in the government and then mutilate and impair our measure in a way that would force us in honour to resign at some point, upon which neither king nor country would support us in making peers.'[13] He also noted Lyndhurst to be 'as manifestly as much agitated and as nervous as his nature, destitute of shame, could be'.[14] In pursuit of such high standards, Lyndhurst proclaimed 'that at no period of the history of the country during the last hundred years had an opposition to Government been carried on less in the spirit of party and personal feeling'.[15]

There ought to have been an award. Lyndhurst, financially off-colour, former radical and political taxicab, hit a high moral tone and stuck to

---

* To the fury of his brother, the King, who for some time refused to speak to him.

it. He was giving the Ultras, his current team, the benefit of their high doctrine that disfranchisement offended against God. What Eldon believed, Lyndhurst with much huffing about the prerogative, was saying. Except that for Lyndhurst, of course, there *would* be enfranchisement, in which case acts of disfranchisement would follow. A frozen prejudice was being adjusted into a procedural wheeze. Objecting to the principle of disfranchisement, they should, like practical men, do the specific acts of enfranchisement first. He was seeking to lead their Lordships round the commitment to get rid of fifty-six rotten boroughs, just possibly use its majority to save some of them, expand the counties, conflate metropolitan boroughs and generally design a minimal Reform Bill tolerable to the old and inheriting order who had not wanted any Reform Bill at all.

The Duke of Newcastle, less subtle, more candid, 'thought it of little consequence whether they proceeded to consider the enfranchising or the disfranchising clauses. The Bill was calculated to produce revolution, and therefore he was determined to oppose it.'[16] But if Lyndhurst's motion was the strategy of aggression, Harrowby's response was the tactic to make its achievement possible. One of the two principle Waverers had announced that 'he did not think it all indispensable for the purpose of supporting the government in the general measure, it was necessary that the decision on the disfranchisement measure should precede the discussion of the enfranchising clauses'.[17] The Waverers were going to defect. And after Brougham had made a cool speech against the amendment and Holland a sharp one, and Wellington had declared with a straight face that the opposition had 'no dirty view of party interest or intention to get rid of the Bill',[18] defect they did.

By a majority of thirty-five (151 to 116) the amendment was carried. Harrowby and Wharncliffe were among the Contents, along with Greville's friend De Ros, who had been scared of consequences at second reading, and Gage, who had recognised the inevitability of Reform during second reading debate. So were thirteen bishops (against four opposed) and three archbishops (including Armagh). It was a terrible mistake, but it was not immediately taken to be one. Ellenborough, as ever full of himself, stepped forward to propose an alternative reform bill. They should acknowledge Schedule A, but resist the notion of any single member constituency. His other central feature was Lord Aberdeen's proposal for the utilisation of the £10 household by scot and lot, the old easy standard in nomination boroughs which admitted, on the face of it, a rougher sort of voter than a £10 valuation. With a burst of democratic feeling, Ellenborough 'threw it out to the consideration of the House whether it would be safe, perspectively [*sic*], to disfranchise all the poorest class of voters and to establish one uniform qualification?'.

It was a wild move based on the acceptability of scot and lot to the borough-owning element in the days when voters were either submissive or open to bidding. Wellington had warned Ellenborough against it. Such franchises were 'all very well while property had a secure responsibility, but would now only add to the democratic influence created by the Bill'.[19] But the move reflected Ellenborough's own innermost thoughts, which were full of dread. He had noted to himself that 'In ten years the poorest class will be unrepresented & then we shall have a servile war or universal suffrage.'[20] Such thinking contradicted the entire Tory line on the £10 householder franchise – votes for beggars, admitting men unable to pay the poor rate, a lazaretto. But it was sincere, the public avowal matching the diary reflection. Grey mockingly echoed Wellington on the point, but chiefly concerned to go away and consider what to do, the Prime Minister obtained an adjournment until Thursday.

'It is no time for conventional politics,' said *The Times*. 'This is no time for dancing minuets and exchanging bows. Life and death are in the scale. Opinion has been provoked into a passion . . .' There existed 'a state of revolution to be terminated only by frank acceptance of the Bill . . .'.[21]

For once, all the Cabinet knew what they had to do and they did it. Althorp and Grey immediately got up and went to the Chancellor's room in the Lords. They were joined there by senior Cabinet ministers and agreed unanimously that they must offer William their resignations if he would not now create the peers needed to pass the Reform Bill.[22] The matter was formalised next day, the 8th, with a Cabinet meeting at the Foreign Office at eleven passing a minute for the King of what had happened and formerly resigning. With only Richmond's ducal reservation, the minute included a requirement of fifty to sixty peers; it would be taken by Grey and Brougham to Windsor.

What followed was a furious dash westward through Hounslow where Prime Minister and Lord Chancellor were involved in a collision with a Lady Glengall; 'they broke the pole of her ladyship's carriage and frightened her proportionately',[23] delivered the ultimatum to the King and had some talk with him, 'gracious but cold',[24] before they returned, adjourning at a Hounslow inn for mutton chops and kidneys, getting back to Downing Street at 9.30 in the evening.

It was the impression of Holland that Grey now expected William to 'reluctantly and somewhat sulkily comply with our suggestion'. He did nothing of the sort, but instead sent a letter accepting the resignations. Perhaps the coldness and the acceptance were all one with the rumour picked up by Denis Le Marchant, startled by the size of the vote and the hostile solidarity of the bishops, that 'the Archbishop of Canterbury had already assured them privately that the king was resolved not to make peers'.[25] *The Times*, which had earlier talked of 'our good and upright King' was subarctic: 'What His Majesty's feelings may be in the new relationship in which he already stands toward a people who within one short week adored him it would be disrespectful, however curious to speculate.'[26]

It was never quite clear in this conflict who consistently intended to do what. Having denied his ministers, William made a great fuss of them and snubbed Wellington at the levee on the 9th where they formally took their leave. In an emotional, affectionate man, that is unlikely to have been feigned. And yet, though William actually wept when taking his farewell of Goderich, Palmerston and (according to Brougham) Brougham, his next act before ministers had left was to send for Lyndhurst. William was not insincere; he was in several emotional states at the same time.

Meanwhile, Grey would shortly get credit for the political stroke of his life, the bold challenge calling the other side's bluff, before emerging on to an open road. But his words immediately after the vote to Wharncliffe, with whom he had readily traded, sound like pique and defeated pique at that: 'We had not the slightest idea you would vote against us. Why did you not tell us? However you may now manage the Bill yourselves, I shall resign tomorrow morning.' As for Althorp, that oddly shuttling personality, affectionate, suicidal, radical, defeatist, showed every sign of delight at departure. Francis Jeffrey, now Lord Advocate, found him in the middle of shaving. 'He gave me the loose finger of his brush hand and with the usual twinkle of his bright eye and a radiant smile, he said "You need not be anxious about your Scotch Bills tonight, as I have the pleasure to tell you that we are no longer His Majesty's Ministers."' This good humour derived, thought Jeffrey, from belief 'that the Tories were prepared to take up the Reform Bill, and that they would carry it, which he now despaired of the Whigs being able to do'.[27]

There was, as so often with the aristocratic core of this Ministry, an element of honour and vanity curiously blended. Graham and Stanley, observed to be in good spirits, told Hobhouse before the King's refusal came in that 'if the Tories had been paid for it, they could not have acted more for the country and the character of the Ministers'. And as Hobhouse, a mere baronet, remarked with some surprise, 'They did not seem to be sure, or indeed to care much, about the result of the proposal.'[28] But in the midst of all this ambiguity, there was an interesting and contrary pointer. The proposal that the King should be presented with an ultimatum might have come from any minister, but it was a little more than interesting that it was the suggestion of Palmerston. The Foreign Secretary had been the least enthusiastic of reformers, the readiest to talk compromise with the Waverers. In his original Reform speech in the Commons he had said 'he must be a bold or a very unshrinking man who did not contemplate the measure with the deepest solicitude and the greatest anxiety; who could calmly and carelessly look at a measure calculated to effect a great change in the character of the House of Commons, a House of Commons which in spite of its defects, had for so many years contributed so effectually to promote the happiness of the people'.[29] But not only was he a very clever, clear-sighted man, but all his life Henry Temple understood power. The flattering of Wharncliffe and the instant opportunism of Lyndhurst were clearly discounted. If there was going to be a fight, Palmerston meant to be in it.

The distinction between Wharncliffe and Lyndhurst soon became apparent. Wharncliffe, bustling round the scene fixing things which failed to stay fixed, but occupying stage and lights, collapsed pitifully when upbraided by the Whig, Edward Littleton, for his vote. 'He attempted no other justification than that "Opposition had made such a point of it."'[30] Yet Palmerston would tell the same Littleton next day that Grey, Brougham and Wharncliffe had met at his, Palmerston's, house. 'When they had put it to Lord Wharncliffe what he would do if it were proposed to postpone Schedule A, he answered that he would vote against the postponement!'[31]

By instructive contrast Lyndhurst knew very well what he wanted. The King was widely alleged, not just by Brougham, to be trying to persuade that lawyer, who was longest with him after the levee, to remain as Lord Chancellor, insisting that it was not a political post. 'This,' muttered Holland, was 'a view which some shrewdly suspected to have been suggested by Lord Lyndhurst. That unblushing lawyer was certainly on the next day, namely on Thursday 10 May, with the King. He saw him frequently in the course of 24 hours and in some sort clandestinely.' The possibility that Lyndhurst who had, of course, been sent for first, might aim beyond his natural berth on the Woolsack, at the Prime Ministership, was not thought beyond the scope of his impudence. In fact, difficult as it might seem, this was unfair. He had been hired only as prospector for Prime Minister, the King's kingmaker, still a remarkable role for the Chief Baron of the Court of Exchequer.

Beyond the littleness and resolution of different sorts of politicians lay other players, 'the People' in exalted language, 'the Populace' as Wetherell saw them. Greville reported that the first thing Wellington advised the

King was that he should reject any advice tendered by the Birmingham Political Union 'which he did, said he knew of no such body. All very proper.'[32] Proper it might be to follow Wellington's obsession with the unions, but the unrecognised hundreds of thousands in Birmingham had had enough of advice. Birmingham expected military intervention, one group offering to assemble 1,500 men under arms. And indeed there were 250 infantrymen in Weedon Barracks in Northamptonshire as reinforcement for the usual contingent of Scots Greys.[33] While a petition was being brought by three of his colleagues to present to Parliament through Daniel O'Connell, a good friend of the union, Attwood stayed in Birmingham, reckoning that he was the only one who could stop the breakdown of order. Drilling began and churches sounded an all-night knell. Private Alexander Somerville of the Scots Greys speaks of the soldiers having often been visited by Birmingham people in the months before that date. 'On the Sunday before the meeting on Newhall Hill, there were upwards of five thousand people within the gates, most of them well-dressed artisans, all wearing ribbons of light blue, knotted in their breasts, indicating that they were members of political unions.'[34] Within days he would repeat something very different.

In London from 7 May onwards, Francis Place reported everything being done except normal work. For these were the Days of May, the phrase echoing the French Days of July nearly two years earlier. But the Parisian episode, however much it might have resembled light relief after 1791–4, still cost many lives. The exemplary non-violence of Attwood and Place, even though Place was cheerful about breaking corners of the law, as with unauthorised meetings, and the fact that Wellington was only at the edge of office and unable to conjure up heirs to the Manchester yeomanry, kept these days unstained. It would be a matter of meetings and mobilisations and publicity. Placards were placed all over London from 7 May onwards: the first of them, pre-vote, read simply 'Seventh of May, Crisis Day'. By way of such headlines, the message, likely to be Place's, was got quickly across. Meanwhile, the overflowing first NPU gathering at the Crown and Anchor sent an address to the King calling on him to create peers. A second, vast, unofficial gathering outside the NPU's office next day, unable to get into the meeting was enrolled for membership on the spot.

At the meeting proper, Place, who thought in terms of means and practicalities, organised a petition to the Commons aimed at any function of a successor government; it said very simply 'Block Supply'. On the 11th, a conference held with the Birmingham delegates and those from many other towns agreed that physical (not violent) resistance in the form of raising barricades should be undertaken in those provincial centres. This peaceful illegality would require a violent initiative from the authorities to remove them. The consensus was action without violence, the object maximum harassment of any forces which a new authority might direct at the unions.

Demonstrations, barricades, the general public mobilised by placards, were steps intended in a dozen or more towns to push the military to the harassed limits of their resources and put the soldiery, whose senior officers had prevented Hobhouse from abolishing flogging, to a tempting test of loyalty. This programme of activities could form the foundations of revolution. Indeed, they are reminiscent of the early stages of East European protests against Soviet rule in East Germany, Hungary, Poland and Czechoslovakia in the twentieth century. Alternatively, as the rumbling accompaniment to an attempt to form a king's government without an elected majority, they would be a serious discouragement. For Holland, looking on from the Lords and the Foreign Office, 'the accounts from the country were appalling, the encrease [sic] of the political unions rapid, and the notions of and preparations for resisting taxes, barricading towns establishing communications and organizing simultaneous movements, more or less questionable, in terms of legality, manifest and undeniable'.[35]

And just such an attempt was now being made. There had been talk of the King wanting Harrowby as his First Minister, but Ellenborough, leaving the Lords, ran into Lyndhurst entering. 'He told me he had been with the king and was in search of the Duke.'[36] On 11 May, Hobhouse noted 'rumours that Peel and the Duke of Wellington are in negotiation with Lord Lyndhurst; the greatest possible excitement prevailing everywhere'. *The Times* had already noted 'the inordinate eagerness with which his Grace does desire to be Minister'.[37] Next day Hobhouse reported a meeting with Graham at the War Office and being told 'that everything was settled, and that the Duke of Wellington was Minister; Baring Chancellor of the Exchequer; [Sir George] Murray, Hardinge etc., in office; and Parliament to be dissolved on Monday'.[38] Another talking point was Brougham. As everyone had noticed, the King had kept the Lord Chancellor much longer than any other minister at the levee, a full half-hour-long private audience. Brougham had at once told Grey that he had been entreated to stay. Given the touch of fantasy in which he had been known to indulge, this might have been thought at least an improvement, but the story was running in the clubs and his man, Le Marchant, stated 'The Tories used every art to spread the report that the Chancellor would join them . . . The king stated openly that the Chancellor and the Duke of Richmond would stay at his desire, and he prided himself upon the circumstance.'[39]

Hobhouse is a good guide at this time. He had lines to Place and other radicals and he was urging his senior colleagues to show spirit, but as a resigning minister he was also a witness to the talents and understanding of William IV. His farewells came several days later, on Monday 14 May, when the crisis was at fever point. The King told him that

> I had too much property to lose, to wish for or assist any attempts at convulsion . . . He then talked of various matters, of my father, of his intimacy with Lord Sidmouth [who had retired from government in 1824] . . . a good speaker and an agreeable man but not a minister of great capacity . . . We talked of the cholera which he said he did not think had been bad in London; then asked if I had a home in Wiltshire and about where I should settle in the summer . . .

Before he 'bowed *backwards* out of the room', Hobhouse observed that the King 'was looking well and in good spirits; and when I told him so, he said "Thank God. I was never better in my life." I thought he seemed pleased to be rid of his Whig tutors.' It is worth noting that later in the year William, who was of course also King of Hanover, had a vote cast for him at the German Diet in favour of what were known as 'the Six Resolutions'. These were in response to a students' club in Hambach drinking the health of General Lafayette, the old American War of Independence hero and French revolutionary moderate. They called on the governments of all the German states to restrict freedom of the press, impose stricter discipline throughout their universities and ban all meetings and badges which it characterised as 'revolutionary'.[40]

Greville, furious with himself for having been out of town at the start of the crisis, remarked airily that 'there will probably be a good deal of bustle and bluster here and elsewhere; but I do not believe in real tumults, particularly when the rabble and the unions know that there is a government which will not stand such things, and that they will not be able to bandy compliments with the Duke as they did with Althorp and Johnny [Russell], not but what much dissatisfaction and disquietude must prevail'.[41] By glaring contrast, Le Marchant, hearing people through Wednesday and Thursday talking 'very openly of civil war and even of a change of dynasty', remembered a conversation he had had in France with a Bourbon minister before the French crisis. 'In England where no one ever dreams of the removal of the Monarch, one can be at no great distance from such an event when it becomes the subject of general conversation.'[42]

The French political class certainly seem to have thought so. Holland, as a Foreign Office minister, engaged in talk with the great Talleyrand,* now ambassador to St James's, and had found that 'so intense was the interest taken in our domestick affairs during these six or seven days that neither the Cholera nor the death of Casimir Perrier (a signal misfortune to Europe and the World) were deemed worthy of much notice, and even at Paris, I have been assured that the Publick were more occupied with the dismissal of our Premier than with the illness and death of their own'.[43] It was more interest than Holland could get from William. At a levee at St James's on 14 May, the very height of the crisis, the King, as with Hobhouse, talked trivialities and irrelevancies, 'pictures, old stories and indifferent matters'.[44] Furthermore, the minister was told at court that William had drunk a toast to 'the virtuous men who are forming my new administration'.[45]

In the House of Lords, political life of a sort had continued. It included a savage little spat between Carnarvon and the resigning Prime Minister. Grey, in moving the order for the day on 9 May, formally announced the tendering of resignations and their acceptance, and in his caretaker capacity proposed that the Reform Bill should not go forward, but that a piece of Admiralty legislation should do so. Carnarvon, a bitter Tory, roundly abused Grey in an uncomprehending way which illustrated the hermetic quality of House of Lords thinking:

> My Lords, I do think we will do our duty to our Sovereign, left by the extraordinary conduct of the noble Earl and his colleagues in a most difficult, if not a most perilous situation, if we permit this order to be contemptuously discharged, and abandon the measure now . . . we know the grounds, the slight grounds, which their defeat on Monday evening afforded them for one of the most atrocious propositions with which a subject ever dared to insult the ears of his Sovereign . . .[46]

Carnarvon wanted the Bill continued in committee and moved that consideration of it should continue on the following Monday.

Grey, who had leant backwards to the point of almost falling over *not* to oppress William with the only mechanism which would carry Commons and electoral wishes into law, wearily disclaimed any atrocious act. He was 'too much accustomed to the ill-timed, violent, personal, and I must add, unparliamentary, language of the noble Earl who has just sat down, as well as to his personal attacks on myself and my colleagues to be much

* Talleyrand, the great anglophile, was a resolute anti-reformer!

affected or even surprised by the very disorderly attack which the noble Earl has considered it necessary to make on this occasion.'[47] And he answered the charge of overreaction by pointing out that the postponement of the principle of the first fifty-six disfranchisements clause had left the whole of Schedule A open to casual dismemberment. Wharncliffe had said that he would go the distance with Schedule A, but no one else had.

Grey dwelt lovingly on the incoherence born of opportunism in the whole Lyndhurst strategy. That 'noble and learned Lord . . . in the course of his speech, stated that he still considered the Bill to be inconsistent with the safety of the Government and subversive of the Constitution'. And by whom was he principally supported? 'In the first place by a noble Duke [Wellington] who has declared that the present state of the Representation is incapable of being amended by human ingenuity or wisdom.'[48] Grey did not think that it was any part of his duty 'to continue the mere shadow of a Minister, and to have the Reform Bill taken out of my hands for the purpose of being cut, carved, mutilated and destroyed just as its opponents might think proper'.[49]

In the Commons, the Tories, especially a very *pro forma* Peel, kept their heads down, and members rallied round, though Hunt, with his usual directness, observed that if Grey 'was never promised the power to create Peers to carry the Reform Bill, it followed that he and his colleagues had for the last twelve months been imposing the grossest delusion on the people'. And he wanted to know 'whether the king had at any time consented to perform what he had yesterday refused'.[50] It was a painful question better not answered off the cuff, though Grey's chief deception had been of himself. As one of the historians of the Reform makes clear, the real deception came, if only through incompetence and muddle, from William IV. The royal and convoluted message had been that 'he will not, after having allowed that the resource should be effectual, and having, indeed insisted upon the absurdity of allowing any risk by an insufficient addition to the House of Lords, if resorted to at all, deny to his Ministers the power "of acting at once up to the full exigency of the case"'.[51]

But the main move in the Commons would be a second motion for an address from Ebrington. That courtesy Viscount had, of course, helped focus attitudes with an address the last time their Lordships had kicked over the table. Ebrington was a very necessary man at this point. Too many ministers, notably Grey and Althorp, were high-mindedly disposed to let a Tory Ministry be formed and a diminished Bill be proposed. The gentility of the Whig leadership could on occasion pass all understanding. There were attempts to persuade Ebrington not to make trouble, all of which he sensibly ignored. Althorp begged him 'not to make his Motion, as it would embarrass the king in the formation of a new government'.[52]

Such meekness was not followed. Indeed, after consultation, Ebrington stiffened the original, politer form of his address. It would stress 'the deep regret of this House at the change which has taken place in the councils of His Majesty by the retirement of those ministers in whom this House continues to repose unaltered confidence'. The House, for Ebrington, could not 'disguise from His Majesty their apprehension that any successful attempt to mutilate or impair the efficiency of the Bill will be productive of great disappointment and dismay'.[53] Finally, after necessary flummery about William, the address implored him 'to call to his councils such persons only as will carry into effect unimpaired in all its essential provisions that Bill for reforming the Representation of the people which has recently passed this House'.[54]

It was a strong line, not the way Grey or Althorp talked. But the leaders were now to a degree leading over their shoulders, ancient deference to the monarch, however dull-minded and erratic, offset by the early stirrings of democratic politics, a force which hitherto had dared not speak its name. And Ebrington found the words. On 10 May the address was debated,* with Alexander Baring speaking for the Tories, but also from limbo. According to most advanced political gossip, Baring's name had been pencilled in for Chancellor of the Exchequer in the Cabinet which the same gossip indicated the Duke of Wellington to be forming. Baring was gracious in the approved, old-school style about Grey: 'He had the sincerest respect for his character and abilities.'[56] But such courtliness was no longer to the point. Far more interestingly, he took issue with Strutt of Derby, radical industrialist and seconder of the address: 'he seemed to think that the House of Commons should do everything . . . the speech of the Hon. Member for Derby implied the House of Commons was everything – That the people who sent them there were to have the sole control – and the King and Lords were to be put out of the question.'[57] To which the best answer was that more people were saying just that than had ever done before the House of Lords had first rejected Reform. And when Baring said, a little later, that 'what was really meant by the address was to tell His Majesty that he had lost Ministers which the House desired he would take back again',[58] he was greeted with Whig cheers. That was exactly what they were saying. He was left complaining in the topical metaphor of the day about the government wanting a 'new, improved patent, steam-engine

---

* *The Times* noted the event by clearing the famous small advertisements – for ladies' maids and curricles – from the front page to make way for reporting the debate on Lord Ebrington's motion.[55]

way of passing a bill through the Lords if indeed the Lords still possessed any power'.[59]

Althorp, for all his longing for ease and release, was pushed forward by mood and events. The day before he had been cheered very loudly all round the House and, an emotional man, he had come close to tears.[60] His speech to the motion carried him beyond his intentions. He could have wished, he said, that Ebrington had not brought an address forward and he did not like to hear Place's parliamentary ally, Joseph Hume, speaking of the people as 'master'. But aware of the pressure for a straight answer, he spelt out what had never before been spelt out, 'that the advice which we thought it our duty to offer to His Majesty was that he should create a number of peers sufficient to enable us to carry the Reform Bill through the other House of Parliament in an efficient form'.[61] When Hume expressed his delight at Althorp's speech, he was rejoicing at the exposure of the real cause of resignation – failure of the King to give an elected government powers to carry the public will. It was a truth painful to the old leadership.

But it was a truth by which they now had to live. And Hume made the point which bolder members of the Cabinet had tried to impress upon Grey in January. 'This he would say, knowing what he did about the other House of Parliament, that he would stake his existence that if the king had given Earl Grey a *Carte blanche* to make as many Peers as were wanted, not ten would have been required.' And pushing the new, brisk, demotic style a little further, Hume added that 'from the course taken by the majority on the late occasion, it was evident that some little bird had whispered to them that the King would not consent to the creation of any Peers'. Hume hoped that 'the House by its vote tonight, would uphold Ministers in the course they had taken and would support the Reform Bill to its triumphant termination'.[62] He was, with Ebrington, making the trenchant case which reminded King, Lords and the Tories that they were the ones threatening constitutional government by a foolish disregard for vulgar majorities among the electors and elected.

Peel would be widely praised for the eloquence of his orthodoxy on 10 May, but the same Peel was being cajoled to join a government whose formation Grey and Althorp did not want to embarrass. And nothing that he said, however exquisitely reasoned, would be as important as what he proceeded not to do. His position was deftly summed up by Daniel O'Connell, who followed him. 'The right hon. Baronet appears to me quite inconsistent in his observations. First Sir, he makes an open and avowed declaration against all Reform, that is against the power of the people honestly and truly expressing their sentiments in this House; and then he is apprehensive that they will obtain the power to which they are entitled: he declares that he will oppose them, and then he thinks that they will be able to beat him.'

The result of the division was probably less important than the impression left by both leaderships. A majority for the address of eighty (288 to 208) was proclaimed a good score by both sides. It was down from the last vote on an address and Croker remarked that the 'Ministers looked, I thought, *abattus*'. But Whigs could point to the fact that it was a much tougher, less respectful affair and that the Commons had passed with quite enough votes what Grey and Althorp had tried to stop. The irony was that while the first and second man in a Whig administration shrank from a fight, the leader of the Tory Party also pulled back.

The strategy of Lyndhurst had been simple partisan politics, to combine the vote of Ultras opposed to any reform with that of those who accepted the inevitability of most of it, thereby scoring a big party point, turning the other fellows out and winning office. It would be no problem for Lyndhurst (whose most recent biography is subtitled 'The Flexible Tory') to put through Russell's bill trimmed of a few seats in Schedule B, with a handful of county seats favoured at the expense of industrial towns within their boundaries and some ineffective test of payment on the £10 franchise. Lyndhurst was a political animal looking for a political kill. A Wellington administration which should pass the essentials of reform would keep the public disquiet down; and the Duke, for a man who made great play of his honour, was potentially of Lyndhurst's party.

Yet the attitude of the King now intruded again at a different angle. William was a sort of reflex Tory and he objected to creation of peers as something which diminished the weight and symmetry of the society at the top of which he stood. But he was not an opponent of parliamentary reform as such. Had he been a middling Viscount with a vote in the Upper House, he would have been a devoted Waverer. Moderate Reform put through by a Tory administration would have left William content in every sense. Wellington, the King's man and Wellington, the dedicated opponent of the last particle of Reform, did not fit. But there existed with Wellington, as he had shown at the end of the first Lords debate, a streak of straightforward opportunism and a desire to hold office again. Apologists could see this as a soldierly instinct for a gap to be charged at, or as simple devotion to the sacred crown. Had not Greville called Wellington 'a little man in great things?'. What certainly played upon him was the charge that his obduracy in November 1830 had put the Tories out when, with a little ambiguity or concession, he could have kept them in. The urge to meet this charge almost certainly lurked behind the set features.

Croker, who had remarked back in February, 'Revolution progresses, and so does cholera',[63] was his usual mellow self, but also a witness and player in what the Tories were doing. He attended at Lord Stormont's house a meeting on 10 May, the morning of the debate on Ebrington's address. There were thirty or so present, including Peel, Goulburn, Herries, Vyvyan, Murray, Hardinge and Alexander Baring. Detached by Peel, Croker was taken to Apsley House to talk with the Duke and Lyndhurst, who now briefed him on the King's instructions to him as commissioner finding a government. When Croker asked whom he would ask to lead the government, Lyndhurst 'made a significant motion with his hand and said "*That*, Peel must answer"'.[64] Peel made it clear that he would not be involved, saying 'with a tone of concentrated resolution, that he could not have and would not have anything to do with the settlement of the Reform Question and that it was evident that it must be settled now, and on the basis as he understood, of the present Bill'.[65] This was Peel's settled view and he would not be shifted from it.

Like Grey, he had a regard for his reputation as a currency. He had changed his position on Catholic emancipation and was not going to go through the experience a second time. He thought that 'public men should maintain a character for consistency and disinterestedness which he would ever forfeit if for a second time, he were on any pretence to act for anything like his part in the Catholic Question'.[66] Croker agreed with him and suggested that the proper person to enact a modified bill was Harrowby. Croker of course blamed Harrowby for supporting the second reading and saw him as having dug the hole the Tories were now in. Rejection at second reading in his view would have allowed the Duke and Peel to form a government.

Rather warmingly, when Croker met him again next day, Saturday 13 May, the Duke summed up the situation as conclusively as when he had once talked of 'Hard pounding, Gentlemen' or 'a damned close-run thing'. 'Well,' he said, 'we are in a fine scrape and I don't see how we are to get out of it.'[67] He related the fact that Lyndhurst had canvassed Charles Manners-Sutton, the Speaker and a Tory, and so far, had been rejected. Accordingly, Wellington had indicated his willingness to function as backstop – his duty to the King! But by this time Croker had changed his mind and wrote to Peel, urging him either to take up the commission or serve under Wellington. The Duke was pleased at least with the second option and wanted Croker to join him. Ironically, Croker himself was resolved not to take part in such a government for, equally ironically, the very reasons of past committed views which he had urged Peel to disregard.

Part of the argument at this stage was that the King, having been told by Lyndhurst that the Tories 'could not swallow schedule A or Schedule B in the lump', had said, woolly as ever, 'Well then an *extensive* reform.'[68] The Duke of Wellington, Horatius of the anti-Reform bridge, was now turning his mind to the assembly of a government which should enact an extensive reform. A fine scrape it was.

TWELVE

The Days of May

'But until this day we had rough-sharpened no swords'

The Duke, less Castilian than the middle-class bureaucrat from Limerick, showed 'pique' at Croker's refusal to join the government but took him to talk with Goulburn, Holmes and Peel. To the latter Croker laid urgent siege, and though at one stage he 'thought his resolution shaken', did so without success. But later in the day, he met Sir Robert again at the Tories' new club, the Carlton, where he learned that, within a few minutes of their meeting, Peel had been summoned by the King. William had told him that he had 'once said that some degree of reform was desirable'. William's systematically imperfect and wish-fulfilling memory was back at work: Peel had said nothing of the sort. The King, equally annoyingly, spoke warmly of his departed ministers. To Croker 'he seemed to have taken his stand where he did without being well aware of the whole importance of the case'.[1]

Rumour now took over: the Duke had kissed hands and was Prime Minister. He hadn't and wasn't. As he told Croker on the Saturday, 12 May, 'His Majesty invited him [Peel] into his service without saying in what post or who was to be his First Minister and that he had shortly but firmly declined, on the same reasons he had before given.'[2] Peel had been followed by the Speaker whom the King invited 'to come in as *leader of the House of Commons*'. Manners-Sutton had declined the offer and asked who should be Premier, leaving William as he reported it '*flabbergasted*', before he 'stammered out "the *Duke of Wellington*"'.[3] The Tories were in no great state of coherence themselves, but William's erratic actions were confounding confusion.

Wellington was only at the contemplating and recruiting stage, with the King evidently trying to help. Manners-Sutton's thinking on what should be done was sensible at least in principle. Though a Tory, he had by reason of his office said nothing against Reform. It would be absurd for him now to become a specifically party leader in the Commons on behalf of the man who had damned all thought of reform. And the thought did occur, to him and others, that he himself was better placed to form a government which should put through the essentials of reform. The precedent of Addington (Lord Sidmouth), undistinguished, but functioning adequately, who had left the Chair to take over from Pitt in 1801, was available. The Whig leadership, if not its 'violent party', would be acquiescent. And Manners-Sutton's neutral status would be turned to use rather than compromised. There was an irony in all this. The Tory leadership was now reconciled to passing the core and essentials of the Bill. They would very soon be derided and denounced in turn not least by some of their own troops, for the contradictions and opportunism involved in such a mood. But the legislative health of the Bill had not been communicated to either Birmingham or the leaders of the Whigs. On Saturday evening 12 May Holland would write in pleased surprise, 'Is it possible that Wellington has announced his adhesion to the Bill, the whole bill and nothing but the Bill?'

Meanwhile, if Croker, the central chronicler of these events, was dining at Lord Lonsdale's on the same Saturday night, hearing Ellenborough confirm that Wellington had not kissed hands, then next day, calling at Apsley House to consult with the Duke, Francis Place had been rather busier. And Place had heard the same rumours as the clubmen: Wellington was to be Prime Minister. The delegates from the midland and northern political unions gathered at noon that Saturday in a Covent Garden public house. It was then that the order to barricade each town was agreed and sent throughout England. Place himself (surprisingly excited for a Utilitarian) believed that 'it was quite certain that the bulk of the people would rise *en masse* at the call of the unions, and the deputies now in London and other cities'.[4] What Wellington had morosely and obsessively feared – armed, fighting unions functioning like the Jacobin clubs of 1789 – looked close to materialising.

It was at this point that Place started sketching a slogan. The words he eventually came up with were an alternative solution, almost the capitalist option. On a piece of paper and in capitals he printed out the words

TO STOP THE
DUKE
GO FOR
GOLD

It was blessedly short, succinct and complete. Money was thrown on the table, printers, then billstickers, were called in. Within four hours, the placards were going up all round the capital, distributed to shops and parcelled off to the towns and cities of the country. With the King giving bad advice and Wellington unsure, the radical tailor of Charing Cross, distrusting the command of Reform, was securing its back.

Wellington, meanwhile, was in trouble with his own side. As Croker, during his Apsley House call, had learnt from both the Duke and Goulburn, Peel's refusal was turning into a sort of unvoiced whip for a broad and substantial category of Conservative. His refusal had kept Goulburn himself from acceptance, Wharncliffe would not come in, Baring, though nominated to the Treasury, was uneasy and Herries declined office. Croker could at that date quote only Sir George Murray and General Hardinge, the closest of Wellington's personal friends and men with military connections, as those who *were* ready to serve. It turned out that the ardently ambitious Ellenborough was also available and there was desperate talk of falling back on the eccentric Duke of Buckingham. Wellington enjoyed, though, the high expectations of the French ambassador. Talleyrand thought he would succeed '*Car il avait un volanté si forte et je crois à la puissance d'une volanté forte*', a judgement which cut neatly through Wellington's pose of painful duty loyally undertaken. Greville was less kind. 'The Duke,' he wrote, comparing his conduct with Peel's, 'is more thick-skinned . . . it was in mere derision that it used to be said that he would very likely be found proposing a Bill of Reform, and here he is coming into office for the express purpose of carrying this very Bill against which the other day, he entered a protest which must stare him in the face during the whole progress of it . . .'. He added that 'the Duke's worshippers (a numerous class) call this the finest action of his life though it is difficult to perceive in what the grandeur of it consists. Or the magnitude of the sacrifice.'[5] 'Who is that would change places with the Duke of Wellington,' asked *The Times*, contemplating 'a cabinet of which the first condition is that every man who enters it must leave his good name behind him'.[6]

The Whigs might have been expected, after gathering in the best intelligence, to have sat back and enjoyed themselves. But this was to reckon without Grey's debilitating sense of propriety. On the following Sunday evening a great meeting was held at Brooks's. The 'violent party', notably Ebrington and Hume, were against acceptance of any Bill that a Tory government was likely to bring in. Althorp and Stanley argued for accepting reform from the other side, but making it clear that no Tory Bill could constitute finality. This was accepted out of deference, it seems, to the elder leadership and as the view of the country gentlemen element in the party. As Le Marchant recorded, 'the feeling of the majority was in favour of violent measures'.[7] What *they* chiefly seem to have amounted to, with

Hume urging it, was the withholding of supply, the ultimate civil weapon of Parliament against Charles I.

And if there were rumours bubbling about what William and Wellington intended, there were now more vivid ones about the people. News was 'pouring in from all parts of the country of the furious hatred that prevailed against Wellington'.[8]

A final fact was recorded by Private Somerville: 'It was rumoured that the Birmingham Political Union was to march for London that night; and that we were to stop it on the road. We had been daily and nightly booted and saddled, with ball cartridge in each man's possession, for three days, ready to mount and turn out at a moment's notice. But until this day we had rough-sharpened no swords.'[9]

Somerville's choice of words referred to the irregular sharpening of swords for the purpose of inflicting 'a ragged wound', one more likely to fester and cause death from septicaemia. In the cause of maintaining public order, it was an act of premeditated viciousness likely to provoke unimaginable public consequences. The Scots Greys, confined to closed barracks, were rough-sharpening their swords on the Sunday Croker conversed urgently with Wellington, that parcels of 'Go for Gold' placards arrived in a score of cities, the Sunday which the Whigs would spend at Brooks's discussing tactics. 'Not since Waterloo had the swords of the Greys undergone the same process. Old soldiers spoke of it and told the young ones. Few words were spoken. We had made more noise and probably looked less solemn at prayers in the morning than we did now grinding our swords.'[10] Fear of what soldiers might do broke both ways. Rumour being what it was, readers of the radical *Morning Herald* would read next day in London that the Scots Greys had gone over to the Birmingham union!

The day after the rough-sharpening, the council of the Birmingham union heard from its main delegate to London, Joshua Scholefield, just returned. The delegates had spoken with Grey as well as Place. The Prime Minister despaired. He had sent a message advising obedience to the laws and patient attendance upon Wellington's bill. The respectable element answered in harmony with Grey's gloomy tune. Attwood did not. It was beyond Wellington's or Croker's political radar that the leader of the largest and most effective of all the political unions was a constitutionalist abhorring violence. That ignorance, across social class and a country Wellington did not understand, was capable, given a particular sequence of events, of creating a revolution and civil war in truth and fact. Wellington was tolerably close to giving his own fantasies life, and, had he held power, tolerably close to a great crime. Back in October 1831 he had said, 'The people of England are very quiet if they are left alone; and if they won't there is a way to make them.'[11]

But Attwood's response now, though it remained constitutional, was braver and more positive than Grey's. If the House of Lords could break a Reform Bill and a government and make a government of its own, he argued, the 'spirit of the people would be utterly broken'.[12]

Attwood and Birmingham could fight only with words, and they would have had some idea of what the Scots Greys would be told to fight with. Attwood prepared, with his mind very much on the Solemn League and Covenant, a declaration against the Duke. It was to be printed, circulated to all rallying points in the country, and when signed, to constitute a national Document.[13] *The Times* had asked on 11 May, 'Will Birmingham be trifled with? Or Sheffield? Or Westminster? Or Portsmouth? Or Brighton (Pavilion Brighton)? Or Bury? Or North Shields?'[14] What mattered in the elaborate game of involuntary bluff now being played was that Attwood, keeping his nerve and pushing protest to obtain maximum publicity, was sustaining all the groups of people and all the pressures which made the formation of any Tory government so intolerable.

Events were moving too forcefully for any of Grey's steps of retreat to affect matters. The Tories were instructing themselves in their own disunity; Peel was the key man and for a congeries of reasons this key declined to turn in that lock. The middle and artisan class showed correspondingly formidable unity in ways which, without serious breach of the law, thoroughly frightened their betters. The menace of the political unions was a menace in prospect, not unlike a sentiment on a stock market. Place's placards were going up in London by early Saturday evening; other cities would have them on Sunday. The banks and markets would remain closed until Monday morning, and on that day a meeting of the Commons would take place at which prospective ministers would face very brisk music.

Wellington would now realise that his personal game at any rate was up. He made two attempts that day to persuade Manners-Sutton to take up the Premiership, an idea which had originated with Croker. At midday he was writing to the King to say the Speaker had refused the offer. At four in the afternoon he tried again, telling Manners-Sutton that he personally could not form a government, but that 'he had no doubt that the Speaker could, and offered to serve with or under him'. He also conveyed Baring's willingness to join them, but Manners-Sutton, after exhausting everyone with a great drawing-room oration, asked for time to reflect. With Lyndhurst – who had characterised him as 'a damned tiresome old bitch' – harrying him, the Speaker, after consulting Peel, on the Monday sent Wellington a letter whose key words were 'I will now say with reference to the proposition made by your Grace yesterday, that if *no other* arrangement can be made, I must give way though with fear and trembling . . .'[15]

A debate in the Commons sometimes matters, sometimes does not. This one, of 14 May, mattered. Formally, it concerned a petition on the change of Ministry. Presented by the radical Alderman Wood, an enemy of the Tories for two decades, it had been agreed by a livery company of the City of London, and it called for 'Supply' to be blocked. But this was a very general debate and a chance to find out what the Tories meant to do. Fire was concentrated on the head of the Duke, Ebrington noting the Duke's demonstration 'by votes – by speeches – and by solemn protests of an uncompromising hostility to the measure'. He asked if it was 'possible that the Duke of Wellington can come down to the House of Lords with a Bill in one hand and with his protest in the other and call upon the House of Peers to pass any portion of that measure that can give the slightest satisfaction to this House or the people?'.[16] Had not Wellington called down 'the vengeance of Heaven upon the principles of this Bill . . .'? It couldn't be done if 'anything like public morality still exists'. This in Tory mouths became a charge of public *immorality*.

It was a bitter, noisy and angry debate: 'such a scene,' wrote Greville, 'of violence and excitement as had never been exhibited within those walls . . . The House was crammed to suffocation; every violent sentiment and vituperative expression was received with shouts of approbation.'[17] There would be much lingering ironic comment that afternoon and evening from the reformers, but the really significant contribution lay in the defensive and fugitive tone of Tory contributors struggling to get a hearing. Sir Henry Hardinge was anxious to defend Wellington against Ebrington's charge of 'public immorality', but Hardinge himself had not accepted office from the King and he did not know whether any putative bill would 'be passed through the House of Lords by the Duke of Wellington, for of that I am ignorant'.[18] For the Tories, having failed to get their act together and with their best chance of a Prime Minister presiding in the Chair, ignorance was unavoidable.

As for public immorality, the age and the social position of most players put the concept of honour very high. Arguments from pragmatism and necessity were not made as they might properly have been over both Catholic emancipation and Reform. No politician of the time could have given 'Events dear boy, events', the languid realism of Harold Macmillan, as the foundation for his thinking. Lyndhurst might have thought it, but could not have said as much. And Tory spokesmen were at a double disadvantage because they spoke without *locus*; they were a mere government in prospect. As Alexander Baring, fighting to be heard, put it, 'Although

I venture to address the House on behalf of the Crown, I beg to say I am not empowered by the Crown.' He was nevertheless caught in defending not only prospective ministers but the Crown itself. He asked whether it was 'generous toward the Crown, whether it is common fairness toward the Crown to irritate the public mind from one end of the country to another before the Crown is in a condition to make an answer?'[19]

'The Crown', of course, means both the head of state and ministers employing his prerogatives. Baring was complaining on behalf of a Crown which, in this full sense, had not yet been reassembled. And he was protesting, understandably but without effect, against a blast which, as spokesman for a man who had stopped trying to form a government and another who had not started, he received upon his uncommissioned head. It was a cry of 'unfair', never one much heeded. However, Baring attempted a sort of dialectic to make sense of the position which not-yet ministers were already in. The Crown had 'given a pledge to the country of extensive reform, and no person could approach His Majesty with the advice, by forfeiting that pledge, to sacrifice his own character and to sacrifice the monarchy'. The Crown's promise was the King's promise and he could not be asked to break faith on it. So the only proper thing for a former opponent to say was 'My own opinion is that the Reform Bill will not promote the good of the country: the Constitution to arise out of it will not be so beneficial as that we are about to abandon; but dangers may arise – an emergency may occur – circumstance may present themselves requiring this concession.'[20]

Baring was feeling his way towards pragmatism, 'events' and retreat. But he would be reproached by Croker for 'having spoken with a kind of Ministerial authority in defence of the supposed Administration'. By doing so he had 'kept up a very damaging debate for several hours'. It was damaging because a ghostly spokesman like Baring had to acknowledge an acceptance of reform in a degree which made the whole enterprise of killing the key clause of the bill in committee quite pointless.

The debate would also be damaging because a number of very good speeches were made on the Whig side, speeches at which even Croker nodded admiration. Duncombe pitched at Wellington, not troubling his honour or his public morality, but giving him a terrible time for all that, getting him laughed at, something new and dangerous to the Duke. His attempt to form a government, not yet generally known to have lapsed, was compared with vehicles of the day, 'crane-necked carriages, the advantage of which is that they turn round in the smallest possible space. In such a vehicle must the Duke of Wellington go down to the House of

Lords. What will be the beasts that draw him, who the charioteer that drives him, or who the pensioned lacquies that stand behind him, I know not; but this I know, that in under such circumstances, I would rather be the tailor that turns his coat than the Duke of Wellington in all his glories.'

And what about the bishops? 'Are the Bishops to hang upon crane-necked carriages too? Are they of a sudden to fling up their mitres and halloo for "the bill, the whole bill and nothing but the bill"?' And with a thrust at the cult of personality which Wellington drew about him, sustained by what Greville called 'the Duke's worshippers', Duncombe quoted a pamphlet put out by a Tory bishop, of his speech at second reading in April. It was, of course, Phillpotts of Exeter, now available in print saying it again. Exeter was a dogmatic believer in the power of the Lords and he had invoked it. 'My Lords but one thing is clear and bright and one thing only; to walk uprightly is within your power. As for the consequences, they are in the power of God. Will you distrust that Power? My Lords, you will not.'[21] 'I say to the House of Peers,' commented Duncombe, 'you will distrust that power unless the Duke of Wellington and place are your God.'

'Place', meaning office in a rather low, cadging sort of way, was a contemptuous expression in those days. And Macaulay, always good with an epigram, had a prim, but perfectly judged shaft for Wellington's movement between 16 April, when he had denounced reform in terms, and 14 May, when he seemed ready to enact it. 'I am willing to let others have infamy and place, only leave us honour and the Bill.'[22] And in the words of Le Marchant, 'The effect was electric. Poor Hardinge's face was swollen with rage.'[23] It was the way of politics that the most bitter things were being said about Wellington at a time when the Duke had just washed his hands of at any rate the premiership. But he had made the attempt and suddenly found that no talk about his honour and integrity altered a startling and widespread contempt. And such sharpness from the Whig ranks, coupled with open embrace of the political unions, something notably done by Duncombe, was at last communicating to the Tories a notion of the world out there where the unenfranchised were now, frighteningly, taking their own steps. But the killer speech against the Tory position came from their own side.

We met Sir Robert Inglis in the very first Reform debate, a historically well-informed and sophisticated debater, but a proper representative of Oxford University as which, to Peel's lasting pain, he had replaced him. He had done so in reflection of the horror felt at Catholic emancipation (and his change of front) by its voters. No high-flyer flew above this most absolute of absolutists; he was Wetherell with dignity and manners. He was also, like the best anti-reformers, coherent. His opposition, he said, was not at all to Lord Grey, but to his main policy, to the Bill itself. It was a great evil in itself, the source of incalculable evils. As such he had opposed it; as such, he should continue to oppose it. He could understand young men changing their views, but when he saw 'men of mature lives, statesmen who all their lives had been opposed to a particular measure, who had in April protested against it as revolutionary, adopting it and making it their own measure in May, he must own that he could acknowledge no consideration which could justify such a change of conduct'. Inglis was an able man and a straight one. He embodied all the Tory qualities. *The Times* would applaud his 'calm condemnation of that ravenous thirst for office'.[24] He had moved against Peel over the Catholic question; he now, without naming names, publicly damned Wellington with the example of Peel. Inglis talked in a very quiet voice which Croker had difficulty in making out. But Peel heard enough to describe the contribution simply as 'fatal and conclusive against any Government to be formed by any class of anti-Reformers'.[25]

If Inglis was the voice of intelligent Ultrism, exposing the leadership's contradictions, Baring, coming back to the despatch box to wind up, had to speak for that leadership and now did so in terms close to surrender. He argued from the isolation of the King: 'A conflict had taken place between the king and his confidential advisers and therefore at present, the king has no confidential advisers.'[26] If in such a case Wellington were asked to form a ministry to pass the Bill and said that he thought it wrong to do so, the King, who had pledged himself to the Bill, was put in a hopeless position. He put forward the hypothesis of the Duke saying 'I will not forsake the king; I know to what I shall be exposed for changing my conduct, but rather than not save the scruples of the king – rather than have the Bill passed by a grievous violation of the constitution, I will give up my own opposition; and I will assist the king in redeeming his pledge in a constitutional manner.'[27] That was a hypothesis and it served – taking Wellington's high line about duty to the throne uncritically – to make an answer of sorts to Inglis and the critics of inconsistency. But that accomplished, Baring now began his retreat by arguing that it had been the intention of the Lords not to touch Schedule A, not, that is, to rescue one of the fifty-six condemned rotten boroughs, the mere mention of which had set the Upper House choking. 'If only Ministers had waited 48 hours,' he said sadly. But having expressed that regret, he suggested that there might be a renewal of Whig ministers' dealing with their Lordships. 'I should think that if Lord Grey goes back to the king and stating his unwillingness to employ those means which he had already admitted, he entertained a repugnance to perform, and stating that he expected with great probability that the Lords would not differ to him except as to the details of the bill; if Lord Grey would so state to the king, I see no difficulty in the Ministers again taking their places.'[28] So here, at about ten at night on 14 May 1832 and towards the bottom of column 957 of *Hansard*, Series Three, volume 12, the spokesman for the Tory Party acknowledged that the Reform Bill should pass and pass by the hands of those who had initiated it.

Baring went on to be even more explicit. Although he would argue that the Bill would prove a great disappointment to its supporters outside, he also thought that 'it would be much for the good of the country if the present Administration were not dissolved. That they should quit office would be one of the greatest calamities imaginable.'[29] It was widely supposed that Baring was taking instructions from the Duke and was only the spokesman for a decision to retreat. But as he explained to Hobhouse walking in Berkeley Square next day, he had made the decision entirely on his own; 'it was his own conviction that it was best to open a loophole of retreat for the Duke'.[30] He had been immediately endorsed by Hardinge and Murray, and the Duke had confirmed his approval later in the evening. Baring's own message to Wellington that night had been 'that he would rather face a thousand devils than such a House of Commons'.[31] The idea of a ministry of Tories and/or Waverers and independent figures handling the Bill was now over. Hobhouse spoke in his diary of 'the *phantom* Ministry'; the Tory Chief Whip, Billy Holmes, called it 'the interlude'.

Meanwhile, a great deal else had been happening. The public was going for Gold. Only Rothschild's intervention stopped the stocks from falling immediately. But over a few days, from specie reserves of £3–4 million, as much as £1.6 million would be withdrawn and it was necessary to withhold the April dividend.[32] Holland believed that Rothschild had given the Duke warning of 'frightful encrease'.[33] Selling would stop when, and only when, Grey returned to office.

Which he would soon do. Althorp, having heard Baring in the debate, had in a brief intervention expressed scepticism about the door being held open for him. He doubted 'that in the present state of the House of Lords, it was possible for the late Administration to carry such a Bill'. And he wondered 'what probability there was the House of Lords would allow the last Administration to carry the Reform Bill?'[34]

There was no scepticism at the centre of London radicalism. Hobhouse went to see his friend, Place, whom he found 'overjoyed' and marking 'the greatest and most surprising Revolution in History'. He had seen in London 'symptoms of fighting. But now, he thought all would be well.' He echoed Lord Holland's comment, 'The debate has produced such a sensation in the publick that Tories, waverers and Court must yield. The Duke of Wellington at ½ past 11 o'clock slunk ignominiously away from the enterprise he had so recently undertaken and told the king he was unable to form a ministry.'[35]

Meanwhile, when 'very full and much expectation alive' the House reassembled next day, 'Lord Althorp, Graham, Stanley and Palmerston entered and took their old seats.'[36] William had written to Grey suggesting that a bill might be passed by agreement without creation of peers. Being William, he still hankered after a watering or moderating of the legislation. The once and future Cabinet met and agreed that the Reform Bill must be passed 'as nearly as possible in its present form'. But to make sure that it did go through, they reiterated their need of a promise to create peers 'if it should be required to give additional strength to your Majesty's Government in the House of Lords'.[37] At the same time, Sir Herbert Taylor for the King sent a note listing twelve peers said to have given written promises that they would oppose the Bill no further.

The Whigs, still quite cagey, held over their reply until the Friday and went to see what the opposition would say in the Upper House. They were rewarded with a squelch of sour grapes being trampled, with Wellington's increasingly familiar recital of his own devotion to the King, another aria on the evils of all reform, a harrumph at the criminality of peer creation and a good deal of *ad hominem* stuff at ministers. One sentence catches the invincibility: 'If I have made a mistake, I regret it; but I am not aware that I have made any mistake.'[38] All of which would be followed by Lyndhurst elaborately exculpating Lyndhurst and praising the 'illustrious Duke' for his matchless integrity and quoting verse about one who:

> *Midst sorrow, cares and dire dismay*
> *Brought calm and sure relief;*
> *He scrutinized his noble heart*
> *Found virtue had performed her part*
> *And peacefully slept the Chief.*[39]

At one point in Wellington's oration, Richmond had leant over to Holland and whispered 'that he began to believe that no declaration would be made'.[40] Grey's quiet, non-triumphalist reply met with attacks from Mansfield, Haddington, Londonderry, Salisbury and Carnarvon, made, said Holland, with 'a virulence of gesture and fury of sentiment such as

I have never witnessed in the House of Lords'.[41] Carnarvon, familiar enemy, said that if Grey 'had already played the part of Necker,* he would hereafter be compelled to play the part of Robespierre.' After which, concluded Carnarvon, 'he would leave it to the noble Lords to do their dirty work themselves.'†[42]

At which signal, Wellington and fifty to sixty Tory peers got up and walked out. Grey's gentlemanliness however occasionally irksome, never encumbered the Ultras who chose to end with neither bang nor whimper but a tantrum. Historically, with however ill a grace, the walkout was surrender.

It did not look like that to the Whigs. The violent tenor of the Lords had contradicted a statement made by Althorp in the Commons that a solution was on the way. They were far from sanguine that all would go smoothly, William's signal was still needed and, though the Duke and Lyndhurst had privately signed off from the struggle, they had told the King but not gone public. It all rather looked as if, Spanish revolutionary style, the struggle continued. Meanwhile, of course, however great Place's immediate relief, the stocks had been falling. William's reply was as obtuse and self-centred as ever. He had made a promise of creation three months before but thought that keeping it was 'against his *honour* and his *conscience* and fatal to his future *peace of mind*'[43] wrote a thoroughly exasperated Holland. The Cabinet, long tolerant of William to the point of culpability, would take no more nonsense. They prepared him a minute requiring enough peers to do the job 'in the event of any fresh obstacle arising which should in the humble judgment of your Ministers, render it necessary for the success of the Bill'. 'Humble' wasn't really the word.

They also spoke of doing so 'for the public safety',[44] for the continued resistance of Lords and King resonated in the country. The measures of resistance organised in expectation of a Wellington government did not end with a strolling back to normality when the Duke desisted from his search. Place and Attwood kept the official political world fully alerted to the state of open-ended disorder likely to commence if Reform were yet

---

* Jacques Necker (1732–1804), Swiss banker and royal Minister in the days immediately preceding the French Revolution.

† Much responsibility for the conduct of some Lords belongs with William's eldest illegitimate son by Dora Jordan, George Augustus, Earl of Munster, a gifted, self-destructively discontented man who, a decade later, would die at his own hand. Munster had put it about that his father would resist Grey's calls for assurance in the Upper House. Oddly *The Times* (12 May 1832) had compared the family influence around William with the court clique which had overthrown Necker. 'The consequences,' it added, 'are well known.'

again evaded. The answer came on 18 May in the House of Commons in a single sentence from Althorp stating that 'Ministers, having what they conceived a sufficient guarantee for being able to pass the Reform Bill unimpaired, retained their office.' They had the King's promise and could bank it in a public statement.

But although that statement was met with delight on the government benches, the victory did not come in a clap of thunder or a plain statement of acceptance. The Ultras carried on where they had left off at the walkout. They sulked and stayed away. At the end of the month, 31 May, Greville, a man with his own priorities, could write, 'Since I came back from Newmarket there has not been much to write about. A calm has succeeded the storm, last night Schedules A and B were galloped through the Committee and they finished the business. On Thursday next (the day of the Derby) the Bill will probably be read a third time . . . In Society the excitement has ceased, but the bitterness remains.'[45] And indeed on 4 June third reading was passed by 106 to 21, with royal assent following by commission on 7 June. It was accomplished. After all the griefs, hesitations, asininity in the monarch, loss of nerve in government, exaltations in opposition and after real fears of a civil war involving an angry people and unsure troops, a modest measure of constitutional amendment had passed into law.

The worst rotten boroughs had gone, the franchise was made uniform, and in most places made rather wider. If it did not fulfil the assurance received by Greville that 'the Reformed Parliament will be the most aristocratic we have ever seen' and Edward Ellice's claim of 'not a single improper person likely to be elected for any of the new places',[46] there would be widespread disappointment. The measure which created shock and amazement in the Commons when Russell read out its schedules on 1 March 1831, was incremental, limited and inordinately safe. Disappointment would show most sharply later in the decade in the Chartist movement. The nomination borough was not dead. At the highest estimate[47] seventy-three MPs would be returned by fifty-four individuals at any given election between the first Reform Act and the second in 1867.

But the Reform Act was real and predicated all the increments which would follow. Though, as Linda Colley has pointed out, whilst the Reform Act would make us at that time 'one of the most democratic nations in Europe',[48] establishment complacency would leave us behind the major states of Europe even after the second Reform Act of 1867. It would take a world war and Stanley Baldwin's plans for the 1929 elections to take us the whole 'revolutionary' hog, by which time 'democracy', an expletive to the Duke of Wellington, would be common and debased currency.

Even so when every caveat has been entered and reservation made, the last word on Reform belongs with Sydney Smith when he assured fellow reformers that 'they had accomplished a very great good'.

Notes

The Cast

1. J.H. Plumb, *The First Four Georges*, p.174.
2. Quoted in E.A. Smith, *Lord Grey*, p.165.
3. Quoted ibid., p.188.
4. John Belchem, *Orator Hunt*, quoted throughout.
5. E.P. Thompson, *The Making of the English Working Class*, p.690.
6. Sir Hughe Knatchbull-Hugessen, *A Kentish Family*, p.195.
7. Quoted ibid., p.172.
8. Ibid., p.176.
9. Ibid., p.198.
10. Quoted ibid., p.201.

Chapter 1 The Old System

1. John Galt, *The Member*, p.18.
2. Arthur Aspinall, ed., *Three Early Nineteenth Century Diaries*, p.89, 27 April 1832 (Ellenborough).
3. *Galt*, The Member, pp.ix–x.
4. Edward and Annie Porritt, *The Unreformed House of Commons*, p.309.
5. Adam Sisman, *Boswell's Presumptuous Task*, p.180.
6. E. and A. Porritt, *The Unreformed House of Commons*, p.318.
7. Ibid.
8. Bacon, 'Memoir of Edward, Lord Suffield', quoted ibid., p.324.
9. J.A. Froude, 'The English in Ireland', vol. II, quoted ibid., p.329.
10. Trevelyan, 'Life of C.J. Fox', quoted ibid., p.330.
11. F.M.L. Thompson, *English Landed Society in the Nineteenth Century*, pp.47–8.
12. Ibid.
13. Ibid., p.47.
14. Ibid., p.49.
15. J.R.M. Butler, *The Passing of the Great Reform Bill*, p.176.
16. Ibid., p.174.
17. Borlase, 'History of Cornwall', 1758, quoted in E. and A. Porritt, *The Unreformed House of Commons*, p.93.

18. Thomas Love Peacock, *Melincourt*, pp.228–9.
19. Butler, *The Passing of the Great Reform Bill*, p.174.
20. E. and A. Porritt, *The Unreformed House of Commons*, p.92.
21. Butler, *The Passing of the Great Reform Bill*, p.106.

Chapter 2 *Tory Disintegration, 1827–30*

1. Sir Herbert Maxwell, ed., *The Creevey Papers*, p.106, 17 February 1827.
2. Ibid.
3. Ibid., p.100, 3 May 1826.
4. Quoted in Sir Hughe Knatchbull-Hugessen, *A Kentish Family*, p.172.
5. Maxwell, *The Creevey Papers*, p.101, 11 May 1826.
6. Ibid., p.101, 12 May 1826.
7. Ibid., p.101, 13 May 1826.
8. William Hazlitt, *The Spirit of the Age*, p.190.
9. Maxwell, *The Creevey Papers*, p.100, 3 May 1826.
10. Lytton Strachey and Roger Fulford, eds, *The Greville Memoirs*, vol. I, p.169.
11. Ibid., p.172, 12 April 1827.
12. Quoted in Wendy Hinde, *George Canning*, p.434.
13. Quoted in Robert Stewart, *Henry Brougham*, p.214.
14. Ibid.
15. Ibid.
16. Strachey and Fulford, *The Greville Memoirs*, vol. I, p.174, 12 May 1827.
17. Ibid., p.177, 17 June 1827.
18. Maxwell, *The Creevey Papers*, 9 August 1827.
19. Strachey and Fulford, *The Greville Memoirs*, vol. I, p.192, 15 December 1827.
20. Ibid., p.208, 12 June 1828.
21. Maxwell, *The Creevey Papers*, p.183, 23 October 1828.
22. Ibid., p.175, 1 October 1828.
23. Ibid., p.180, 7 October 1828.
24. Ibid.
25. Charles Chevenix Trench, *The Great Dan*, p.145.
26. Ibid.
27. Oliver MacDonagh, 'The Politicisation of Irish Bishops 1800–1850', *The Historical Journal*, vol. xviii, March 1975. Quoted in Chevenix Trench, *The Great Dan*, p.149.

28. *Journal of Mrs Arbuthnot*, vol. I, pp.198–200. Quoted in Elizabeth Longford *Wellington*, p.168.

29. Knatchbull-Hugessen, *A Kentish Family*, p.175.

30. Ibid.

31. Maxwell, *The Creevey Papers*, p.196, 2 March 1829.

32. Ibid., pp.198–9, 6 March 1829.

33. Quoted in Knatchbull-Hugessen, *A Kentish Family*, p.186.

34. Lorne, 'Lord Palmerston', 1892. Quoted in Knatchbull-Hugessen, *A Kentish Family*, p.180.

35. Ibid.

36. Ibid., p.183.

37. Ibid., p.179.

38. Strachey and Fulford, *The Greville Memoirs*, vol. I, p.369, 5 February 1830.

39. Letter to Thomas Creevey. Maxwell, *The Creevey Papers*, p.208, February 1830.

40. Quoted in J.R.M. Butler, *The Passing of the Great Reform Bill*.

41. Strachey and Fulford, *The Greville Memoirs*, vol. I, p.237, 12 January 1829.

42. Quoted in Duff Cooper, *Talleyrand*, p.313.

43. Ibid., p.316.

44. Strachey and Fulford, *The Greville Memoirs*, vol. II, p.19, 30 July 1830.

45. Nowell C. Smith ed., *The Letters of Sydney Smith*, p.514, letter 554, late in 1829, exact date not given.

46. Strachey and Fulford, *The Greville Memoirs*, vol. II, p.46, 18 September 1830.

47. Ibid., p.47.

48. Longford, *Wellington*, p.222.

49. Charles Lamb, *The Letters of Charles Lamb*, letter to George Dyer, 20 December 1830, letter dxx, pp.288–9.

50. Strachey and Fulford, *The Greville Memoirs*, vol. II, p.51, 25 October 1830.

51. Salisbury MSS, 9 December 1836. Quoted in Longford, *Wellington*, p.224.

52. Smith, *The Letters of Sydney Smith*, p.523, letter 567.

53. David J. Moss, *Thomas Attwood*, p.185.

54. Quoted in Butler, *The Passing of the Great Reform Bill*, p.97.

55. Strachey and Fulford, *The Greville Memoirs*, vol. II, pp.52–3, 8 November 1830.

56. Ibid., p.59, 16 November 1830.

Chapter 3 The First Bill

1. Francis Bamford and the Duke of Wellington, eds, *The Journal of Mrs Arbuthnot*, p.401.
2. Ibid., p.402.
3. Ibid.
4. Ibid., p.404.
5. Quoted in Robert Stewart, *Henry Brougham*, p.248.
6. Alexander Somerville, *The Autobiography of a Working Man*, quoted in Stewart, *Henry Brougham*, p.247.
7. Lytton Strachey and Roger Fulford, eds, *The Greville Memoirs*, vol. II, pp.64–5, 20 November 1830.
8. Bamford and Wellington, *The Journal of Mrs Arbuthnot*, pp.310–11, 16 October 1829.
9. Ibid., p.343, 8 March 1830.
10. Poor Law Commission report 1836, quoted in E.P. Thompson, *The Making of the English Working Class*, p.247.
11. Lord Byron speech, House of Lords, 27 February 1812, quoted in Raymond Wright, 'Prose of the Romantic Period', in Raymond Wright, ed., *The Pelican Book of Selected Nineteenth-Century English Prose*, p.118.
12. A. Prentice 'Historical Sketches of Manchester', quoted ibid., p.250.
13. Nowell C. Smith, ed., *The Letters of Sydney Smith*, p.522.
14. Ibid., p.525.
15. Strachey and Fulford, *The Greville Memoirs*, vol. II, p.116, 15 February 1831.
16. Ibid., p.118, 24 February 1831.
17. Michael Brock, *The Great Reform Act*, p.140.
18. Ibid., p.150.
19. Strachey and Fulford, *The Greville Memoirs*, vol. II, p.123, 2 March 1831.
20. *Hansard's Parliamentary Debates*, Third Series (henceforth *PD*), vol. 2, 1 March, col. 1072.
21. Ibid.
22. Ibid., col. 1074.
23. Ibid., col. 1077.
24. Ibid.
25. Strachey and Fulford, *The Greville Memoirs*, vol. II, p.123, 2 March 1831.
26. *PD*, col. 1083.

27. Ibid., col. 1084.
28. Ibid.
29. Ibid., col. 1085.
30. Ibid.
31. Ibid.
32. Ibid., cols 1086–7.
33. Ibid., col. 1102.
34. Ibid., col. 1106.
35. Ibid., col. 1101.
36. Ibid.
37. Ibid., col. 1103.
38. Ibid., col. 1104.
39. Ibid., col. 1113.
40. Ibid., col. 1090.
41. Ibid., cols 1090–91.
42. All ibid., col. 1091.
43. Ibid., col. 1097.
44. Ibid., col. 1096.
45. Ibid., col. 1094.
46. Ibid., col. 1095.
47. Ibid., col. 1129.
48. Ibid., col. 1133.
49. Ibid., col. 1135.
50. All ibid., cols 1134–5.
51. Ibid., col. 1141.
52. Ibid.
53. Ibid., col. 1143.
54. Ibid.
55. Ibid., col. 1184.
56. Ibid., col. 1186.
57. Ibid., col. 1190.
58. Ibid., col. 1191.
59. Ibid., cols 1191–2.
60. Ibid., col. 1192.
61. Ibid., col. 1193.
62. Ibid.
63. Ibid., cols 1193–4.
64. Ibid., col. 1194.
65. Ibid., col. 1196.
66. Ibid.
67. Ibid.

68. Ibid., cols 1196–7.
69. Ibid., col. 1198.
70. Ibid., col. 1199.
71. Ibid.
72. Ibid.
73. Ibid.
74. Ibid., cols 1199–1200.
75. Ibid., col. 1203.
76. Ibid.
77. Ibid., col. 1204.
78. Ibid.
79. Ibid.
80. Arthur Aspinall, ed., *Three Early Nineteenth Century Diaries*, p.48, 9 February 1831 (Ellenborough).
81. Bamford and Wellington, *The Journal of Mrs Arbuthnot*, p.400.
82. *PD*, col. 1109.
83. Ibid.
84. Ibid.
85. Ibid., col. 1218.
86. Ibid., col. 1211.
87. Ibid.
88. Ibid., col. 1215.
89. Ibid., col. 1217.
90. All Strachey and Fulford, *The Greville Memoirs*, vol. I, 21 March 1829.
91. *PD*, col. 1224.
92. Ibid., col. 1229.
93. Ibid.
94. Ibid., col. 1230.
95. Ibid., col. 1232.
96. Ibid., cols 1237–8.
97. Ibid., col. 1238.
98. Ibid.
99. Strachey and Fulford, *The Greville Memoirs*, vol. II, pp.124–5, 3–5 March 1831.
100. Croker to Hertford, 15 March 1831, quoted in Louis J. Jennings, ed., *Croker's Correspondence and Papers*, p.110.
101. Quoted in Denis Le Marchant, *Memoir of Viscount Althorp*, pp.309–10.
102. Ibid., p.310.
103. Ibid.

104. Norman Gash, *Sir Robert Peel*, p.11.
105. *PD*, col. 1282.
106. All at ibid., col. 1282.
107. Ibid., col. 1337.
108. Ibid., col. 1338.
109. Ibid., col. 1340.
110. Ibid., cols 1342–3.
111. Ibid., col. 1346.
112. Ibid., col. 1355.
113. Ibid., col. 1358.

Chapter 4 On to the Vote

1. Arthur Aspinall, ed., *Three Early Nineteenth Century Diaries*, p.62 (Ellenborough).
2. Ibid.
3. All at ibid., pp.62–3.
4 *PD*, vol. 3, col. 39.
5. Louis J. Jennings, ed., *Croker's Correspondence and Papers*, p.110, 15 March 1831.
6. Sir Herbert Maxwell, ed., *The Creevey Papers*, p.221, 3 March 1831.
7. Ibid., p.221, 5 March 1831.
8. *PD*, col. 38.
9. Ibid., col. 39.
10. Ibid., col. 97.
11. Ibid., col. 99.
12. Ibid., col. 101.
13. Ibid., cols 106–7.
14. Aspinall, *Three Early Nineteenth Century Diaries*, p.64, 6 March 1831 (Ellenborough).
15. Strachey and Fulford, *The Greville Memoirs*, vol. II, p.127, 10 March 1831.
16. Ibid., p.128, 11 March 1831.
17. *PD*, cols 141–2.
18. Ibid., col. 143.
19. Ibid., col. 147.
20. Ibid.
21. Ibid., col. 151.
22. Ibid., col. 161.
23. Ibid., col. 162.
24. Ibid., col. 177.

25. Francis Bamford and the Duke of Wellington, eds, *The Journal of Mrs Arbuthnot*, p.285.
26. Aspinall, *Three Early Nineteenth Century Diaries*, p.65, 9 March 1831 (Ellenborough).
27. *PD*, col. 181.
28. Ibid., col. 184.
29. Ibid., col. 194.
30. Ibid., cols 205–6.
31. Ibid., col. 197.
32. Ibid., cols 208–9.
33. Ibid., col. 229.
34. Ibid., col. 230.
35. Aspinall, *Three Early Nineteenth Century Diaries*, p.65, 9 March 1831 (Ellenborough).
36. *PD*, col. 241.
37. Ibid., cols 243–4.
38. Ibid., col. 245.
39. Ibid., col. 246.
40. All at ibid., cols 246–7.
41. Ibid., col. 256.
42. Ibid., col. 259.
43. Ibid., cols 259–60.
44. Ibid., col. 262.
45. Ibid., col. 277.
46. Ibid.
47. Ibid., col. 283.
48. Ibid., col. 289.
49. Ibid., col. 290.
50. Ibid., col. 291.
51. Ibid., cols 300–301.
52. Ibid., col. 302.
53. Ibid.
54. Maxwell, *The Creevey Papers*, p.224, 21 March 1831.
55. *PD*, col. 304.
56. Ibid., col. 310.
57. Ibid., cols 310–11.
58. Ibid., col. 311.
59. Ibid., col. 313.
60. Ibid., col. 315.
61. All at ibid., cols 315–16.
62. Ibid., col. 317.

63. Ibid.
64. Aspinall, *Three Early Nineteenth Century Diaries*, p.66, 11 March 1831 (Ellenborough).
65. Ibid., p.66.
66. Ibid., p.67, 14 March 1831
67. Lytton Strachey and Roger Fulford, *The Greville Memoirs*, vol. II, pp.128–9, 15 March 1831.
68. Ibid., p.131, 20 March 1831.
69. Ibid., p.132.
70. Lord Broughton, *Recollections of a Long Life* p.94, 19 March 1831.
71. Ibid., p.94.
72. Ibid., p.95.
73. Ibid., p.96.
74. Quoted in Michael Brock, *The Great Reform Act*, p.174.
75. *PD*, col. 599, 21 March 1831.
76. Ibid., cols 599–600.
77. Ibid., cols 600–601.
78. Ibid., col. 602.
79. Charles Dickens, *The Pickwick Papers*, p.238.
80. *PD*, col. 608.
81. Ibid., cols 611–12.
82. Ibid., col. 644.
83. Ibid., col. 650.
84. Ibid., col. 655.
85. Ibid., col. 664.
86. Ibid.
87. Ibid., col. 665.
88. Ibid., col. 669.
89. Ibid., cols 673–4.
90. Ibid., col. 683.
91. Ibid., col. 686.
92. Ibid., col. 718.
93. Ibid., col. 716.
94. Ibid., col. 719.
95. Ibid., col. 727.
96. Ibid.
97. Ibid., col. 728.
98. All at Strachey and Fulford, *The Greville Memoirs*, vol. II, p.132, 20 March 1831.
99. *PD*, col. 733.
100. Ibid., col. 738.

101. Ibid., col. 737.
102. Ibid., col. 741.
103. Ibid., col. 744.
104. Ibid., col. 751.
105. Ibid., col. 754.
106. Ibid., col. 761.
107. Ibid., col. 772.
108. Ibid., col. 782.
109. Ibid., col. 789.
110. Ibid., col. 797.
111. Ibid., col. 796.
112. Ibid., col. 803.
113. Ibid., cols 803–4.
114. Strachey and Fulford, *The Greville Memoirs*, vol. II, p.134, 24 March 1831.
115. Broughton, *Recollections of a Long Life*, p.96.
116. Ibid.
117. Strachey and Fulford, *The Greville Memoirs*, vol. II, p.133, 23 March 1831.
118. Quoted in Brock, *The Great Reform Act*, p.180.

Chapter 5 Gascoyne's Motion, Dissolution and Election

1. Lytton Strachey and Roger Fulford, eds., *The Greville Memoirs*, vol. II, p.135, 24 March 1831.
2. Francis Bamford and the Duke of Wellington, eds, *The Journal of Mrs Arbuthnot*, p.415, 29 March 1831.
3. Strachey and Fulford, *The Greville Memoirs*, vol. II, p.135, 28 March 1831.
4. Lord Broughton, *Recollections of a Long Life*, p.100.
5. Sir Herbert Maxwell, ed., *The Creevey Papers*, p.225, 24 March 1831.
6. Michael Brock, *The Great Reform Act*, p.188.
7. *PD*, vol. 3, col. 1529.
8. Ibid., col. 1528.
9. Ibid., col. 1529.
10. Broughton, *Recollections of a Long Life*, p.101.
11. *PD*, col. 1568.
12. Broughton, *Recollections of a Long Life*, pp.101–2.
13. *PD*, col. 1618.
14. Ibid., col. 1620.
15. Ibid., cols 1620–21.

16.   Ibid., cols 1621–2.
17.   Ibid., col. 1622.
18.   Ibid., col. 1623.
19.   Ibid., cols 1623–4.
20.   Ibid., col. 1624.
21.   Ibid., col. 1627.
22.   Ibid., cols 1628–9.
23.   Ibid., col. 1629.
24.   Ibid., col. 1637.
25.   Ibid., col. 1638.
26.   Ibid., col. 1640.
27.   Ibid.
28.   Ibid.
29.   Broughton, *Recollections of a Long Life*, p.102.
30.   *PD*, col. 1641.
31.   Ibid., col. 1658.
32.   Ibid., col. 1659.
33.   Ibid., col. 1667.
34.   Ibid.
35.   Ibid.
36.   Ibid., col. 1671.
37.   Ibid., col. 1672.
38.   Ibid.
39.   Ibid., col. 1673.
40.   Ibid., col. 1672.
41.   Ibid., col. 1678.
42.   Ibid., col. 1683.
43.   Ibid.
44.   Broughton, *Recollections of a Long Life*, p.103.
45.   Charles Chevenix-Trench, *The Great Dan*, p.192.
46.   Ibid., p.193.
47.   Broughton, *Recollections of a Long Life*, p.104.
48.   *PD*, col. 1778.
49.   Ibid.
50.   Strachey and Fulford, *The Greville Memoirs*, vol. II, p.137, 24 April 1831.
51.   Ibid.
52.   J.R.M. Butler, *The Passing of the Great Reform Bill*, p.213.
53.   Henry Lord Brougham, *The Life and Times of Henry Lord Brougham Written by Himself*, p.115.
54.   Ibid.
55.   Quoted in Butler, *The Passing of the Great Reform Bill*, p.217.

56. Strachey and Fulford, *The Greville Memoirs*, vol. II, p.137, 24 April 1831.
57. Ibid., pp.137–8, 24 April 1831.
58. *PD*, col. 1822.
59. Ibid.
60. Broughton, *Recollections of a Long Life*, p.106.
61. *PD*, col. 1822.
62. Broughton, *Recollections of a Long Life*, p.138, 24 April 1831.
63. Ibid.
64. Ibid., p.106.
65. *PD*, col. 1808.
66. Ibid.
67. Ibid., col. 1809.
68. Ibid., col. 1810.
69. Strachey and Fulford, *The Greville Memoirs*, vol. II, p.139, 24 April 1831.
70. *PD*, col. 1810.
71. Strachey and Fulford, *The Greville Memoirs*, vol. II, p.141, 26 April 1831.
72. Brock, *The Great Reform Act*, p.200.
73. Butler, *The Passing of the Great Reform Bill*, p.222.
74. Brock, *The Great Reform Act*, p.198.
75. Arthur Aspinall, ed., *Three Early Nineenth Century Diaries*, p.88, 25 April 1831 (Ellenborough).
76. Ibid., p.87.
77. Brock, *The Great Reform Act*, p.196.
78. Aspinall, *Three Early Nineteenth Century Diaries*, p.90, 3 May 1831 (Ellenborough).
79. Ibid.
80. Brock, *The Great Reform Act*, p.196.
81. Strachey and Fulford, *The Greville Memoirs*, Vol. II, p.143, 11 May 1831.
82. Ibid., p.144.
83. Broughton, *Recollections of a Long Life*, p.112.
84. Daniel Green, *Cobbett* p.436.
85. Sir Walter Scott, *The Journal of Sir Walter Scott*, p.736, 18 May 1831.
86. Ibid., p.737.
87. Ibid., p.736.
88. Quoted in Butler, *The Passing of the Great Reform Bill*, p.224.
89. Strachey and Fulford, *The Greville Memoirs*, vol. II, p.144, 14 May 1831.
90. Ibid., p.147, 22 May 1831.
91. 'Friendly Advice to the Lords', article in the *Quarterly Review*, vol. XLV, April–July, p.538.

92. Ibid.
93. Ibid., p.548.

Chapter 6 *The Second Bill*

1. Quoted in J.R.M. Butler, *The Passing of the Great Reform Bill*, p.278.
2. William Hazlitt, *The Spirit of the Age*, pp.96–7.
3. Abraham D. Kriegel, ed., *The Holland House Diaries*, p.16, 24 July 1831, p.69, 13 October 1831.
4. John Davies, *A History of Wales*, pp.366–7.
5. Quoted in David J. Moss, *Thomas Attwood*, p.197.
6. Quoted in Michael Brock, *The Great Reform Act*, p.202.
7. *The Mirror of Parliaments*, John Henry Borrow, ed. (henceforth *Mirror*), p.313, 4 July 1831.
8. Ibid., p.384, 6 July 1831.
9. Ibid.
10. Ibid.
11. Ibid.
12. Ibid., p.348, 5 July 1831.
13. Ibid., p.349.
14. Ibid.
15. Ibid., p.400, 6 July 1831.
16. Ibid.
17. Lytton Strachey and Roger Fulford, eds, *The Greville Memoirs*, Vol. II, p.159, 5 July 1831.
18. Ibid., pp.159–60, 8 July 1831.
19. *PD*, vol. 7, 9 September 1831, col. 134.
20. Ibid.
21. Ibid., 17 July 1831, col. 162.
22. Strachey and Fulford, *The Greville Memoirs*, Vol. II, p.165, 14 July 1831.
23. Kriegel, *The Holland House Diaries*, p.6.
24. *PD*, vol. 7, 9 September 1831, col. 153.
25. All ibid., 19 September 1831, col. 213.
26. Ibid., col. 309.
27. Ibid., 20 September 1831, col. 309.
28. Ibid., col. 315.
29. Ibid., cols 435–6.
30. Ibid., col. 447.
31. Ibid., col. 455.
32. Ibid., col. 459.

33. Lord Broughton, *Recollections of a Long Life*, p.132, 21 September 1831.

34. Quoted in Butler, *The Passing of the Great Reform Bill*, p.278 (from Wellington's Despatches).

35. Moss, *Thomas Attwood*, p.199.

36. Ibid., pp.201–2.

37. *Manchester Guardian*, 24 September 1831. Quoted in Butler, *The Passing of the Great Reform Bill*, p.282.

38. All at Strachey and Fulford, *The Greville Memoirs*, vol. II, p.201, 22 September 1831.

39. Arthur Aspinall, ed., *Three Early Nineteenth Century Diaries*, pp.131–2, 21 September 1831 (Ellenborough).

40. Broughton, *Recollections of a Long Life*, p.133, 22 September 1831.

41. Ibid.

42. Ibid., p.134, and Aspinall, *Three Early Nineteenth Century Diaries*, p.134, 26 September 1831 (Ellenborough).

43. Aspinall, *Three Early Nineteenth Century Diaries*, p.134, 28 September 1831 (Ellenborough), and Chester New, *Lord Durham*, pp.149–50.

44. Aspinall, *Three Early Nineteenth Century Diaries*, pp.136–7, 29 September 1831 (Ellenborough).

45. Ibid., p.140, 2 October 1831 (Ellenborough).

46. Quoted in Elizabeth Longford, *Wellington*, pp.268–9.

47. Both at ibid., p.268.

48. Strachey and Fulford, *The Greville Memoirs*, vol. II, p.208, 11 October 1831.

49. Ibid.

50. *PD*, vol. 7, 3 October 1831, col. 921.

51. Ibid., cols 929–30.

52. Ibid., col. 931.

53. Ibid., col. 943.

54. Ibid.

55. Ibid., col. 944.

56. Ibid., col. 951.

57. Ibid., col. 953.

58. Ibid., col. 955.

59. Ibid.

60. Ibid., col. 956.

61. Ibid., col. 959.

62. Ibid., col. 958.

63. Ibid., col. 965.

64. Ibid., col. 967.

65. Ibid.
66. Ibid., col. 969.

Chapter 7 The Lords: The Outcome

1. *PD*, vol. 7, 3 October 1831, col. 987.
2. Ibid., col. 972.
3. Ibid.
4. Ibid., col. 981.
5. Ibid.
6. Ibid., col. 986.
7. Ibid., all at cols 1009–10.
8. Ibid., col. 1012.
9. Ibid., col. 1011.
10. Ibid., col. 1013.
11. Michael Brock, *The Great Reform Act*, p.243.
12. *PD*, vol. 7, 4 October 1831, col. 1150.
13. Ibid., col. 1153.
14. Ibid., col. 1174.
15. All at ibid., col. 1169.
16. Ibid., col. 1175.
17. Ibid., col. 1176.
18. Ibid.
19. Ibid., col. 1178.
20. Ibid., col. 1180.
21. Ibid., col. 1185.
22. Ibid., col. 1187.
23. Ibid., col. 1188.
24. Ibid.
25. Ibid., col. 1193.
26. Ibid.
27. Ibid., cols 1193–4.
28. Ibid., col. 1198.
29. Ibid., col. 1201.
30. Ibid., cols 1202–3.
31. Ibid., col. 1205.
32. Lord Broughton, *Recollections of a Long Life*, p.134, 4 October 1831.
33. *PD*, vol. 7, 5 October 1831 col. 1308.
34. Ibid., col. 1312.
35. Ibid., col. 1313.
36. Ibid., col. 1324.

37. Ibid., col. 1368.
38. Ibid., col. 1369.
39. Ibid.
40. Ibid., col. 1372.
41. Ibid., col. 1374.
42. Ibid., col. 1375.
43. All at ibid., col. 1376.
44. Ibid., cols 1376–7.
45. *PD*, vol. 8, 6 October 1831, cols 72–3.
46. Ibid., col. 74.
47. Ibid., cols 74–5.
48. Ibid., col. 88.
49. Ibid., col. 89.
50. Ibid.
51. Ibid., cols 98–9.
52. Ibid., col. 104.
53. Ibid., col. 103.
54. Ibid., col. 122.
55. Ibid., col. 119.
56. Ibid.
57. Ibid., col. 123.
58. Ibid.
59. Ibid., col. 125.
60. Ibid.
61. Ibid., col. 126.
62. Ibid., col. 128.
63. Ibid.
64. Quoted in Hesketh Pearson, *The Smith of Smiths*, p.211.
65. *PD*, vol. 8, 7 October 1831, col. 193.
66. Ibid., cols 196–7.
67. Ibid., col. 204.
68. Ibid., col. 205.
69. Ibid., col. 211.
70. Ibid., col. 225.
71. All at ibid., col. 233.
72. Ibid., col. 242.
73. Ibid., col. 243.
74. Ibid., col. 244.
75. Ibid., col. 246.
76. Ibid.
77. Ibid., col. 248.

78. Ibid., col. 251.
79. Ibid.
80. Ibid., col. 252.
81. All at ibid., cols 259–61.
82. Ibid., col. 270.
83. Ibid.
84. Ibid., cols 274–5.
85. Ibid., col. 280.
86. Ibid., col. 294.
87. Ibid., col. 296.
88. Norman Gash, *Sir Robert Peel*, p.592.
89. *PD*, vol. 8, col. 297.
90. Ibid., col. 298.
91. All at ibid., cols 298–9.
92. J.H. Plumb, *The First Four Georges*, p.150.
93. *PD*, vol. 8, col. 306.
94. Ibid.
95. Ibid., col. 311.
96. Ibid., col. 319.
97. Ibid., col. 323.
98. Ibid., col. 337.
99. Francis Bamford and the Duke of Wellington, eds, *The Journals of Mrs Arbuthnot*, p.437.
100. *PD*, vol. 8, cols 337–8.
101. Bamford and Wellington, *The Journals of Mrs Arbuthnot*, p.429.

Chapter 8 Bristol, Birmingham and After

1. Lord Broughton, *Recollections of a Long Life*, p.137.
2. Adam Sisman, *Boswell's Presumptuous Task*, p.295.
3. Broughton, *Recollections of a Long Life*, p.138.
4. Quoted in Hesketh Pearson, *The Smith of Smiths*, p.213.
5. Broughton, *Recollections of a Long Life*, p.140.
6. Ibid., p.139.
7. Abraham D. Kriegel, *The Holland House Diaries*, p.67.
8. Quoted in Dudley Miles, *Francis Place*, p.183.
9. Quoted in David Moss, *Thomas Attwood*, p.202.
10. Ibid.
11. Quoted ibid.
12. E.P. Thompson, *The Making of the English Working Class*, p.697.
13. Norman Gash, *Sir Robert Peel*, p.24.

14. Quoted in J.R.M. Butler, *The Passing of the Great Reform Bill*, p.296.

15. *PD*, vol. 8, col. 458.

16. Ibid., cols 474–5.

17. Lytton Strachey and Roger Fulford, eds, *The Greville Memoirs*, vol. II, p.208, 14 October 1831.

18. *PD*, col. 479.

19. Strachey and Fulford, *The Greville Memoirs*, vol. II, p.211.

20. Michael Brock, *The Great Reform Act*, pp.251–2.

21. Quoted in Thompson, *The Making of the English Working Class*, p.281.

22. Strachey and Fulford, *The Greville Memoirs*, vol. II p.211.

23. Ibid., pp.211–12, 11 November 1831.

24. Ibid., p.212.

25. Ibid.

26. Recorded in Cobbett's, *Political Register*, quoted here from Anthony Burton, *William Cobbett*, pp.235–6.

27. Brock, *The Great Reform Act*, p.253.

28. *PD*, vol. 8, cols 898–9.

29. Ibid., col. 901.

30. Strachey and Fulford, *The Greville Memoirs*, vol. II, p.212, 11 November 1831.

31. Ibid., p.213.

32. Ibid., p.219, 23 November 1831.

33. Broughton, *Recollections of a Long Life*, p.148.

34. Strachey and Fulford, *The Greville Memoirs*, vol. II, p.214, 19 November 1831.

35. Ibid., p.215.

36. Letter, 19 October 1831, from Parker, 'Life of Sir James Graham' 1907. Quoted in Butler, *The Passing of the Great Reform Bill*, p.318.

37. Wellington Despatches VIII, 30, quoted in Butler, *The Passing of the Great Reform Bill*, p.315.

38. Moss, *Thomas Attwood*, p.207.

39. Wellington Despatches, quoted in Moss, ibid., pp.206–7.

40. Ibid., p.208.

41. Kriegel, *The Holland House Diaries*, p.77.

42. Strachey and Fulford, *The Greville Memoirs*, vol. II, p.216, 19 November 1831.

43. Ibid.

44. Ibid.

45. Ibid.

46. Kriegel, *The Holland House Diaries*, p.81.

47. Ibid.
48. Ibid., p.82.
49. Strachey and Fulford, *The Greville Memoirs*, vol. II, p.220, 27 November 1831.
50. Ibid., p.220, 27 November 1831.
51. Kriegel, *The Holland House Diaries*, p.82.
52. Ibid., p.83.
53. Ibid., p.84.
54. Ibid., p.82.
55. Quoted in Brock, *The Great Reform Act*, p.259.
56. Kriegel, *The Holland House Diaries*, p.83.
57. Quoted in Brock, *The Great Reform Act*, p.264.
58. *Mirror*, vol. I, p.62.
59. Ibid., pp.64–5.
60. Ibid., pp.65–6.
61. Gash, *Sir Robert Peel*, pp.25–6.
62. *Mirror*, p.71.
63. Ibid., p.68.
64. Ibid.
65. Arthur Aspinall, ed., *Three Early Nineteenth Century Diaries*, pp.167–8, 12 December 1831 (Le Marchant).
66. Ibid., p.168.
67. Ibid.
68. Ibid., p.169.
69. *Mirror*, p.146.
70. Ibid., p.152.
71. Ibid., p.149.
72. Ibid., p.153.
73. Ibid., p.182.
74. Ibid., p.186.
75. Ibid.
76. Ibid., p.184.
77. Ibid., p.190.
78. Gash, *Sir Robert Peel*, p.40.
79. *Mirror*, p.191.
80. *The Times*, 19 December 1831.
81. *Mirror*, p.191.

Chapter 9 The Second Bill and Hopes for Peer Creation

1. *The Times*, 19 December 1831.

2. Arthur Aspinall, ed., *Three Early Nineteenth Century Diaries*, p.173, 28 December 1831 (Le Marchant).

3. Henry, Lord Brougham, *The Life and Times of Henry Lord Brougham*, p.158.

4. Ibid., p.160.

5. Ibid.

6. Ibid., p.151.

7. *The Times*, 19 December 1831.

8. Brougham, *The Life and Times of Henry Lord Brougham*, p.156.

9. Ibid., p.165.

10. Ibid., p.166.

11. Ibid., p.165.

12. Abraham D. Kriegel, *The Holland House Diaries*, p.108, 2 January 1832.

13. Ibid., p.108.

14. Ibid., p.167.

15. Aspinall, *Three Early Nineteenth Century Diaries*, p.173, 28 December 1831 (Le Marchant).

16. Francis Bamford and the Duke of Wellington, eds, *The Journal of Mrs Arbuthnot*, pp.437–8.

17. Ibid., p.437.

18. Aspinall, *Three Early Nineteenth Century Diaries*, p.177, 18 January 1832 (Ellenborough).

19. Kriegel, *The Holland House Diaries*, p.115.

20. Lytton Strachey and Roger Fulford, *The Greville Memoirs*, vol. II, p.237, 15 January 1832.

21. Lloyd C. Sanders, ed., *Lord Melbourne's Papers*.

22. Lord Broughton, *Recollections of a Long Life*, p.163.

23. J.R.M. Butler, *The Passing of the Great Reform Bill*, p.338.

24. Ibid., p.339.

25. *Mirror*, p.332.

26. Ibid.

27. Ibid.

28. Ibid., p.333.

29. Ibid.

30. Ibid.

31. Ibid.

32. Ibid., p.334.

33. Broughton, *Recollections of a Long Life*, p.163.

34. Ibid., p.173, 8 February 1832.

35. Ibid., p.176.

36. Ibid., p.178.

37. Ibid., p.179.

38. Ibid., p.180.

39. Ibid.

40. Aspinall, *Three Early Nineteenth Century Diaries*, p.196, 16 February 1832 (Le Marchant).

41. Ibid., p.183, 22 January 1832 (Ellenborough).

42. Quoted in Norman Gash, *Sir Robert Peel*, p.38.

43. Ibid.

44. Myron Brightfield, *John Wilson Croker*, p.403.

45. Gash, *Sir Robert Peel*, p.39.

46. Strachey and Fulford, *The Greville Memoirs*, vol. II, p.265, 24 February 1832.

47. Ibid.

48. Aspinall, *Three Early Nineteenth Century Diaries*, p.201, 22 February 1832 (Le Marchant).

49. Ibid.

50. Ibid.

51. Strachey and Fulford, *The Greville Memoirs*, vol. II, p.266, 6 March 1832.

52. Ibid.

53. Quoted in Denis Le Marchant, *Memoir of Viscount Althorp*, p.410.

54. Ibid., p.412.

55. Ibid., p.413.

56. Nowell C. Smith, ed., *The Letters of Sydney Smith*, p.554.

57. Lambton MS, quoted in Chester New, *Lord Durham*, p.165.

58. Ibid.

59. Sir Herbert Maxwell, ed., *The Creevey Papers*, pp.241–2, 13 March 1832.

60. *PD*, vol. 11, col. 417.

61. Ibid., col. 421.

62. Ibid., col. 436.

63. Ibid.

64. Ibid., col. 438.

65. Ibid., col. 462.

66. Ibid.

67. All ibid.

68. Ibid., col. 463.

69. Ibid.

70. Ibid., cols 466–7.

71.   Ibid., cols 480–81.
72.   Ibid., cols 474–5.
73.   Ibid., col. 560.
74.   Ibid., col. 561.
75.   Ibid., col. 570.
76.   Aspinall, *Three Early Nineteenth Century Diaries*, p.211, 10 March 1832 (Le Marchant).
77.   Ibid., p.213, 20 March 1832.
78.   *PD*, col. 578.
79.   Ibid., col. 580.
80.   Ibid., col. 581.
81.   Kriegel, *The Holland House Diaries*, p.157, 21 March 1832.
82.   Butler, *The Passing of the Great Reform Bill*, pp.350–51.
83.   *PD*, col. 739.
84.   Ibid., col. 752.
85.   Ibid.
86.   Ibid., col. 763.
87.   Kriegel, *The Holland House Diaries*, p.158, 21 March 1832.
88.   Broughton, *Recollections of a Long Life*, p.204, 24 March 1832.
89.   Kriegel, *The Holland House Diaries*, pp.158–9, 22 March 1832,
90.   *The Times*, 23 March 1832.
91.   All at Broughton, *Recollections of a Long Life*, p.208.
92.   Ibid., p.210.
93.   Ibid.
94.   Kriegel, *The Holland House Diaries*, p.164, 30 March 1832.
95.   Ibid., p.165.
96.   Ibid.
97.   Ibid., p.166.
98.   Ibid., pp.166–7.
99.   Ibid., p.167.
100.   Ibid., p.168.
101.   Ibid., p.169.
102.   Broughton, *Recollections of a Long Life*, p.209, 4 April 1832.

Chapter 10 Back in the Lords

1.   *The Times*, 26 March 1832.
2.   Lytton Strachey and Roger Fulford, eds, *The Greville Memoirs*, vol. II, p.282, 6 April 1832.
3.   *The Times*, 26 March 1832.
4.   Strachey and Fulford, *The Greville Memoirs*, p.282, 6 April 1832.

5. Ibid., p.284, 8 April 1832.
6. Arthur Aspinall, ed., *Three Early Nineteenth Century Diaries*, p.222, 10 April 1832 (Le Marchant).
7. *PD*, Third Series, vol. 12, col. 16.
8. Ibid., col. 25.
9. Ibid.
10. Ibid.
11. Aspinall, *Three Early Nineteenth Century Diaries*, p.221, 9 April 1832 (Ellenborough).
12. *PD*, col. 26.
13. Aspinall, *Three Early Nineteenth Century Diaries*, p.222, 10 April 1832 (Le Marchant).
14. *PD*, col. 42.
15. Ibid., col. 49.
16. All at Ibid., col. 50.
17. Ibid., col. 73.
18. Ibid., col. 77.
19. Quoted ibid., at cols 75–6.
20. Ibid., col. 78.
21. Ibid., col. 79.
22. Ibid., col. 123.
23. Ibid., col. 124.
24. Ibid.
25. All at ibid., col. 125.
26. Ibid., col. 126.
27. All at ibid., col. 128.
28. All at Strachey and Fulford, *The Greville Memoirs*, vol. II, pp.286–7, 11 April 1832.
29. Aspinall, *Three Early Nineteenth Century Diaries*, p.222, 10 April 1832 (Le Marchant).
30. *PD*, col. 150.
31. Ibid., col. 154.
32. All at ibid.
33. All at ibid., col. 157.
34. Ibid., cols 156–7.
35. Ibid., col. 160.
36. All at ibid., col. 161.
37. All at ibid.
38. Ibid.
39. Ibid., col. 166.
40. Abraham D. Kriegel, ed., *The Holland House Diaries*, p.169.

41. Aspinall, *Three Early Nineteenth Century Diaries*, p.223, 10 April 1832 (Le Marchant).
42. *PD*, col. 180.
43. Ibid., col. 187.
44. Ibid., col. 219.
45. Ibid., col. 233.
46. Ibid., col. 234.
47. Ibid., cols 245–6.
48. Ibid., col. 259.
49. Ibid.
50. Ibid., col. 267.
51. Ibid., col. 271.
52. Both at ibid., col. 277.
53. Ibid., col. 277.
54. Ibid., col. 351.
55. All at ibid., col. 354.
56. Ibid., col. 357.
57. Ibid., col. 358.
58. Ibid., col. 359.
59. Ibid., col. 360.
60. Ibid., col. 361.
61. Ibid., col. 368.
62. Ibid., col. 385.
63. Ibid., col. 392.
64. Ibid., col. 400.
65. Ibid., cols 402–3.
66. Ibid., col. 420.
67. Kriegel, *The Holland House Diaries*, p.169.
68. *PD*, col. 435.
69. Ibid., col. 440.
70. Quoted in Chester New, *Lord Durham*, p.173.
71. *PD*, col. 441.
72. Ibid., col. 442.
73. Ibid., col. 446.
74. Ibid.
75. All at ibid., col. 452.
76. Ibid., cols 452–3.
77. Strachey and Fulford, *The Greville Memoirs*, vol. II, p.288, 15 April 1832.
78. Quoted in New, *Lord Durham*, p.174.

Chapter 11 The Bill in the Lords

1. Arthur Aspinall, ed., *Three Early Nineteenth Century Diaries*, p.230, 12 April 1832 (Ellenborough).
2. Abraham D. Kriegel, ed., *The Holland House Diaries*, p.173, 1 May 1832.
3. Lytton Strachey and Roger Fulford, eds, *The Greville Memoirs*, vol. II, p.290, 22 May 1832.
4. Kriegel, *The Holland House Diaries*, p.172, 28 April 1832.
5. Ibid.
6. All at Aspinall, *Three Early Nineteenth Century Diaries*, p.238, 6 May 1832 (Ellenborough).
7. Ibid., p.225, 10 April 1832 (Le Marchant).
8. Ibid., p.236, 3 May 1832 (Ellenborough).
9. Strachey and Fulford, *The Greville Memoirs*, vol. II p.292, 12 May 1832.
10. Dudley Miles, *Francis Place*, p.194.
11. *PD*, vol. 12. col. 677.
12. Ibid., cols 677–8.
13. Kriegel, *The Holland House Diaries*, p.176, 7 May 1832.
14. All at ibid., p.176.
15. *PD*, col. 679.
16. Ibid., col. 709.
17. Ibid., col. 692.
18. Ibid., col. 698.
19. Aspinall, *Three Early Nineteenth Century Diaries*, p.237, 4 May 1832 (Ellenborough).
20. Ibid., p.237.
21. *The Times*, 8 May 1832.
22. Denis Le Marchant, *Memoir of Viscount Althorp*, pp.419–20.
23. Aspinall, *Three Early Nineteenth Century Diaries*, p.241, 8 May 1832 (Le Marchant).
24. Ibid., p.242.
25. Ibid., p.241.
26. *The Times*, 10 May 1832.
27. Le Marchant, *Memoir of Viscount Althorp*, p.422.
28. Lord Broughton, *Recollections of a Long Life*, p.219, 8 May 1832.
29. Quoted in Jasper Ridley, *Palmerston*, p.205.
30. Aspinall, *Three Early Nineteenth Century Diaries*, p.240, 7 May 1832 (Littleton).
31. Ibid., p.242, 8 May 1832 (Littleton).

32. Strachey and Fulford, *The Greville Memoirs*, vol. II, p.294, 12 May 1832.

33. David Moss, *Thomas Attwood*, p.218.

34. Alexander Somerville, *The Autobiography of a Working Man*, p.155.

35. Kriegel, *The Holland House Diaries*, p.178, 10 May 1832.

36. Aspinall, *Three Early Nineteenth Century Diaries*, p.244, 9 May 1832 (Ellenborough).

37. *The Times*, 8 May 1832.

38. All at Broughton, *Recollections of a Long Life*, p.223.

39. Aspinall, *Three Early Nineteenth Century Diaries*, p.246, 9 May 1832 (Le Marchant).

40. Ridley, *Palmerston*, p.215.

41. Strachey and Fulford, *The Greville Memoirs*, vol. II, p.296, 12 May 1832.

42. Both at Aspinall, *Three Early Nineteenth Century Diaries*, p.246, 9 May 1832 (Le Marchant).

43. Kriegel, *The Holland House Diaries*, p.178, 10 May 1832.

44. Ibid., p.179, 14 May 1832.

45. Ibid.

46. *PD*, col. 762.

47. Ibid., col. 763.

48. Ibid., col. 765.

49. Ibid., col. 766.

50. Ibid., col. 780.

51. Correspondence 113, quoted in J.R.M. Butler, *The Passing of the Great Reform Bill*.

52. Aspinall, *Three Early Nineteenth Century Diaries*, p.248, 10 May 1832 (Ellenborough).

53. *PD*, col. 787.

54. Ibid., col. 788.

55. *The Times*, 11 May 1832.

56. *PD*, col. 792.

57. Ibid., col. 793.

58. Ibid., col. 795.

59. Ibid., col. 797.

60. Aspinall, *Three Early Nineteenth Century Diaries*, p.247, 11 May 1832 (Le Marchant).

61. *PD*, col. 805.

62. All at ibid., col. 822.

63. Louis J. Jennings, ed., *Croker's Correspondence and Papers*, p.149, 14 February 1832.

64. Ibid., p.155.
65. Ibid.
66. Ibid.
67. Ibid., p.157.
68. Ibid., p.155.

Chapter 12 *The Days of May*

1. Louis J. Jennings, ed., *Croker's Correspondence and Papers*, p.160.
2. Ibid.
3. All at ibid., p.161 (Croker's italics).
4. Quoted in Dudley Miles, *Francis Place*, p.196.
5. All at Lytton Strachey and Roger Fulford, eds, *The Greville Memoirs*, vol. II, p.296, 12 May 1832.
6. *The Times*, 15 May 1832.
7. Arthur Aspinall, ed., *Three Early Nineteenth Century Diaries*, p.252, 13 May 1832 (Le Marchant).
8. Ibid., 13 May 1832.
9. Alexander Somerville, *The Autobiography of a Working Man*, p.155.
10. Ibid., p.156.
11. Quoted in J.R.M. Butler, *The Passing of the Great Reform Bill*, p.409.
12. David Moss, *Thomas Attwood*, p.220.
13. See generally ibid., pp.220–21.
14. *The Times*, 11 May 1832.
15. Quoted Jennings, *Croker's Correspondence and Papers*, p.164.
16. *PD*, vol. 12, col. 907.
17. Strachey and Fulford, *The Greville Memoirs*, vol. II, p.299, 17 May 1832.
18. *PD*, col. 910.
19. All at ibid., col. 912.
20. Ibid., col. 913.
21. Quoted here from *PD*, supra col. 287.
22. All at *PD*, cols 917–18.
23. Aspinall, *Three Early Nineteenth Century Diaries*, p.255, 14 May 1832 (Le Marchant).
24. *The Times*, 16 May 1832.
25. Jennings, *Croker's Correspondence and Papers*, p.166.
26. *PD*, col. 954.
27. Ibid., cols 955–6.
28. Ibid., col. 957.
29. Ibid.

30.   Lord Broughton, *Recollections of a Long Life*, p.229.

31.   Strachey and Fulford, *The Greville Memoirs*, vol. II, p.299, 17 May 1832.

32.   Miles, *Francis Place*, p.197.

33.   Abraham D. Kriegel, ed., *The Holland House Diaries*, p.180, 15 May 1832.

34.   *PD*, col. 970.

35.   Kriegel, *The Holland House Diaries*, p.180, 15 May 1832.

36.   All at Broughton, *Recollections of a Long Life*, p.277.

37.   Quoted at Butler, *The Passing of the Great Reform Bill*, pp.402–3.

38.   *PD*, col., 997.

39.   Ibid., col. 1015.

40.   Kriegel, *The Holland House Diaries*, p.182.

41.   Ibid., p.183, 16 May 1832.

42.   *The Times*, 12 May 1832.

43.   Kriegel, *The Holland House Diaries*, p.183, 17 May 1832.

44.   All at Michael Brock, *The Great Reform Act*, p.302.

45.   Strachey and Fulford, *The Greville Memoirs*, vol. II, pp.303–4, 31 May 1832.

46.   Ibid., p.307, 18 June 1832.

47.   Norman Gash, 'Politics in the Age of Peel', in *Sir Robert Peel*, Appendix D, pp.438–9.

48.   Linda Colley, *Britons*, p.349.

Bibliography

Hansard's Parliamentary Debates, Third Series, Volumes 2, 3, 7, 8, 11, 12.
The Mirror of Parliament, Sixth Series, Volume 1. First Session commencing 14 June 1831; Second Session commencing 6 December 1831, ed. John Henry Barrow

Newspapers and Journals
The Times (*Passim*)
Quarterly Review, vol. XLV, April–July (John Murray, 1831)
Edinburgh Review, vol. LIV, August–December 1831

Books
Aspinall, Arthur, ed., *Three Early Nineteenth Century Diaries* (Williams and Norgate, 1952)
Bamford, Francis and the Duke of Wellington, eds, *The Journal of Mrs Arbuthnot, 1820–32*, vol. II (Macmillan, 1950)
Belchem, John, *Orator Hunt* (Clarendon Press, 1985)
Brightfield, Myron, *John Wilson Croker* (1940)
Brock, Michael, *The Great Reform Act* (Hutchinson University Library, 1973)
Brougham, Henry Lord, *The Life and Times of Henry Lord Brougham Written by Himself*, vol. III (William Blackwood, 1871)
Broughton, Lord (John Cam Hobhouse) *Recollections of a Long Life*, vol. 4, 1829–34 (John Murray, 1909–11)
Burton, Anthony, *William Cobbett, Englishman* (Aurum Press, 1997)
Butler, J.R.M., *The Passing of the Great Reform Bill* (Longmans, Green, 1914)
Colley, Linda, *Britons: Forging the Nation 1707–1837* (Pimlico, 1992)
Cooper, Duff, *Talleyrand* (Jonathan Cape, 1971)
Cooper, Leonard, *Radical Jack* (Cresset Press 1959)
Davies, John, *A History of Wales* (originally published as *Hanes Cymru*) (Penguin, 1993)
Derry, John W., *Charles Earl Grey* (Blackwell, 1992)
Dickens, Charles, *The Pickwick Papers* (1836)
Disraeli, Benjamin, *Coningsby* (Dent Dutton, 1911)
Eagles, John, a citizen, *The Bristol Riots* (Gutch and Martin, 1832)
Galt, John, *The Member*, ed. Ian A. Gordon (Scottish Academic Press, 1975)
Gash, Norman, *Sir Robert Peel*, vol. II (Longman, 1972)

——*Pillars of Government* (Edward Arnold, 1986)

Green, Daniel, *Cobbett; The Noblest Agitator* (OUP, 1985)

Hazlitt, William, *The Spirit of the Age* (1825, this edition Northcote House, 1991)

Hibbert, Christopher, *George IV* (Readers Union, 1975)

Hinde, Wendy, *George Canning* (Collins/Purnell, 1973)

Jennings, Louis J., ed., *Croker's Correspondence and Papers*, vol. II (John Murray, 1911)

Knatchbull-Hugessen, Sir Hughe, *A Kentish Family* (Methuen, 1960)

Kriegel, Abraham D., ed., *The Holland House Diaries, 1831–1840* (Routledge and Kegan Paul, 1977)

Lamb, Charles, *The Letters of Charles Lamb*, vol. II (Everyman, 1912)

Lee, Dennis, *Lord Lyndhurst: The Flexible Tory* (University Press of Colorado, 1994)

Le Marchant, Denis, *Memoir of Viscount Althorp* (Richard Bentley, 1876)

Longford, Elizabeth, *Wellington: Pillar of State* (Weidenfeld & Nicolson, 1972)

Maxwell, Sir Herbert, ed., *The Creevey Papers*, vol. II (John Murray, 1904)

Miles, Dudley, *Francis Place 1771–1854* (Harvester/St Martin's Press, 1988)

Mitchell, Austin, *The Whigs in Opposition 1815–1830* (Clarendon Press, 1967)

Morgan, Kenneth, *The Great Reform Act* (The Reform Club, 2000)

Moss, David J., *Thomas Attwood: The Biography of a Radical* (McGill-Queen's University Press, 1990)

Myers, Ernest, *Lord Althorp* (Richard Bentley, 1890)

New, Chester, *Lord Durham* (Oxford, 1929)

Peacock, Thomas Love, *Melincourt* (1817), this edition published in David Garnett, ed., *The Novels of Thomas Love Peacock* (Rupert Hart Davis, 1948)

Pearson, Hesketh, *The Smith of Smiths* (Hogarth Press, 1984)

Petrie, Sir Charles, *Lord Liverpool and His Times* (James Barrie, 1954)

Plumb, J. H. *The First Four Georges* (Fontana, 1966)

Porritt, Edward and Annie, *The Unreformed House of Commons*, vol. I (CUP, 1903)

Ridley, Jasper, *Palmerston* (Granada, 1972)

Sanders, Lloyd C., ed., *Lord Melbourne's Papers* (Longmans, Green, 1889)

Scott, Sir Walter, *The Journal of Sir Walter Scott* (Canongate, 1971)

Sisman, Adam, *Boswell's Presumptuous Task* (Penguin, 2001)

Smith, E. A., *Lord Grey* (Clarendon Press, 1990)

Smith, Nowell. C., ed., *The Letters of Sydney Smith* (Clarendon Press, 1953)

Somerville, Alexander, *The Autobiography of a Working Man*, ed. John Carswell (Turnstile Press, 1951)

Stewart, Robert, *Henry Brougham, 1778–1868* (Bodley Head, 1986)

Strachey, Lytton and Roger Fulford, eds, *The Greville Memoirs*, vol. I,

1814–1830 (Macmillan, 1938), vol. II, July 1830–December 1833 (Macmillan, 1938)

Thompson, E.P., *The Making of the English Working Class* (Gollancz, 1963)

Thompson, F.M.L., *English Landed Society in the Nineteenth Century* (Routledge and Kegan Paul, 1963)

Trench, Charles Chevenix, *The Great Dan: A Biography of Daniel O'Connell* (Triad/Grafton, 1985)

Wiener, Joel H., *Radicalism and Free Thought in Nineteenth Century Britain* (Greenwood Press, 1983)

Wright, Raymond, ed., *The Pelican Book of Selected Nineteenth-Century English Prose* (Pelican, 1956)

Ziegler, Philip, *Melbourne* (Fontana, 1978)

Index

The Term 'MP' was not widely used in the 1830s,
but it is used here to indicate members of parliament.